The Penguin
Touring Atlas
of Australia

Penguin Books

CONTENTS

Inside front cover
Major Highways Route-planner

HOLIDAY REGIONS

Blue Mountains	v
Hunter Valley & Coast	vi
Great Ocean Road	vii
Grampians & Beyond	viii
Fleurieu Peninsula	ix
Flinders Ranges & Outback	x
South-West Corner	xi
The Kimberley	xii
Kakadu	xiii
The Red Centre	xiv
Tropical North	xv
Sunshine Coast	xvi
Gold Coast & Hinterland	xvii
South-East Tasmania	xviii

AUSTRALIA-WIDE MAPPING

Sydney Approach and Bypass Routes	xix
Melbourne Approach and Bypass Routes	xx
Adelaide Approach and Bypass Routes	xxi
Perth Approach and Bypass Routes	xxii
Brisbane Approach and Bypass Routes	1

NEW SOUTH WALES

New South Wales Location Map	2
Central Sydney	3
Sydney & Surrounds	4
Central Eastern New South Wales	6
North Eastern New South Wales	8
North Western New South Wales	10
South Western New South Wales	12
South Eastern New South Wales	14

AUSTRALIAN CAPITAL TERRITORY

Central Canberra	15
Canberra & Surrounds	16

VICTORIA

Victoria Location Map	18
Central Melbourne	19
Melbourne & Surrounds	20
Southern Central Victoria	22
South Western Victoria	24
Central Western Victoria	26
North Western Victoria	28
North Central Victoria	30
North Eastern Victoria	32

SOUTH AUSTRALIA

South Australia Location Map	34
Central Adelaide	35
Adelaide & Surrounds, North	36
Adelaide & Surrounds, South	37
South Central South Australia	38
Central South Australia	40
South Western South Australia	42
North Western South Australia	44
North Eastern South Australia	46
South Eastern South Australia	48
Barossa Valley	49

WESTERN AUSTRALIA

Western Australia Location Map	50
Central Perth	51
Perth & Surrounds	52
The South-West	53
South Western Western Australia	54
Central Western Western Australia	55
Southern Western Australia	56
Central Western Australia	58
Northern Western Australia	60

NORTHERN TERRITORY

Northern Territory Location Map	62
Central Darwin	63
Darwin & Surrounds	64
Northern Northern Territory	66
Central Northern Territory	68
Southern Northern Territory	70

QUEENSLAND

Queensland Location Map	72
Central Brisbane	73
Brisbane & Surrounds, North	74
Brisbane & Surrounds, South	75
South Eastern Queensland	76
North Eastern Queensland	78
Far North Eastern Queensland	80
Cape York Peninsula	82
Far North Western Queensland	83
North Western Queensland	84
South Western Queensland	86

TASMANIA

Tasmania Location Map	88
Central Hobart	89
Hobart & Surrounds	90
Southern Tasmania	92
Northern Tasmania	94
INDEX OF PLACE NAMES	96

Inside back cover
Inter-city Route Maps

MAP SYMBOLS

- Freeway
- Freeway under construction
- Highway, sealed, with National Highway Route Marker
- Highway, sealed, with National Route Marker
- Highway, sealed, with Metroad Route Marker
- Highway, unsealed
- Highway under construction
- Main road, sealed, with State Route Marker
- Main road, unsealed, with Tourist Route
- Main road under construction
- Secondary road, sealed, (central city maps only)
- Other road, sealed, with traffic direction arrow
- Other road, unsealed
- Mall
- Vehicle track
- Walking track
- Paratoo — Railway, with station
- Flagstaff — Underground railway, with station
- 114 — Total kilometres between two points
- 45 — Intermediate kilometres
- State border
- Fruit fly exclusion zone boundary
- SYDNEY — State capital city
- GEELONG — Town, over 50 000 inhabitants
- Bundaberg — Town, 10 000–50 000 inhabitants
- Katherine — Town, 5 000–10 000 inhabitants
- Narrogin — Town, 1 000–5 000 inhabitants
- Robe — Town, 200–1 000 inhabitants
- Miena — Town, under 200 inhabitants
- LIVERPOOL — Suburb, on state and region maps
- Liverpool — Suburb, on approach & bypass maps
- Williamsford — Locality
- Alroy Downs — Pastoral station homestead
- Borroloola — Major Aboriginal community
- Murgenella — Aboriginal community
- Fortesque Roadhouse — Roadhouse
- Commercial airport
- Place of interest
- Landmark feature
- General interest feature
- Accommodation
- Hill, mountain
- Mine site
- Lighthouse
- River, waterfall
- Lake
- Intermittent lake
- TO GAWLER — Route destination
- 44 — Adjoining page number
- National park
- Other reserve
- Other named area
- Aboriginal / Torres Strait Islander land
- Prohibited area

HOLIDAY REGIONS

There is much to see in Australia and many ways in which to see it. When touring by car, the opportunities for exploration are endless; take your time and enjoy all there is to see and do enroute to your destination. Discover the history, the natural beauty and the diversity of wonderful attractions that this country has to offer.

This section covers 14 popular holiday regions. These are places where you will find world famous natural landforms, beaches without peer, fascinating animals, and picturesque wine-growing regions. Included, among others, are Tasmania's South-East, with its forested mountains, orchards, glassy waters and convict history; the glamorous, sun-drenched Gold Coast; the ecological wonderland of Kakadu and the grandeur of the Red Centre.

A few of these regions, including the Blue Mountains in New South Wales and Fleurieu Peninsula in South Australia are within a day's drive of a capital city and can be explored with little or no effort. Travellers should, however, consider planning activities in advance in order to make the most of the experience, particularly if time is limited. Make the local visitor information centre the first port of call to collect detailed maps and brochures of the areas you intend to visit. This is particularly useful in winegrowing districts where 50 or more wineries can compete for attention with a range of other attractions.

With the more remote destinations – the Red Centre, the Kimberley, and Flinders Ranges and Outback – forward planning is strongly advised. Large sections of all these areas are suitable only for four-wheel-drive vehicles and are subject to extreme weather conditions that can result in road closures. In many instances there are hundreds, if not thousands, of kilometres between fuel and water stops. Travellers should familiarise themselves with prevailing conditions and carry adequate supplies.

The pages that follow provide a snapshot of the best attractions, highlights, events, and experiences in each area. The detailed maps in this atlas will help you plan your journey and ensure you make the most of your trip. Whatever your inclination, these holiday regions will offer you a wealth of experiences and opportunities from the best of Australia. Happy travelling!

Bungle Bungles, Western Australia

Kakadu National Park, Northern Territory

Daintree National Park, Queensland

Three Sisters, New South Wales

Cape Leeuwin Lighthouse, Western Australia

Aroona Valley, South Australia

Trout fishing, Tasmania

Blue Mountains

The misty, bush-clad cliffs and valleys of the Blue Mountains are the eroded remains of a giant plateau that rose up out of a river delta 80 million years ago. Occupied for at least 20 000 years by Aboriginal peoples, the mountains proved an impenetrable barrier until 1813 to the European settlers of Sydney seeking westward expansion. These days the area provides an accessible and spectacularly beautiful nature retreat for the city's residents, with bushwalking, adventure sports, gourmet retreats and cool-climate gardens among the many attractions.

TOP EVENTS

Feb.	Blue Mountains Festival of Folk, Roots and Blues (Katoomba)
Mar.	Blue Mountains Herb Fest (Medlow Bath)
Apr.	Autumn Gardens Festival (Mt Wilson)
May	Songs of the Wind Festival (throughout region)
June	Winter Magic Festival (Katoomba)
June–Aug.	Yulefest (throughout region)
Sept.–Nov.	Spring Gardens Festival (throughout region)
Oct.	Village Fair (Leura)
Nov.	Rhododendron Festival (Blackheath)

EXPERIENCE IT!

1. **Go** canyoning in the Grand Canyon, south-east of Blackheath
2. **Book** a weekend at Cleopatra, a French-style gourmet retreat in Blackheath
3. **Descend** the Giant Stairway into the Jamison Valley, south of Katoomba

Grose Valley
A visit to the National Parks and Heritage Centre on Govetts Leap Road is a must for visitors who are keen to explore the network of trails overlooking and leading into the Grose Valley. The escarpment in this area east of Blackheath is particularly dramatic and the views are breathtaking.

Jenolan Caves
Formed 400 million years ago in a belt of limestone, this is one of the most extensive and complex underground limestone cave systems in the world. Of the 300 or so 'rooms', 9 are open to the public – by tour only.

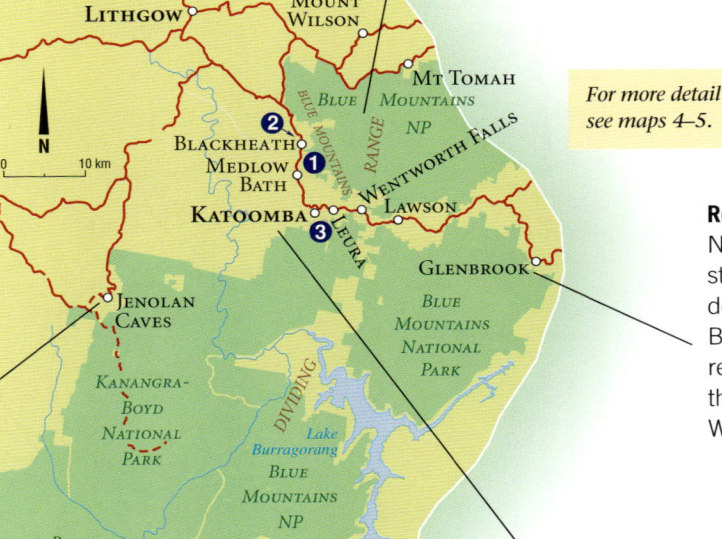

VISITOR INFORMATION
Blue Mountains Visitor Information Centre
Echo Point Rd, Katoomba and Glenbrook: 1300 653 408
www.bluemountainstourism.org.au

FOCUS ON

Gardens
Volcanic soil and cool-climate conditions have made the Blue Mountains one of the best known gardening regions in Australia. Visit Everglades near Leura, a 6-ha classically designed garden that melds with the surrounding bush. Mount Wilson is a tiny village of grand estates, nearly all with large historic gardens of formal lawns, cool-climate plantings, woodlands and huge European trees; many properties are open to the public. Mount Tomah Botanic Garden is the cool-climate annexe of Sydney's Botanic Garden. Here, specialist displays in terraces bring together thousands of worldwide rare species, including the Wollemi Pine, discovered 1994 in Wollemi National Park.

CLIMATE KATOOMBA

	J	F	M	A	M	J	J	A	S	O	N	D
Max. °C	23	22	20	17	13	10	9	11	14	17	20	22
Min. °C	13	13	11	9	6	4	2	3	5	8	10	12
Rain mm	160	170	169	126	103	123	89	81	74	93	103	125
Raindays	13	12	13	10	9	9	9	9	9	10	11	12

For more detail see maps 4–5.

Red Hands Cave
Near Glenbrook, Aboriginal red-ochre hand stencils, between 500 and 1600 years old, decorate the walls of the Red Hands Cave in Blue Mountains National Park. The stencils recall the presence of the first inhabitants of the mountains, the people of the Darug, Wiradjuri and Gandangara tribes.

Three Sisters and Echo Point
This feature has been carved by millions of years of erosion, although Aboriginal legend has it that the rock was formed when a father turned his daughters to stone to protect them from an evil figure. Nearby, visitors can ride into or across the Jamison Valley aboard the Scenic Railway or Scenic Skyway.

Hunter Valley & Coast

The Hunter is one of Australia's top wine-producing regions, but this is only a small part of its charm for visitors. Rich alluvial plains, historic towns and tree-lined country avenues create one of the State's most attractive rural landscapes. In the north-east is the rainforest wilderness of Barrington Tops National Park. Over on the coast is Lake Macquarie, a saltwater paradise for boaters and anglers, while to its north lies Newcastle, a major port and industrial centre. Further north again is Port Stephens, a vast semi-enclosed body of water ringed by near-perfect beaches.

TOP EVENTS
Feb.	Vintage Festival (Lower Hunter)
Mar.	Beaumont Street Jazz and Arts Festival (Newcastle)
Apr.	Heritage Month (Maitland)
May	Lovedale Long Lunch (Lovedale, near Cessnock)
Sept.	Folk Festival (Wollombi)
Oct.	Jazz in the Vines (Cessnock)
Oct.	Opera in the Vineyards (Cessnock)

EXPERIENCE IT!
1. **Trek** the 4-hour-return Rocky Crossing Walk through subtropical rainforest in Barrington Tops National Park
2. **Shop** for antiques, crafts and curios at heritage-listed Morpeth, Australia's oldest river port
3. **Take** a tour to see Aboriginal hand stencils at Wollombi

CLIMATE CESSNOCK
	J	F	M	A	M	J	J	A	S	O	N	D
Max. °C	31	31	29	26	21	19	18	19	23	25	29	30
Min. °C	17	17	16	12	7	7	4	6	9	12	14	16
Rain mm	80	84	79	64	59	59	45	41	43	57	60	76
Raindays	8	8	8	7	6	7	6	6	6	7	7	8

VISITOR INFORMATION
Hunter Valley (Cessnock): (02) 4990 4477
Newcastle: (02) 4974 2999
Port Stephens (Nelson Bay): (02) 4981 1579; 1800 808 900
www.winecountry.com.au

FOCUS ON

Top Wines
The Tyrrell family pioneered the wine industry in the Pokolbin district late in the 1850s. The McWilliams and the Draytons soon followed. Premium wines made from shiraz and semillon grapes grown on the lower Hunter's alluvial red soils are unique. In good years, Hunter chardonnay ranks with Australia's best; Tyrrells Vat 47 Chardonnay is notable. McWilliam's Mount Pleasant Elizabeth (semillon) and Philip (shiraz) offer a relatively inexpensive introduction to the delights of Hunter wines while McWilliam's more expensive Rosehill Shiraz is a top-quality red. The Allandale and Capercaillie estates offer splendid chardonnay and semillon and very accessible shiraz.

Upper Hunter
This striking landscape of alluvial plains and rugged mountains supports 7 wineries, including the large estates of Rosemount and Arrowfield. The area just to the north, around Scone, is one of the world's largest thoroughbred horse breeding centres, and boasts some spectacular rural scenery.

Barrington Tops National Park
Barrington Tops is the most southerly of the State's World Heritage Rainforest Reserves. Rugged basalt cliffs, cool-temperate and subtropical rainforests, gorges, waterfalls and a touch of light snow in winter make this stunning landscape a popular spot with walkers, campers and climbers.

Port Stephens
Port Stephens, reached via the township of Nelson Bay, offers excellent boating, fishing and swimming. It is also something of a wildlife haven: about 160 bottlenose dolphins have permanent residence here, migrating whales can be seen in season from a cruise of Stockton Sand Dunes, and koalas can be spotted near Tilligerry Habitat.

Lower Hunter
The Lower Hunter is Australia's oldest and best known winegrowing district. Around 3000 ha of vines and over 60 wineries are set across rolling hills against the backdrop of the Broken Back Range. A day's tour should start at the wine and information centre in Cessnock.

Lake Macquarie
This is a magnificent saltwater expanse, four times the size of Sydney Harbour, offering every kind of water sport from angling to skiing, swimming, diving, sailing or kayaking. Don't miss Dobell House at Wangi Wangi (Sundays only), former home of prominent Australian painter William Dobell.

Newcastle
Australia's second oldest city was founded as a penal colony in 1804. Newcastle rises up the surrounding hills from a spectacular surf coastline, its buildings a pleasant chaos of architectural styles. The city boasts a range of attractions including good restaurants, a premier regional gallery and many historic sites.

GREAT OCEAN ROAD

The south-west coast of Victoria is one of Australia's great scenic destinations. The Great Ocean Road, the region's main touring route, weaves a breathtaking course across a coastal landscape of rugged cliffs and unique geological formations, quiet bays and wild surf beaches, rainforests and waterfalls. En route is a string of charming holiday towns, with many attractions, including heritage sites and wildlife. Inland, the geological theme continues in the craters and lakes of the region's volcanic landscape. The accommodation choices throughout the region include everything from gourmet retreats to B&Bs, hillside cabins and remote camping spots.

TOP EVENTS

Jan.	Pier to Pub Swim; Mountain to Surf Footrace (Lorne)
Feb.	Food and Wine Festival (Heywood, near Portland)
Mar.	Folk Festival (Port Fairy)
Easter	Bells Beach Surfing Classic (Torquay)
Apr.	Country Music Festival (Colac)
May	Racing Carnival (horseracing, Warrnambool)
July	Fun 4 Kids (children's festival, Warrnambool)
Sept.	Angair Wildflower Festival (Anglesea)
Dec.	Falls Festival (Lorne)

EXPERIENCE IT!

1. **Spot** southern right whales at Logans Beach, Warrnambool (June to September)
2. **Walk** the Alan Marshall Memorial Walking Track to the summit of Mt Noorat, near Terang
3. **Take** a boat trip at Cape Bridgewater to see Australian fur seals at play

VISITOR INFORMATION
Lorne: (03) 5289 1152
Warrnambool: (03) 5564 7837
www.greatoceanrd.org.au

FOCUS ON
Maritime history
There are about 160 wrecks along the vital though treacherous south-west coast shipping route. Victoria's Historic Shipwreck Trail, between Moonlight Head (in Port Campbell National Park) and Port Fairy, marks 25 sites with plaques telling the history of the wrecks. Not to be missed is the evocative *Loch Ard* site, near Port Campbell. Maritime history is preserved in the superb streetscape of Port Fairy, an 1830s whaling port, and in the 200 heritage buildings of Portland, Victoria's first settlement. At Flagstaff Hill Maritime Museum in Warrnambool you'll find a completely rebuilt 19th-century maritime village, and a collection of seafaring treasures.

CLIMATE WARRNAMBOOL

	J	F	M	A	M	J	J	A	S	O	N	D
Max. °C	24	23	22	20	17	15	14	15	16	18	20	22
Min. °C	13	14	13	11	9	7	6	7	8	9	10	12
Rain mm	33	34	48	60	78	77	88	86	74	67	55	44
Raindays	8	8	10	13	17	17	20	19	17	15	13	11

Mount Eccles National Park
Mount Eccles is at the far edge of the 20 000-year-old volcanic landscape that extends west from Melbourne. Geological features of the park include a complex cave system, scoria cones and a large lake (suitable for swimming), enclosed within three volcanic craters. There are excellent walking trails and camping is available.

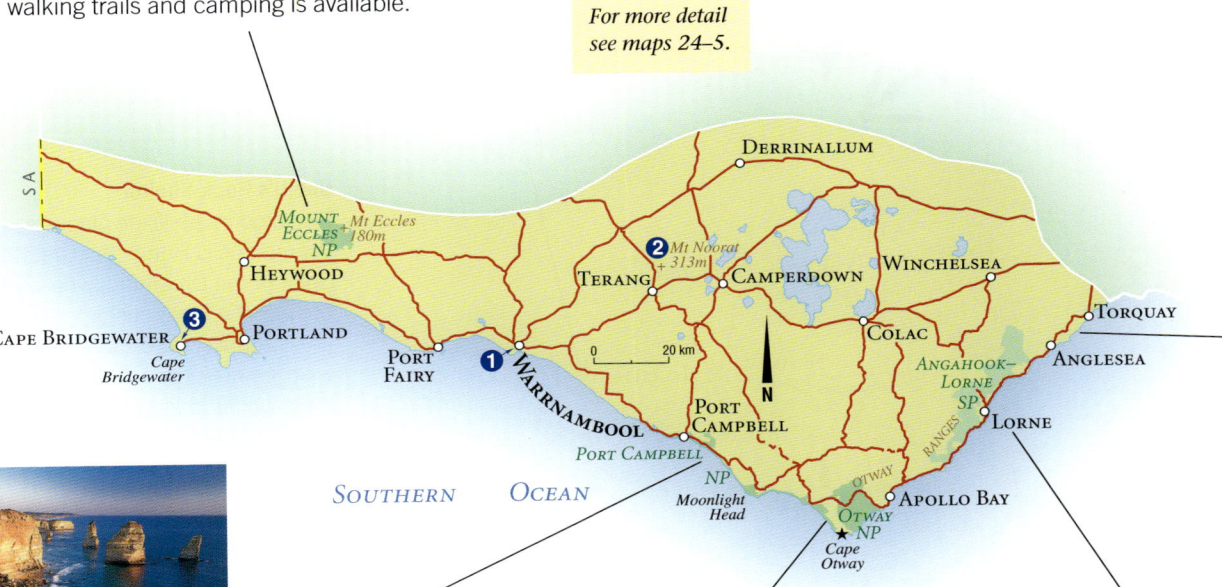

For more detail see maps 24–5.

Surf coast
Torquay is Victoria's premier surfing town. This is where young surfers start out and old surfers settle down, where surfing is business as well as fun. Factory outlets offer great bargains on surf gear and the local Surfworld Surfing Museum celebrates the wonders of the wave. Bells and Jan Juc beaches are just around the corner.

The Twelve Apostles
These spectacular sandstone stacks were part of the original cliffs until wind and water carved them into their present shape and left them stranded in wild surf off the shoreline. Preserved within Port Campbell National Park, they are one of Australia's most photographed sights and the region's signature attraction.

The Otways
Ancient southern temperate rainforest is preserved in the hills and gullies of this magical landscape. Follow a rainforest boardwalk at Maits Rest in Otway National Park, drive along the 20-km scenic Turtons Track, north-east of Apollo Bay, and visit historic Cape Otway Lighthouse.

Lorne
This popular resort village is the inner city of the south-west coast: it has excellent cafes and restaurants and a lively summertime crowd. As well, it offers good beaches and surfing opportunities. Nearby, in Angahook–Lorne State Park (pictured), beautiful forests and waterfalls provide time out for walkers and nature lovers.

Grampians & Beyond

Victoria's central west is a mix of ancient mountains, semi-arid plains and classic farming landscapes. In the south, the rugged 400 million-year-old blue-grey shapes of the Grampians rise from the cleared plains, a dense and awe-inspiring environment of forests, fern gullies, soaring cliffs, waterfalls, creeks, lakes and swampland. In the many rock shelters of the area, details of pre-European Aboriginal life are impressively recorded. Anglo-Celtic settlement has made its mark with the hundred of thousands of hectares of wheat crops and sheep paddocks that dominate what is Australia's richest farming country, while the proliferation of olive groves and vineyards signal a more Mediterranean landscape.

TOP EVENTS

Jan.	Champagne Picnic Races (Great Western, near Ararat)
Feb.	Grampians Jazz Festival (Halls Gap)
Mar.	Vintage Car Rally (Casterton)
Easter	Stawell Easter Gift (professional foot race)
May	Grampians Gourmet Weekend (Halls Gap)
Sept.	Cymbidium Orchid Festival (Ararat)
Oct.	Spring Garden Festival (Horsham)

EXPERIENCE IT!

1. **Visit** Mount Zero Olives at Laharum, the largest olive plantation in the Southern Hemisphere
2. **Choose** one of the short walks through the eastern part of Little Desert National Park, near Nhill
3. **Drive** to the top of One Tree Hill at Ararat for a 360° view of the region

VISITOR INFORMATION

Halls Gap: (03) 5356 4616
Hamilton: (03) 5572 3746; 1800 807 056
Horsham: (03) 5382 1832; 1800 633 218
www.grampians.org.au

FOCUS ON

Aboriginal culture in the Grampians
The Djab Wurrung and Jardwadjali peoples shared the territory they called Gariwerd, for at least 5000 years before European settlement, though some evidence points to 30 000 years of habitation. The Brambuk Aboriginal Cultural Centre at Halls Gap, run by five Koorie communities, is an excellent first stop for information about the region's heritage. There are 100 recorded rock-art sites in this area, representing more than 80 per cent of all sites found in Victoria. A Brambuk-guided tour of some of the sites is a rewarding way to experience the meaning and nature of the art. Notable 'shelter' sites include: Gulgurn Manja, featuring over 190 kangaroo, emu and handprint motifs; and Ngamadidj, a site consisting of 16 figures painted with white clay. Bunjil's Rock Shelter is just outside the park.

Mount Arapiles
Mount Arapiles, part of the Mount Arapiles–Tooan State Park, is regarded as Australia's best rock-climbing venue. It attracts interstate and international enthusiasts with its 2000 rock-climbing routes marked out across 365 m of sandstone cliffs. Courses and tours are available.

Halls Gap
Halls Gap, 24 km south-west of Stawell and surrounded by Grampians National Park, is the gateway to the central Grampians. This little village is connected to a network of scenic drives and walking tracks into the mountains. The area attracts bushwalkers, campers, abseilers and, between August and October, wildflower enthusiasts.

CLIMATE STAWELL

	J	F	M	A	M	J	J	A	S	O	N	D
Max. °C	28	28	25	20	16	13	12	14	16	19	22	26
Min. °C	13	13	12	9	7	4	4	5	6	8	9	11
Rain mm	37	28	37	46	63	46	67	63	60	61	40	28
Raindays	6	4	7	9	12	14	18	17	13	11	9	7

Bunjil's Rock Shelter
Depicted in a hillside alcove east of the Grampians is Bunjil, the Great Ancestor Spirit of the Dreaming, who created the people, the land, customs and law. In the Grampians area it is the only art site where more than one colour is used and a known figure is represented. Approach from the Western Highway, near Stawell.

Hamilton
Hamilton is the commercial hub of the wool-rich Western District. Gracious houses and churches on its tree-lined streets testify to over a century of prosperity. The town boasts botanic gardens and an excellent gallery. Close to town are historic homesteads in magnificent gardens; these properties are generally open in spring.

For more detail see maps 24–5 & 26–7.

Wines of Great Western
Grapevines were first planted at Seppelt's Great Western vineyards in 1865. Seppelt Winery is best known for its red and white sparkling wines, cellared in 1.6 km of National Trust-classified tunnels dug by miners late in the 19th century. Other wineries in the area include Best's and Garden Gully.

FLEURIEU PENINSULA

This peninsula is one of the most popular and accessible holiday destinations in South Australia. It is known for its wineries, magnificent coastline, scenic landscapes and gourmet produce. Some of the Fleurieu's rural villages date back 160 years. Many of the attractions are only an hour or so from Adelaide and visitors can schedule day tours using the city as a base. Travellers heading for the Victor Harbor district, on the far side of the peninsula, might consider booking a night or two of accommodation to take account of longer distances.

TOP EVENTS

Jan.	Granite Island Regatta (Victor Harbor)
Jan.	Milang to Goolwa Freshwater Sailing Classic
May	Vintage Affair (Langhorne Creek)
June	Sea and Vines Festival (McLaren Vale)
June	Whale Season Launch (Victor Harbor)
July	Almond Blossom Festival (Willunga)
Aug.	Collectors, Hobbies and Antique Fair (Strathalbyn)
Oct.	Wine Bushing Festival (McLaren Vale)
Oct.	Folk and Music Festival (Victor Harbor)

EXPERIENCE IT!

1. **Lunch** amid the vines at the Salopian Inn, McLaren Vale
2. **Cruise** from the river port of Goolwa to the mouth of the Murray
3. **Ride** the horse-drawn tram from the township of Victor Harbor to Granite Island, to see fairy penguins

VISITOR INFORMATION
McLaren Vale and Fleurieu Visitor Centre
McLaren Vale: (08) 8323 9944
Victor Harbor: (08) 8552 5738
www.fleurieu.com.au/tourism

FOCUS ON

Wine districts
The McLaren Vale winegrowing district, just 45 minutes from Adelaide, has 53 wineries offering tastings, set against a landscape of weathered hills and rolling acres of almond and olive groves. With a viticultural history dating back to 1838, the region is highly regarded, particularly for its full-bodied reds and notably its shiraz. It supports a wide range of wineries from boutique outfits to some of the big players. In the highly productive Langhorne Creek area a few wineries offer tastings, although many of the grapes grown here are used by wineries in other regions around the country.

McLaren Vale
This is the heart of the winegrowing region. Several wineries are near the town's centre, as are the olive and almond groves, where visitors can buy local produce. Maps are available at the visitor information centre in the main street.

CLIMATE VICTOR HARBOR

	J	F	M	A	M	J	J	A	S	O	N	D
Max. °C	24	24	23	21	19	16	15	16	18	20	22	23
Min. °C	16	16	15	12	10	8	8	8	9	11	12	14
Rain mm	22	20	23	43	62	71	74	67	55	46	28	23
Raindays	4	4	6	10	14	15	16	16	14	11	8	6

Strathalbyn
Picturesque Strathalbyn was settled in 1839 by Scottish immigrants and is a heritage town. The thirty or so listed buildings are fine examples of the State's 19th-century rural architecture. Shop here for antiques, bric-a-brac and arts and crafts.

For more detail see maps 37 & 39.

Gulf St Vincent coast
Enjoy the scenery at Second Valley and Cape Jervis or go snorkelling at Port Noarlunga. Bathe at one of a number of family beaches, or wine and dine on superb local produce at the Star of Greece at Port Willunga.

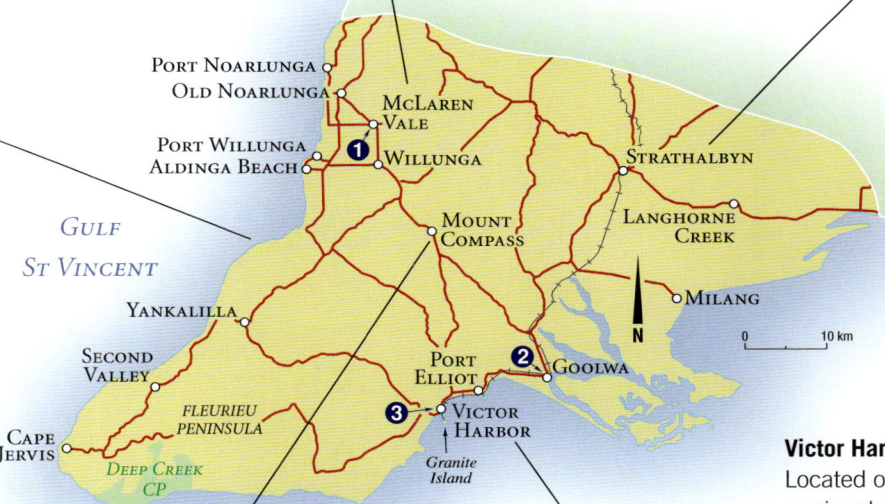

Victor Harbor
Located on the Southern Ocean side of the peninsula, historic Victor Harbor has long been a popular holiday resort. Attractions include the horse-drawn tram, heritage sites, penguins, dolphins, whales and the bush trails in wilderness parks west of town.

Mount Compass Gourmet Trail
Mount Compass is the centre of gourmet food production in this region, with trout, berry, deer, pheasant and marron farms open for viewing and sales. Pick up a touring map from the visitor information centre in McLaren Vale.

FLINDERS RANGES & OUTBACK

This vast, varied region, covering about 70 per cent of the State, offers spectacular scenery and abundant flora and fauna. While many attractions are easily reached along well-maintained roads, other spots are remote and require special preparations and, in some cases, a four-wheel drive vehicle. Always check weather conditions ahead. Camping and caravanning holidays are very popular in these parts, a fact reflected by the high quality of many facilities. Fees are charged for entry to national parks; a pass should be bought in advance for the desert parks in the north. Conditions apply to travel in Aboriginal lands.

TOP EVENTS

Easter	Opal Festival (Coober Pedy)
Apr.	Antique and Craft Fair (Port Augusta)
May	Race Meeting and Gymkhana (Oodnadatta)
June	Glendi Festival (Greek culture, Coober Pedy)
July	Australian Camel Cup (Marree)
Aug.	Races (Innamincka)
Sept.	Art Exhibition (Hawker)
Sept.	Opal Festival (Andamooka)

EXPERIENCE IT!

1. **Take** a Ridgetop Tour via Arkaroola for a taste of the ancient world of the Flinders Ranges
2. **Admire** desert flora at Port Augusta's Australian Arid Lands Botanic Gardens
3. **Visit** Kanyaka Homestead Historic Site, south of Hawker

VISITOR INFORMATION
Wadlata Outback Centre
Port Augusta: (08) 8641 0793
www.flinders.outback.on.net

FOCUS ON

Ancient landforms
Traces of the first life on earth, marine animal fossils, have been found in the Flinders Ranges. There are numerous places to experience the geological and scenic wonders of these ancient peaks and valleys. In the south around Wilpena, attractions include the Great Wall of China (a massive limestone ridge) and Bunyeroo and Brachina gorges, where an interpretative walk retraces 1000 million years of fossil history. In the north, in and around the Gammon Ranges National Park, visit the Bararrana, Wearing, Mount Chambers, Big Moro, Italowie and Weetootla gorges, and the Bolla Bollana and Nooldoonooldoona waterholes.

CLIMATE HAWKER

	J	F	M	A	M	J	J	A	S	O	N	D
Max. °C	34	33	30	25	20	16	16	18	21	26	29	32
Min. °C	17	18	15	11	7	5	4	4	7	10	13	16
Rain mm	20	21	17	20	31	39	35	33	28	24	22	21
Raindays	3	2	2	3	5	7	7	7	6	5	4	3

Coober Pedy
This town is famous for its opal production (70 per cent of world's supply), and for buildings constructed underground to protect residents against extreme temperatures. Visit the museums and mines, try your hand at prospecting, and shop for opals.

Lake Eyre
Australia's largest salt lake, in Lake Eyre National Park, is also the continent's lowest lying land at 15 metres below sea level. A few times each century the dry lake fills and hundreds of thousands of birds flock to the area to feed and breed.

Innamincka and Cooper Creek
Near Innamincka is the part of Cooper Creek where the Burke and Wills expedition ended in tragedy. Memorials include the Dig Tree, across the Queensland border. The nearby Coongie Lakes form a remarkable wetland in the midst of gibber plains.

Yourambulla Caves
One of several Aboriginal rock-art sites in the Flinders Ranges, these caves are reached via a 15-minute walk off the road south of Hawker. The images are characterised by the use of black and yellow pigment rather than the common red ochre.

For more detail see maps 40–1, 44–5 & 46–7.

Wildflowers of the ranges
In spring, rainfall permitting, native flowers carpet the semi-arid landscape of the Flinders Ranges. Stunning displays can be seen throughout the region, including around the popular Wilpena Pound in Flinders Ranges National Park. Favourites include Sturt's nightshade, silver tails, yellow buttons and the brilliant Sturt's desert pea (pictured).

SOUTH-WEST CORNER

Western Australia's south-west corner, with a climate comfortable enough to allow year-round visits, is about three-and-a-half hours' drive from Perth. Mandurah, at the beginning of a stretch of low, sandy inlets and lakes, is the first of a number of seaside resorts. The rocky Limestone Coast beyond Cape Naturaliste, broken by good surf beaches, ends at Cape Leeuwin where the Indian and Southern oceans meet. The State's premier winegrowing region, at Margaret River, is a few kilometres inland. The old-growth jarrah and karri forests on the low plateau 30 km from the coast are one of the south-west's unique features.

TOP EVENTS
Jan.	Summerfest (Busselton)
Feb.	Amberley Semillon and Seafood Weekend (Amberley Estate, near Yallingup)
Feb.	Crab Festival (Mandurah)
Feb.–Mar.	Leeuwin Estate Concert (Leeuwin Estate, near Margaret River)
Mar.	Margaret River Masters (surfing competition, Margaret River)
June	15 000 Motocross (Manjimup)
Aug.	Tulip Festival (Balingup, near Donnybrook)
Nov.	Wine Festival (Australind, even-numbered years)
Nov.	Spring Festival (Rockingham)

EXPERIENCE IT!
1. **Climb** the spiral ladder to the top of the 61-m karri Gloucester Tree in Gloucester National Park
2. **Cruise** to see dolphins in Koombana Bay at Bunbury
3. **Visit** the restored 1859 homestead Wonnerup House, 10 km east of Busselton

VISITOR INFORMATION
Mandurah: (08) 9550 3999
Margaret River: (08) 9757 2911
www.margaretriverwa.com

FOCUS ON
Old-growth forests
Western Australia's only forests are in the cool, well-watered south-west. Jarrah, a beautifully grained, deep-red hardwood, flourishes between Dwellingup and Collie. Forests of karri, one of the world's tallest trees, reaching 90 m in a hundred years, are found in the wetter areas, from Manjimup to Walpole. Pemberton is the focus of a struggle over logging between the timber industry and conservationists that has become a State and Federal political issue. Dwellingup's Forest Heritage Centre shows both sides of the controversy and features the forest (at treetop level, from the Canopy Walk) and the furniture made from forest timbers, in the workshops below.

CLIMATE BUSSELTON
	J	F	M	A	M	J	J	A	S	O	N	D
Max. °C	29	28	26	23	19	17	16	17	18	20	24	27
Min. °C	14	14	13	11	9	8	8	8	9	11	13
Rain mm	10	11	22	42	118	175	167	117	75	52	24	13
Raindays	3	2	4	8	15	19	22	19	16	13	7	4

Peel Coast
The coastal towns south of Rockingham offer swimming, boating, fishing and crabbing. The Yalgorup National Park protects ten coastal lakes, with views over ocean and dunes at high points. From Preston Beach, a walking track crosses tuart and peppermint woodlands to Lake Pollard, where black swans gather from October to March.

Limestone Coast
Protected by the Leeuwin–Naturaliste National Park, the Limestone Coast offers a splendid stretch of rocky headlands, wild beaches and limestone caves. Walking, surfing at Yallingup beach, scuba-diving, and whale-watching and salmon fishing from September to December, are other attractions.

Margaret River wine styles
The region's reputation for premium wines rests principally on cabernet sauvignon and chardonnay grown on grey-brown, gravelly-sandy soils. Try the cabernet from Vasse Felix, Moss Wood and Cullen and the chardonnays from Leeuwin Estate, Voyager Estate (pictured) and Ashbrook.

For more detail see maps 52, 53 & 54.

Blackwood Valley
The Blackwood River meanders for 500 km through wheat-belt plains and forested valleys to its broad estuary at Augusta. Secluded spots along the river between Nannup and Alexandra Bridge offer tranquil camping, fishing, swimming and canoeing. The Sheoak Walk is a 1-hour loop through the forest close to Nannup.

Pemberton
At tiny Pemberton you can take the tramway (pictured) through the heart of the great karri and marri forests, and visit the virgin forests in Warren and Beedelup national parks. You can also sample the marron – freshwater cray – grown in local hatcheries, and tour the 28 or so wineries.

THE KIMBERLEY

The Kimberley, bigger than Germany, has a population of just 25 000 people. It is one of Australia's true frontiers, with an ancient, reddened landscape of rivers and gorges, a wild inhabited coastline, and the signature beehive shapes of the Bungle Bungles. Visitors will find the grandeur largely untouched and travelling conditions highly variable. While the coastal town of Broome is becoming increasingly well known as a resort destination, there are large tracts of this region that are completely inaccessible by road – or accessible by 4WD only. Travellers should familiarise themselves with prevailing conditions and carry adequate supplies.

CLIMATE HALLS CREEK

	J	F	M	A	M	J	J	A	S	O	N	D
Max. °C	37	36	36	34	30	27	27	30	34	37	38	38
Min. °C	24	24	23	20	17	14	13	15	19	23	25	25
Rain mm	153	137	74	22	13	5	6	2	4	17	37	77
Raindays	13	13	8	3	2	1	1	1	1	3	6	11

TOP EVENTS
- **Easter** Dragon Boat Regatta (Broome)
- **May** King Tide Day (festival celebrating highest tide in Australia, Derby)
- **June** Dam to Dam Dinghy Race (Kununurra)
- **June** Mowanjum Festival (indigenous art and culture, Derby)
- **Aug.** Opera Under the Stars (Broome)
- **Aug.–Sept.** Shinju Matsuri (Festival of the Pearl, Broome)
- **Sept.** Munumburra Music Festival (Wyndham)

EXPERIENCE IT!
1. **View** the multi-coloured cliffs of Geikie Gorge on a boat trip up the Fitzroy River
2. **Stay** at El Questro Station, Australia's most luxurious outback resort, and enjoy the hot springs
3. **Ride** a camel along the magnificent Cable Beach in Broome

VISITOR INFORMATION
Broome: (08) 9192 2222
Kununurra: (08) 9168 1177

FOCUS ON

Aboriginal art
The Kimberley region is renowned for two styles – the Bradshaw and the Wandjina. The Bradshaw 'figures' as they are known, are painted in red ochre. According to one Aboriginal legend, birds drew the figures using their beaks. One rock-face frieze depicts figures elaborately decorated with headdresses, tassels, skirts and epaulets. Significant Bradshaw sites have been found on the Drysdale River. The more recent Wandjina figures, named for ancestor spirits from the sky and sea who brought rain and fertility, are in solid red or black, outlined in red ochre, and sometimes on a white background. Wandjina figures are typically human-like, with pallid faces and wide, staring eyes and, for reasons of religious belief, no mouth. Good examples of Wandjina art have been found near Kalumburu on the King Edward River.

Gibb River Road
This unsealed road, starting at Derby and running 649 km through The Kimberley, provides a true outback adventure. River crossings, passable only during the Dry, offer scenic campsites. Along the way are spectacular gorges and swimming spots. Read the *Gibb River Road Guide* before commencing your journey.

Port of pearls
Broome has a balmy winter climate, the white, palm-fringed Cable Beach, and a multicultural heritage. In Chinatown there are Chinese merchants, pearl dealers, and restaurants serving a variety of cuisines. The history of pearling is told at the old customs house, the pearling luggers display, and the Japanese Cemetery (pictured).

Lake Argyle and Kununurra
Lake Argyle was formed in the 1960s as part of the Ord River Scheme, the success of which is evident in the lush crops of the area (pictured). The lake is so large that it has developed its own ecosystems. By taking a boat cruise you can experience the magnificent scenery and abundant wildlife of the area. Start from Kununurra, which has excellent tourist facilities.

Purnululu National Park
A rough 50-km track off the Great Northern Highway leads to the spectacular Bungle Bungle Range in Purnululu National Park on the Ord River. A fantastic landscape of huge black-and-orange sandstone domes is intersected by narrow, palm-lined gorges where pools reflect sunlight off sheer walls.

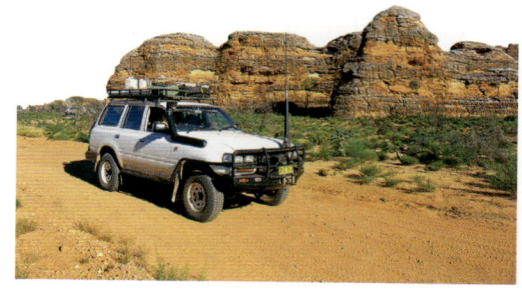

Wolfe Creek Meteorite Crater
Two hours by unsealed road south of Halls Creek, and across some inhospitable country, is the world's second largest meteorite crater. It is 850 m across and was probably formed by a meteorite, weighing at least several thousand tons, crashing to earth a million years ago.

For more detail see map 60–1.

KAKADU

The ancient Arnhem Land escarpment meanders 500 km north to south, separating Kakadu National Park in the west from Arnhem Land in the east. World Heritage-listed Kakadu is of enormous cultural and environmental significance; it is a place of overwhelming natural beauty and grand landscapes. The area is also a birdwatcher's paradise, being home to one-third of all of Australia's bird species. The main access to Kakadu is via the sealed Arnhem Highway from Darwin. Some park areas are 4WD only. Facilities are excellent and park accommodation ranges from resort-style to camping. During the Wet (November to April) some areas of this region may be inaccessible by road.

TOP EVENT
Aug. Wind Festival (Jabiru)

EXPERIENCE IT!
1. **Fish** for barramundi in one of the many beautiful billabongs
2. **Follow** the nature trail through the Mamukala Wetlands where thousands of waterbirds congregate towards the end of the Dry
3. **Take** an Aboriginal-guided cultural tour of the East Alligator River, via Border Store

VISITOR INFORMATION
Tourism Top End
Darwin: (08) 8936 2499
www.nttc.com.au
Bowali Visitor Centre
Kakadu: (08) 8938 1121

FOCUS ON

Natural and cultural Kakadu
Kakadu is one of only a few World Heritage sites worldwide that are listed for both their natural and cultural value. It contains most habitats of northern Australia, including monsoonal rainforest, tidal estuary and floodplain, and riverine floodplain and woodland. One of the most biologically diverse areas of the country, Kakadu is home to 50 or more mammal species, 280 bird species, 123 reptile species, 52 freshwater fish species and 1600 plant species. Culturally, Kakadu's credentials are just as impressive. With an estimated 5000 rock-art sites, it has the world's oldest and largest rock-art collection. Some of the work records important events over the millennia, such as the presence and extinction of the thylacine and the contact between Aboriginal people and Macassan traders.

Ubirr
Ubirr, on the Arnhem Land escarpment, houses one major rock-art gallery and some 36 smaller sites nearby. The paintings are predominantly in the X-ray style, although there are also Mimi paintings (depictions of delicate spirit figures), believed to be older. A circuit walk takes in the main sites.

Bowali Visitor Centre
Dynamic displays in Kakadu National Park's main visitor centre tell the story of Kakadu from indigenous and non-indigenous perspectives. An excellent first stop on any tour of the area, Bowali has a theatrette that shows audio-visuals of the park's highlights. Park headquarters is on the same site.

CLIMATE JABIRU
	J	F	M	A	M	J	J	A	S	O	N	D
Max. °C	34	33	33	34	33	31	32	34	36	37	36	35
Min. °C	25	24	24	24	22	19	18	19	21	24	25	25
Rain mm	347	332	318	66	11	1	3	4	9	27	158	211
Raindays	22	21	20	7	2	0	0	0	1	3	12	16

Ranger Uranium Mine
Uranium was discovered in the region in 1953. The Ranger mine opened in 1981 and the nearby township of Jabiru was established to accommodate mine workers. Tours of the mine are run in the Dry (May to October).

For more detail see maps 65 & 66–7.

Yellow Water
Yellow Water (Ngurrungurrudjba) is a spectacular wetlands area with prolific birdlife, particularly in the dry season. Boat tours give visitors a close-up view of the birdlife and the Territory's crocodiles; the sunrise and sunset tours are particularly rewarding. Tours depart from Gagudju Lodge, Cooinda.

Jim Jim and Twin Falls
Jim Jim Falls (Barrkmalam) and Twin Falls (Gungkurdul) are reached via a 4WD track, 60 and 70 km respectively off the Kakadu Hwy. Both falls are best seen early in the Dry. Jim Jim, a 215-m drop, has a sand-fringed pool for year-round swimming. Twin Falls (pictured) has grand rock formations.

Nourlangie Rock
Nourlangie on the Arnhem Land escarpment is one of Kakadu's main Aboriginal rock-art areas. On the Nourlangie Art Site Walk visitors see a variety of styles, including prime examples of Kakadu X-ray art, which shows the anatomy of humans and animals in rich detail. Enjoy splendid views as you walk.

THE RED CENTRE

This is Australia's geographical, scenic and mythic heart. With its spectacular landforms, deserts, blue skies and monumental sense of scale, it has become a powerful symbol of the ancient grandeur of the Australian continent. For many thousands of years the region has been home to Aboriginal people from numerous groups – including the Arrernte and the Anangu – who named, mapped and inscribed with spiritual meaning almost every one of the landforms, from the massive Uluru to ancient riverbeds and obelisks. The Europeans colonised the area in the 1870s with the building of the Overland Telegraph Line. Tourism began in the 1940s and has flourished since the 1970s.

TOP EVENTS
- **Apr.** Country Music Festival (Alice Springs)
- **May** Bangtail Muster (Alice Springs)
- **June** Finke Desert Race (vehicle-racing, Alice Springs)
- **July** Camel Cup (Alice Springs)
- **Aug.** Rodeo (Alice Springs)
- **Aug.** Henley-on-Todd Regatta (Alice Springs)
- **Sept.** Desert Harmony Festival (Tennant Creek)

EXPERIENCE IT!
1. **Take** a 4WD trip to Palm Valley to see the ancient red fan palms of Finke Gorge
2. **Swim** in the refreshingly cold waters of Trephina Gorge
3. **Explore** the ruins at Arltunga Historical Reserve, site of Central Australia's first gold rush in 1887

VISITOR INFORMATION
Central Australian Tourism Industry Association
Alice Springs: (08) 8952 5800
www.centralaustraliantourism.com

FOCUS ON
The story of Uluru
Uluru lies in the territory of the Anangu people. European explorer William Gosse named it Ayers Rock in 1873. Along with The Olgas (now Kata Tjuta) and surrounding land it became a national park in 1958. In 1985 it was returned to its traditional owners and was gazetted as Uluru. The rock is Australia's most identifiable natural icon. It is a massive, red, rounded monolith rising 348 m above the plain and 863 m above sea level, and reaching 6 km below the earth's surface. Uluru's circumference measures 9.4 km. For the Anangu, the rock is not a single spiritual object but a thing of many parts: along with Kata Tjuta, it is the physical evidence of the deeds and journeys of the Tjukurpa, the ancestral beings of creation times.

CLIMATE ALICE SPRINGS

	J	F	M	A	M	J	J	A	S	O	N	D
Max. °C	36	35	32	28	23	20	19	22	27	31	33	35
Min. °C	21	21	17	13	8	5	4	6	10	15	18	20
Rain mm	36	42	37	14	17	15	16	12	9	21	26	37
Raindays	5	5	3	2	3	3	3	2	2	5	6	5

West MacDonnell Ranges
The traditional home of the Arrernte people, these ranges offer extraordinarily diverse flora (about 600 species, 75 of them rare) and some of Australia's best gorge scenery. Sites to visit include Simpsons Gap, Ellery Creek Big Hole, Serpentine Gorge and Ormiston Gorge. All are accessible in a 2WD vehicle. For walkers, there is the Larapinta Trail.

Kings Canyon
Spectacular Kings Canyon features sandstone walls rising to 100 m. A 6-km-return trail scales the side of the canyon and leads past beehive formations to the Garden of Eden. The surrounding Watarrka National Park, traditional land of the Luritja people, includes lush relic vegetation and classic red sand dunes.

Devils Marbles
This collection of huge, precarious-looking spherical boulders lies in clusters in a shallow valley. The area is protected as an Aboriginal site. According to legend, the Marbles are the Rainbow Serpent's eggs.

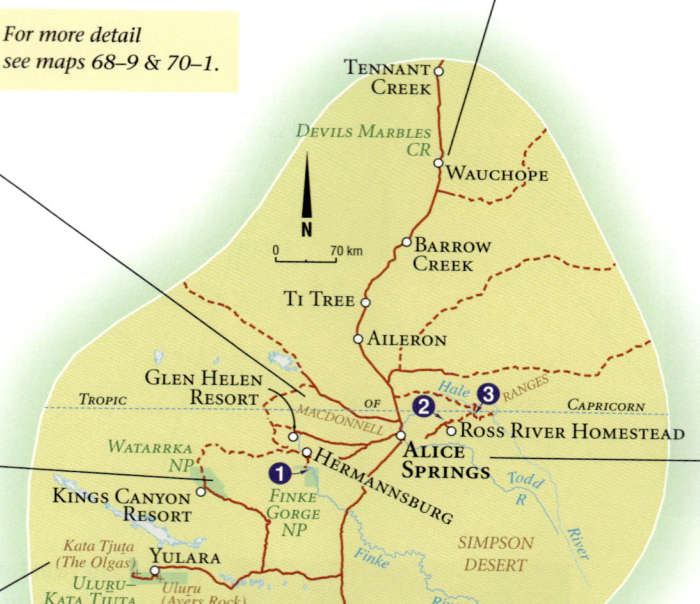

For more detail see maps 68–9 & 70–1.

Kata Tjuta
Uluru's sister rock formation Kata Tjuta, meaning 'many heads' comprises 36 magnificently rounded and coloured dome-like shapes covering about 35 sq km. The 3-hour Valley of the Winds walk winds through the crevices and gorges of the rock system.

Alice Springs
Australia's best-known country town was originally a waterhole, named for a telegraph official's wife. Alice Springs today is a lively, well-serviced centre with around 400 000 visitors each year. Attractions include the Museum of Central Australia, Araluen Galleries and the Telegraph Station Historical Reserve.

Exploring Uluru
The Anangu prefer tourists not to climb Uluru. There are four guided walks: a 9.5-km walk around the base; the Mala walk to art sites; the Liru walk explaining the use of bush materials; and the Kuniya walk, during which creation stories are told.

TROPICAL NORTH

Cairns, capital of tropical Australia, is a major destination for tourists from around the world. It is also within easy reach of some of the country's most famous natural landscapes. At Cape Tribulation, north of Cairns, the rainforest meets the sea; the coastline, already blessed with dazzling white sands and turquoise waters, takes on a beauty so intense as to be almost surreal. Off the coast, and easily explored by boat, is the Great Barrier Reef, one of the natural wonders of the world. A maze of coral reefs and cays, the reef extends for thousands of kilometres along the coast and supports an extraordinary collection of marine life.

TOP EVENTS
May	Village Carnivale (Port Douglas)
May	Races, Concert and Rodeo (Chillagoe)
May	Folk Festival (Kuranda)
July	Jazz Festival (Yungaburra)
Oct.	Reef Festival and Hook, Wine and Sinker Festival (Cairns)
Oct.	Country Music Festival (Mareeba)
Oct.	Folk Festival (Yungaburra)

EXPERIENCE IT!
1. **Ride** a raft on the white water of the Tully River which descends from the Atherton Tableland through rainforest gorges
2. **Climb** Mount Bartle Frere, Queensland's highest mountain, on a 12-hour walk through Wooroonooran National Park
3. **Dive**, snorkel or just gaze at the wonder of the Great Barrier Reef on a boat trip from Cairns or Port Douglas

CLIMATE CAIRNS
	J	F	M	A	M	J	J	A	S	O	N	D
Max.°C	31	31	30	29	28	26	26	27	28	29	31	31
Min. °C	24	24	23	22	20	18	17	18	19	21	22	23
Rain mm	413	435	442	191	94	49	28	27	36	38	90	175
Raindays	18	19	20	17	14	10	9	8	8	8	10	13

VISITOR INFORMATION
Tourism Tropical North Queensland
Cairns: (07) 4051 3588
www.tnq.org.au

FOCUS ON

Tropical rainforests
The World Heritage Wet Tropics area covers 894 000 ha along the eastern escarpment of the Great Dividing Range between Townsville and Cooktown, and features rainforest, mountains, gorges, fast-flowing rivers and numerous waterfalls. The rainforest here is one of the most biologically diverse and ancient environments on Earth. Australia's largest area of rainforest wilderness is in the Daintree River valley just north of Mossman. At Cape Tribulation two World Heritage areas come together: rainforest and reef along the coast. Queensland's tropical rainforests can be seen on short walks, or on hikes lasting days; on sealed roads or 4WD treks along rutted tracks that cross creek fords; from scenic railways and cableways; and by boat or raft on forest rivers.

Tropical cuisine
A menu at a restaurant in the exclusive holiday town of Port Douglas might offer Gulf bug tempura skewered on lemongrass accompanied by a Tableland salad of greens, mango slices, coconut slivers and wasabi mayonnaise, and with a tropical-fruit ice-cream for dessert. Chefs are using the abundant local produce to create a true regional cuisine.

Daintree National Park
The Mossman Gorge section of this World Heritage park takes visitors into the rainforest's green shady heart via an easy 2.7-km walk to the Mossman River. The Cape Tribulation section is a rich mix of coastal rainforest, mangroves, swamp and heath. There is camping at Noah Beach. From here, walking trails lead to spectacular reef and rainforest scenery.

For more detail see map 81.

Chillagoe Caves
This outstanding cave system is in a limestone belt extending north to the Palmer River. Vine thickets, towering above-ground structures, bat colonies and richly decorative stalactites and stalagmites create an unforgettable natural environment. There are regular tours of some caves, and visitors can wander through others without a guide.

Atherton Tableland
This 900-m-high tableland south-west of Cairns is a productive farming district, thanks to its high rainfall and rich volcanic soil. The historic town of Yungaburra is listed with the National Trust. Nearby is the remarkable Curtain Fig Tree, a strangler fig that has subsumed its host, sending down a curtain of roots. Volcanic lakes and spectacular waterfalls, including Millaa Millaa Falls (pictured) and Zillie Falls, are among the other scenic attractions.

Scenic routes to Kuranda
Kuranda, an Aboriginal word for 'village in the rainforest', can be reached from Cairns via a couple of spectacularly scenic routes. A 19th-century steam-train carries visitors 34 km up steep slopes, through rainforest, along Barron Gorge and past Barron Falls. The Skyrail Rainforest Cableway (pictured) is a gondola cableway, passing through and above the rainforest canopy.

Cairns
Cairns, located on the edge of two extraordinary natural environments, the reef and the rainforest, is an ideal base for activities ranging from big-game fishing to diving, walking and 4WD touring. A casino, five-star hotels, excellent restaurants and pulsating nightclubs cater for the most sophisticated travellers, while cafes, backpacker lodges and a lively atmosphere attract the backpacker crowd.

SUNSHINE COAST

Beautiful beaches, bathed by the blue South Pacific and fringed by native bush, stretch from Rainbow Beach southward to the tip of Bribie Island to form the Sunshine Coast. The weather is near perfect, with winter temperatures around 25°C. Well-serviced holiday towns cater to all interests from golf and fishing to fine dining and cafe-squatting. Inland lie the forested folds and ridges of the hinterland, where visitors can enjoy hillside villages, waterfalls, walks, scenic drives, superb views and a couple of trademark Queensland holiday attractions. In the south of this area, the Glass House Mountains loom above the surrounding plains.

TOP EVENTS

Jan.	Ginger Flower Festival (Yandina)
Easter	Easter Festival (Tin Can Bay)
Apr.	Sunshine Coast Festival of the Sea
June	William Landsborough Day (Landsborough)
Aug.	National Country Music Muster (Gympie)
Sept.–Oct.	Jazz Festival (Noosa Heads)
Oct.	Gold Rush Festival (Gympie)
Oct.	Nambour Yarn Festival (Mapleton, near Nambour)
Oct.–Nov.	Triathlon Multi Sport Festival (Noosa Heads)

EXPERIENCE IT!

1. **Glide** along Noosa River in a gondola at sunset, with champagne and music
2. **Experience** the transparent tunnel at the UnderWater World complex at Mooloolaba
3. **Fish** for bream, flathead, whiting and dart in the surf along Rainbow Beach

CLIMATE NAMBOUR

	J	F	M	A	M	J	J	A	S	O	N	D
Max.°C	30	29	28	26	24	22	21	22	25	27	28	29
Min.°C	19	20	18	15	12	9	8	8	10	14	16	18
Rain mm	242	262	236	149	143	91	92	53	48	105	141	176
Raindays	16	18	18	13	13	9	9	8	9	12	12	13

VISITOR INFORMATION

Caloundra: (07) 5491 0202; 1800 644 969
Cooloola area: (07) 5483 5554
Maroochydore: (07) 5479 1566; 1800 882 032
Noosa Heads: (07) 5447 4988; 1800 448 833
www.sunshinecoast.org

FOCUS ON

Tropical produce

The Sunshine Coast hinterland, with its subtropical climate and volcanic soils, is renowned for its produce. Nambour's Big Pineapple symbolises the importance of food as a tourist attraction in the region. Visitors can take a train, trolley and boat through a plantation growing pineapples and other fruit, macadamia nuts, spices and flowers. Yandina's Ginger Factory, the world's largest, sells ginger products including ginger ice-cream. For freshly picked local fruit and vegetables, visit the Saturday morning markets at Eumundi, north of Yandina. The Superbee Honey Factory, south of Buderim, has beekeeping demonstrations and 28 varieties of honey for tasting.

The coloured sands of Teewah

Located in the Cooloola section of Great Sandy National Park, the coloured sands rise in 40 000-year-old, 200-m-high multicoloured cliffs. It is thought that oxidisation or the dye of vegetation decay has caused the colouring; Aboriginal legend attributes it to the slaying of a rainbow serpent.

Mountain villages

The 70-km scenic drive here is one of Queensland's best. Starting on the Bruce Highway near Landsborough, it passes the antiques shops, B&Bs, galleries and cafes of the pretty mountain villages of Maleny, Montville, Flaxton and Mapleton, offering beautiful coastal and mountain views as well. The drive ends near the town of Nambour.

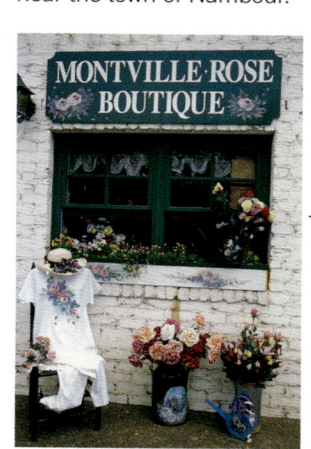

Noosa Heads

Noosa Heads offers luxury hotels, top restaurants, hip bars and stylish boutiques. The town is flanked by ocean on one side and an estuary on the other, and is overlooked by the headland of Noosa National Park with its pandanus-fringed beaches.

Southern coastal

The towns of Caloundra, Mooloolaba and Maroochydore make a pleasant daytrip from Brisbane, as well as being good spots for a family holiday. The area offers patrolled surfing beaches, protected lakes and rivers for boating and fishing, holiday flats and caravan parks, boat hire, and a range of child-friendly attractions.

Glass House Mountains

These 20-million-year-old crags, the giant cores of extinct volcanoes, mark the southern entrance to the Sunshine Coast. Glasshouse Mountains Road leads to sealed and unsealed drives through the mountains, with some spectacular lookouts along the way. There are walking trails, picnic grounds and challenges aplenty for rock-climbers.

For more detail see maps 74 & 77.

GOLD COAST & HINTERLAND

Each year, some 4 million visitors holiday along the Gold Coast's 70 km of coastline, which includes no less than 35 beaches stretching from South Stradbroke Island to the New South Wales border. Shopping, restaurants, nightlife, family entertainment, golf, fishing, sailing, surfing and unbelievably good weather are the trademark features of what has become Australia's biggest and busiest holiday destination. To the west lies the Gold Coast hinterland, another kind of world altogether. Here a superb natural landscape of tropical rainforests, unusual rock formations and cascading waterfalls offers visitors opportunities for such nature-based activities as bushwalking, camping, and wildlife-watching.

TOP EVENTS

Jan.	New Age of Aquarius Expo (Southport)
May–June	Gold Coast Cup Outrigger Canoe Ultra Marathon (Coolangatta)
June	Wintersun Festival (Coolangatta)
June	Gold Coast City Marathon (Runaway Bay, near Main Beach)
Aug.	Australian Arena Polo Championships (Nerang)
Aug.–Sept.	Gold Coast Show (Southport)
Oct.	Honda Indy 300 (Surfers Paradise)

EXPERIENCE IT!

1. **Try** your luck at the popular Conrad Jupiters Casino at Broadbeach
2. **Board** a charter to fish for mackerel, tuna, bonito and snapper, just offshore at Surfers Paradise
3. **Tee** off on one of the championship golf courses at Sanctuary Cove, one of the Southern Hemisphere's great golfing destinations

CLIMATE COOLANGATTA

	J	F	M	A	M	J	J	A	S	O	N	D
Max.°C	28	28	27	25	23	21	20	21	22	24	26	26
Min.°C	20	20	19	17	13	11	9	10	12	15	17	19
Rain mm	184	181	213	114	124	122	96	103	49	108	137	166
Raindays	14	15	16	14	10	9	7	9	9	11	11	13

VISITOR INFORMATION

Gold Coast Tourism Bureau
Coolangatta: (07) 5536 7765
Surfers Paradise: (07) 5538 4419
www.goldcoasttourism.com.au

FOCUS ON

Theme parks and family attractions

The Gold Coast theme parks are one of the region's most popular attractions. Warner Bros Movie World, south of Oxenford, is based on the legendary Hollywood movie set. It is a fully operational film set as well as a theme park. Nearby is Wet 'n' Wild Water World, Australia's largest aquatic park. At Coomera to the north is Dreamworld, which includes Tiger Island, the Tower of Terror and the Giant Drop. Sea World, north of Main Beach is the largest marine park in the Southern Hemisphere, offering performances by dolphins and penguins, among others. At Surfers Paradise, Ripleys Believe it or Not Museum exhibits oddities that stretch credibility. Other attractions in the region include the David Fleay Wildlife Park at West Burleigh, Currumbin Wildlife Sanctuary and, further south, Tropical Fruit World (in NSW).

For more detail see map 75.

Tamborine Mountain
This 552-m plateau lies on the Darlington Range, a spur of the McPherson Range. It is a picturesque and popular spot for hang-gliders (pictured). Tamborine National Park comprises seventeen small areas including Witches Falls, the first national park area in the State. Visitors will also find villages full of galleries, cafes, antique stores and craft shops, and a couple of splendid gardens.

Lamington National Park
Part of a World Heritage area, this popular park preserves a wonderland of rainforest and volcanic ridges, criss-crossed by 160 km of walking tracks. Visitors will experience rich plant and animal life. The main picnic, camping and walking areas are at Binna Burra and Green Mountains, sites of the award-winning Binna Burra Lodge and O'Reilly's Rainforest Guest House.

South Stradbroke Island
South Stradbroke, separated from North Stradbroke by the popular fishing channel Jumpinpin, is a peaceful alternative to the Gold Coast. Access is by launch from Runaway Bay. Cars are not permitted; visitors walk or cycle. There are two resorts, a camping ground, a range of leisure activities, and beautiful beaches.

Surfers Paradise
Surfers Paradise is the Gold Coast's signature settlement. The first big hotel was built here in the 1930s among a clutch of shacks along one of the State's most beautiful beaches. Since then the area has become an international holiday metropolis attracting every kind of visitor, from backpacker to jetsetter.

Standout beaches
The Gold Coast is a surfers' mecca. The southern beaches are the best, including Currumbin (pictured), and Kirra Point (in Coolangatta) said to have one of the 10 best breaks in the world. Greenmount Beach (also in Coolangatta) is great for families, as is Tallebudgera (north of Palm Beach), offering both estuary and ocean swimming.

SOUTH-EAST TASMANIA

Rivers, sea and mountains dominate the landscape of this extraordinarily rich and interesting region. The coastline fronting the Tasman Sea is a long, ragged and spectacularly beautiful strip of peninsulas, islands, inlets and channels. Imposing mountains shadow the coast in scenes more reminiscent of the seasides of Europe than those of Australia where the coastal plain is typically broad. Two major rivers, the Huon and Derwent, rise in the high country and meander through heavily pastured valleys. A leisurely pace of development over the last 200 years has kept much of the natural landscape intact and ensured the preservation of many colonial sites.

TOP EVENTS
- **Jan.** Huon Valley Folk and Music Festival (Cygnet)
- **Feb.** Royal Hobart Regatta
- **Mar.** Hop Harvest Festival (New Norfolk)
- **Oct.** Village Fair (Richmond)
- **Oct.** Spring in the Valley (incl. open gardens, New Norfolk)
- **Oct.** Olie Bollen (Dutch community festival, Kingston)
- **Dec.** Boxing Day Woodchop (Port Arthur)

EXPERIENCE IT!
1. **Enjoy** the views in Hartz Mountains National Park, a window onto Tasmania's trackless wildernesses
2. **Visit** Devils Kitchen, Tasman Blowhole and Tasmans Arch, dramatic rock formations on Tasman Peninsula
3. **Swim** in the thermal pool and take an underground cave tour at Hastings Caves

CLIMATE NEW NORFOLK

	J	F	M	A	M	J	J	A	S	O	N	D
Max. °C	24	24	21	18	14	11	11	13	15	17	19	21
Min. °C	11	11	10	7	5	3	2	3	5	6	8	10
Rain mm	40	35	39	48	45	49	48	47	49	55	47	50
Raindays	8	7	9	10	11	12	13	14	13	14	12	11

For more detail see maps 90–1 & 93.

VISITOR INFORMATION
Tasmanian Travel and Information Centre
Hobart: (03) 6230 8233
www.tourism.tas.gov.au

FOCUS ON

The convict system
Reminders of Australia's convict years are a feature of Tasmania's south-east. The island was colonised in 1803 as a penal settlement and over the next 50 years 52 227 males and 12 595 females were transported to its shores. Many prisoners worked on public buildings and other infrastructure until the early 1820s, after which most were assigned to private settlers. Re-offending convicts from other colonies were sent to Port Arthur on the Tasman Peninsula from 1830; later, a penal settlement for re-convicted criminals was built there. Transportation to Tasmania ended in 1852 after a bitter public campaign. Other convict sites on the Tasman Peninsula include the Coal Mines Historic Site and Eaglehawk Neck.

Mount Field National Park
Tasmania's oldest national park, 80 km north-west of Hobart, is a wilderness for beginners and daytrippers. The 40-m Russell Falls (pictured) is a wheelchair-friendly 15 minutes from the car park. Other trails wind through moorland, past lakes, and vistas of mountain and forest.

Derwent Valley
In the rolling country around New Norfolk rows of poplars mark the old hop fields. The Oast House at New Norfolk is a hop industry museum. Hops are still grown at Bushy Park, Glenora and Westerway, where shingled barns and waterwheels recall farming life over a century ago.

Richmond
This historic town 26 km from Hobart has 50 National Trust-classified 19th-century buildings. Some, like the courthouse and old post office, date from the 1820s. Convict-built Richmond Bridge (1823–25), is Australia's oldest bridge. Old Richmond Gaol (1825) retains its original cells and has displays on the convict system.

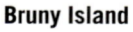

Bruny Island
Bruny Island was home to the Nuenonne people, of whom Truganini, Tasmania's most famous Aboriginal, was one. Ferries run from Kettering. In the north are farms and holiday shacks; the south is part national park. Visitors can fish, swim, bushwalk and see penguins at The Neck Reserve on the isthmus.

Southern Tasmanian Wine Route
Tasmania's first vineyard was established at New Town in 1821. The modern industry began in 1958 when Claudio Alcorso set up the acclaimed Moorilla Estate on the Derwent. There are now about 18 boutique wineries fanning out from Hobart. Start with a map from information centres in the area.

Port Arthur Historic Site
Port Arthur is Tasmania's most popular tourist attraction and one of Australia's most significant historic sites. Imposing sandstone prison buildings are set in 40 ha of spectacular landscaping. There are ghost tours and summer boat trips to Isle of the Dead, final resting-place for convicts and prison personnel alike.

Approach & Bypass Routes SYDNEY xix

Thick roads represent recommended approach and bypass routes.

Approach & Bypass Routes MELBOURNE

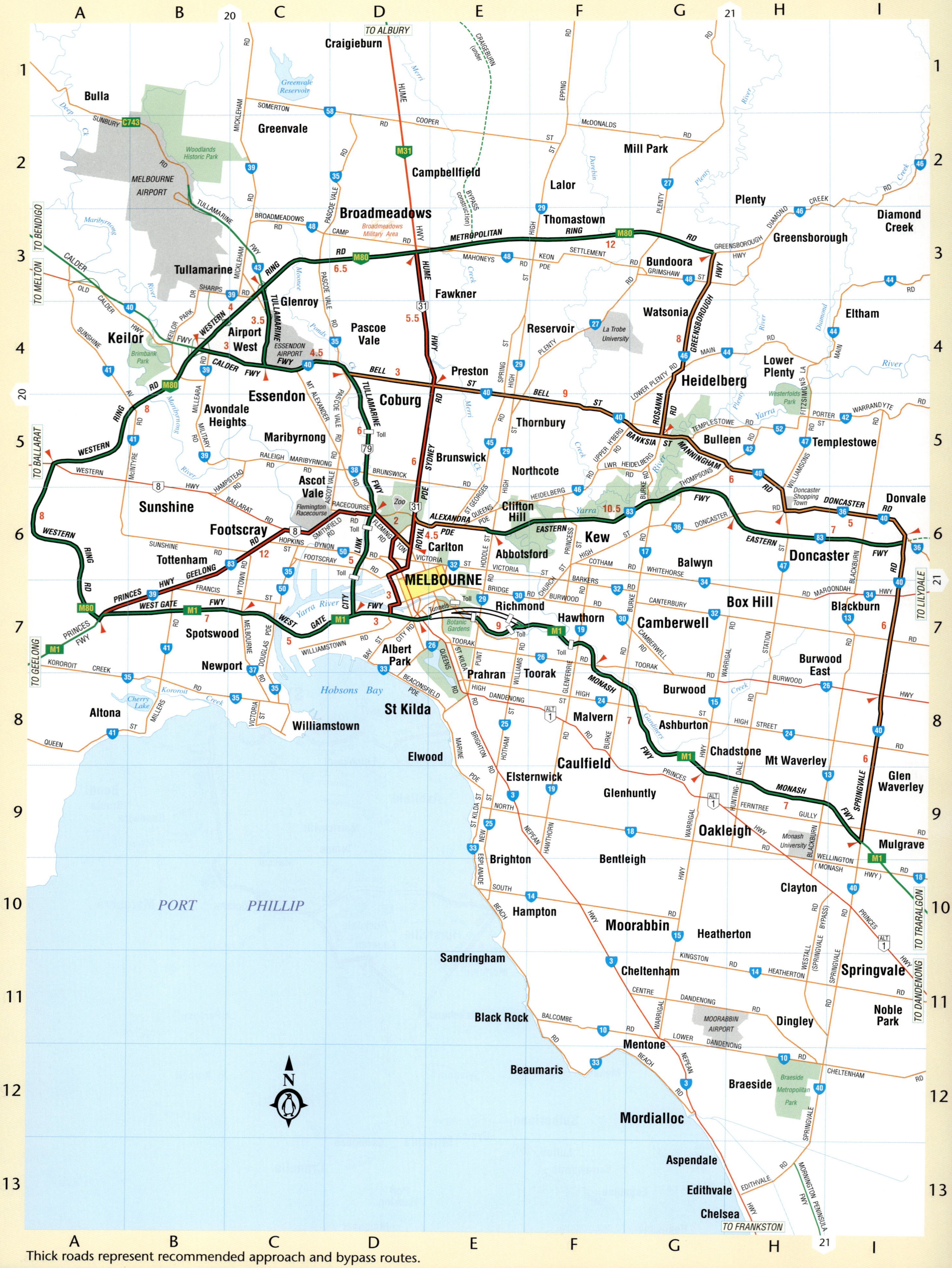

Thick roads represent recommended approach and bypass routes.

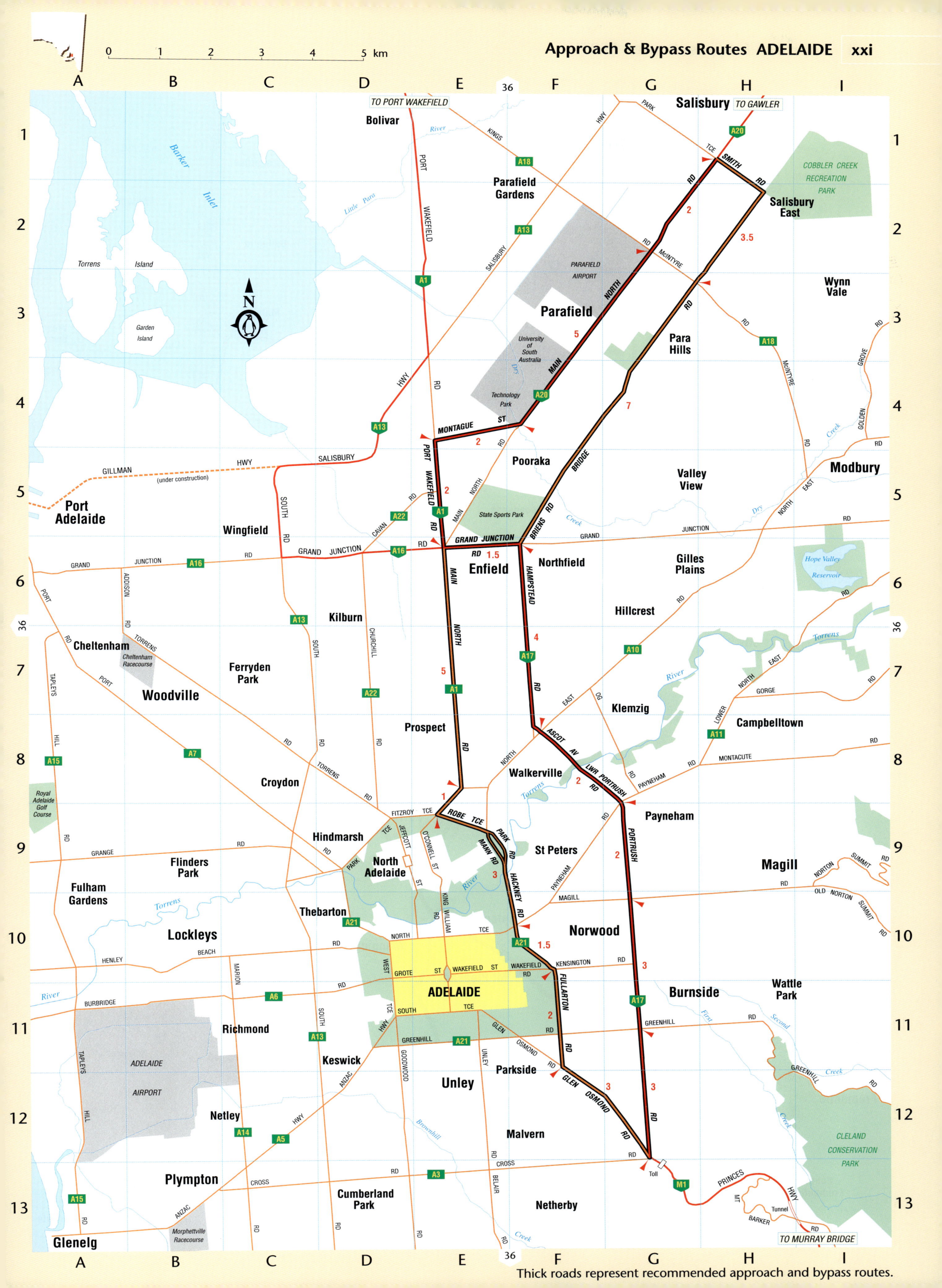

Approach & Bypass Routes ADELAIDE xxi

Thick roads represent recommended approach and bypass routes.

xxii Approach & Bypass Routes PERTH

Approach & Bypass Routes BRISBANE 1

Thick roads represent recommended approach and bypass routes.

New South Wales
Location Map

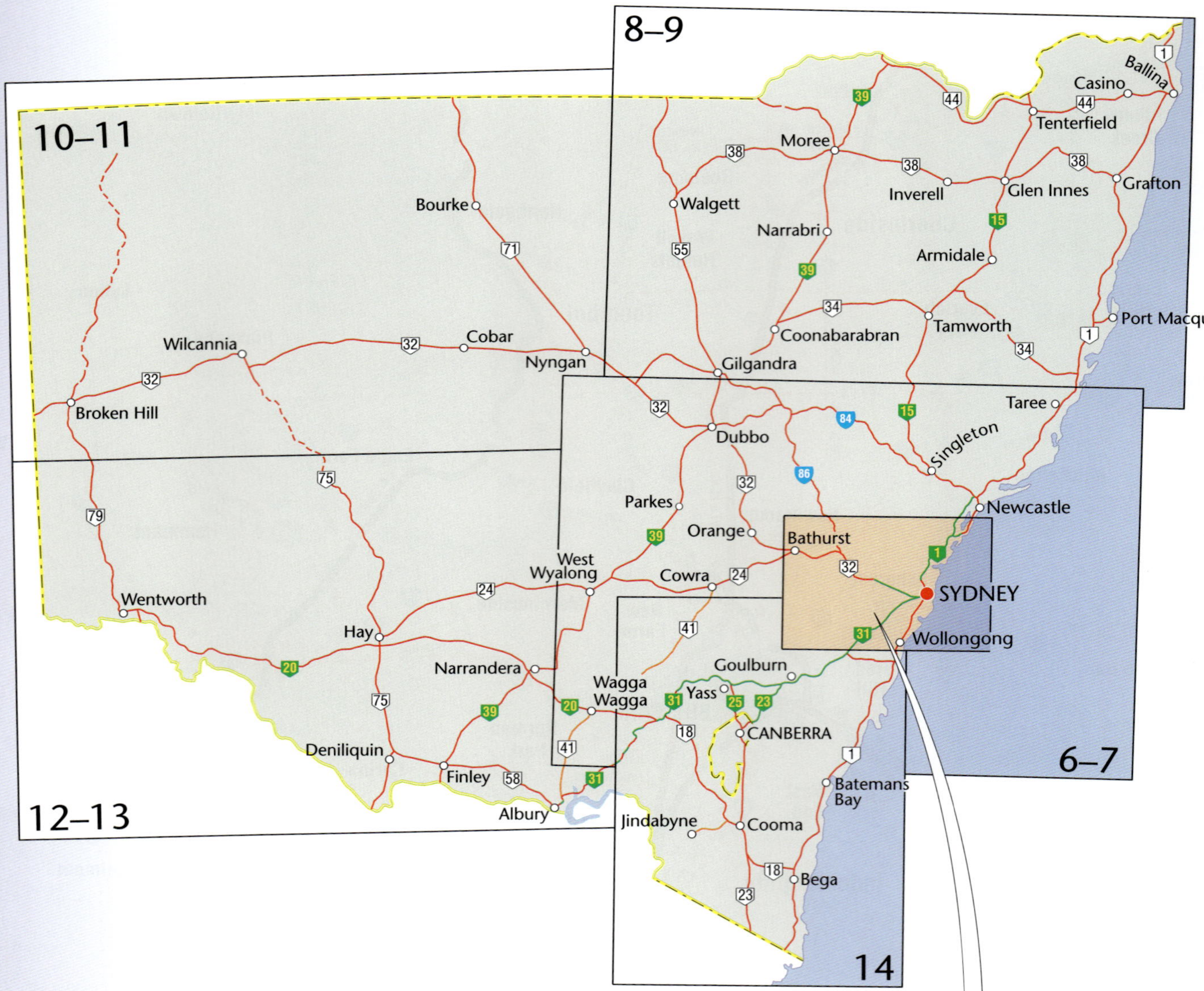

Sydney and Suburbs	
Central Sydney	3
Sydney Approach and Bypass Routes	xix
Touring New South Wales	
Sydney & Surrounds	4–5
Complete State Coverage	
Central Eastern New South Wales	6–7
North Eastern New South Wales	8–9
North Western New South Wales	10–11
South Western New South Wales	12–13
South Eastern New South Wales	14

Central Sydney 3

Accommodation
- ANA Hotel Sydney 1 D5
- Four Points Sheraton 2 C8
- Hilton Sydney 3 E9
- Hotel Intercontinental Sydney 4 F5
- Novotel Sydney on Darling Harbour 5 B9
- Park Hyatt Sydney 6 E2
- Parkroyal at Darling Harbour 7 C9
- The Regent Sydney 8 E5
- Renaissance Sydney Hotel 9 E5
- Sydney Central YHA 10 D12
- The Westin Sydney 11 E7
- The York Apartment Hotel 12 D6

General Information
- Cadmans Cottage (NPWS Info. Centre) 13 E4
- Central Railway Station 14 D13
- City Central Police Station 15 D10
- Coach Tour Departures 16 E3
- General Post Office 17 E7
- Interstate & Country Coach Terminal 18 E12
- Motoring Organisation (NRMA) 19 D7
- Qantas Travel Centre 20 E6
- Sydney Ferries 21 F4
- Sydney Visitor Centre 22 E3

Places of Interest
- AMP Tower Centrepoint 23 E8
- Art Gallery of New South Wales 24 H7
- Australian Museum 25 F9
- Australian National Maritime Museum 26 B8
- Campbell's Storehouse 27 E3
- Chinatown 28 D11
- Chinese Garden 29 C10
- Government House 30 G4
- Hyde Park Barracks Museum 31 F8
- IMAX Theatre 32 C9
- Justice & Police Museum 33 F5
- Museum of Contemporary Art 34 E4
- Museum of Sydney 35 F5
- Parliament of NSW 36 F7
- Powerhouse Museum 37 B11
- Queen Victoria Building 38 D8
- Royal Botanic Gardens 39 H6
- St Mary's Cathedral 40 F8
- Star City (casino, hotel & theatres) 41 A7
- State Library of NSW 42 F6
- Susannah Place 43 D4
- Sydney Aquarium 44 C8
- Sydney Harbour Bridge 45 F1
- Sydney Observatory 46 D4
- Sydney Opera House 47 G3
- Sydney Town Hall 48 D9
- Victoria Barracks 49 I13

Accommodation Only a sample range is listed; inclusion is not necessarily a recommendation.

4 Sydney & Surrounds

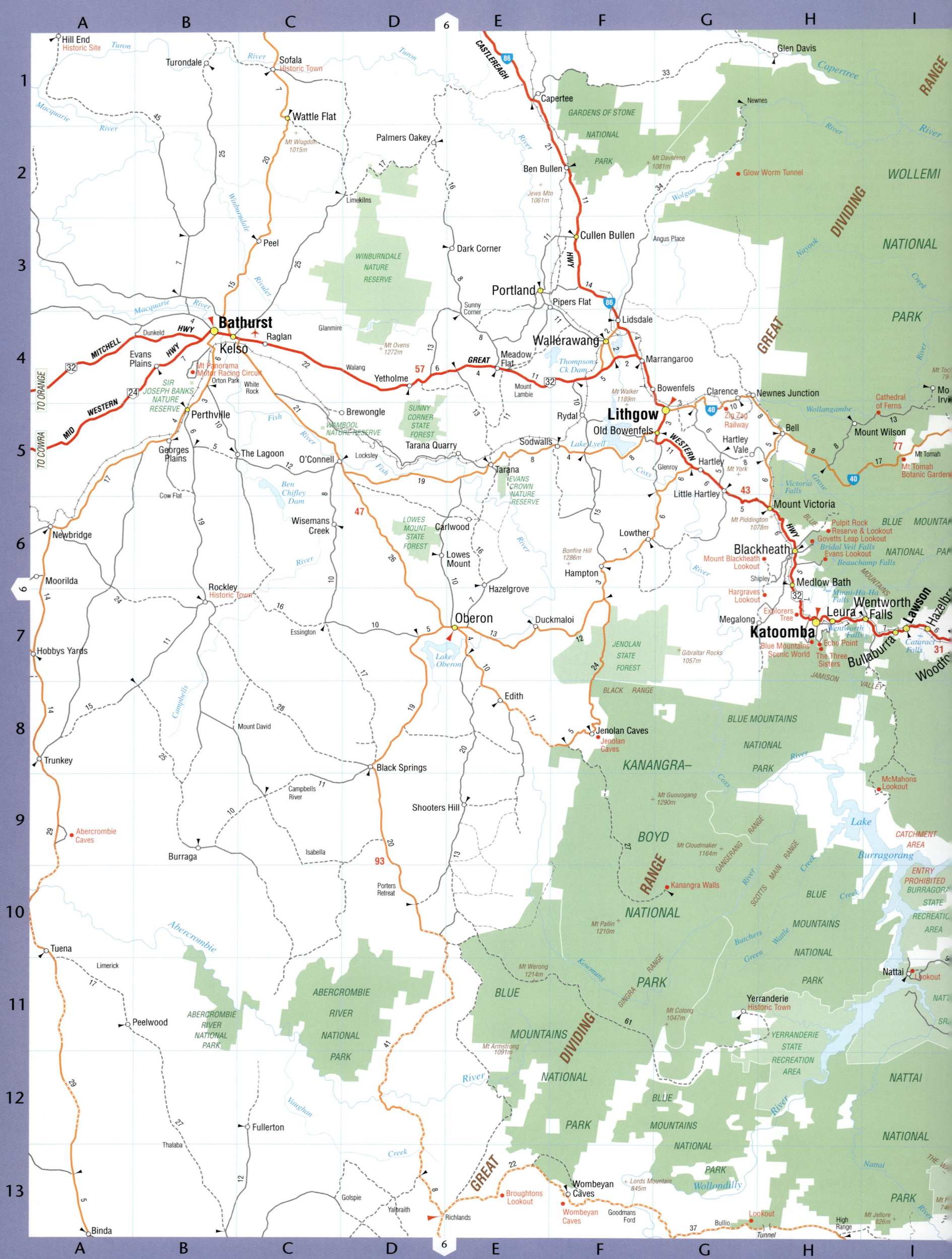

0 5 10 15 20 25 30 km
J K L M N O P Q R
1 2 3 4 5 6 7 8 9 10 11 12 13
YENGO NATIONAL PARK
PARR STATE RECREATION AREA
DHARUG NATIONAL PARK
MARRAMARRA NATIONAL PARK
KU-RING-GAI CHASE NATIONAL PARK
BRISBANE WATER NATIONAL PARK
OLNEY STATE FOREST
WYRRABALONG NATIONAL PARK
BOUDDI NATIONAL PARK
SYDNEY HARBOUR NP
BOTANY BAY NATIONAL PARK
ROYAL NATIONAL PARK
HEATHCOTE NATIONAL PARK
DHARAWAL STATE RECREATION AREA
DHARAWAL NATURE RESERVE
MILITARY RESERVE
MUNMORAH STATE RECREATION AREA
SOUTH PACIFIC OCEAN
CENTRAL COAST
TO NEWCASTLE
TO SHELLHARBOUR
Morisset
Brightwaters
Sunshine
Gwandalan
Nords Wharf
Catherine Hill Bay
Mannering Park
Wyee
Lake Munmorah
Doyalson
Budgewoi
Toukley
Noraville
Norah Head
Mandalong
Cedar Brush
Ravensdale
Dooralong
Kulnura
Yarramalong
Jilliby
Wyong Creek
Wyong
Gorokan
Tuggerah
The Entrance North
The Entrance
Toowoon Bay
Long Jetty
Bateau Bay
Forresters Beach
Ourimbah
Tumbi Umbi
Lisarow
Narara
Matcham
Gosford
Wamberal
Terrigal
The Skillion
Erina
Point Clare
Kincumber
Avoca Beach
Woy Woy
Ettalong
Umina
Macmasters Beach
Killcare
Wagstaffe
Patonga
Mooney Mooney
Brooklyn
Somersby
Palmdale
Palm Grove
Peats Ridge
Central Mangrove
Mangrove Mountain
Upper Mangrove Creek
Ten Mile Hollow
Mangrove Creek
Lower Mangrove
Calga
Glenworth Valley
Mount White
Spencer
Gunderman
Laughtondale
Wisemans Ferry
St Albans
Webbs Creek
Maroota
Leets Vale
Upper Colo
Colo
Sackville North
East Kurrajong
Blaxlands Ridge
Comleroy Road
Glossodia
Kurmond
Kurrajong Heights
Kurrajong
Bowen Mountain
North Richmond
Agnes Banks
Freemans Reach
Wilberforce
Ebenezer
Cattai
Richmond
Windsor
Pitt Town
McGraths Hill
Maraylya
Clarendon
Londonderry
Vineyard
Windsor Downs
Marsden Park
Riverstone
Schofields
Quakers Hill
Kenthurst
Annangrove
Glenhaven
Glenorie
Galston
Berowra
Cowan
Hornsby
Castle Hill
St Ives
Pymble
Terrey Hills
Frenchs Forest
Mona Vale
Elanora Heights
Narrabeen
Collaroy
Dee Why
Manly
Balgowlah
Mosman
Watsons Bay
Dover Heights
Bondi
Paddington
Coogee
Kingsford
Maroubra
La Perouse
Kurnell
Cronulla
Bundeena
Maianbar
Audley
Palm Beach
Whale Beach
Avalon
Newport
Chatswood
North Sydney
Lane Cove
Ryde
Balmain
SYDNEY
Gladesville
Homebush Bay
Strathfield
Marrickville
Sydney Airport
Botany
Parramatta
Merrylands
Fairfield
Blacktown
Rooty Hill
Mount Druitt
Kingswood
Penrith
St Marys
Eastern Creek
Horsley Park
Cecil Park
Erskine Park
Cabramatta
Liverpool
Milperra
Bankstown
Belfield
Bexley
Revesby
Hurstville
Peakhurst
Brighton Le Sands
Blakehurst
Sylvania
Sutherland
Miranda
Heathcote
Waterfall
Helensburgh
Otford
Stanwell Tops
Stanwell Park
Coalcliff
Clifton
Scarborough
Wombarra
Coledale
Austinmer
Thirroul
Bulli
Corrimal
Springwood
Faulconbridge
Winmalee
Valley Heights
Warrimoo
Blaxland
Glenbrook
Hawkesbury Heights
Mulgoa
Wallacia
Luddenham
Warragamba
Silverdale
Badgerys Creek
Bringelly
Rossmore
Austral
Leppington
Catherine Field
Werombi
Theresa Park
Oran Park (Raceway)
Cobbitty
Orangeville
Brownlow Hill
Narellan
Camden
Grasmere
Glenmore
Mount Hunter
The Oaks
Oakdale
Cawdor
Menangle Park
Menangle
Macquarie Fields
Minto
Leumeah
Campbelltown
Wedderburn
Mowbray Park
Picton
Thirlmere
Maldon
Douglas Park
Appin
Tahmoor
Wilton
Bargo
Yanderra
Hilltop
Yerrinbool
Mittagong
Buxton
For more detail on Central Sydney see page 3
Wonderland Sydney
Featherdale Wildlife Park
Australian Reptile Park & Wildlife Sanctuary
Old Sydney Town
Fowlers Lookout
Warrah Lookout
Hawkesbury Museum
Hawkesbury Lookout
Bellbird Hill Lookout
Vale of Avoca Lookout
Martins Lookout
Rouse Hill Estate
Lawrence Hargrave Memorial & Lookout
Sublime Point Lookout
PACIFIC HWY
NEWCASTLE FWY
SYDNEY NEWCASTLE FWY
WESTERN MWY
HILLS MWY
M5
HUME HWY
SOUTHERN FWY
PRINCES HWY
PUTTY RD
Hawkesbury River
Nepean River
Georges River
Port Jackson
Botany Bay
Port Hacking
Broken Bay
Pittwater
Brisbane Water
Tuggerah Lake
Budgewoi Lake
Lake Cataract
Woronora Reservoir
Prospect Reservoir
Nepean Reservoir
Cordeaux Reservoir
Avon Reservoir
Mangrove Reservoir

6 Central Eastern New South Wales

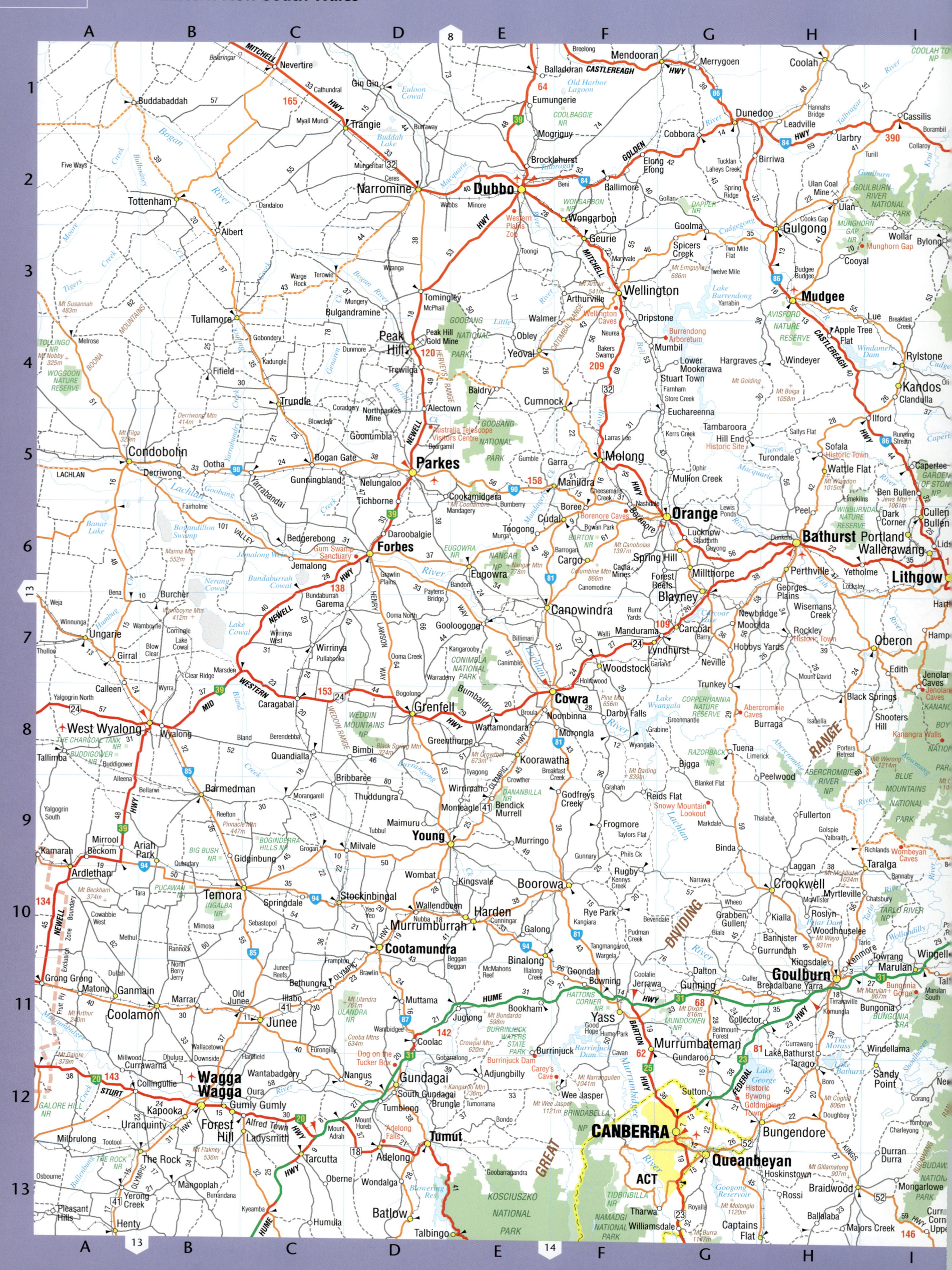

0 20 40 60 80 100 km
J K L M N O P Q R
1 2 3 4 5 6 7 8 9 10 11 12 13
SOUTH
PACIFIC
OCEAN
TASMAN
SEA
CENTRAL
COAST
ILLAWARRA
COAST
For more detail on Sydney & Surrounds see pages 4–5
N
SYDNEY
NEWCASTLE
WOLLONGONG
MAITLAND
Cessnock
Singleton
Muswellbrook
Scone
Aberdeen
Denman
Merriwa
Wingen
Parkville
Bunnan
Gundy
Moonah Flat
Ellerston
Gloucester
Barrington
Copeland
Stratford
Craven
Wards River
Stroud Road
Stroud
Dungog
Gresford
East Gresford
Paterson
Vacy
Clarence Town
Seaham
Karuah
Limeburners Creek
Bulahdelah
Booral
Bunyah
Coolongolook
Wootton
Nabiac
Krambach
Taree
Wingham
Tinonee
Coopernook
Lansdowne
Moorland
Harrington
Crowdy Head
CROWDY BAY NP
Old Bar
Wallabi Point
Rainbow Flat
Diamond Beach
Hallidays Point
Forster–Tuncurry
BOOTI BOOTI NATIONAL PARK
Green Point
Coomba
Pacific Palms
Smiths Lake
Bluey's Beach
Seal Rocks
MYALL LAKES NATIONAL PARK
Broughton Island
Tea Gardens
Hawks Nest
Shoal Bay
Nelson Bay
TOMAREE NATIONAL PARK
Anna Bay
Lemon Tree Passage
Williamtown
Raymond Terrace
Morpeth
Beresfield
Hexham
Minmi
Branxton
Lochinvar
Greta
Bellbird
Kurri Kurri
Weston
Abermain
Paxton
Millfield
Ellalong
Wollombi
Broke
Bulga
Warkworth
Jerrys Plains
Camberwell
Ravensworth
Mt Olive
CHARLESTOWN
Rathmines
Swansea
Mannering Park
Catherine Hill Bay
Lake Munmorah
Doyalson
Morisset
Cooranbong
Avondale
Wyee
TOUKLEY
WYONG
THE ENTRANCE
OURIMBAH
GOSFORD
TERRIGAL
KINCUMBER
WOY WOY
UMINA
Broken Bay
Jilliby
Palmdale
Kulnura
Peats Ridge
St Albans
Wisemans Ferry
Mount White
Bilpin
Kurrajong Heights
Richmond
Windsor
Wilberforce
Freemans Reach
Galston
Mount Victoria
Blackheath
Lawson
Springwood
Katoomba
Glenbrook
Blaxland
PENRITH
PARRAMATTA
MANLY
Port Jackson
HOMEBUSH
LIVERPOOL
Botany Bay
Mulgoa
Wallacia
Warragamba
Silverdale
Cobbitty
CAMDEN
CAMPBELLTOWN
HEATHCOTE
Waterfall
ROYAL NP
Helensburgh
Stanwell Park
Coalcliff
Scarborough
Thirroul
CORRIMAL
PORT KEMBLA
SHELLHARBOUR
Kiama
Gerringong
Jamberoo
Robertson
Burrawang
Bundanoon
Kangaroo Valley
Fox Ground
Berry
Bomaderry
Nowra
Shoalhaven Heads
Greenwell Point
Culburra
Callala Bay
Currarong
Huskisson
Vincentia
Sanctuary Point
St Georges Basin
Jervis Bay
Sussex Inlet
Swanhaven
BOODEREE NP
Conjola
Lake Conjola
Yatte Yattah
Milton
Ulladulla
Burrill Lake
Kings Point
Termeil
Bawley Point
Kioloa
Moss Vale
Bowral
Mittagong
Berrima
Colo Vale
Hilltop
Yerrinbool
Yanderra
Bargo
Buxton
Thirlmere
Picton
Wilton
Appin
The Oaks
Oakdale
Nattai
WOLLEMI NATIONAL PARK
YENGO NATIONAL PARK
GREAT DIVIDING RANGE
BARRINGTON TOPS NATIONAL PARK
BLUE MOUNTAINS NATIONAL PARK
MARRAMARRA NATIONAL PARK
KU-RING-GAI CHASE NATIONAL PARK
DHARUG NATIONAL PARK
PACIFIC HWY
PRINCES HWY
NEW ENGLAND HWY
GOLDEN HWY

8 North Eastern New South Wales

0 20 40 60 80 100 km
J K L M N O P Q R
1 2 3 4 5 6 7 8 9 10 11 12 13
77
7
QUEENSLAND
NEW SOUTH WALES
SOUTH
PACIFIC
OCEAN
N
GREAT DIVIDING RANGE
NEW ENGLAND
COOLANGATTA
TWEED HEADS
Fingal
Banora Point
Terranora
Chinderah
Kingscliff
Tumbulgum
Cudgen
Bogangar
Hastings Point
Pottsville
Murwillumbah
Mooball
New Brighton
Ocean Shores
Brunswick Heads
Mullumbimby
Tyagarah
Cape Byron
Byron Bay
Suffolk Park
Lennox Head
Lismore
Wollongbar
Alstonville
Ballina
Casino
Coraki
Woodburn
Evans Head
Iluka
Yamba
Angourie
Maclean
Harwood
Chatsworth
Grafton
Ulmarra
Brooms Head
Minnie Water
Wooli
Red Rock
Corindi
Arrawarra
Mullaway
Woolgoolga
Sandy Beach
Emerald Beach
Moonee Beach
Korora
Coffs Harbour
Sawtell
Boambee
Bonville
Mylestom
Urunga
Bellingen
Dorrigo
Valla Beach
Hyland Park
Nambucca Heads
Macksville
Bowraville
Scotts Head
Stuarts Point
South West Rocks
Kempsey
Crescent Head
Port Macquarie
Wauchope
Lake Cathie
Bonny Hills
North Haven
Dunbogan
Laurieton
Kendall
Harrington
Taree
Wingham
Warwick
Yangan
Killarney
Stanthorpe
Tenterfield
Texas
Inglewood
Yelarbon
Yetman
Bonshaw
Ashford
Inverell
Delungra
Gilgai
Glen Innes
Deepwater
Emmaville
Guyra
Armidale
Uralla
Walcha
Kentucky
Manilla
Tamworth
Kootingal
Moonbi
Nemingha
Quirindi
Nundle
Murrurundi
Wingen
Bundarra
Tingha
Warialda
Drake
Tabulam
Kyogle
Nimbin
Bangalow
Junction Hill
Ebor
Wollomombi
Hillgrove
Comboyne
Yarras
Ellenborough
Long Flat
Beechwood
Gladstone
Smithtown
Frederickton
Hat Head
Wooloweyah Estuary
Pacific Hwy
New England Hwy
Gwydir Hwy
Oxley Hwy
Waterfall Way

North Western New South Wales

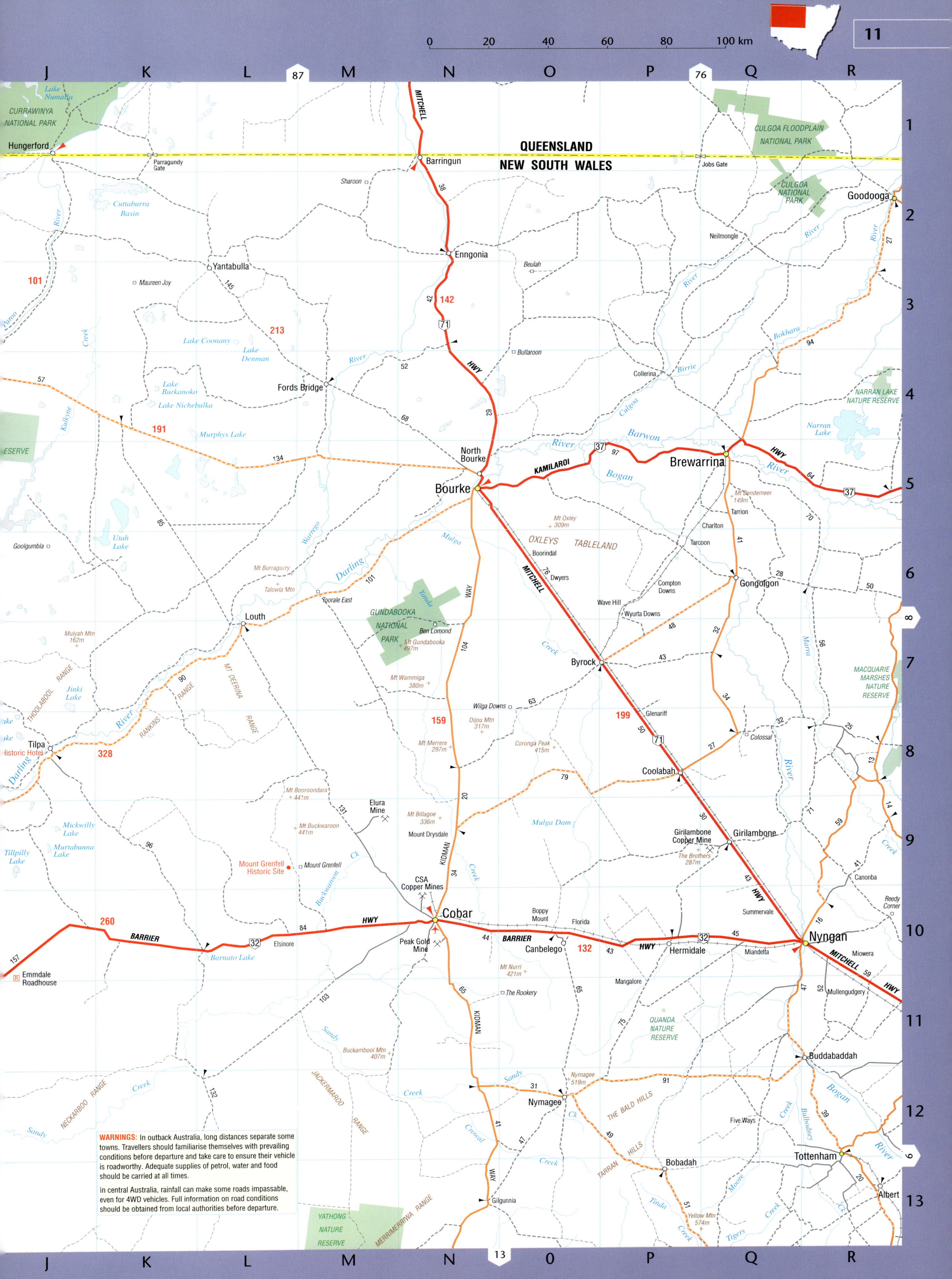

12 South Western New South Wales

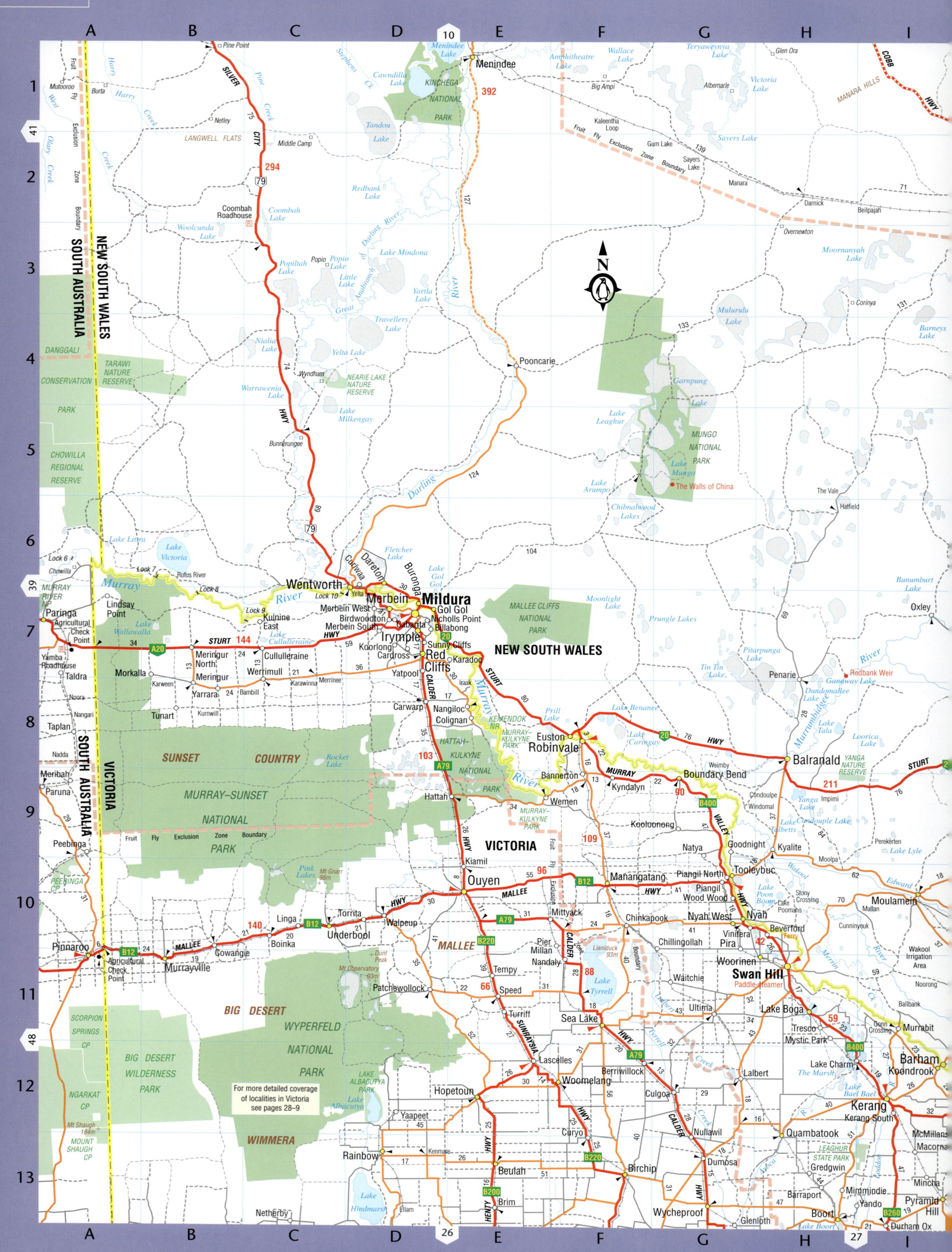

0 20 40 60 80 100 km

J K L M N O P Q R

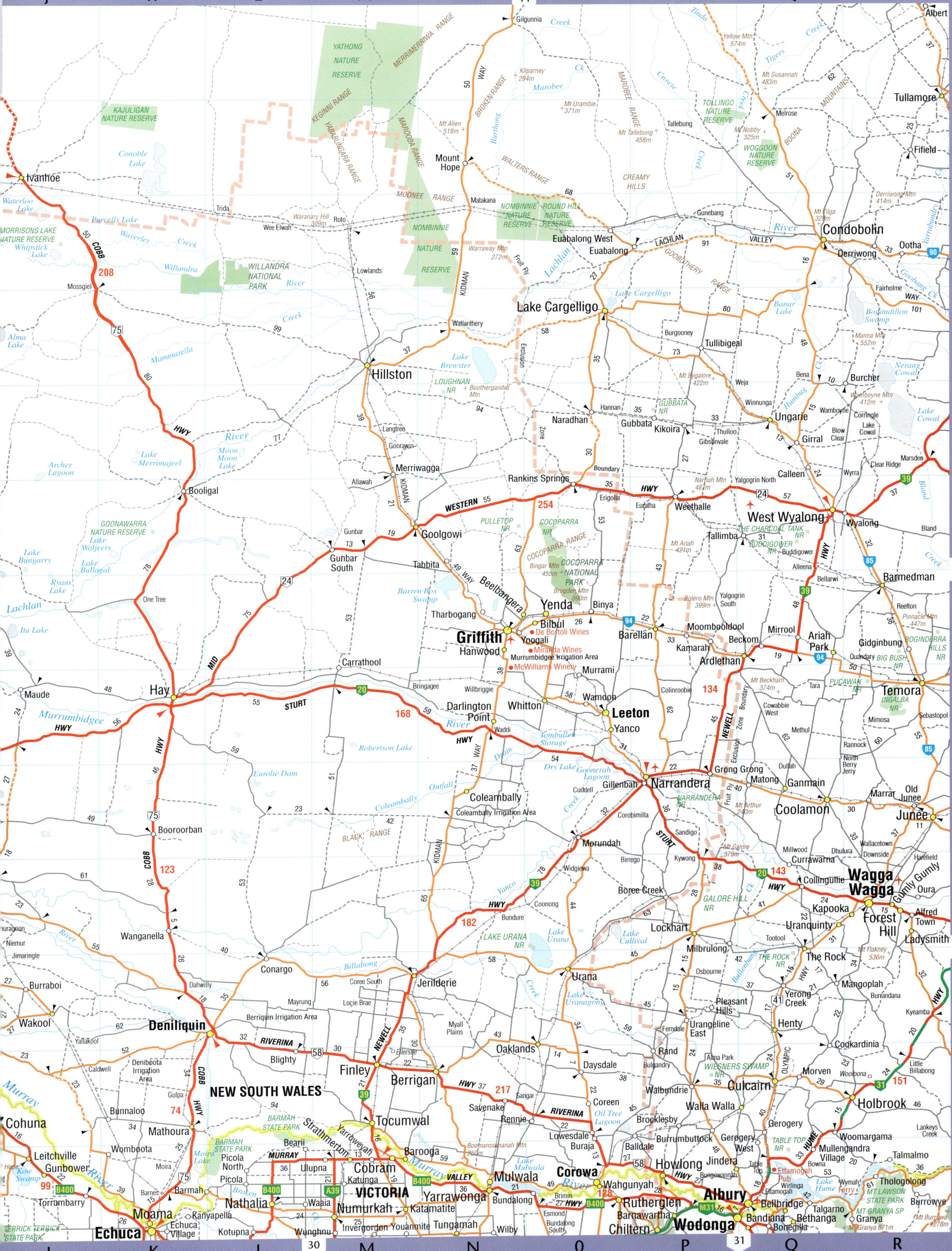

J K L M N O P Q R

0 20 40 60 80 100 km
CANBERRA
ACT
Queanbeyan
Goulburn
Yass
Cooma
Young
Cootamundra
Tumut
Gundagai
Junee
Temora
Harden
Murrumburrah
Boorowa
Crookwell
Braidwood
Batemans Bay
Moruya
Narooma
Bermagui
Bega
Merimbula
Eden
Nowra
Ulladulla
Milton
Bowral
Moss Vale
Mittagong
Picton
Jindabyne
Thredbo
Corryong
Khancoban
Tumbarumba
Adaminaby
Bombala
Delegate
Mallacoota
Cann River
NEW SOUTH WALES
VICTORIA
KOSCIUSZKO NATIONAL PARK
NAMADGI NATIONAL PARK
GREAT DIVIDING RANGE
SNOWY MOUNTAINS
SOUTH PACIFIC OCEAN
TASMAN SEA
EAST GIPPSLAND
For more detail on Canberra & Surrounds see pages 16–17

Central Canberra

Accommodation
- Best Western Motel Monaro 1 G13
- Brassey of Canberra 2 E12
- Crowne Plaza Canberra 3 E4
- The Griffin Apartment Hotel 4 F12
- Hyatt Hotel Canberra 5 C8
- James Court Apartment Hotel 6 D2
- Hotel Kurrajong 7 E10
- Olims Canberra 8 G3
- Rydges Canberra 9 C5
- Rydges Capital Hill 10 D12

General Information
- Bus Terminal 11 D3
- Canberra Railway Station 12 H13
- General Post Office 13 D3
- Jolimont Centre 14 D3
- Motoring Organisation (NRMA) 15 D2
- Police Station 16 C4
- Qantas Travel Centre 17 D3

Accommodation Only a sample range is listed; inclusion is not necessarily a recommendation.

Places of Interest
- Australian National University 18 B5
- Australian War Memorial 19 H4
- Blundell's Cottage 20 F7
- Canberra Museum and Gallery 21 D4
- Canberra Theatre Centre 22 D4
- Captain Cook Memorial Water Jet 23 D7
- High Court of Australia 24 E8
- Legislative Assembly of the ACT 25 D4
- The Lodge 26 A11
- Manuka Oval 27 E13
- National Capital Exhibition 28 D6
- National Carillon 29 F8
- National Gallery of Australia 30 F9
- National Library of Australia 31 D8
- National Museum of Australia 32 B7
- Old Parliament House 33 D9
- Parliament House 34 C11
- Questacon – The National Science & Technology Centre 35 D8
- St John the Baptist Church & Schoolhouse Museum 36 F6
- ScreenSound Australia 37 B4

16 Canberra & Surrounds

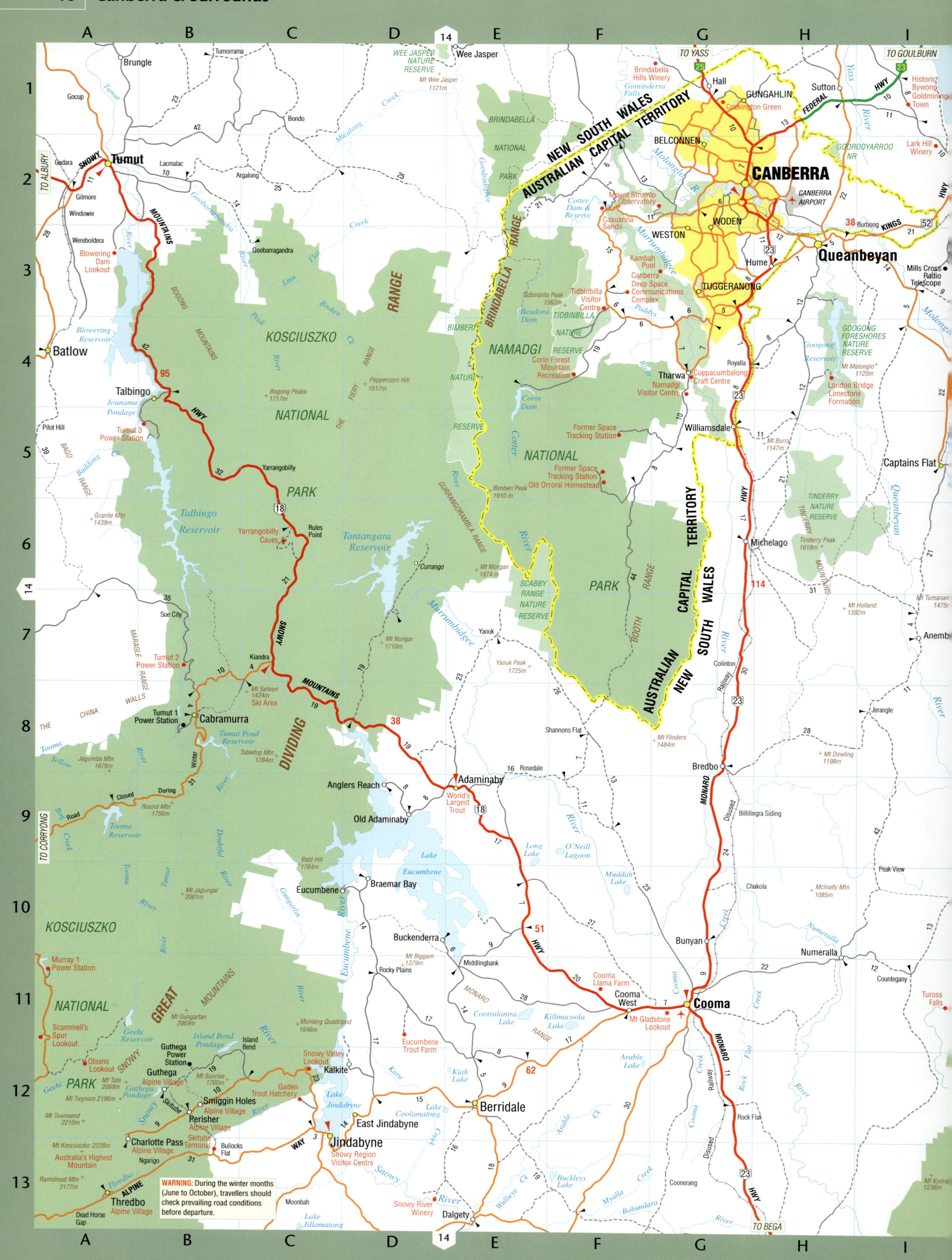

0 5 10 15 20 km
J K L M N O P Q R
1 2 3 4 5 6 7 8 9 10 11 12 13
14
TO NOWRA
TO BEGA
Lake George
Sandy Point
Sassafras
Boro
Mt Coghill 806m
Mt Fairy
Lower Boro
Butmaroo
Bungendore
KINGS HWY
Doughboy
Nerriga
Bulea Brook
MORTON NATIONAL PARK
Mt Sassafras 823m
Main Ck
Corang
Charleyong
Tomboye
Shoalhaven
River
Mt Tianjara 768m
Mt Corang 863m
RANGE
Freeman
Creek
BUDAWANG
Durran Durra
Hoskinstown
Mt Gillamatong 907m
BUDAWANG NATIONAL PARK
Currockbilly Mtn 823m
Pigeon House Mtn 719m
Braidwood
Historic Town
Mongarlowe
Rossi
Mt Mogood 391m
Ballalaba
Majors Creek
Reidsdale
Currowan Corner Upper
Shallow Crossing
Clyde Mtn 850m
Monga
Carters Ck
Bimberamala
Toggannoggera
Araluen North
Araluen
Round Mtn 1224m
Oranmeir
Kain
Bettowynd
Buckenbowra
Clyde
Nelligen
Runnyford
The Big Hole and Marble Arch
Gundillion
Mt Tamanmang 1419m
Jerrabattgulla
Deua
Wandera Mtn 580m
DEUA NATIONAL PARK
Mt Anembo 1416m
Jinden
Mt Donovan 784m
Bald Mtn 1469m
Bendethera Mtn 997m
Burra Ck
Donalds Ck
Running Creek
BADJA SWAMPS NATURE RESERVE
Badja Mill
Sandy Point
TO NOWRA
NSW JERVIS BAY NP
Callala Bay
Huskisson
NSW JERVIS BAY NP
Tomerong
St Georges Basin
Vincentia
Wandandian
Basin View
Erowal Bay
Hyams Beach
Jervis Bay
NSW JERVIS BAY NP
Sanctuary Point
Sussex Inlet
Swan Lake
JERVIS BAY TERRITORY
Green Patch
CUDMIRRAH NATIONAL PARK
BOODEREE NATIONAL PARK
Berrara
Swanhaven
Cudmirrah
Conjola
Fishermans Paradise
CONJOLA NP
Lake Conjola
Bendalong
Manyana
Cunjurong
Lake Conjola
Pointer Gap Lookout
Yatte Yattah
NARRAWALLEE CREEK NR
Narrawallee
Milton
Mollymook
COAST
Kings Point
Ulladulla
Burrill Lake
Tabourie Lake
Burrill Lake
Lake Tabourie
Termeil
Bawley Point
MURRAMARANG ABORIGINAL RESERVE
Kioloa
ILLAWARRA
PRINCES HWY
East Lynne
Benandarah
Durras Lake
Pebbly Beach
Depot Beach
Cullendulla
Durras
Long Beach
Batemans Bay
Shell Museum
Batehaven
Batemans Bay
Surf Beach
MURRAMARANG NATIONAL PARK
Malua Bay
Mogo
Rosedale
Bimbimbie
Tomakin
Mossy Point
Broulee
Mogendoura
Yarragee
Gundary
Mullenderee
Moruya
Moruya Heads
The Anchorage
Kiora
Congo
EUROBODALLA NATIONAL PARK
Bergalia
Coila Lake
Meringo
Turlinjah
Tuross Lake
Tuross Head
Bodalla
Potato Point
Nerrigundah
Lake Brou
EUROBODALLA NP
Mummuga Lake
Eurobodalla
Dalmeny
Belowra
Tuross
Wagonga
Billa Billa Ck
Kianga
Narooma
WADBILLIGA NATIONAL PARK
Wadbilliga
BODALLA STATE FOREST
Montague Island
MONTAGUE ISLAND NATURE RESERVE
Tilba Valley Vineyard
Corunna Lake
Corunna
Mt Dromedary
Wandella
Yowrie
Peak Alone 954m
Central Tilba Historic Village
Tilba Tilba
GOURA NR
Tilba Tilba Lake
EUROBODALLA NATIONAL PARK
WALLAGA LAKE NP
Wallaga Lake
Cobargo
Narira Creek
Bermagui
Bermagui South
BERMAGUEE NATURE RESERVE
Quaama
TASMAN SEA
SOUTH PACIFIC OCEAN
SOUTH COAST
N

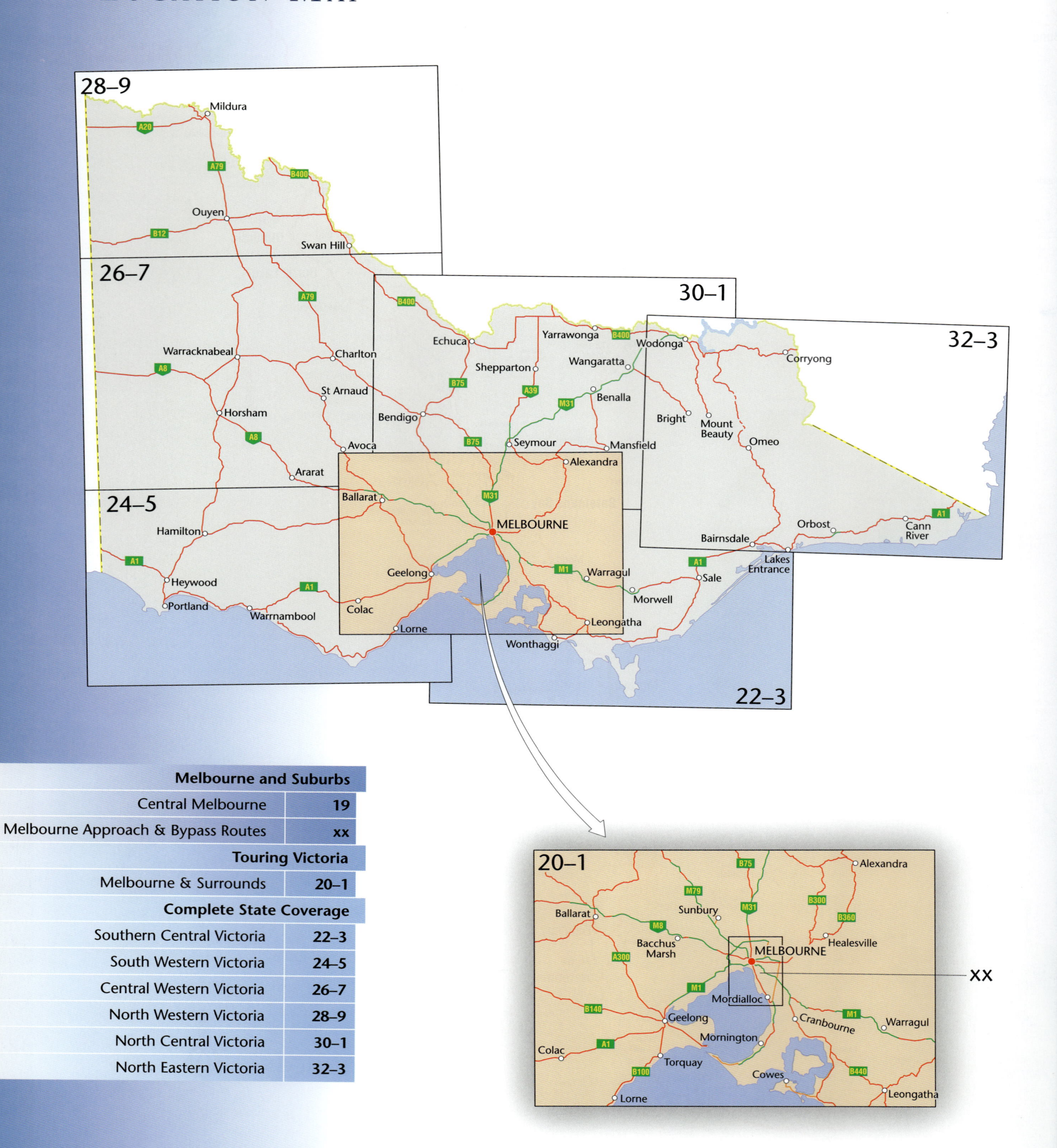

VICTORIA
LOCATION MAP

Melbourne and Suburbs	
Central Melbourne	19
Melbourne Approach & Bypass Routes	xx
Touring Victoria	
Melbourne & Surrounds	20–1
Complete State Coverage	
Southern Central Victoria	22–3
South Western Victoria	24–5
Central Western Victoria	26–7
North Western Victoria	28–9
North Central Victoria	30–1
North Eastern Victoria	32–3

Central Melbourne

Accommodation
- All Seasons Premier Grand Hotel 1 B9
- Crown Towers 2 C10
- Grand Hyatt Melbourne 3 F7
- The Hotel Y (YMCA) 4 C5
- Le Meridien at Rialto 5 C8
- Lygon Lodge 6 E3
- Novotel Melbourne on Collins 7 E7
- Oakford Gordon Place 8 F6
- Radisson on Flagstaff Gardens 9 B6
- Rockman's Regency 10 F5
- Sheraton Towers Southgate 11 E9
- Hotel Sofitel Melbourne 12 G7
- The Windsor 13 G6

General Information
- Bus Day Tour Departure Point 14 E7
- City Police Station 15 E8
- Flinders Street Station 16 E8
- General Post Office 17 D7
- Melbourne River Cruises 18 F8
- The Melbourne Transit Centre 19 C5
- Melbourne Visitor Information Centre 20 E7
- Motoring Organisation (RACV) 21 D7
- Qantas Travel Centre 22 C5, C8, E7,
- Spencer Street Coach Terminal 23 A8
- Spencer Street Station 24 A8

Places of Interest
- Aust. Centre for Contemporary Art 25 G13
- The Block Arcade 26 D7
- Captain Cook's Cottage 27 H7
- Chinatown 28 E6
- Chinese Museum 29 F6
- Crown Entertainment Complex 30 C10
- Fire Services Museum 31 G5
- IMAX Theatre 32 F3
- La Trobe's Cottage 33 G13
- Melbourne Aquarium 34 C9
- Melbourne Baptist Church 35 E7
- Melbourne Central 36 D6
- Melbourne Convention Centre 37 B9
- Melbourne Cricket Ground (MCG) 38 I9
- Melbourne Museum 39 F3
- Melbourne Park 40 H9
- Melbourne Town Hall 41 E7
- National Gallery of Victoria on Russell 42 E5
- Old Melbourne Gaol 43 E5
- Parliament of Victoria 44 G6
- Performing Arts Museum 45 E9
- Polly Woodside Melbourne Maritime Museum 46 A10
- Queen Victoria Market 47 B4
- Rialto Towers Observation Deck 48 C8
- Royal Arcade 49 D7
- Royal Botanic Gardens 50 I12
- Royal Exhibition Building 51 F4
- St Patrick's Cathedral 52 G5
- St Paul's Anglican Cathedral 53 E8
- Shrine of Remembrance 54 G12
- Sidney Myer Music Bowl 55 G10
- Southgate 56 E9
- State Library of Victoria 57 D5
- Victoria Police Museum 58 A10
- Victorian Arts Centre 59 E9

Accommodation Only a sample range is listed; inclusion is not necessarily a recommendation.

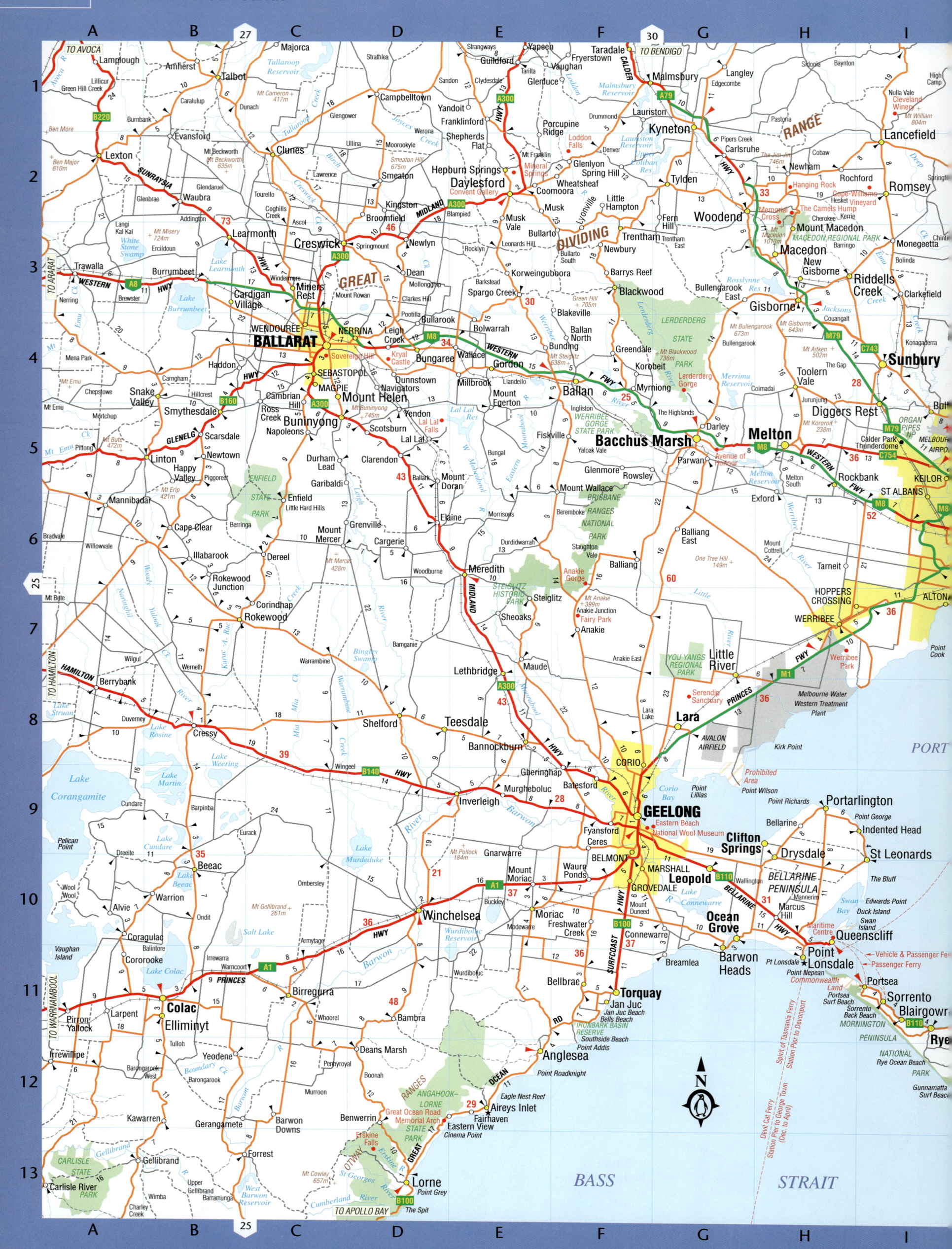

20 Melbourne & Surrounds

21

22 Southern Central Victoria

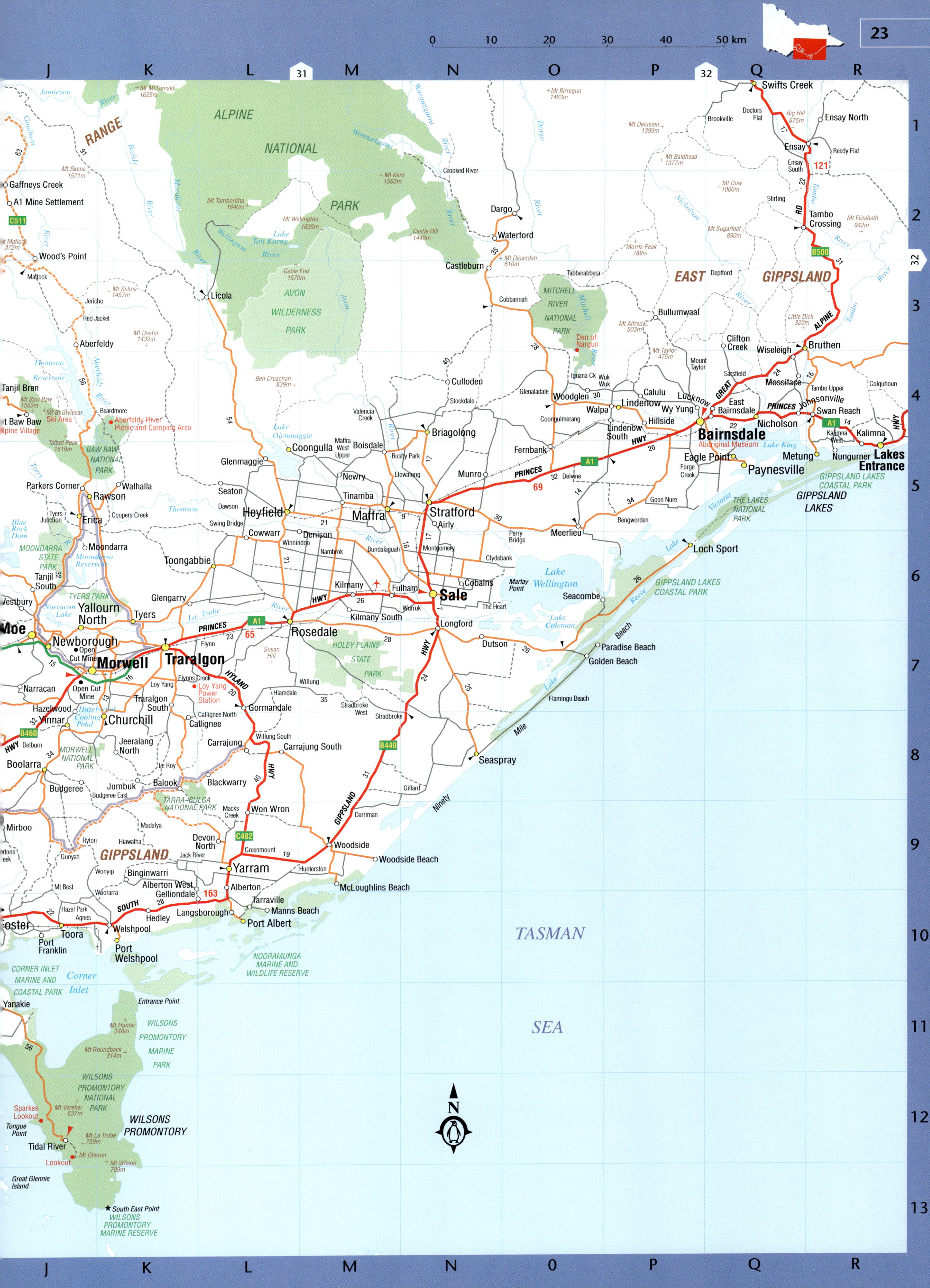

0 10 20 30 40 50 km
J K L M N O P Q R
31 32
1 2 3 4 5 6 7 8 9 10 11 12 13
Jamieson
RANGE
ALPINE
NATIONAL
PARK
Mt McDonald 1625m
Mt Skene 1571m
Gaffneys Creek
A1 Mine Settlement
C511
Matlock 372m
Wood's Point
Matlock
Jericho
Mt Selma 1457m
Red Jacket
Mt Useful 1432m
Aberfeldy
Thomson Reservoir
Tanjil Bren
Mt Baw Baw 1563m
Mt St Gwinear
Baw Baw Ski Area
Baw Baw Alpine Village
Beardmore
Aberfeldy River Picnic and Camping Area
Talbot Peak 1519m
BAW BAW NATIONAL PARK
Parkers Corner
Rawson
Walhalla
Tyers Junction
Erica
Blue Rock Dam
Coopers Creek
MOONDARRA STATE PARK
Moondarra
Moondarra Reservoir
Tanjil South
Westbury
TYERS PARK
Narracan Lake
Yallourn North
Tyers
Moe
Newborough
Open Cut Mine
Morwell
Traralgon
Narracan
Open Cut Mine
Hazelwood
Hazelwood Cooling Pond
Yinnar
Churchill
B460
HWY
Delburn
Boolarra
MORWELL NATIONAL PARK
Budgeree
Budgeree East
Jumbuk
Balook
TARRA-BULGA NATIONAL PARK
Mirboo
Ryton
Gunyah
Hiawatha
GIPPSLAND
Wonyip
Binginwarri
Mt Best
Woorarra
Hazel Park
Agnes
SOUTH
Foster
Toora
Welshpool
Port Franklin
Port Welshpool
CORNER INLET MARINE AND COASTAL PARK
Corner Inlet
Yanakie
Entrance Point
Mt Hunter 348m
WILSONS PROMONTORY MARINE PARK
Mt Roundback 314m
WILSONS PROMONTORY NATIONAL PARK
Sparkes Lookout
Tongue Point
Mt Vereker 637m
Mt La Trobe 759m
Tidal River
Lookout
Mt Oberon
Mt Wilson 709m
WILSONS PROMONTORY
Great Glennie Island
South East Point
WILSONS PROMONTORY MARINE RESERVE
Mt Tamboritha 1640m
Wellington River
Lake Tali Karng
Mt Wellington 1635m
Gable End 1570m
AVON WILDERNESS PARK
Mt Kent 1563m
Wonnangatta
Castle Hill 1448m
Licola
Ben Cruachan 839m
Lake Glenmaggie
Glenmaggie
Coongulla
Seaton
Dawson
Swing Bridge
Heyfield
Cowwarr
Thomson
Toongabbie
Glengarry
La Trobe River
PRINCES
A1
Rosedale
Flynn
Flynns Creek
Loy Yang
Loy Yang Power Station
Traralgon South
HYLAND
Gormandale
Callignee North
Callignee
Jeeralang North
Carrajung
Le Roy
Blackwarry
HWY
Carrajung South
Willung South
Macks Creek
Won Wron
C482
Madalya
Devon North
Greenmount
Jack River
Yarram
Alberton West
Gelliondale
163
Alberton
Tarraville
Hedley
Langsborough
Manns Beach
Port Albert
NOORAMUNGA MARINE AND WILDLIFE RESERVE
Hunterston
McLoughlins Beach
Woodside
Woodside Beach
Darriman
GIPPSLAND
B440
Giffard
Ninety
Seaspray
Mile
Stradbroke
Stradbroke West
Willung
Hiamdale
Susan Hill
HOLEY PLAINS STATE PARK
Kilmany
Kilmany South
HWY
Fulham
Wurruk
Sale
The Heart
Longford
Dutson
Winnindoo
Denison
Nambrok
Maffra
Tinamba
Newry
Maffra West Upper
Boisdale
Valencia Creek
Bushy Park
Llowalong
Briagolong
Stratford
Airly
Bundalaguah
Montgomery
Cobains
Clydebank
Munro
Culloden
Stockdale
Crooked River
Dargo
Waterford
Castleburn
Mt Djoandah 610m
Cobbannah
Mt Birregun 1463m
MITCHELL RIVER NATIONAL PARK
Den of Nargun
Glenaladale
Iguana Ck
Wuk Wuk
Woodglen
Coongulmerang
Fernbank
Perry Bridge
Meerlieu
Marlay Point
Lake Wellington
Seacombe
Lake Coleman
Reeve
Beach
Paradise Beach
Golden Beach
Lake
Flamingo Beach
Loch Sport
GIPPSLAND LAKES COASTAL PARK
THE LAKES NATIONAL PARK
Lake Victoria
Goon Nure
Bengworden
Delvine
69
Forge Creek
Eagle Point
Paynesville
Bairnsdale
Aboriginal Museum
Lake King
Metung
Nungurner
Lakes Entrance
GIPPSLAND LAKES COASTAL PARK
GIPPSLAND LAKES
East Bairnsdale
Nicholson
Lucknow
GREAT
Wy Yung
Hillside
Lindenow
Lindenow South
Walpa
Calulu
Tabberabbera
Mt Alfred 503m
Bullumwaal
Mt Taylor 475m
Mount Taylor
Morris Peak 789m
Mt Delusion 1399m
Mt Baldhead 1377m
Mt Dow 1000m
Mt Sugarloaf 890m
EAST
GIPPSLAND
Deptford
Brookville
Doctors Flat
Swifts Creek
Big Hill 675m
Ensay North
Ensay
Reedy Flat
Ensay South
121
Stirling
RD
Tambo Crossing
Mt Elizabeth 942m
B500
ALPINE
Little Dick 320m
Bruthen
Wiseleigh
Clifton Creek
Sarsfield
Mossiface
Tambo Upper
Colquhoun
Johnsonville
PRINCES
Swan Reach
Kalimna
Kalimna West
HWY
TASMAN
SEA
N

24 South Western Victoria

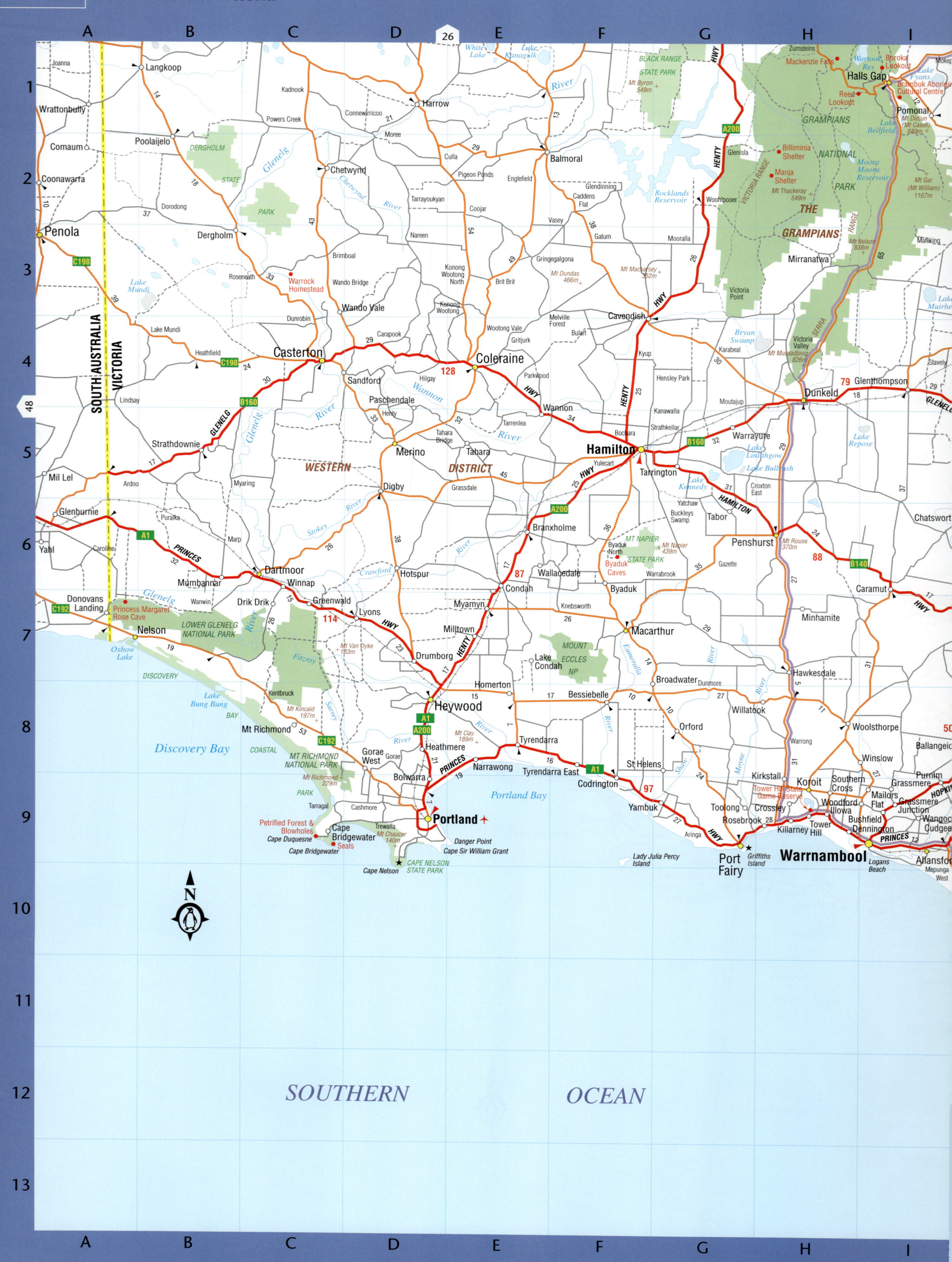

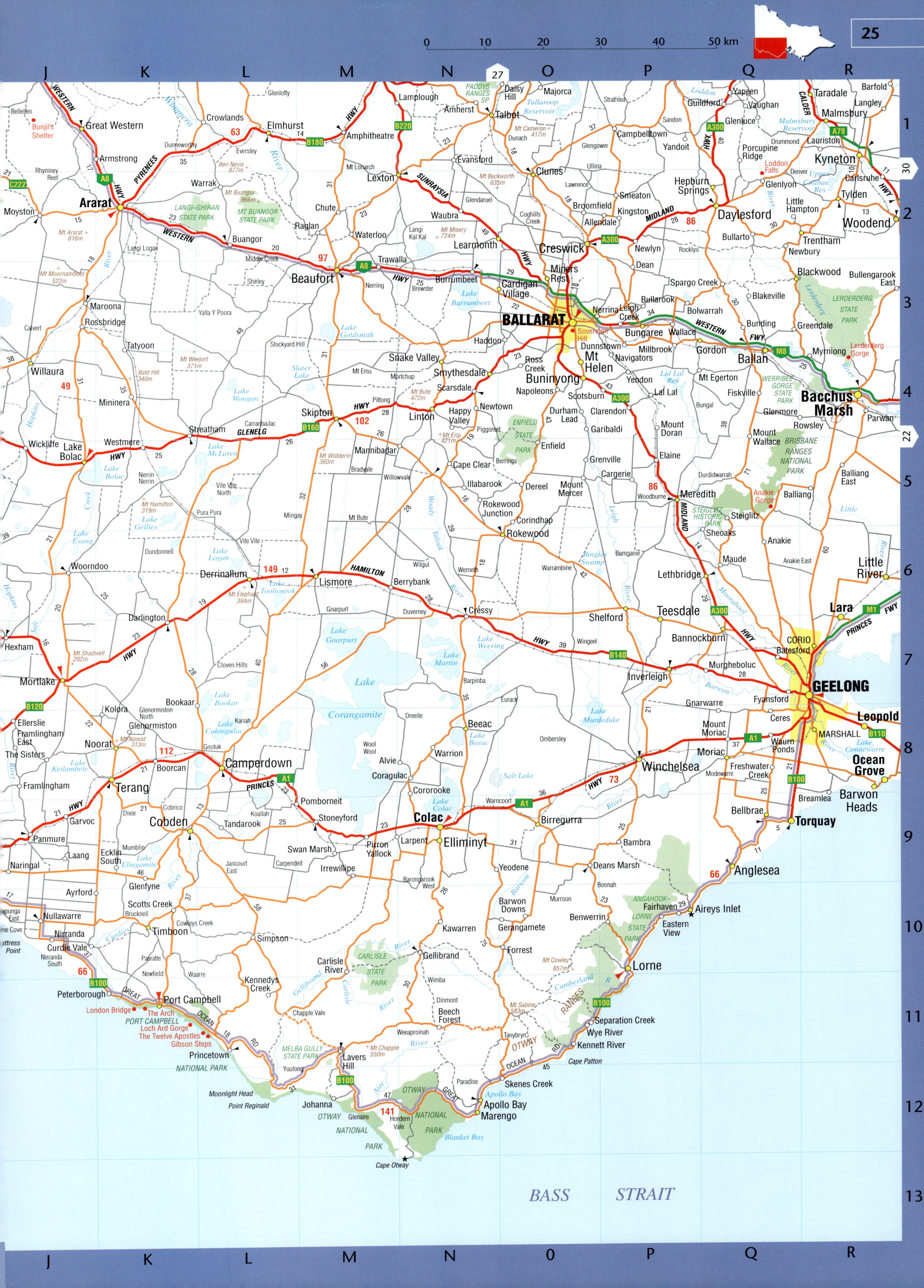
0 10 20 30 40 50 km
J K L M N O P Q R
27
30
22
1 2 3 4 5 6 7 8 9 10 11 12 13
Bellellen
Bunjil's Shelter
Great Western
WESTERN
Crowlands
Glenlofty
Elmhurst
Amphitheatre
Lamplough
Amherst
PADDYS RANGES SP
Daisy Hill
Talbot
Majorca
Tullaroop Reservoir
Mt Cameron 417m
Dunach
Strathlea
Loddon
Yapeen
Guildford
Vaughan
Sandon
Glenluce
Taradale
Barfold
Langley
Malmsbury
Malmsbury Reservoir
Lauriston
Drummond
Kyneton
Carlsruhe
Tylden
Woodend
Trentham
Newbury
Armstrong
Rhymney Reef
Moyston
Ararat
Mt Ararat 616m
PYRENEES HWY
Dunneworthy
Eversley
Ben Nevis 877m
Warrak
Mt Buangor 966m
LANGI-GHIRAN STATE PARK
MT BUANGOR STATE PARK
Buangor
Langi Logan
Middle Creek
Shirley
Raglan
Chute
Mt Lonarch
Lexton
SUNRAYSIA
Evansford
Campbelltown
Yandoit
Glengower
Clunes
Mt Beckworth 635m
Ullina
Lawrence
Smeaton
Kingston
Broomfield
Allendale
Creswick
Coghills Creek
Glendaruel
Waubra
Learmonth
Mt Misery 724m
Langi Kal Kal
Waterloo
Trawalla
Beaufort
Nerring
Brewster
Burrumbeet
Lake Burrumbeet
Cardigan Village
Miners Rest
BALLARAT
Sovereign Hill
Hepburn Springs
Daylesford
Porcupine Ridge
Loddon Falls
Denver
Glenlyon
Upper Coliban Res
Little Hampton
Bullarto
Newlyn
Dean
Rocklyn
MIDLAND
Spargo Creek
Blackwood
Bullengarook East
Blakeville
LERDERDERG STATE PARK
Bolwarrah
Bullarook
Leigh Creek
Nerrina
Bungaree
Wallace
Bunding
Greendale
Gordon
Ballan
Myrniong
Lerderderg Gorge
Millbrook
Navigators
Dunnstown
Mt Helen
Buninyong
Ross Creek
Haddon
Snake Valley
Smythesdale
Scarsdale
Napoleons
Scotsburn
Yendon
Lal Lal
Lal Lal Res
Mt Egerton
Fiskville
WERRIBEE GORGE STATE PARK
Bacchus Marsh
Glenmore
Parwan
Rowsley
Maroona
Rossbridge
Tatyoon
Calvert
Willaura
Mt Moornambool 522m
Mininera
Bald Hill 340m
Mt Weejort 371m
Yalla Y Poora
Stockyard Hill
Lake Goldsmith
Slater Lake
Mt Emu
Mortchup
Pittong
Mt Bute 472m
Linton
Happy Valley
Newtown
Piggoreet
Durham Lead
Clarendon
Garibaldi
Bungal
Mount Doran
Elaine
Mount Wallace
BRISBANE RANGES NATIONAL PARK
Lake Wongan
Skipton
GLENELG
Streatham
Carranballac
Westmere
Wickliffe
Lake Bolac
Lake McLaren
Nerrin Nerrin
Mannibadar
Bradvale
Willowvale
Mt Widderin 360m
ENFIELD STATE PARK
Enfield
Mt Erip 421m
Cape Clear
Berringa
Illabarook
Dereel
Mount Mercer
Grenville
Cargerie
Durdidwarrah
Meredith
Woodburne
Anakie Gorge
Balliang
Balliang East
Rokewood Junction
Rokewood
Corindhap
Vite Vite North
Vite Vite
Mt Hamilton 319m
Lake Gellies
Pura Pura
Mingay
Mt Bute
Lake Eyang
Dundonnell
Lake Logan
Woorndoo
Derrinallum
Lake Tooliorook
Mt Elephant 394m
Lismore
HAMILTON
Berrybank
Wilgul
Werneth
Warrambine
Bingles Swamp
Bamganie
STEIGLITZ HISTORIC PARK
Steiglitz
Sheoaks
Anakie
Maude
Anakie East
Little River
Lethbridge
Hexham
Darlington
Gnarpurt
Duverney
Cressy
Shelford
Teesdale
Bannockburn
Lara
PRINCES FWY
Mt Shadwell 292m
Mortlake
Cloven Hills
Lake Gnarpurt
Lake Weering
Lake Martin
Wingeel
Inverleigh
Murgheboluc
CORIO
Batesford
GEELONG
Barpinba
Lake Corangamite
Eurack
Bookaar
Lake Bookaar
Kolora
Glenormiston North
Glenormiston
Kariah
Lake Colongulac
Dreeite
Beeac
Lake Beeac
Lake Murdeduke
Gnarwarre
Fyansford
Ceres
Leopold
Ellerslie
Framlingham East
Noorat
Mt Noorat 313m
Gnotuk
Camperdown
Wool Wool
Alvie
Warrion
Ombersley
Mount Moriac
Moriac
Waurn Ponds
MARSHALL
Lake Connewarre
Ocean Grove
The Sisters
Lake Keilambete
Boorcan
Terang
Framlingham
Coragulac
Cororooke
Lake Colac
Salt Lake
Winchelsea
Modewarre
Freshwater Creek
Barwon Heads
Breamlea
Garvoc
Dixie
Cobrico
Cobden
Koallah
Tandarook
Pomborneit
Stoneyford
Colac
Warncoort
Birregurra
Bellbrae
Torquay
Panmure
Laang
Ecklin South
Mumblin
Lake Elingamite
Naringal
Swan Marsh
Jancourt East
Carpendeit
Pirron Yallock
Larpent
Elliminyt
Irrewillipe
Barongarook West
Yeodene
Bambra
Deans Marsh
Anglesea
Ayrford
Glenfyne
Scotts Creek
Brucknell
Cowleys Creek
Boonah
Murroon
Barwon Downs
Gerangamete
Benwerrin
ANGAHOOK-LORNE STATE PARK
Fairhaven
Aireys Inlet
Eastern View
Nullawarre
Nirranda
Timboon
Curdie Vale
Nirranda South
Curdies River
Simpson
Kawarren
Forrest
Paaratte
Newfield
Waarre
Carlisle River
CARLISLE STATE PARK
Gellibrand
Mt Cowley 657m
Lorne
Cumberland R
Peterborough
London Bridge
The Arch
PORT CAMPBELL
Loch Ard Gorge
The Twelve Apostles
Gibson Steps
Port Campbell
GREAT OCEAN RD
Kennedys Creek
Chapple Vale
Wimba
Dinmont
Beech Forest
Mt Sabine 583m
OTWAY RANGES
Separation Creek
Wye River
Kennett River
Princetown
NATIONAL PARK
MELBA GULLY STATE PARK
Lavers Hill
Yuulong
Weeaproinah
Mt Chapple 550m
Tanybryn
Cape Patton
Moonlight Head
Point Reginald
Johanna
Glenaire
Hordern Vale
Aire
OTWAY NATIONAL PARK
Paradise
Skenes Creek
Apollo Bay
Marengo
Blanket Bay
Cape Otway
BASS STRAIT

26 Central Western Victoria

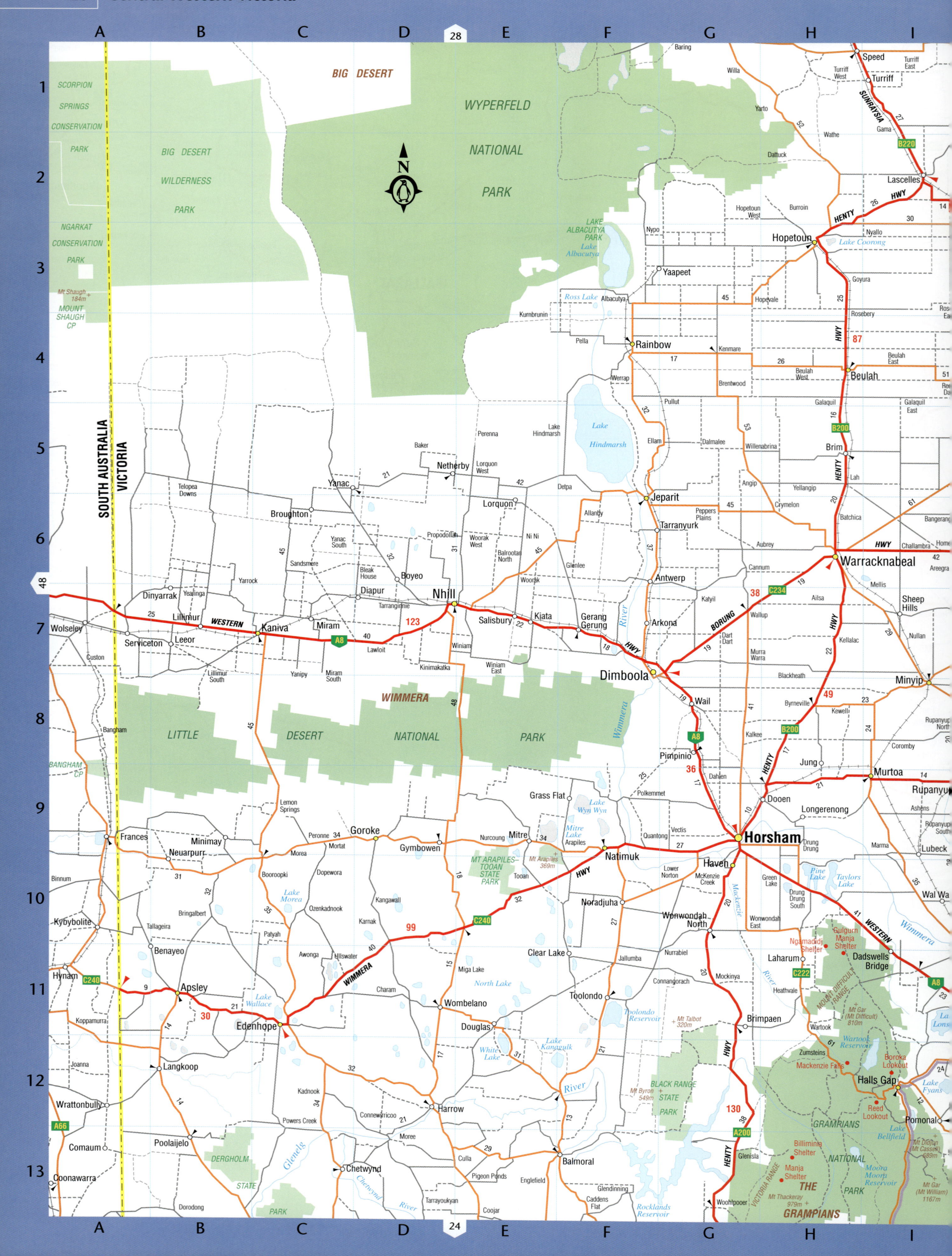

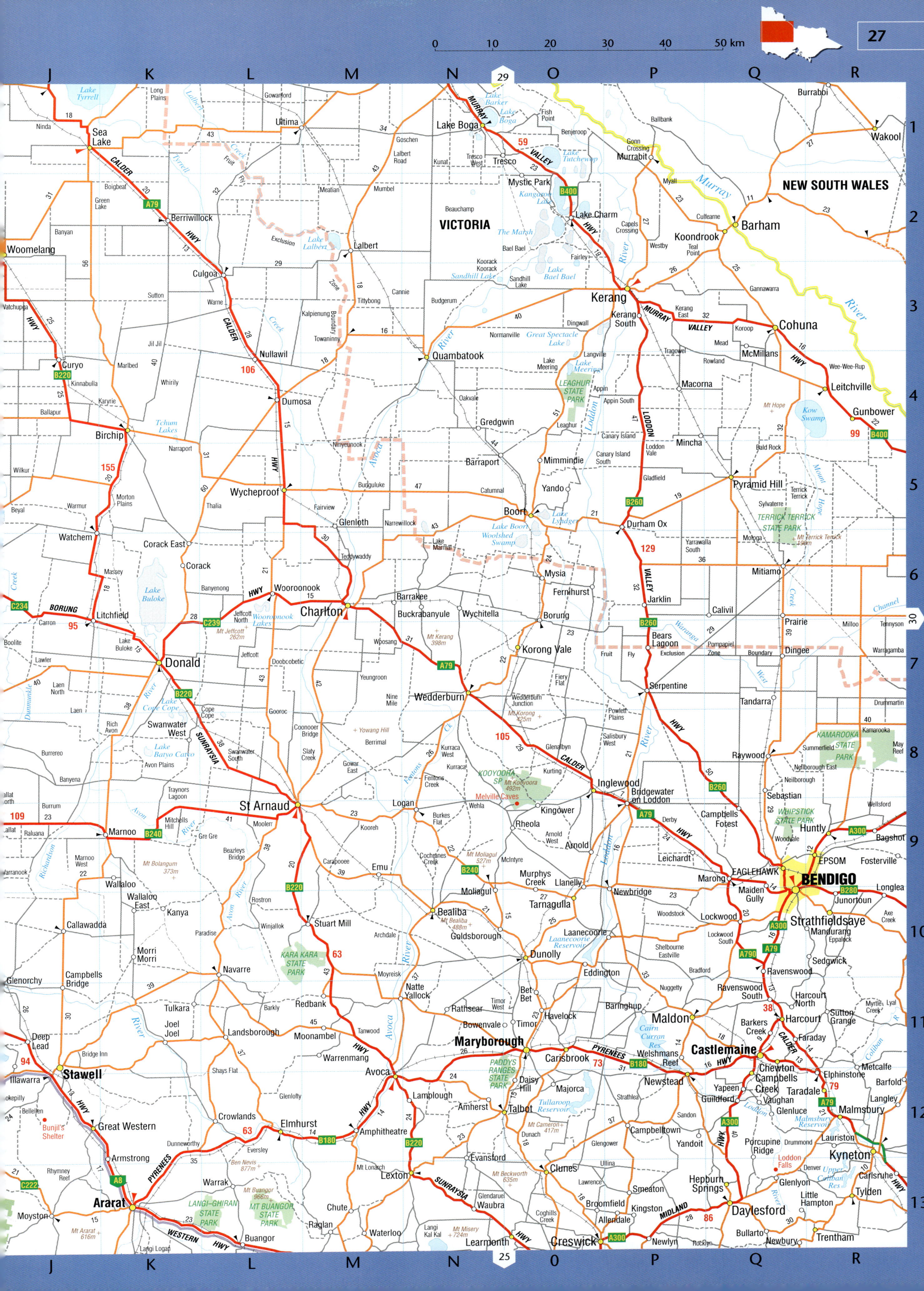
0 10 20 30 40 50 km
J K L M N O P Q R
1 2 3 4 5 6 7 8 9 10 11 12 13
29
30
25
VICTORIA
NEW SOUTH WALES
Lake Tyrrell
Long Plains
Gowanford
Sea Lake
Ninda
Ultima
Lake Boga
Lake Barker
Fish Point
Burraboi
Wakool
Ballbank
Benjeroop
Goschen
Lalbert Road
Gonn Crossing
Murrabit
Tresco West
Tresco
Kunat
Lake Tutchewop
Mystic Park
Kangaroo Lake
Myall
Murray
Meatian
Mumbel
Boigbeat
Green Lake
Berriwillock
Beauchamp
Lake Charm
Capels Crossing
Westby
Cullfearne
Barham
Koondrook
Teal Point
Banyan
Woomelang
Exclusion
Lake Lalbert
Lalbert
The Marsh
Bael Bael
Fairley
Kooorack Koorack
Sandhill Lake
Lake Bael Bael
Culgoa
Sutton
Warne
Vatchupga
Tittybong
Cannie
Budgerum
Kerang
Kerang East
Kerang South
Gannawarra
Cohuna
Koroop
Mead
Tragowel
Rowland
McMillans
Wee-Wee-Rup
Leitchville
Gunbower
Kow Swamp
Mt Hope
Kalpienung
Towaninny
Jil Jil
Nullawil
Curyo
Kinnabulla
Marlbed
Whirily
Quambatook
Normanville
Great Spectacle Lake
Dingwall
Lake Meering
Langville
Appin
Appin South
LEAGHUR STATE PARK
Loddon
Macorna
Karyrie
Dumosa
Ballapur
Birchip
Tchum Lakes
Narraport
Oakvale
Gredgwin
Leaghur
Canary Island
Canary Island South
Loddon Vale
Mincha
Bald Rock
Nineyeunook
Barraport
Mimmindie
Wilkur
Gladfield
Pyramid Hill
Terrick Terrick
Sylvaterre
Beyal
Warmur
Morton Plains
Wycheproof
Thalia
Fairview
Bunguluke
Catumnal
Yando
Boort
Durham Ox
Lake Boort
Lake Lyndger
Woolshed Swamp
TERRICK TERRICK STATE PARK
Mologa
Mt Terrick Terrick
Yarrawalla South
Watchem
Corack East
Glenloth
Narrewillock
Teddywaddy
Lake Marmal
Corack
Massey
Lake Buloke
Banyenong
Wooroonook
Mysia
Fernihurst
Mitiamo
Jarklin
Calivil
Prairie
Milloo
Tennyson
Channel
Borung
Litchfield
Carron
Jeffcott North
Wooroonook Lakes
Mt Jeffcott
Charlton
Barrakee
Buckrabanyule
Wychitella
Korong Vale
Bears Lagoon
Exclusion
Pompapiel
Boundary
Dingee
Warragamba
Boolite
Lake Buloke
Jeffcott
Woosang
Mt Kerang
Fruit
Fly
Zone
Lawler
Donald
Doobcobetic
Yeungroon
Fiery Flat
Serpentine
Laen North
Laen
Lake Cope Cope
Cope Cope
Gooroc
Nine Mile
Wedderburn
Wedderburn Junction
Mt Korong
Powlett Plains
Tandarra
Drummartin
Rich Avon
Swanwater West
Coonooer Bridge
Yowang Hill
Berrimal
Salisbury West
Kamarooka
KAMAROOKA STATE PARK
May Reef
Burrereo
Lake Batyo Catyo
Swanwater South
Slaty Creek
Kurraca West
Kurraca
Glenalbyn
Raywood
Summerfield
Neilborough East
Neilborough
Banyena
Avon Plains
Traynors Lagoon
Gowar East
Fentons Creek
KOOYOORA SP
Mt Kooyoora
Kurting
Inglewood
Bridgewater on Loddon
Sebastian
Wellsford
Burrum
St Arnaud
Logan
Melville Caves
Wehla
Kingower
Campbells Forest
WHIPSTICK STATE PARK
Huntly
Bagshot
Raluana
Marnoo
Mitchells Hill
Mooleer
Kooreh
Burkes Flat
Rheola
Derby
Woodvale
Marnoo West
Gre Gre
Beazleys Bridge
Arnold West
Arnold
Leichardt
EPSOM
Fosterville
Mt Bolangum
Carapooee
Emu
Cochranes Creek
Mt Moliagul
McIntyre
Murphys Creek
Llanelly
Marong
EAGLEHAWK
BENDIGO
Maiden Gully
Longlea
Wallaloo
Wallaloo East
Kanya
Rostron
Moliagul
Newbridge
Junortoun
Winjallok
Stuart Mill
Bealiba
Mt Bealiba
Tarnagulla
Woodstock
Lockwood
Strathfieldsaye
Axe Creek
Callawadda
Paradise
Archdale
Goldsborough
Laanecoorie
Laanecoorie Reservoir
Lockwood South
Mandurang
Eppalock
Morri Morri
KARA KARA STATE PARK
Dunolly
Shelbourne
Eastville
Sedgwick
Glenorchy
Campbells Bridge
Navarre
Moyreisk
Eddington
Bradford
Ravenswood
Natte Yallock
Bet Bet
Nuggetty
Ravenswood South
Harcourt North
Tulkara
Barkly
Redbank
Rathscar
Timor West
Havelock
Baringhup
Myrtle Creek
Lyal
Sutton Grange
Joel Joel
Landsborough
Tanwood
Bowenvale
Timor
Maldon
Cairn Curran Res
Barkers Creek
Harcourt
Faraday
Deep Lead
Moonambel
Maryborough
Carisbrook
Welshmans Reef
Castlemaine
Bridge Inn
Shays Flat
Warrenmang
PADDYS RANGES STATE PARK
Chewton
Metcalfe
Elphinstone
Stawell
Illawarra
Avoca
Daisy Hill
Majorca
Newstead
Campbells Creek
Barfold
Taradale
Yapeen
Vaughan
Guildford
Strathlea
Langley
Glenlofty
Lamplough
Glenluce
Malmsbury
Malmsbury Reservoir
Bellellen
Bunjil's Shelter
Great Western
Crowlands
Amherst
Talbot
Tullaroop Reservoir
Sandon
Elmhurst
Amphitheatre
Mt Cameron
Dunach
Campbelltown
Yandoit
Lauriston
Porcupine Ridge
Drummond
Armstrong
Dunneworthy
Eversley
Ben Nevis
Glengower
Kyneton
Carlsruhe
Loddon Falls
Upper Coliban Res
Rhymney Reef
Evansford
Ullina
Denver
Mt Lonarch
Lexton
Clunes
Mt Beckworth
Smeaton
Hepburn Springs
Glenlyon
Tylden
Warrak
Mt Buangor
LANGI-GHIRAN STATE PARK
MT BUANGOR STATE PARK
Glendaruel
Waubra
Lawrence
Broomfield
Allendale
Kingston
Daylesford
Little Hampton
Ararat
Moyston
Chute
Coghills Creek
Raglan
Langi Kal Kal
Mt Misery
Waterloo
Bullarto
Trentham
Mt Ararat
Buangor
Langi Logan
Learmonth
Creswick
Newlyn
Rocklyn
Newbury
CALDER HWY
MURRAY VALLEY HWY
LODDON VALLEY HWY
BORUNG HWY
SUNRAYSIA HWY
PYRENEES HWY
WESTERN HWY
MIDLAND HWY
A79
A8
A300
A790
B220
B240
B260
B280
B180
B400
C220
C222
C234
C239
59
106
155
95
109
105
129
63
94
73
99
86
38

28 North Western Victoria

0 10 20 30 40 50 km

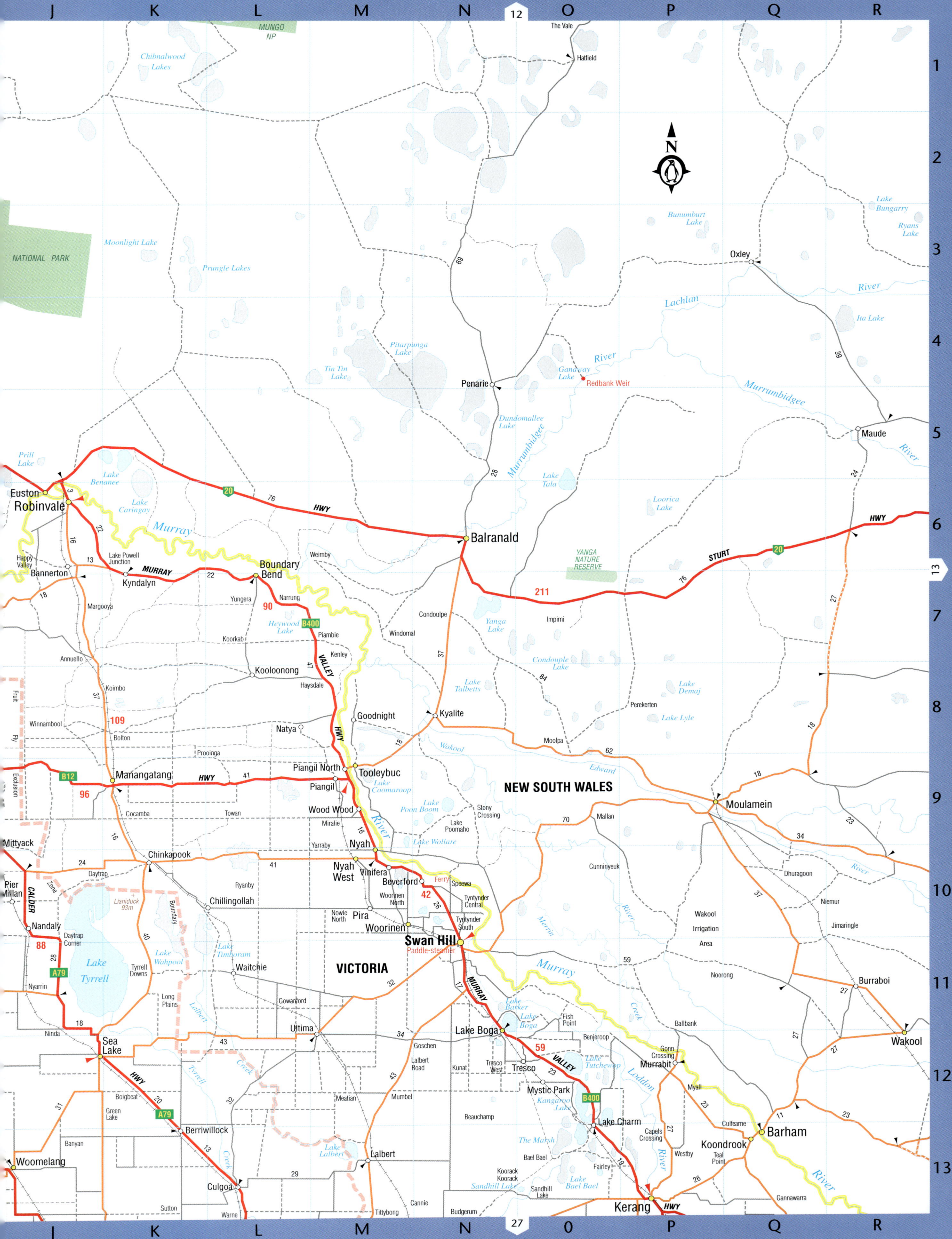

30 North Central Victoria

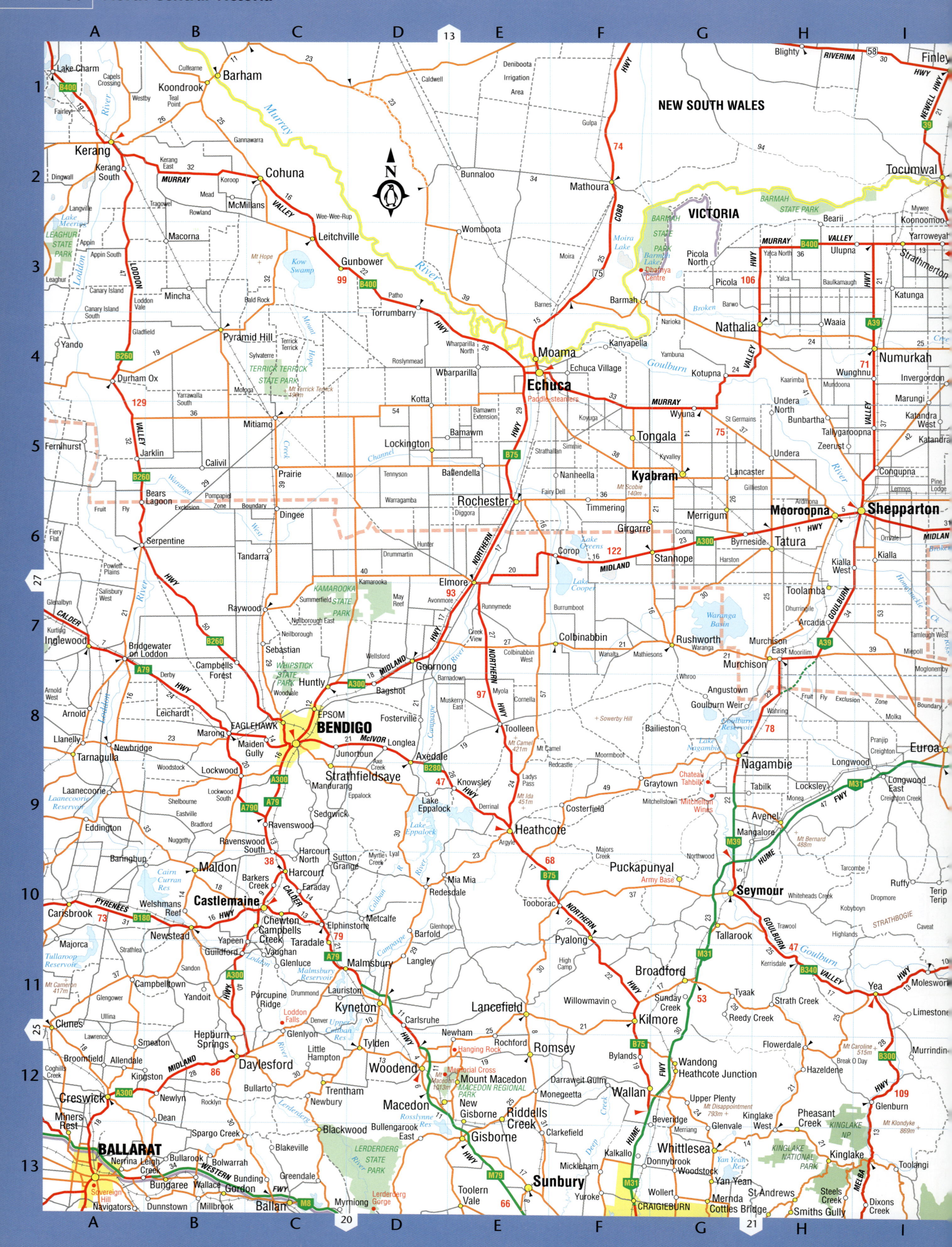

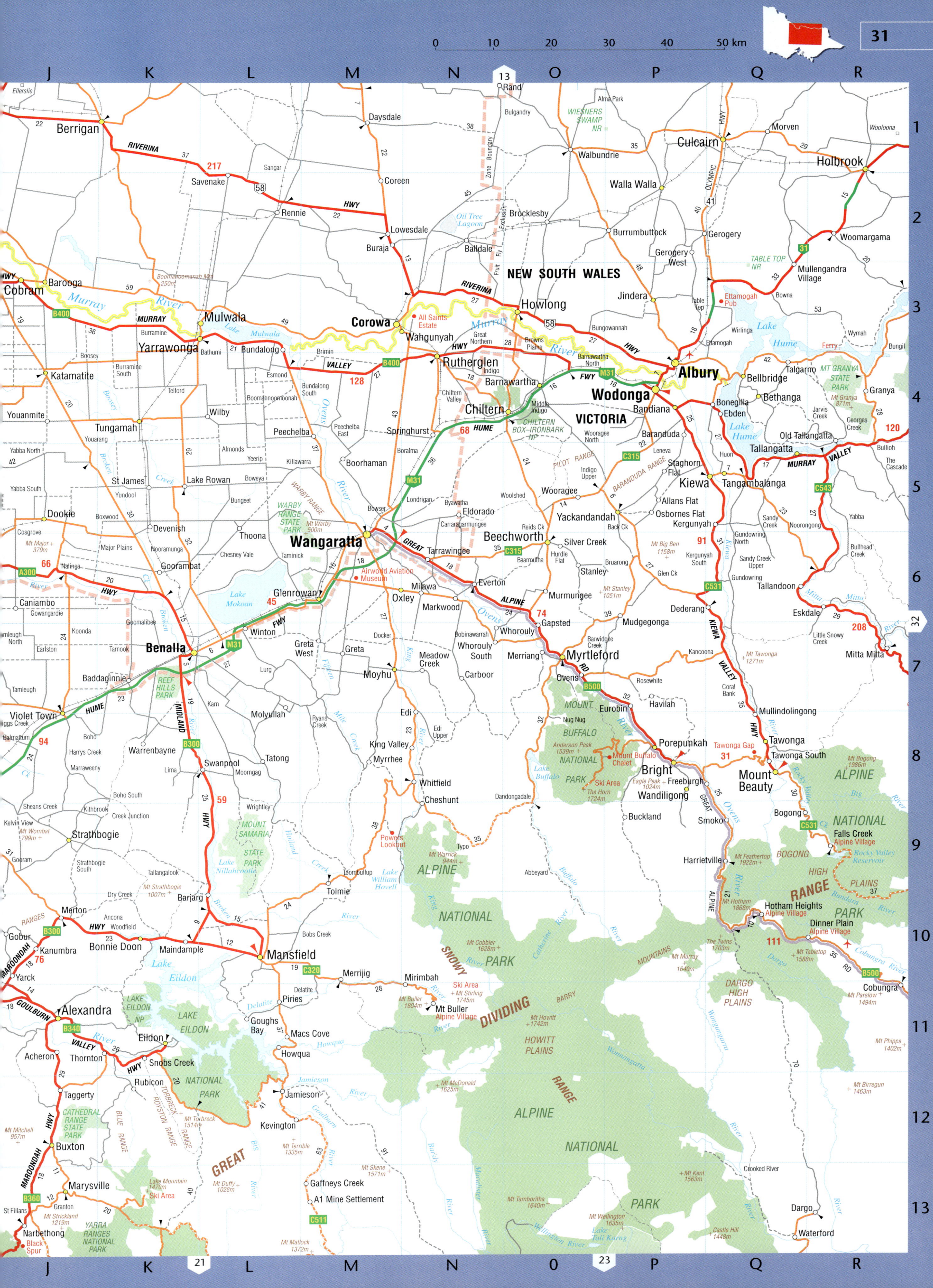

0 10 20 30 40 50 km
J K L M N O P Q R
1 2 3 4 5 6 7 8 9 10 11 12 13
NEW SOUTH WALES
VICTORIA
Berrigan
Ellerslie
RIVERINA
Savenake
Sangar
Rennie
HWY
Daysdale
Coreen
Lowesdale
Buraja
Rand
Bulgandry
Alma Park
WIESNERS SWAMP NR
Walbundrie
Culcairn
Morven
Wooloona
Holbrook
Walla Walla
Brocklesby
Oil Tree Lagoon
Balldale
Burrumbuttock
Gerogery
Gerogery West
Woomargama
TABLE TOP NR
Mullengandra Village
Cobram
Barooga
Boomahnoomanah Mt 250m
Murray River
Mulwala
Lake Mulwala
Corowa
All Saints Estate
Wahgunyah
Howlong
Jindera
Ettamogah Pub
Table Top
Bowna
Wirlinga
Lake Hume
Wymah
Bungil
Ferry
Ettamogah
Bungowannah
Brimin
Yarrawonga
Bundalong
Burramine
Burramine South
Bathumi
Katamatite
Boosey
Esmond
VALLEY
Rutherglen
Great Northern
Browns Plains
Barnawartha North
Albury
Wodonga
Bellbridge
Talgarno
MT GRANYA STATE PARK
Granya
Bundalong South
Indigo
Barnawartha
Bonegilla
Ebden
Bethanga
Mt Granya 871m
Jarvis Creek
Georges Creek
Youanmite
Telford
Boomahnoomoonah
Wilby
Chiltern Valley
Chiltern
Middle Indigo
Bandiana
CHILTERN BOX-IRONBARK NP
Baranduda
Tungamah
Youarang
Peechelba
Peechelba East
Springhurst
HUME
Wooragee North
Old Tallangatta
Tallangatta
Huon
Bullioh
The Cascade
Yabba North
Almonds
Yeerip
Killawarra
Boorhaman
Boralma
PILOT RANGE
Leneva
Staghorn Flat
Indigo Upper
BARANDUDA RANGE
Kiewa
Tangambalanga
Yabba South
St James
Lake Rowan
Boweya
Bungeet
Yundool
Woolshed
Wooragee
Allans Flat
Osbornes Flat
Kergunyah
Sandy Creek
Noorongong
Yabba
Dookie
Boxwood
WARBY RANGE STATE PARK
Mt Warby 500m
Londrigan
Byawatha
Eldorado
Carraragarmungee
Yackandandah
Back Ck
Cosgrove
Devenish
Thoona
Bowser
Wangaratta
Reids Ck
Beechworth
Silver Creek
Mt Big Ben 1158m
Kergunyah South
Gundowring North
Bullhead Creek
Mt Major 379m
Major Plains
Nooramunga
Chesney Vale
Taminick
Tarrawingee
Hurdle Flat
Baarmutha
Stanley
Bruarong
Glen Ck
Sandy Creek Upper
Gundowring
Tallandoon
Nalinga
Goorambat
Airworld Aviation Museum
Everton
Mt Stanley 1051m
Dederang
Mitta River
Caniambo
Gowangardie
Glenrowan
Lake Mokoan
Milawa
Oxley
Markwood
ALPINE
Murmungee
Gapsted
Mudgegonga
Eskdale
Goomalibee
Winton
Koonda
Docker
Bobinawarrah
Whorouly
Barwidgee Creek
Kancoona
Little Snowy Creek
Mitta Mitta
Mt Tawonga 1271m
Earlston
Tarnook
Benalla
Greta West
Greta
Meadow Creek
Whorouly South
Merriang
Myrtleford
Baddaginnie
REEF HILLS PARK
Lurg
Moyhu
Carboor
Ovens
Rosewhite
KIEWA VALLEY
Coral Bank
Tamleugh
MIDLAND
Karn
Molyullah
Ryans Creek
Edi
MOUNT BUFFALO NATIONAL PARK
Nug Nug
Eurobin
Havilah
Mullindolingong
Violet Town
Boho
Harrys Creek
Edi Upper
King Valley
Anderson Peak 1539m
Porepunkah
Tawonga Gap
Tawonga
Tawonga South
Mt Bogong 1986m
Balmattum
Warrenbayne
Swanpool
Tatong
Myrrhee
Mount Buffalo Chalet
Bright
Mount Beauty
Marraweeny
Lima
Moorngag
Whitfield
Lake Buffalo
Ski Area
Eagle Peak 1024m
Freeburgh
The Horn 1724m
Wandiligong
Boho South
Wrightley
Cheshunt
Dandongadale
Sheans Creek
Kithbrook
Creek Junction
Buckland
Smoko
Bogong
Kelvin View
Mt Wombat 799m
Strathbogie
MOUNT SAMARIA STATE PARK
Powers Lookout
Typo
Mt Warrick 944m
ALPINE
Falls Creek Alpine Village
Rocky Valley Reservoir
Goorum
Strathbogie South
Lake Nillahcootie
Toombullup
Lake William Hovell
Abbeyard
Harrietville
Mt Feathertop 1922m
BOGONG HIGH PLAINS
RANGE
Tallangalook
Mt Strathbogie 1007m
Dry Creek
Barjarg
Tolmie
Mt Hotham 1868m
Hotham Heights Alpine Village
Merton
RANGES
Ancona
Woodfield
Bonnie Doon
Maindample
Mansfield
Bobs Creek
KING NATIONAL PARK
Mt Cobbler 1628m
SNOWY
The Twins 1703m
MOUNTAINS
Dinner Plain Alpine Village
Mt Tabletop 1588m
Cobungra
Gobur
Kanumbra
Yarck
MAROONDAH
Lake Eildon
Merrijig
Mirimbah
Delatite
Mt Stirling 1745m
Mt Buller 1804m
Mt Buller Alpine Village
DIVIDING
BARRY
Mt Murray 1640m
DARGO HIGH PLAINS
Mt Parslow 1494m
Alexandra
GOULBURN
LAKE EILDON NP
Eildon
Piries
Goughs Bay
Macs Cove
Mt Howitt 1742m
HOWITT PLAINS
Wonnangatta River
Mt Phipps 1402m
Acheron
Thornton
Snobs Creek
Howqua
Rubicon
Taggerty
Jamieson
Mt McDonald 1625m
RANGE
Mt Birregun 1463m
TORBRECK ROYSTON RANGE
CATHEDRAL RANGE STATE PARK
BLUE RANGE
Mt Torbreck 1514m
Kevington
ALPINE
NATIONAL
PARK
Mt Mitchell 957m
Buxton
GREAT
Mt Terrible 1335m
Crooked River
Mt Kent 1563m
Lake Mountain 1470m Ski Area
Mt Duffy 1028m
Mt Skene 1571m
Gaffneys Creek
Marysville
A1 Mine Settlement
Dargo
Mt Strickland 1219m
Granton
St Fillans
YARRA RANGES NATIONAL PARK
Mt Tamboritha 1640m
Mt Wellington 1635m
Castle Hill 1448m
Narbethong
Black Spur
Mt Matlock 1372m
Lake Tali Karng
Wellington River
Waterford
21 23 13 32

32 North Eastern Victoria

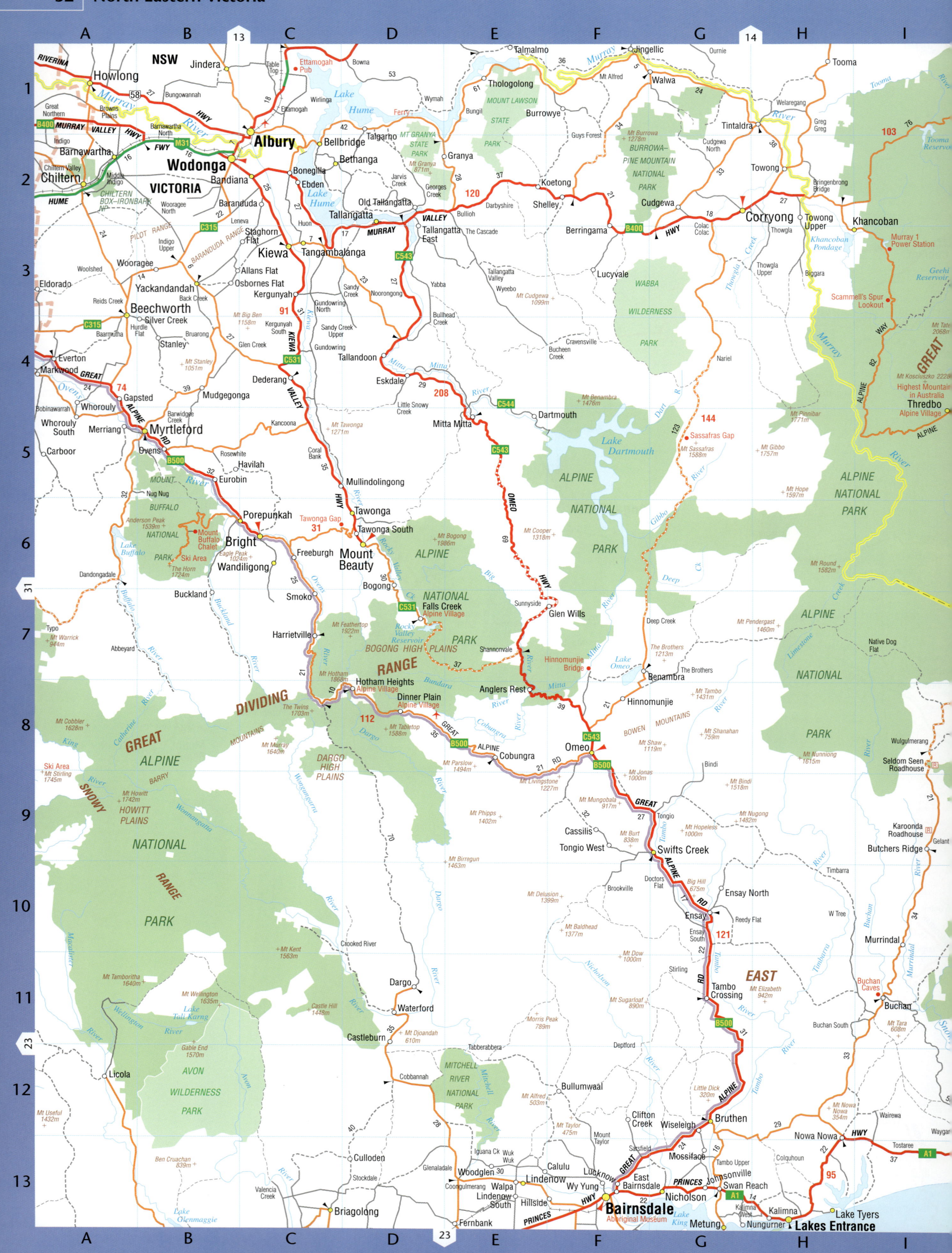

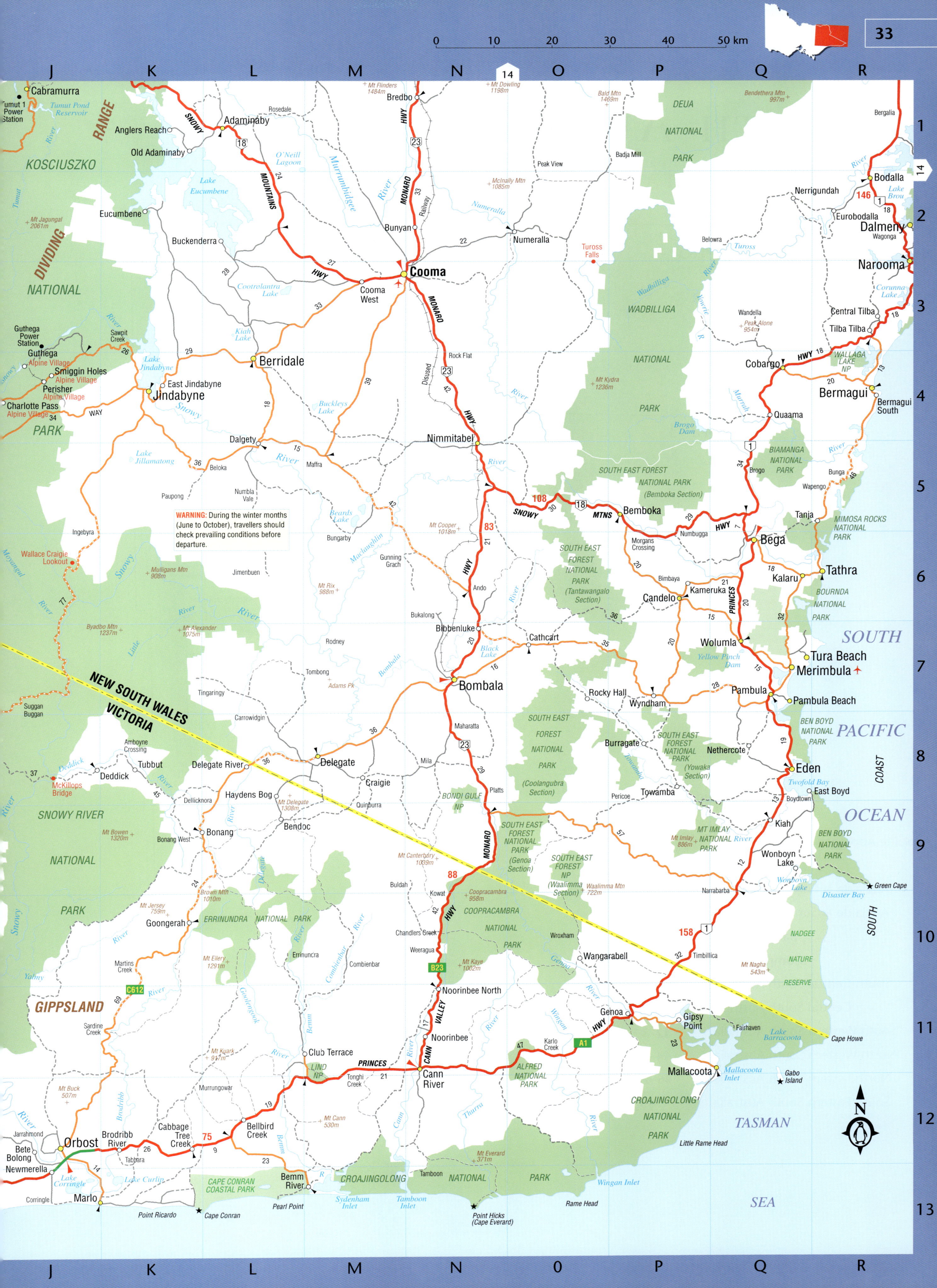
0
10
20
30
40
50 km
J
K
L
M
N
O
P
Q
R
14
1
2
3
4
5
6
7
8
9
10
11
12
13
Cabramurra
Tumut 1 Power Station
Tumut Pond Reservoir
RANGE
SNOWY
Adaminaby
Rosedale
Mt Flinders 1484m
Bredbo
Mt Dowling 1198m
Bald Mtn 1469m
DEUA
NATIONAL
PARK
Bendethera Mtn 997m
Bergalia
Anglers Reach
Old Adaminaby
O'Neill Lagoon
Murrumbidgee
MOUNTAINS
MONARO
HWY
Railway
Peak View
Badja Mill
KOSCIUSZKO
Lake Eucumbene
Mt McInally Mtn 1085m
Numeralla
Bodalla
Nerrigundah
Lake Brou
Eurobodalla
Dalmeny
Wagonga
Eucumbene
Mt Jagungal 2061m
Bunyan
Numeralla
Tuross Falls
Belowra
Tuross
Narooma
Buckenderra
DIVIDING
Cooma
Cooma West
Coorolantra Lake
NATIONAL
WADBILLIGA
Wadbilliga
Corunna Lake
Central Tilba
Tilba Tilba
Wandella
Peak Alone 954m
Guthega Power Station
Guthega
Alpine Village
Sawpit Creek
Smiggin Holes
Alpine Village
Perisher
Alpine Village
Charlotte Pass
Alpine Village
Kiah Lake
Lake Jindabyne
Berridale
East Jindabyne
Jindabyne
Rock Flat
Disused
Cobargo
WALLAGA LAKE NP
Bermagui
Bermagui South
Mt Kydra 1236m
WAY
PARK
Buckleys Lake
Quaama
Brogo Dam
Dalgety
Maffra
Nimmitabel
Lake Jillamatong
Beloka
Paupong
Numbla Vale
BIAMANGA NATIONAL PARK
Brogo
Bunga
Wapengo
SOUTH EAST FOREST NATIONAL PARK (Bemboka Section)
WARNING: During the winter months (June to October), travellers should check prevailing conditions before departure.
Beards Lake
Mt Cooper 1018m
Bemboka
MTNS
Numbugga
Tanja
MIMOSA ROCKS NATIONAL PARK
Bega
Ingebyra
Bungarby
Maclaughlin
Gunning Grach
SOUTH EAST FOREST NATIONAL PARK (Tantawangalo Section)
Morgans Crossing
Wallace Craigie Lookout
Mulligans Mtn 908m
Jimenbuen
Mt Rix 988m
Ando
Bimbaya
Kameruka
Candelo
PRINCES
Kalaru
Tathra
BOURNDA NATIONAL PARK
Bukalong
Bibbenluke
Cathcart
Wolumla
Yellow Pinch Dam
SOUTH
Tura Beach
Merimbula
Byadbo Mtn 1237m
Mt Alexander 1075m
Rodney
Black Lake
Tombong
Adams Pk
Bombala
Tingaringy
Rocky Hall
Wyndham
Pambula
Pambula Beach
NEW SOUTH WALES
VICTORIA
Suggan Buggan
Carrowidgin
Maharatta
SOUTH EAST FOREST NATIONAL PARK (Coolangubra Section)
Burragate
SOUTH EAST FOREST NATIONAL PARK (Yowaka Section)
Nethercote
BEN BOYD NATIONAL PARK
PACIFIC
Amboyne Crossing
Tubbut
Deddick
Delegate River
Delegate
Mila
Craigie
Eden
Twofold Bay
COAST
McKillops Bridge
Dellicknora
Haydens Bog
Mt Delegate 1308m
Quinburra
BONDI GULF NP
Platts
Pericoe
Towamba
East Boyd
Boydtown
SNOWY RIVER
Bonang
Bonang West
Bendoc
Mt Bowen 1320m
SOUTH EAST FOREST NATIONAL PARK (Genoa Section)
MT IMLAY NATIONAL PARK
Mt Imlay 886m
Kiah
OCEAN
NATIONAL
Mt Canterbury 1039m
SOUTH EAST FOREST NP (Waalimma Section)
Waalimma Mtn 722m
Wonboyn Lake
BEN BOYD NATIONAL PARK
Green Cape
Disaster Bay
Buldah
Kowat
Coopracambra 958m
Narrabarba
Brown Mtn 1010m
Mt Jersey 759m
PARK
Goongerah
ERRINUNDRA NATIONAL PARK
COOPRACAMBRA NATIONAL PARK
Chandlers Creek
Wroxham
Timbillica
NADGEE NATURE RESERVE
Weeragua
Errinundra
Combienbar
Wangarabell
Mt Nagha 543m
Martins Creek
Mt Ellery 1291m
Mt Kaye 1002m
Noorinbee North
GIPPSLAND
VALLEY
Genoa
Gipsy Point
Fairhaven
Lake Barracoota
Cape Howe
Sardine Creek
Mt Kuark 917m
Club Terrace
Noorinbee
Karlo Creek
CANN
PRINCES
LIND NP
Tonghi Creek
Cann River
ALFRED NATIONAL PARK
Mallacoota
Mallacoota Inlet
Gabo Island
Mt Buck 507m
Murrungowar
CROAJINGOLONG NATIONAL PARK
TASMAN
N
Jarrahmond
Orbost
Brodribb River
Cabbage Tree Creek
Bellbird Creek
Mt Cann 530m
Little Rame Head
Bete Bolong
Newmerella
Tabbara
Lake Corringle
Lake Curlip
Mt Everard 371m
Tamboon
CROAJINGOLONG NATIONAL PARK
Wingan Inlet
CAPE CONRAN COASTAL PARK
Bemm River
Corringle
Marlo
Point Ricardo
Cape Conran
Pearl Point
Sydenham Inlet
Tamboon Inlet
Point Hicks (Cape Everard)
Rame Head
SEA

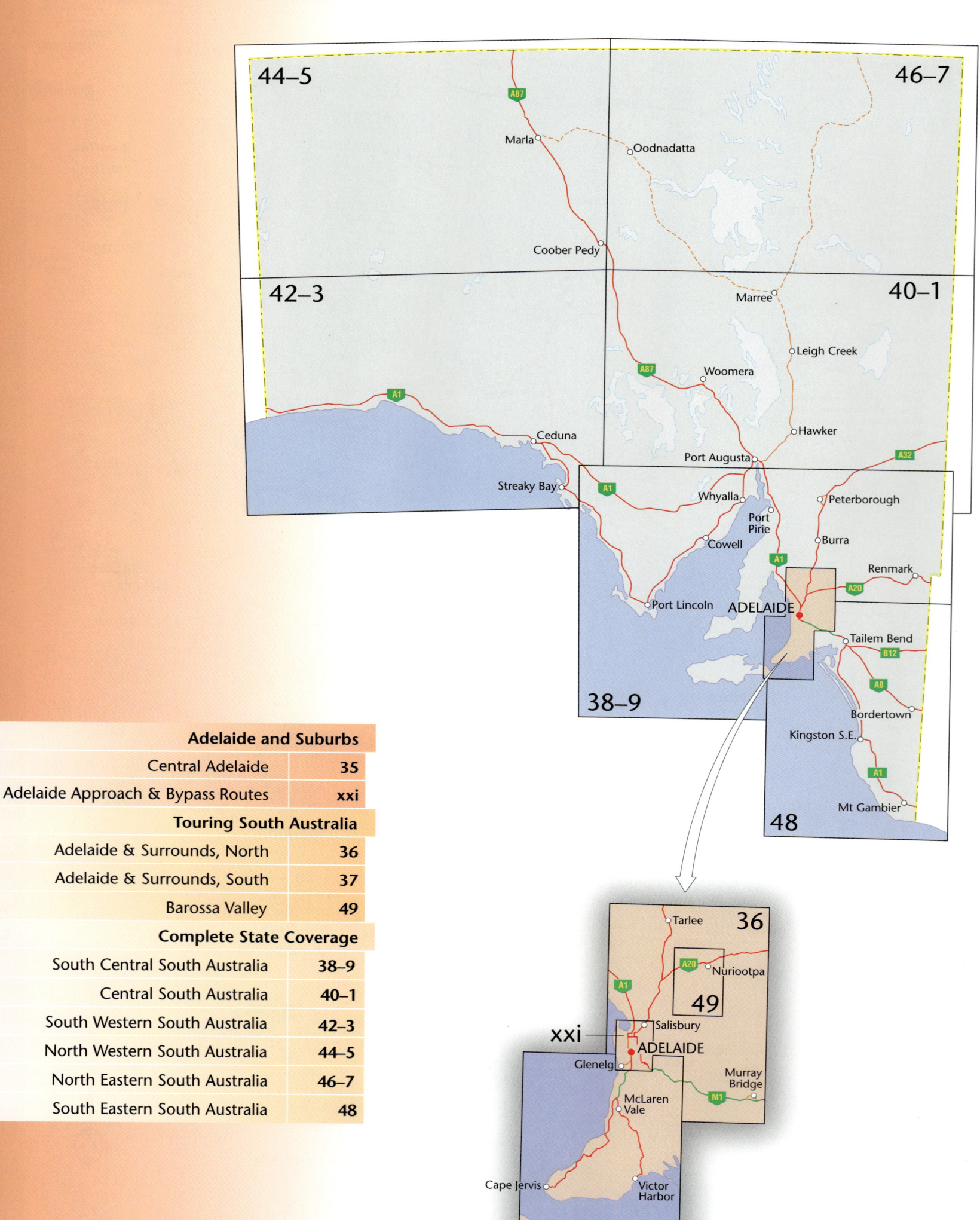

SOUTH AUSTRALIA
Location Map

Adelaide and Suburbs	
Central Adelaide	35
Adelaide Approach & Bypass Routes	xxi
Touring South Australia	
Adelaide & Surrounds, North	36
Adelaide & Surrounds, South	37
Barossa Valley	49
Complete State Coverage	
South Central South Australia	38–9
Central South Australia	40–1
South Western South Australia	42–3
North Western South Australia	44–5
North Eastern South Australia	46–7
South Eastern South Australia	48

Central Adelaide 35

Accommodation
- Adelaide Paringa Motel 1 E8
- Apartments on the Park 2 G11
- Austral Hotel 3 F8
- Centra Adelaide 4 F11
- The Chifley on South Terrace 5 F11
- Hilton 6 E10
- Hyatt Regency 7 D8
- Novotel Adelaide on Hindley 8 D8
- Radisson Playford Hotel 9 D8
- Royal Oak Hotel 10 D4
- Stag Hotel 11 G8
- Stamford Plaza 12 E8
- YMCA 13 F9

General Information
- Adelaide Police Station 14 E10
- Central Bus Station 15 D9
- Explorer Tram Depot 16 E8
- General Post Office 17 E9
- Glenelg Tram Terminus 18 E10
- Interstate/Country Rail Terminal 19 A11
- Motoring Organisation (RAA) 20 F9
- Popeye Motor Launch Cruises 21 D7
- Qantas Travel Centre 22 E8
- Railway Station (Metro) 23 D8
- SA Visitor & Travel Centre 24 E8
- Visitor Information 25 E8

Places of Interest
- Adelaide Casino 26 E8
- Adelaide Convention Centre 27 D8
- Adelaide Festival Centre 28 E7
- Adelaide Oval 29 D6
- Adelaide Town Hall 30 E9
- Adelaide Zoo 31 F6
- Art Gallery of SA 32 F8
- Ayers House 33 G8
- Botanic Gardens of Adelaide 34 G7
- Central Market 35 D10
- Chinatown 36 D10
- Edmund Wright House 37 E8
- Elder Hall 38 F8
- Elder Park 39 E7
- Entertainment Centre 40 A4
- Exhibition Hall 41 D8
- Government House 42 E8
- Historic Adelaide Gaol 43 B7
- Investigator Science & Technology Centre 44 B13
- Jam Factory Craft & Design Centre 45 D8
- Light's Vision 46 D6
- Lion Arts Centre 47 D8
- Migration Museum 48 E7
- Museum of Classical Archaeology 49 F8
- National Wine Centre 50 H7
- Parliament House 51 E8
- South Australian Museum 52 F8
- State Library 53 E8
- Tandanya 54 G9
- University of Adelaide 55 F7

Accommodation Only a sample range is listed; inclusion is not necessarily a recommendation.

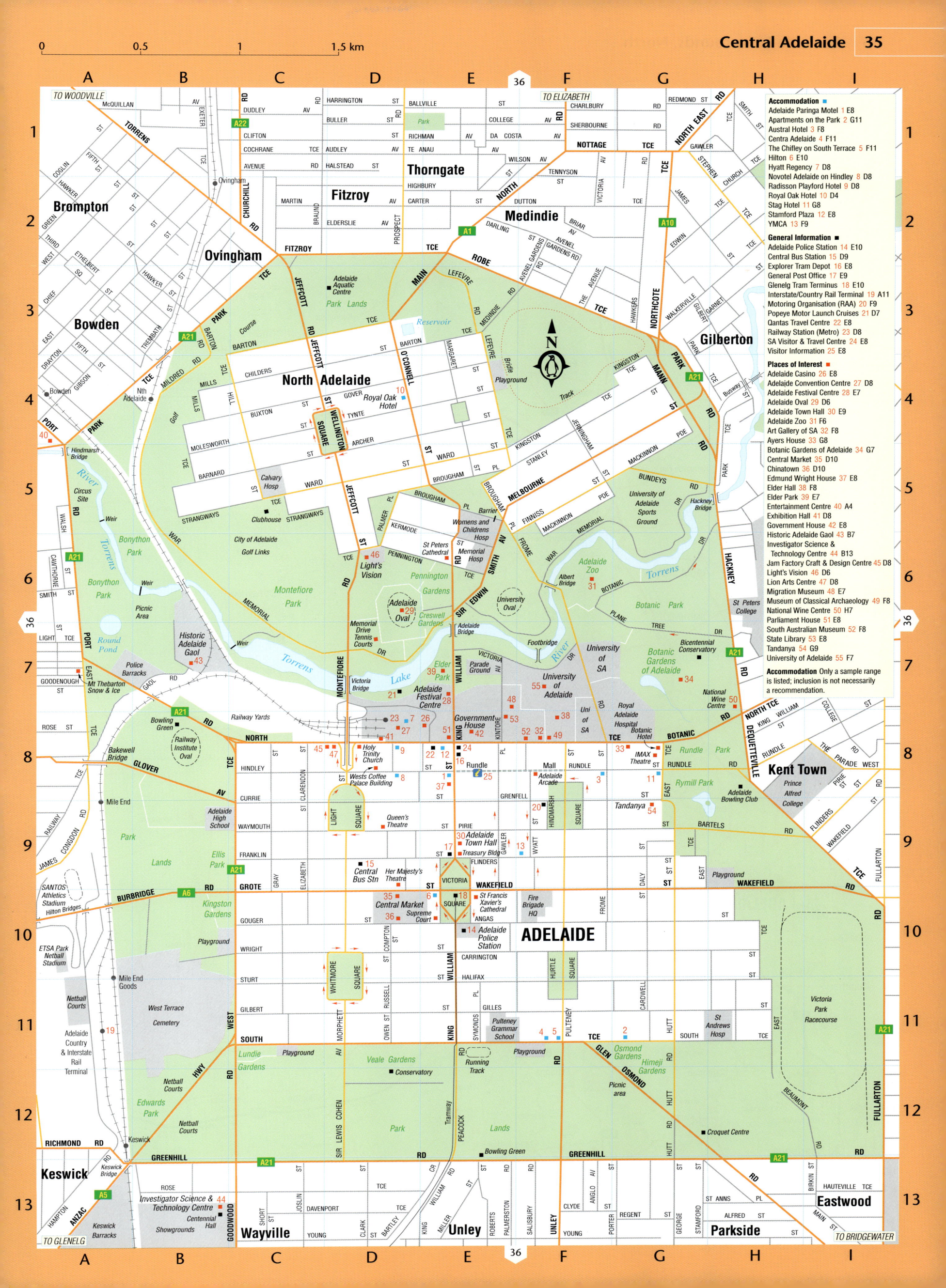

36 Adelaide & Surrounds, North

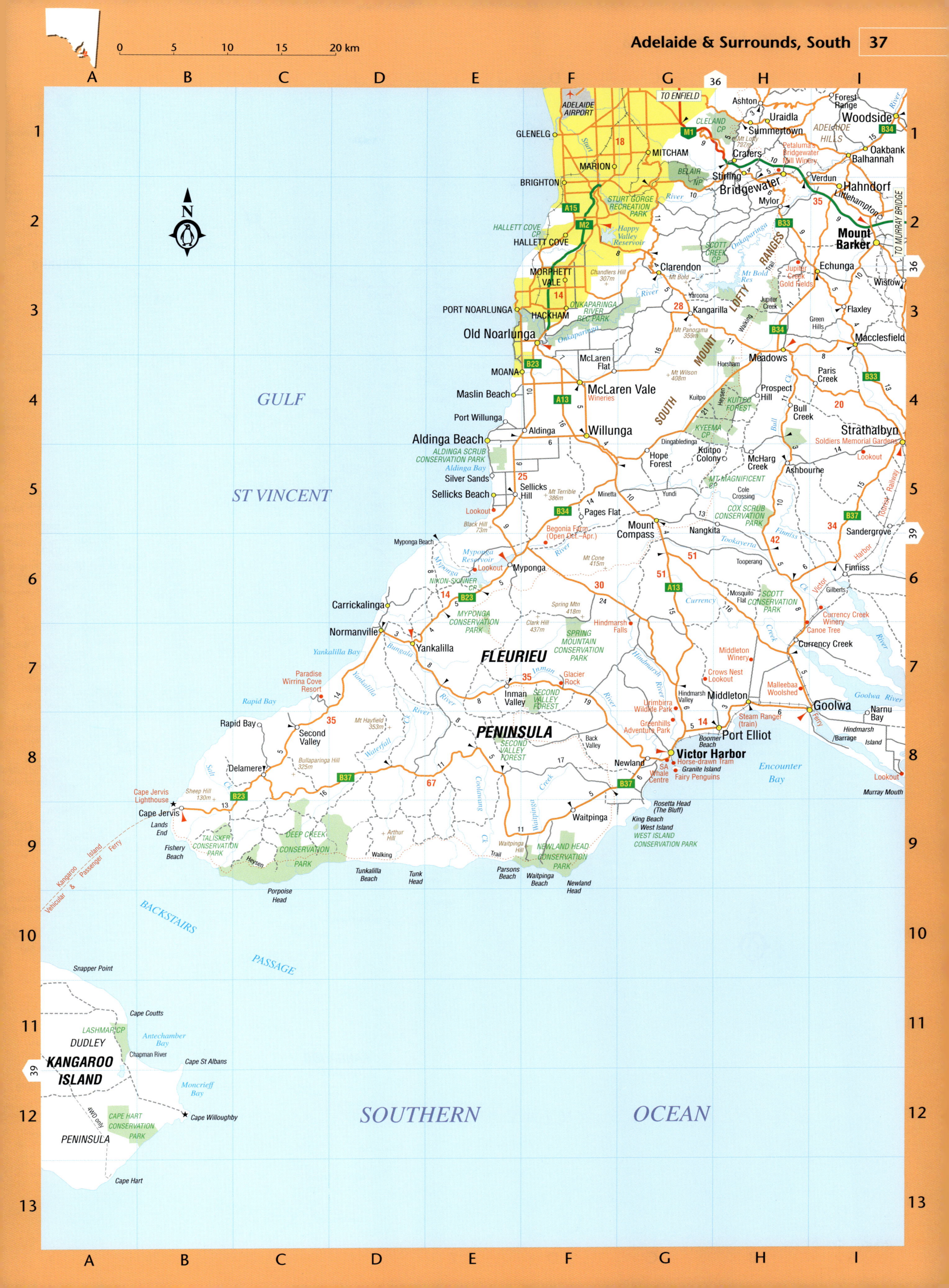

Adelaide & Surrounds, South 37

38 South Central South Australia

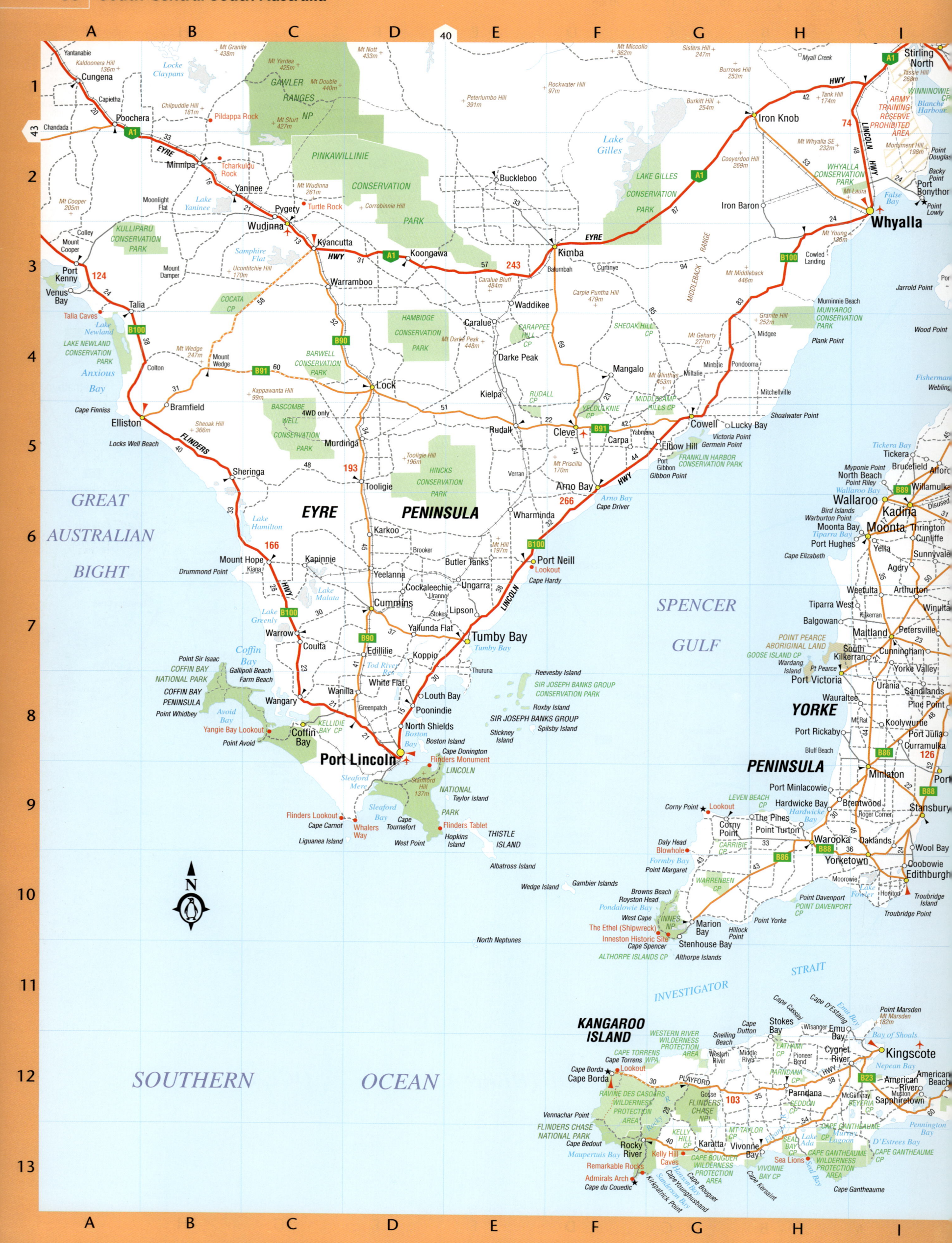

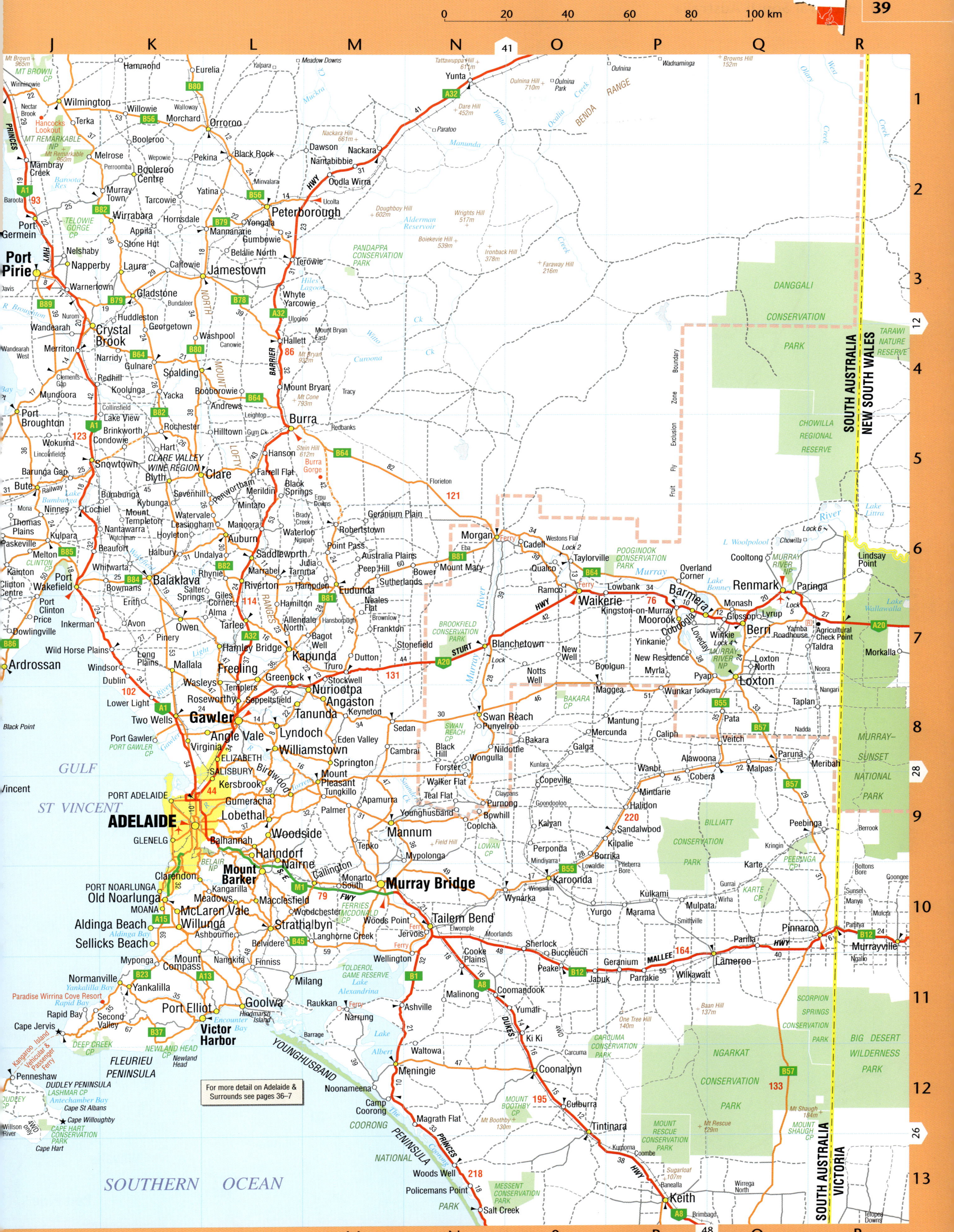
0 20 40 60 80 100 km
J K L M N O P Q R
1 2 3 4 5 6 7 8 9 10 11 12 13
41
12
28
26
48
MT BROWN CP
Hammond
Eurelia
Yalpara
Meadow Downs
Tattawuppa Hill 611m
Yunta
Oulnina Hill 710m
Oulnina Park
Oulnina
Wadnaminga
Browns Hill 152m
Wilmington
Willowie
Walloway
Terka
Hancocks Lookout
MT REMARKABLE NP
Mt Remarkable 960m
Morchard
Orroroo
Booleroo
Dare Hill 452m
Paratoo
BENDA RANGE
Nackara Hill 661m
Dawson
Nackara
Nantabibbie
Melrose
Wepowie
Pekina
Black Rock
Mambray Creek
Booleroo Centre
Minvalara
Oodla Wirra
Murray Town
Tarcowie
Yatina
Ucolta
PRINCES HWY
Baroota
Port Germein
TELOWIE GORGE CP
Wirrabara
Hornsdale
Yongala
Mannanarie
Peterborough
Doughboy Hill 602m
Alderman Reservoir
Wrights Hill 517m
Boiekevie Hill 539m
Ironback Hill 378m
Faraway Hill 216m
Appila
Stone Hut
Gumbowie
Belalie North
Nelshaby
Napperby
Laura
Caltowie
Jamestown
Terowie
PANDAPPA CONSERVATION PARK
Port Pirie
Warnertown
Gladstone
Whyte Yarcowie
Hiles Lagoon
Bundaleer
Huddleston
Georgetown
Ulooloo
Crystal Brook
Wandearah
Washpool
Canowie
Hallett
Mount Bryan East
Merriton
Narridy
Gulnare
Spalding
Mt Bryan 932m
Wandearah West
Redhill
Koolunga
Yacka
Booborowie
Mount Bryan
Tracy
Mt Cone 793m
Mundoora
Clements Gap
Andrews
Leighton
Port Broughton
Collinsfield
Lake View
Brinkworth
Rochester
Burra
Redbanks
Condowie
Hart
Hilltown
Gum Ck
Wokurna
CLARE VALLEY WINE REGION
Hanson
Stein Hill 612m
Burra Gorge
Lincolnfields
Snowtown
Blyth
Clare
Farrell Flat
Barunga Gap
Bute
Railway
Lake Bumbunga
Bumbunga
Sevenhill
Penwortham
Merildin
Black Springs
Emu Downs
Florieton
Mona
Ninnes
Lochiel
Kybunga
Mintaro
Mount Templeton
Watervale
Brady Creek
Geranium Plain
Thomas Plains
Kulpara
Nantawarra
Leasingham
Manoora
Waterloo
Robertstown
Paskeville
Watchman
Hoyleton
Auburn
Ngapal
Morgan
Cadell
Westons Flat
Lock 2
Taylorville
POOGINOOK CONSERVATION PARK
Murray
Overland Corner
Lock 6
Chowilla
MURRAY RIVER NP
Halbury
Saddleworth
Point Pass
Australia Plains
Eba
Mount Mary
Qualco
Cooltong
Lindsay Point
Melton
Beaufort
Undalya
Julia
Peep Hill
Kainton
CLINTON CP
Whitwarta
Rhynie
Marrabel
Tarnma
Hampden
Bower
Clinton Centre
Port Wakefield
Bowmans
Balaklava
Salter Springs
Riverton
Eudunda
Sutherlands
Ramco
Ferry
Waikerie
Lowbank
Barmera
Lake Bonney
Renmark
Paringa
Port Clinton
Erith
Giles Corner
Hamilton
Neales Flat
Brownlow
Kingston-on-Murray
Moorook
Monash
Glossop
Lyrup
Price
Inkerman
Avon
Owen
Alma
Tarlee
Allendale North
Hansborough
Frankton
Cobdogla
Loveday
Winkie
Lock 4
Berri
Yamba Roadhouse
Agricultural Check Point
Dowlingville
Pinery
Bagot Well
Stonefield
STURT HWY
Blanchetown
New Well
Yinkanie
Taldra
Morkalla
Lake Wallawalla
Wild Horse Plains
Long Plains
Hamley Bridge
Kapunda
BROOKFIELD CONSERVATION PARK
Lock 1
Notts Well
Boolgun
New Residence
Myrla
Pyap
Loxton North
Noora
Ardrossan
Windsor
Mallala
Freeling
Dutton
Truro
Loxton
Dublin
Wasleys
Templers
Greenock
Stockwell
Nuriootpa
Maggea
Wunkar
Tookayerta
Nangari
Roseworthy
Seppeltsfield
Angaston
BAKARA CP
Taplan
Lower Light
Tanunda
Keyneton
Two Wells
Gawler
Swan Reach
Punyelroo
Mantung
Pata
Black Point
Port Gawler
PORT GAWLER CP
Angle Vale
Lyndoch
Eden Valley
Sedan
SWAN REACH CP
Mercunda
Caliph
Veitch
Nadda
Virginia
ELIZABETH
Williamstown
Cambrai
Black Hill
Nildottie
Bakara
Galga
Alawoona
Paruna
Meribah
MURRAY–SUNSET NATIONAL PARK
GULF
ST VINCENT
Vincent
SALISBURY
Birdwood
Springton
Wongulla
Forster
Kunlara
Wanbi
Cobera
Malpas
Kersbrook
Mount Pleasant
Tungkillo
Copeville
Mindarie
PORT ADELAIDE
Gumeracha
Lobethal
Apamurra
Walker Flat
Teal Flat
Claypans
Purnong
Goondooloo
Halidon
ADELAIDE
Palmer
Younghusband
Bowhill
Kalyan
Sandalwood
BILLIATT CONSERVATION PARK
Peebinga
Berrook
GLENELG
Woodside
Mannum
Copiha
Field Hill
LOWAN CP
Perponda
Kilpalie
Kringin
Balhannah
Hahndorf
Tepko
Mypolonga
Mindiyarra
Borrika
Karte
Nairne
BELAIR NP
Callington
Lowaldie
Pfeiffer Bore
PEEBINGA CP
Boltons Bore
Goongee
Mount Barker
Monarto South
Murray Bridge
Karoonda
Wynarka
Gurrai
Wirha
KARTE CP
Sunset
PORT NOARLUNGA
Clarendon
Kangarilla
Wanghalin
Kulkami
Mulpata
Manya
Mulcra
Old Noarlunga
Meadows
Macclesfield
FWY
Yurgo
Marama
MOANA
McLaren Vale
Woodchester
FERRIES McDONALD CP
Tailem Bend
Smithville
Pinnaroo
Parilla
Aldinga Beach
Willunga
Strathalbyn
Woods Point
Elwomple
Moorlands
Aldinga Bay
Ashbourne
Langhorne Creek
Jervois
Ferry
Sherlock
Buccleuch
MALLEE HWY
Lameroo
Murrayville
Sellicks Beach
Belvidere
Cooke Plains
Peake
Geranium
Wilkawatt
Ngallo
Myponga
Mount Compass
Nangkita
Finniss
Wellington
TOLDEROL GAME RESERVE
Jabuk
Parrakie
Normanville
Milang
Coomandook
Yankalilla
Yankalilla Bay
Lake Alexandrina
Malinong
Paradise Wirrina Cove Resort
Rapid Bay
Goolwa
Raukkan
Ashville
Yumali
Baan Hill 137m
SCORPION SPRINGS CONSERVATION PARK
Rapid Bay
Second Valley
Port Elliot
Hindmarsh Island
Narrung
One Tree Hill 140m
Cape Jervis
Victor Harbor
Encounter Bay
Barrage
Lake Albert
Ki Ki
DUKES HWY
4WD
Carcuma
CARCUMA CONSERVATION PARK
NGARKAT CONSERVATION PARK
BIG DESERT WILDERNESS PARK
DEEP CREEK CP
NEWLAND HEAD CP
Newland Head
Waltowa
FLEURIEU PENINSULA
Kangaroo Island Vehicular & Passenger Ferry
YOUNGHUSBAND
Meningie
Coonalpyn
Penneshaw
DUDLEY PENINSULA
LASHMAR CP
Antechamber Bay
Cape St Albans
Cape Willoughby
CAPE HART CONSERVATION PARK
Cape Hart
Willson River
DUDLEY CP
For more detail on Adelaide & Surrounds see pages 36–7
PENINSULA
Noonameena
Camp Coorong
COORONG
BOOTHBY CP
MOUNT BOOTHBY CP
Mt Boothby 130m
Culburra
Magrath Flat
THE PENINSULA
NATIONAL
Tintinara
MOUNT RESCUE CONSERVATION PARK
Mt Rescue 129m
Mt Shaugh 184m
MOUNT SHAUGH CP
Kumorna
Coombe
PRINCES HWY
SOUTHERN OCEAN
Woods Well
Sugarloaf 107m
Baneella
Wirrega North
Policemans Point
MESSENT CONSERVATION PARK
PARK
Salt Creek
Keith
Brimbago
Telopea Downs
DANGGALI CONSERVATION PARK
TARAWI NATURE RESERVE
CHOWILLA REGIONAL RESERVE
Fruit Fly Exclusion Zone Boundary
SOUTH AUSTRALIA
NEW SOUTH WALES
VICTORIA
Lake Littra
L. Woolpolool
NORTH MOUNT LOFTY RANGES
BARRIER HWY
A1 A20 A32 A8 A13 A15 B1 B12 B23 B37 B45 B55 B56 B57 B64 B78 B79 B80 B81 B82 B84 B85 B86 B89 M1
93 123 102 114 121 131 44 79 76 220 164 133 195 218 86

40 Central South Australia

WARNING: While visitors are permitted in the township of Woomera, entry to the Woomera Prohibited Area is by permit only, except in the immediate corridors of the Stuart Highway and the road from Coober Pedy to William Creek. Camping is not permitted in the area.

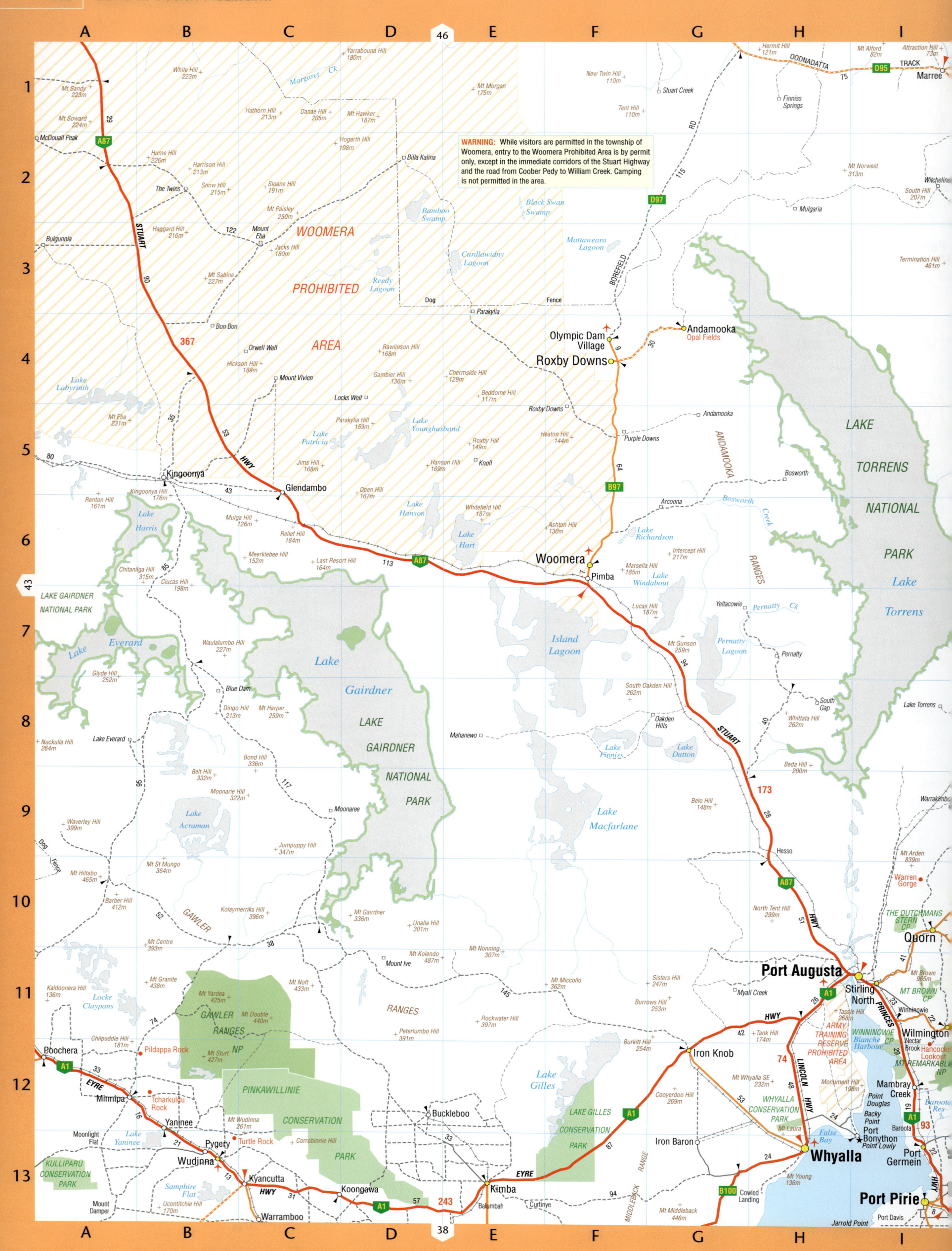

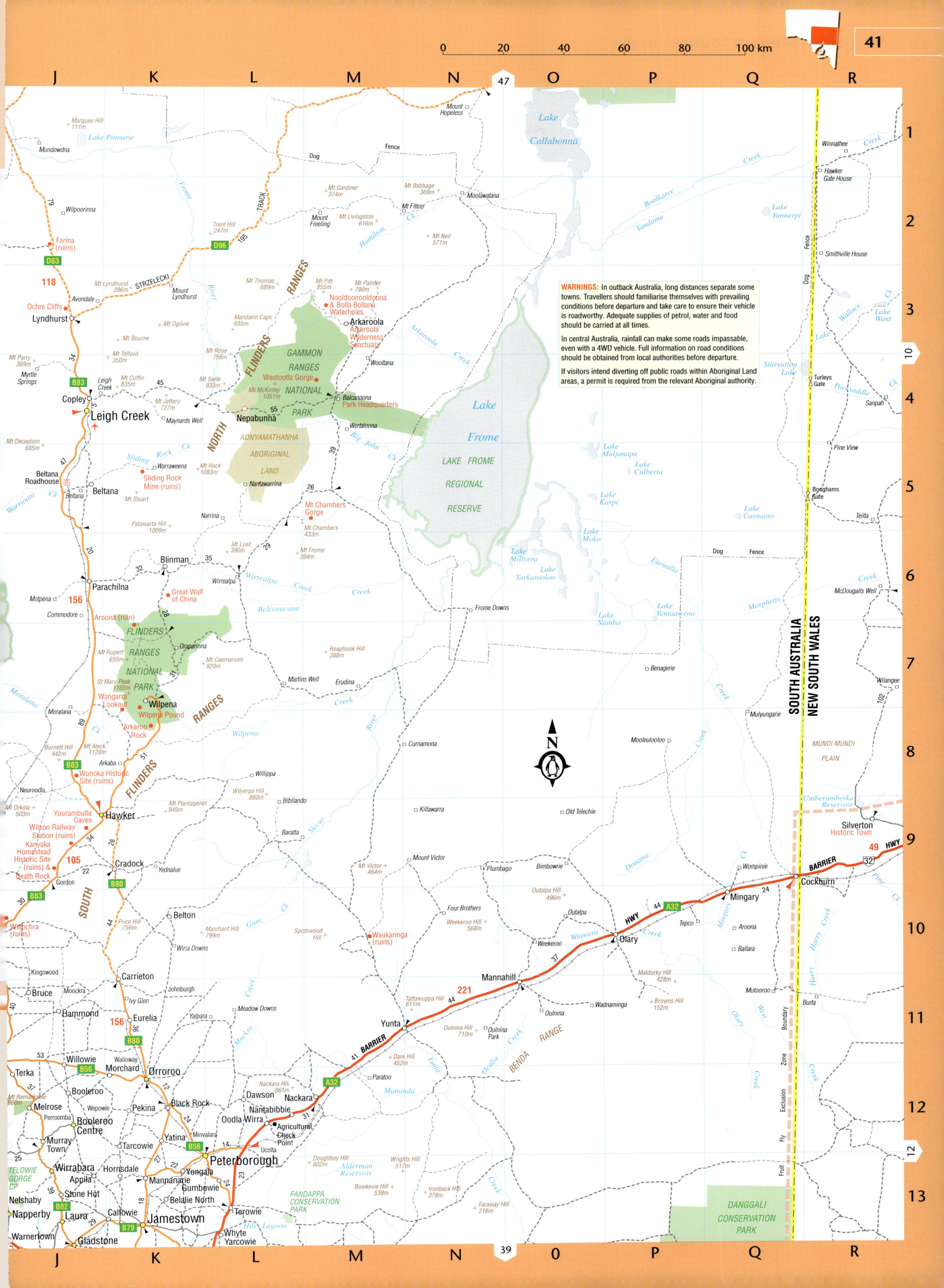

WARNINGS: In outback Australia, long distances separate some towns. Travellers should familiarise themselves with prevailing conditions before departure and take care to ensure their vehicle is roadworthy. Adequate supplies of petrol, water and food should be carried at all times.

In central Australia, rainfall can make some roads impassable, even with a 4WD vehicle. Full information on road conditions should be obtained from local authorities before departure.

If visitors intend diverting off public roads within Aboriginal Land areas, a permit is required from the relevant Aboriginal authority.

42 South Western South Australia

Map grid: columns A–I, rows 1–13

- Great Victoria Desert Nature Reserve (A1–A2)
- Unnamed Conservation Park (B1–B2)
- Maralinga Tjarutja Aboriginal Land (D1–H3)
- Ooldea Range (H2–I3)
- Maralinga (H3)
- Nullarbor Plain (C3–F4)
- Trans Australia Railway (A5–I4)
  - Deakin, Hughes, Denman, Cook, Fisher, O'Malley, Watson, Ooldea
- Western Australia / South Australia border (A1–A8, yellow dashed)
- Nullarbor Regional Reserve (C5–H6)
- Nullarbor National Park (C7–F7)
- Yalata Aboriginal Land (G7–I8)
- Nullarbor Roadhouse (G7)
- Yalata, Yalata Roadhouse (I7)
- Whale-watching (G7)
- Head of Bight (G8)
- Great Australian Bight Marine Park (G8)
- Eyre Hwy (A8–I7), with Lookouts; distances 13, 89, 293, 55, 42, 94
- Eucla, Agricultural Check Point, Border Village, Eucla NP (A8–B8)
- Great Australian Bight (ocean, C10–H10)

THE GREAT AUSTRALIAN BIGHT MARINE PARK: Extends almost 6 km off the coastline around Head of Bight. Between June and Oct., this area is transformed into a maritime nursery for visiting southern right whales and their calves. Permits for whale-watching can be purchased from the White Well Ranger Station near the viewing platform.

N (compass, Penguin logo)

0 20 40 60 80 100 km

J K L M N O P Q R

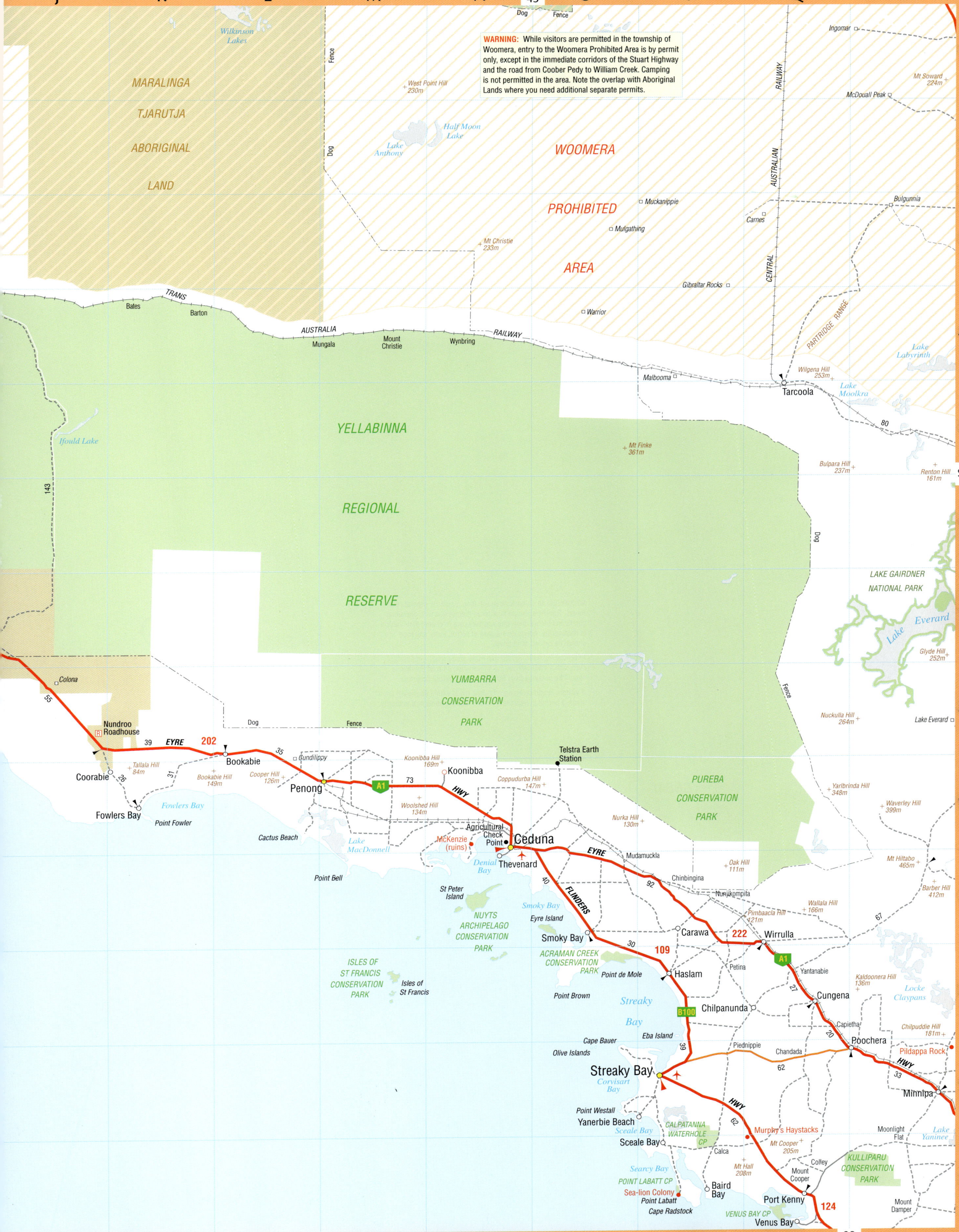

J K L M N O P Q R

44 North Western South Australia

WARNINGS: In outback Australia, long distances separate some towns. Travellers should familiarise themselves with prevailing conditions before departure and take care to ensure their vehicle is roadworthy. Adequate supplies of petrol, water and food should be carried at all times.

In central Australia, rainfall can make some roads impassable, even with a 4WD vehicle. Full information on road conditions should be obtained from local authorities before departure.

If visitors intend diverting off public roads within Aboriginal Land areas, a permit is required from the relevant Aboriginal authority.

Locations and features

- Surveyor Generals Corner
- Mt Hinckley 1018m
- Kalka
- Pipalyatjara
- Mt Cockburn 1138m
- Mt Davies 1058m
- Aparawatatja
- MANN RANGES
- Mt Edwin 1193m
- Mt Whinham 1231m
- Kanypi
- Feltham Hill 863m
- Alpara
- Mt Woodward 1227m
- Mt Morris 1288m
- Amata
- Ayliffe Hill (trig) 1044m
- Mulga Park
- Mt Davenport 1139m
- Mt Woodroffe 1440m
- MUSGRAVE RANGES
- Mt Cooperinna 1045m
- PITJANTJATJARA ABORIGINAL LAND
- Mt Caroline 1042m
- Mt Kintore 1070m
- Mt Harriet 938m
- Mt Crombie 835m
- Mt Agnes 671m
- Permano Hill 719m
- Mt Lindsay 819m
- Oonmooninna Hill 600m
- Maryinna Hill (trig) 622m
- Davies Hill
- EVERARD
- Mt Poondinna 678m
- SOUTH AUSTRALIA / WESTERN AUSTRALIA
- NORTHERN TERRITORY / SOUTH AUSTRALIA
- GREAT VICTORIA DESERT
- UNNAMED CONSERVATION PARK
- Vokes Hill Corner
- Serpentine Lakes
- MARALINGA TJARUTJA ABORIGINAL LAND
- Nurrari Lakes
- Wyola Lake
- Halinor Lake
- Lake Dey Dey
- Forrest Lakes
- Lake Maurice
- GREAT VICTORIA DESERT NATURE RESERVE

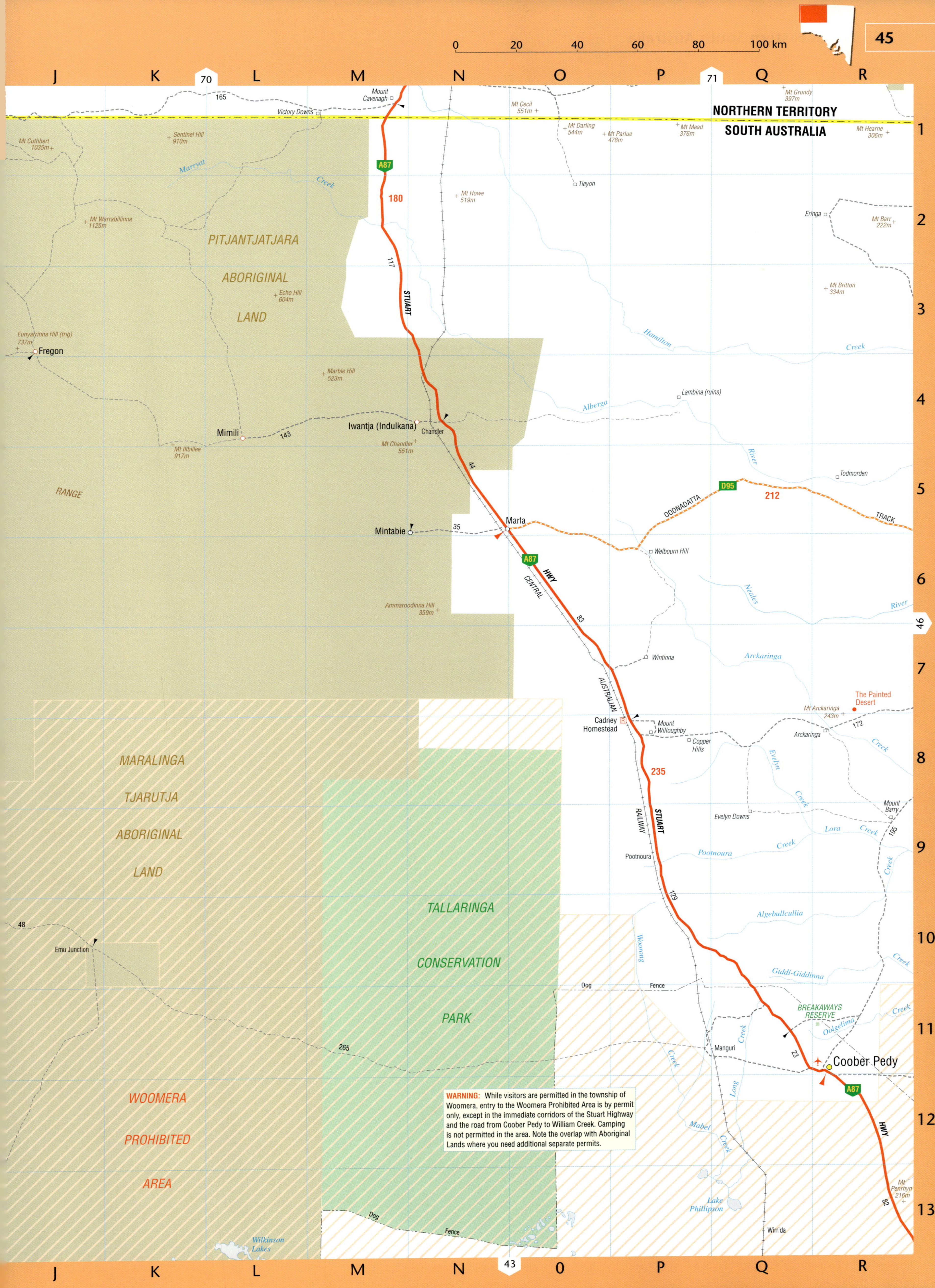

0 20 40 60 80 100 km
J K L M N O P Q R
70
71
43
46
1 2 3 4 5 6 7 8 9 10 11 12 13
NORTHERN TERRITORY
SOUTH AUSTRALIA
Mount Cavenagh
Victory Downs
165
Mt Cecil 551m
Mt Grundy 397m
Mt Darling 544m
Mt Parlue 478m
Mt Mead 376m
Mt Hearne 306m
Mt Cuthbert 1035m
Sentinel Hill 910m
Marryat
Creek
A87
180
Tieyon
Mt Howe 519m
Eringa
Mt Barr 222m
Mt Warrabillinna 1125m
PITJANTJATJARA
ABORIGINAL
LAND
Echo Hill 604m
117
STUART
Mt Britton 334m
Eunyarinna Hill (trig) 737m
Fregon
Hamilton
Creek
Marble Hill 523m
Lambina (ruins)
Alberga
Mimili
143
Iwantja (Indulkana)
Chandler
Mt Chandler 551m
Mt Illbillee 917m
River
Todmorden
44
D95
212
RANGE
OODNADATTA
TRACK
Marla
Mintabie
35
Welbourn Hill
A87
HWY
CENTRAL
Neales
River
Ammaroodinna Hill 359m
83
Wintinna
Arckaringa
AUSTRALIAN
The Painted Desert
Mt Arckaringa 243m
172
Cadney Homestead
Mount Willoughby
Arckaringa
Copper Hills
Creek
MARALINGA
TJARUTJA
ABORIGINAL
LAND
235
Evelyn
Creek
Mount Barry
RAILWAY
STUART
Evelyn Downs
Lora
Creek
195
Pootnoura
Pootnoura
Creek
Creek
129
TALLARINGA
CONSERVATION
PARK
Algebullcullia
48
Emu Junction
Woorong
Creek
Giddi-Giddinna
Dog
Fence
BREAKAWAYS RESERVE
Creek
Ooldgelina
265
Manguri
Creek
Creek
23
Coober Pedy
A87
WOOMERA
PROHIBITED
AREA
WARNING: While visitors are permitted in the township of Woomera, entry to the Woomera Prohibited Area is by permit only, except in the immediate corridors of the Stuart Highway and the road from Coober Pedy to William Creek. Camping is not permitted in the area. Note the overlap with Aboriginal Lands where you need additional separate permits.
Long
Mabel
Creek
HWY
Mt Penrhyn 216m
82
Lake Phillipson
Dog
Fence
Wirrida
Wilkinson Lakes

46 North Eastern South Australia

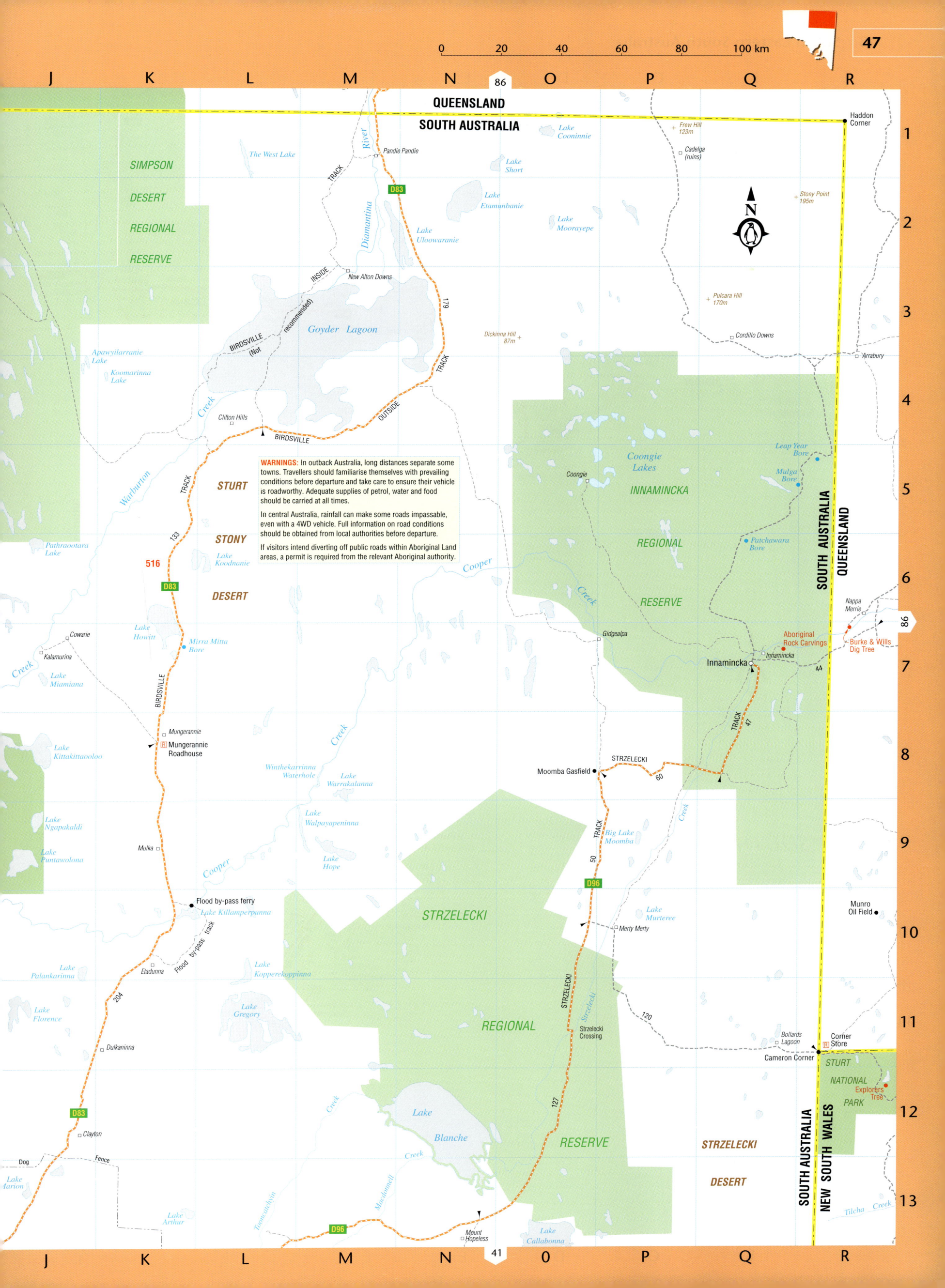

WARNINGS: In outback Australia, long distances separate some towns. Travellers should familiarise themselves with prevailing conditions before departure and take care to ensure their vehicle is roadworthy. Adequate supplies of petrol, water and food should be carried at all times.

In central Australia, rainfall can make some roads impassable, even with a 4WD vehicle. Full information on road conditions should be obtained from local authorities before departure.

If visitors intend diverting off public roads within Aboriginal Land areas, a permit is required from the relevant Aboriginal authority.

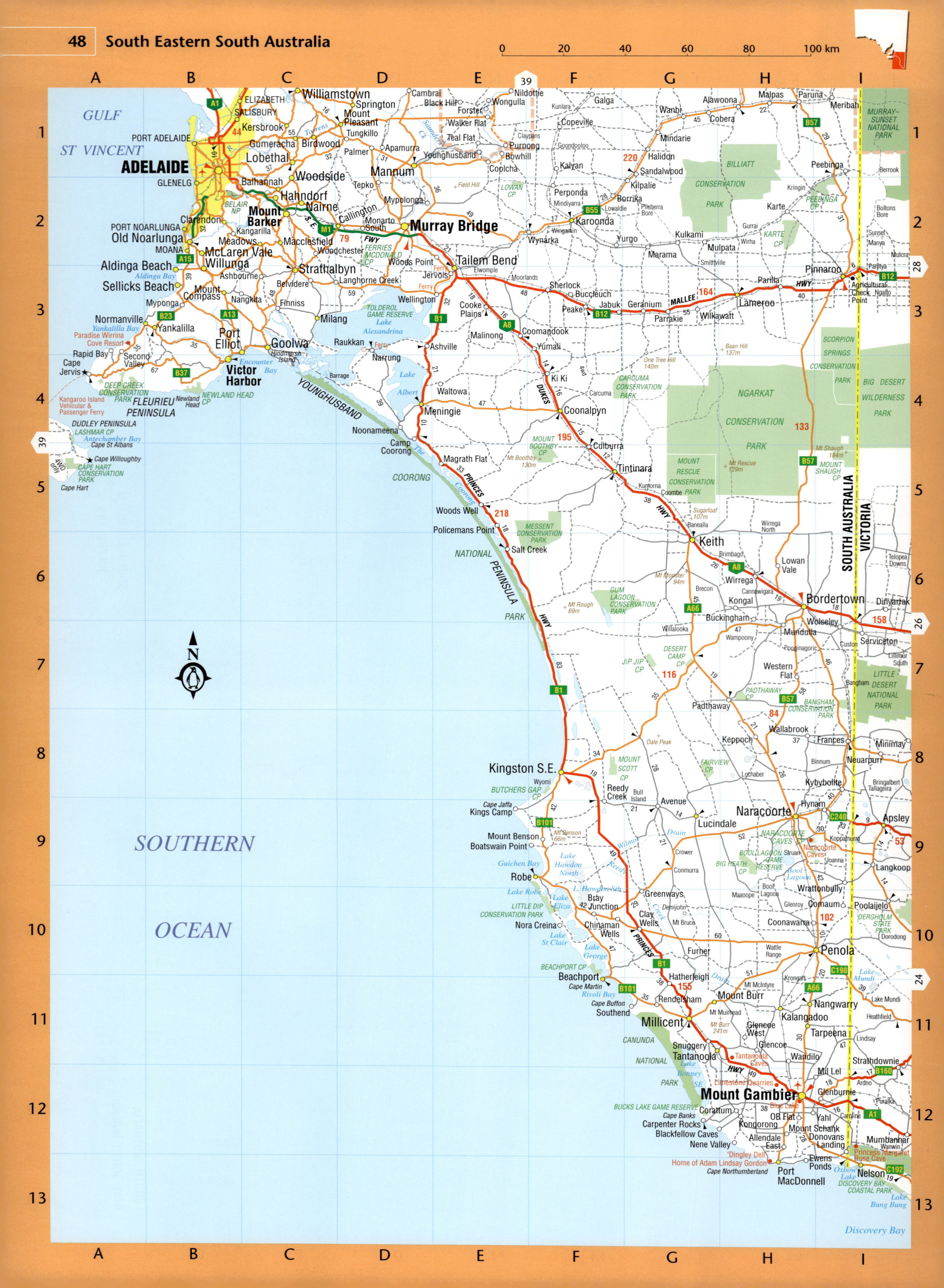

South Eastern South Australia

Barossa Valley

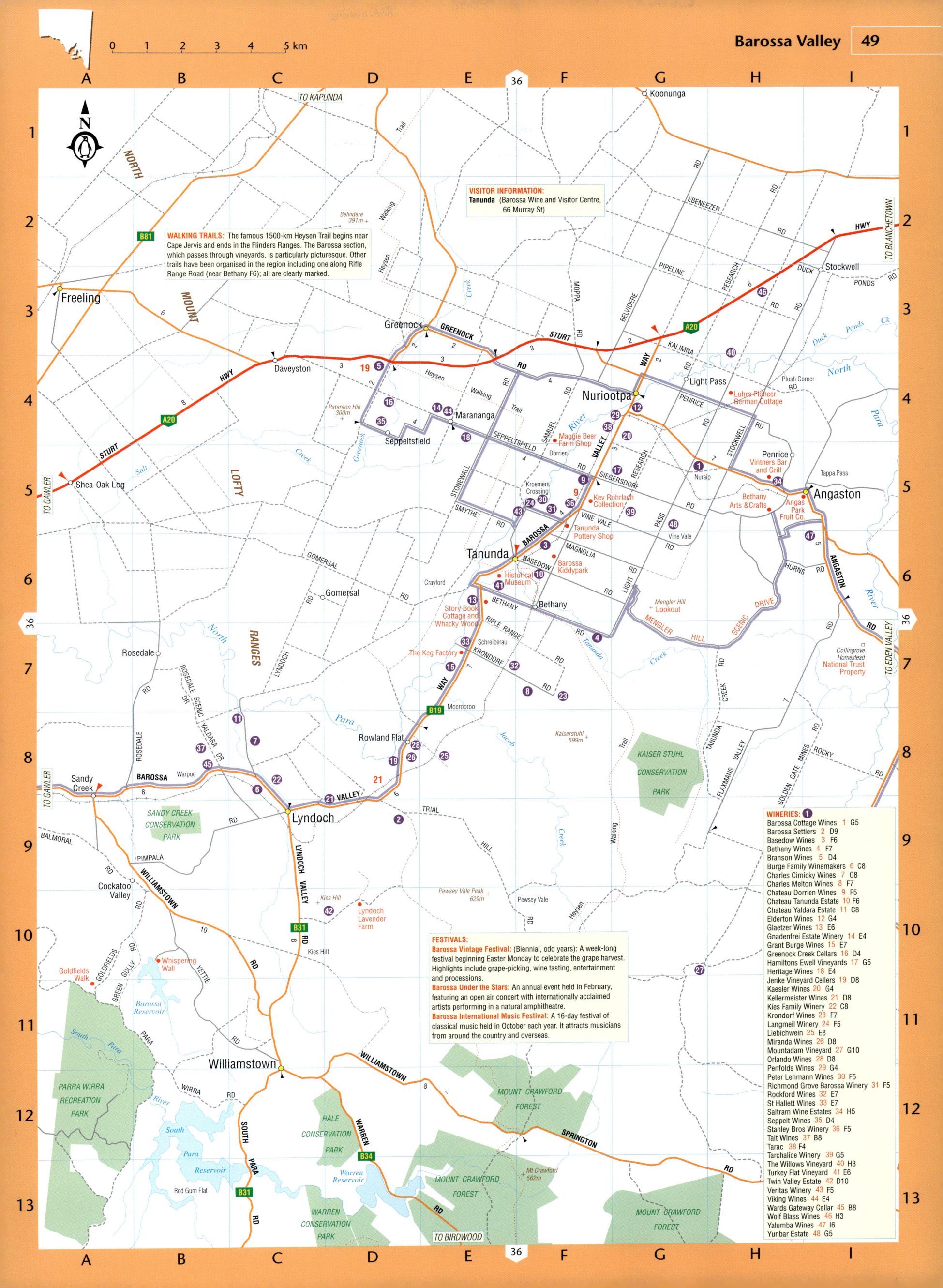

VISITOR INFORMATION:
Tanunda (Barossa Wine and Visitor Centre, 66 Murray St)

WALKING TRAILS: The famous 1500-km Heysen Trail begins near Cape Jervis and ends in the Flinders Ranges. The Barossa section, which passes through vineyards, is particularly picturesque. Other trails have been organised in the region including one along Rifle Range Road (near Bethany F6); all are clearly marked.

FESTIVALS:
Barossa Vintage Festival: (Biennial, odd years) A week-long festival beginning Easter Monday to celebrate the grape harvest. Highlights include grape-picking, wine tasting, entertainment and processions.
Barossa Under the Stars: An annual event held in February, featuring an open air concert with internationally acclaimed artists performing in a natural amphitheatre.
Barossa International Music Festival: A 16-day festival of classical music held in October each year. It attracts musicians from around the country and overseas.

WINERIES

Winery	No.	Grid
Barossa Cottage Wines	1	G5
Barossa Settlers	2	D9
Basedow Wines	3	F6
Bethany Wines	4	F7
Branson Wines	5	D4
Burge Family Winemakers	6	C8
Charles Cimicky Wines	7	C8
Charles Melton Wines	8	F7
Chateau Dorrien Wines	9	F5
Chateau Tanunda Estate	10	F6
Chateau Yaldara Estate	11	C8
Elderton Wines	12	G4
Glaetzer Wines	13	E6
Gnadenfrei Estate Winery	14	E4
Grant Burge Wines	15	E7
Greenock Creek Cellars	16	D4
Hamiltons Ewell Vineyards	17	G5
Heritage Wines	18	E4
Jenke Vineyard Cellers	19	D8
Kaesler Wines	20	G4
Kellermeister Wines	21	D8
Kies Family Winery	22	C8
Krondorf Wines	23	F7
Langmeil Winery	24	F5
Liebichwein	25	E8
Miranda Wines	26	D8
Mountadam Vineyard	27	G10
Orlando Wines	28	D8
Penfolds Wines	29	G4
Peter Lehmann Wines	30	F5
Richmond Grove Barossa Winery	31	F5
Rockford Wines	32	E7
St Hallett Wines	33	E7
Saltram Wine Estates	34	H5
Seppelt Wines	35	D4
Stanley Bros Winery	36	F5
Tait Wines	37	B8
Tarac	38	F4
Tarchalice Winery	39	G5
The Willows Vineyard	40	H3
Turkey Flat Vineyard	41	E6
Twin Valley Estate	42	D10
Veritas Winery	43	F5
Viking Wines	44	E4
Wards Gateway Cellar	45	B8
Wolf Blass Wines	46	H3
Yalumba Wines	47	I6
Yunbar Estate	48	G5

Western Australia
Location Map

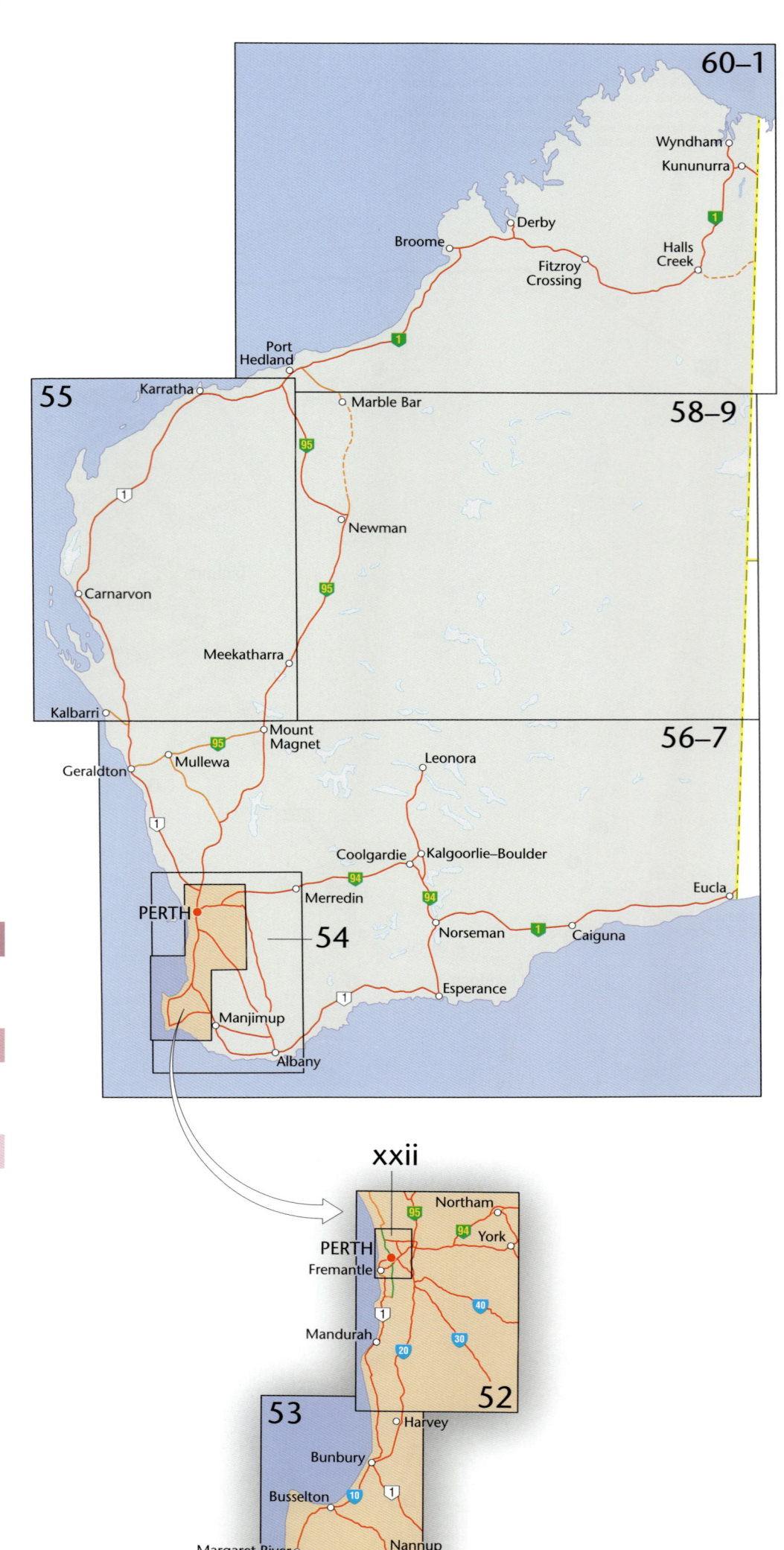

Perth and Suburbs	
Central Perth	51
Perth Approach & Bypass Routes	xxii
Touring Western Australia	
Perth & Surrounds	52
The South-West	53
Complete State Coverage	
South Western Western Australia	54
Central Western Western Australia	55
Southern Western Australia	56–7
Central Western Australia	58–9
Northern Western Australia	60–1

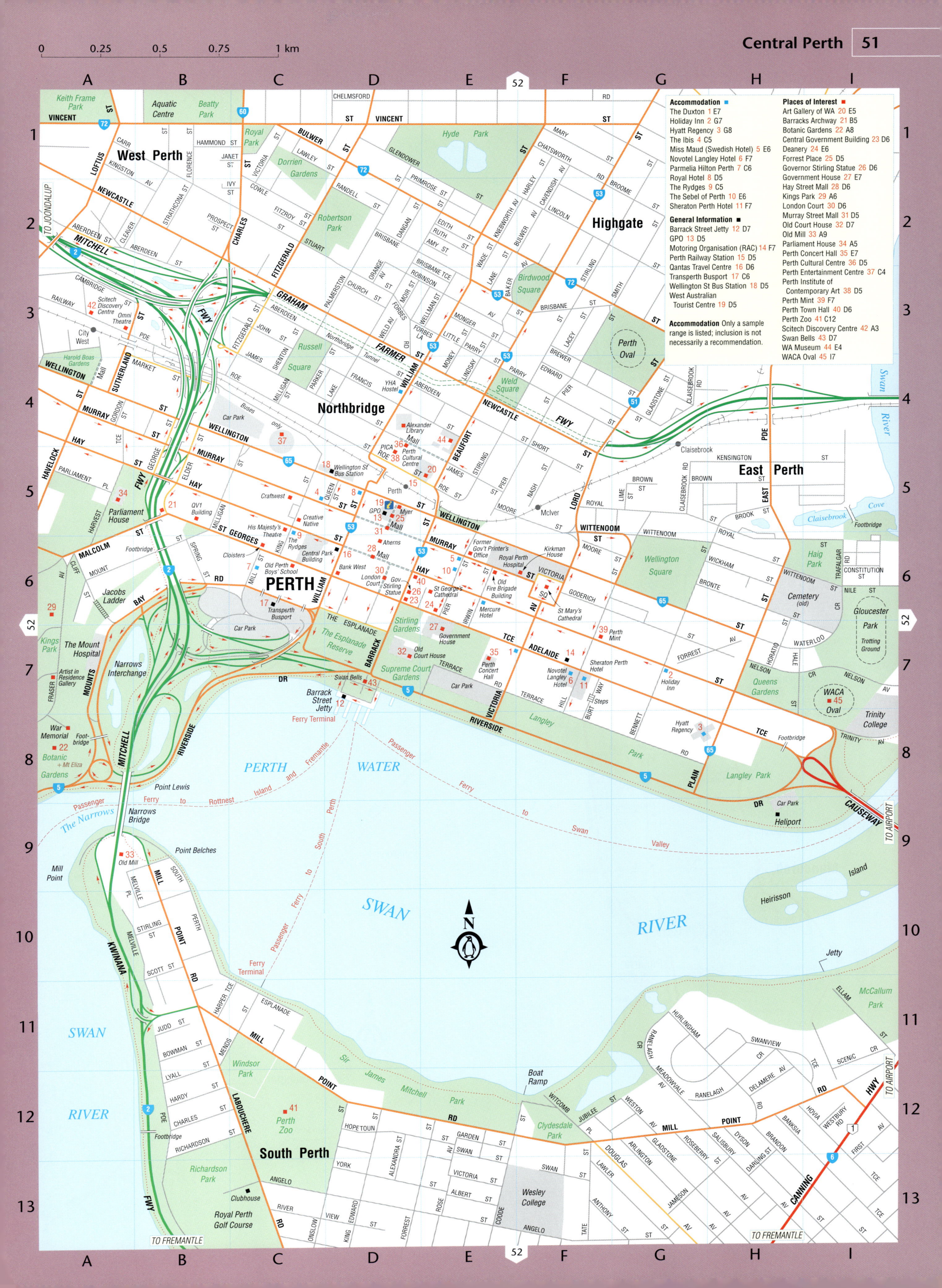

Central Perth 51

Accommodation
- The Duxton 1 E7
- Holiday Inn 2 G7
- Hyatt Regency 3 G8
- The Ibis 4 C5
- Miss Maud (Swedish Hotel) 5 E6
- Novotel Langley Hotel 6 F7
- Parmelia Hilton Perth 7 C6
- Royal Hotel 8 D5
- The Rydges 9 C5
- The Sebel of Perth 10 E6
- Sheraton Perth Hotel 11 F7

General Information
- Barrack Street Jetty 12 D7
- GPO 13 D5
- Motoring Organisation (RAC) 14 F7
- Perth Railway Station 15 D5
- Qantas Travel Centre 16 D6
- Transperth Busport 17 C6
- Wellington St Bus Station 18 D5
- West Australian Tourist Centre 19 D5

Accommodation: Only a sample range is listed; inclusion is not necessarily a recommendation.

Places of Interest
- Art Gallery of WA 20 E5
- Barracks Archway 21 B5
- Botanic Gardens 22 A8
- Central Government Building 23 D6
- Deanery 24 E6
- Forrest Place 25 D5
- Governor Stirling Statue 26 D6
- Government House 27 E7
- Hay Street Mall 28 D6
- Kings Park 29 A6
- London Court 30 D6
- Murray Street Mall 31 D5
- Old Court House 32 D7
- Old Mill 33 A9
- Parliament House 34 A5
- Perth Concert Hall 35 E7
- Perth Cultural Centre 36 D5
- Perth Entertainment Centre 37 C4
- Perth Institute of Contemporary Art 38 D5
- Perth Mint 39 F7
- Perth Town Hall 40 D6
- Perth Zoo 41 C12
- Scitech Discovery Centre 42 A3
- Swan Bells 43 D7
- WA Museum 44 E4
- WACA Oval 45 I7

0 5 10 15 20 25 km

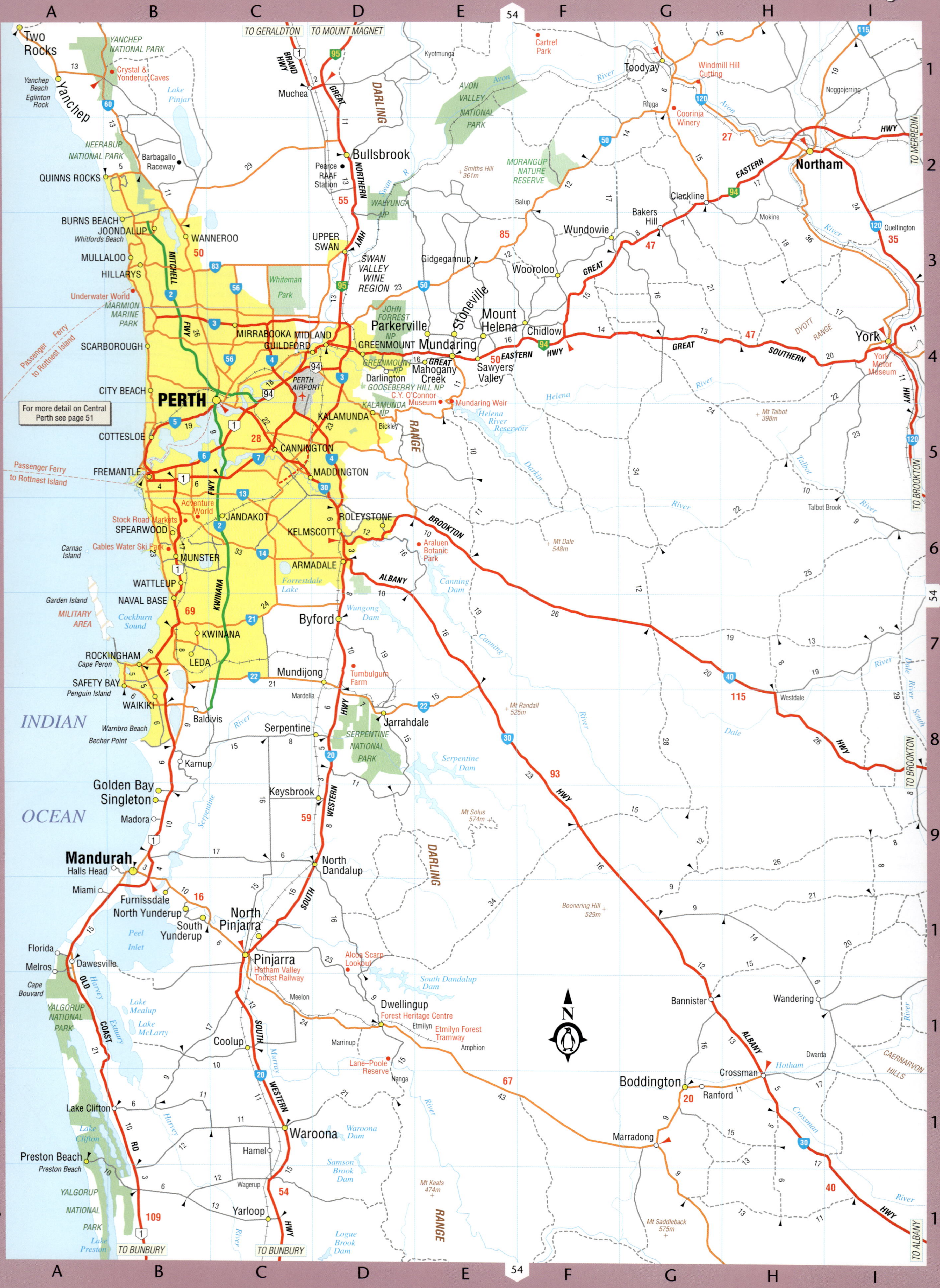

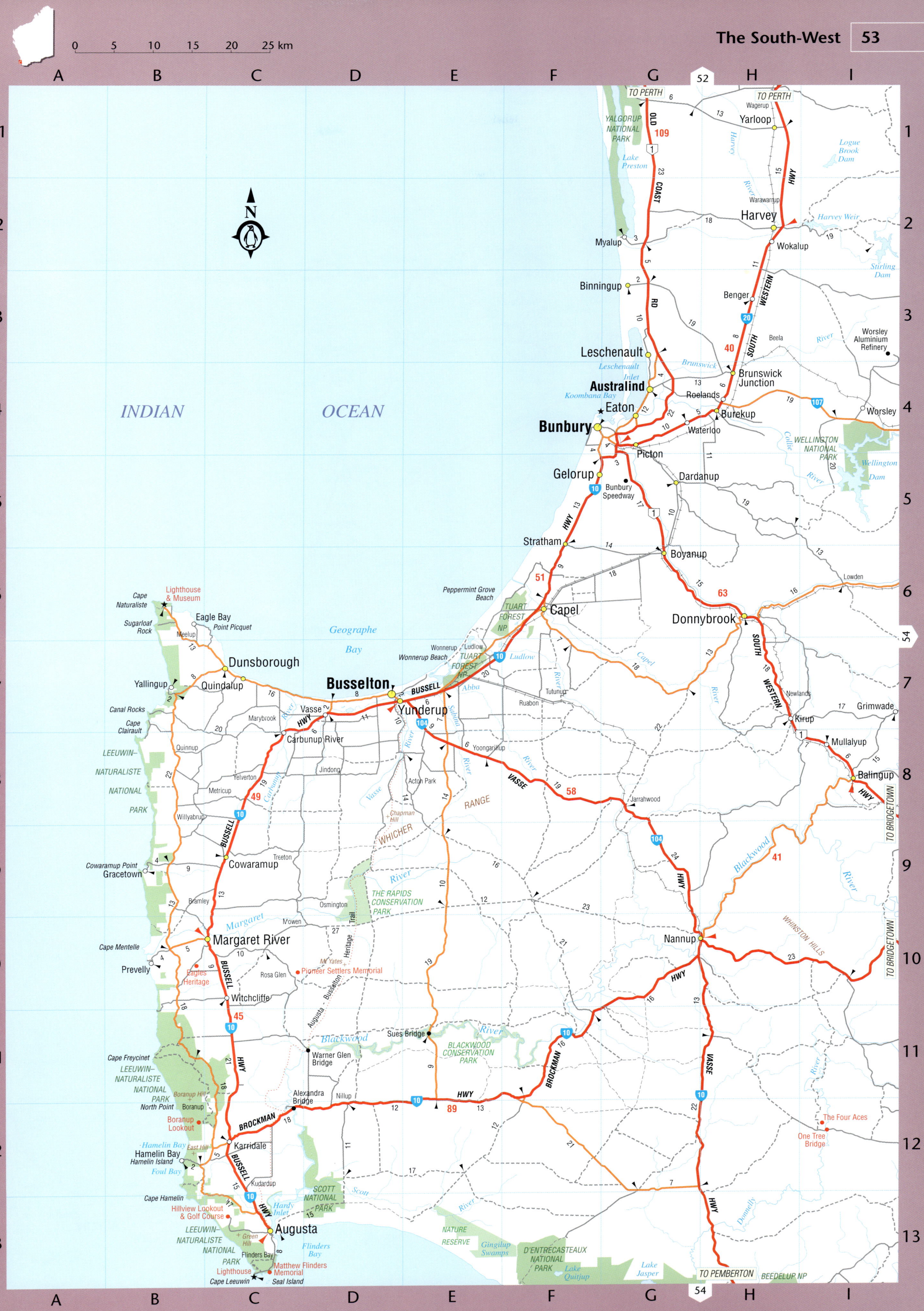
0 5 10 15 20 25 km
INDIAN OCEAN
Geographe Bay
TO PERTH
Yalgorup National Park
Lake Preston
Old Coast Rd
Wagerup
Yarloop
Harvey
Warawarrup
Logue Brook Dam
Harvey Weir
Wokalup
Stirling Dam
Myalup
Binningup
Benger
South Western Hwy
Beela
Worsley Aluminium Refinery
Leschenault
Leschenault Inlet
Brunswick
Brunswick Junction
Australind
Koombana Bay
Roelands
Eaton
Burekup
Worsley
Bunbury
Waterloo
Picton
Wellington National Park
Wellington Dam
Collie River
Gelorup
Bunbury Speedway
Dardanup
Stratham
Boyanup
Lowden
Peppermint Grove Beach
Tuart Forest NP
Capel
Donnybrook
Ludlow
Wonnerup
Wonnerup Beach
Busselton
Yunderup
Bussell Hwy
Abba
Sabina
Tutunup
Ruabon
Newlands
Grimwade
Kirup
Mullalyup
Balingup
TO BRIDGETOWN
Cape Naturaliste
Lighthouse & Museum
Sugarloaf Rock
Eagle Bay
Point Picquet
Meelup
Dunsborough
Yallingup
Quindalup
Canal Rocks
Cape Clairault
Vasse
Marybrook
Carbunup River
Quinnup
Jindong
Yoongarillup
Leeuwin–Naturaliste National Park
Yelverton
Metricup
Acton Park
Vasse Hwy
Whicher Range
Chapman Hill
Jarrahwood
Willyabrup
Treeton
Cowaramup Point
Gracetown
Cowaramup
The Rapids Conservation Park
Blackwood River
Bramley
Osmington
Mowen
Whinston Hills
Margaret River
Cape Mentelle
Prevelly
Eagles Heritage
Mt Yates
Pioneer Settlers Memorial
Rosa Glen
Augusta–Busselton Heritage Trail
Nannup
Witchcliffe
Sues Bridge
Blackwood Conservation Park
Cape Freycinet
Warner Glen Bridge
Brockman Hwy
Boranup Hill
Boranup
North Point
Boranup Lookout
Alexandra Bridge
Nillup
The Four Aces
One Tree Bridge
Hamelin Bay
East Hill
Karridale
Hamelin Island
Foul Bay
Kudardup
Scott National Park
Scott River
Cape Hamelin
Hillview Lookout & Golf Course
Hardy Inlet
Augusta
Green Hill
Flinders Bay
Lighthouse
Matthew Flinders Memorial
Cape Leeuwin
Seal Island
Nature Reserve
Gingilup Swamps
D'Entrecasteaux National Park
Lake Quitjup
Lake Jasper
Donnelly River
TO PEMBERTON
Beedelup NP

54 South Western Western Australia

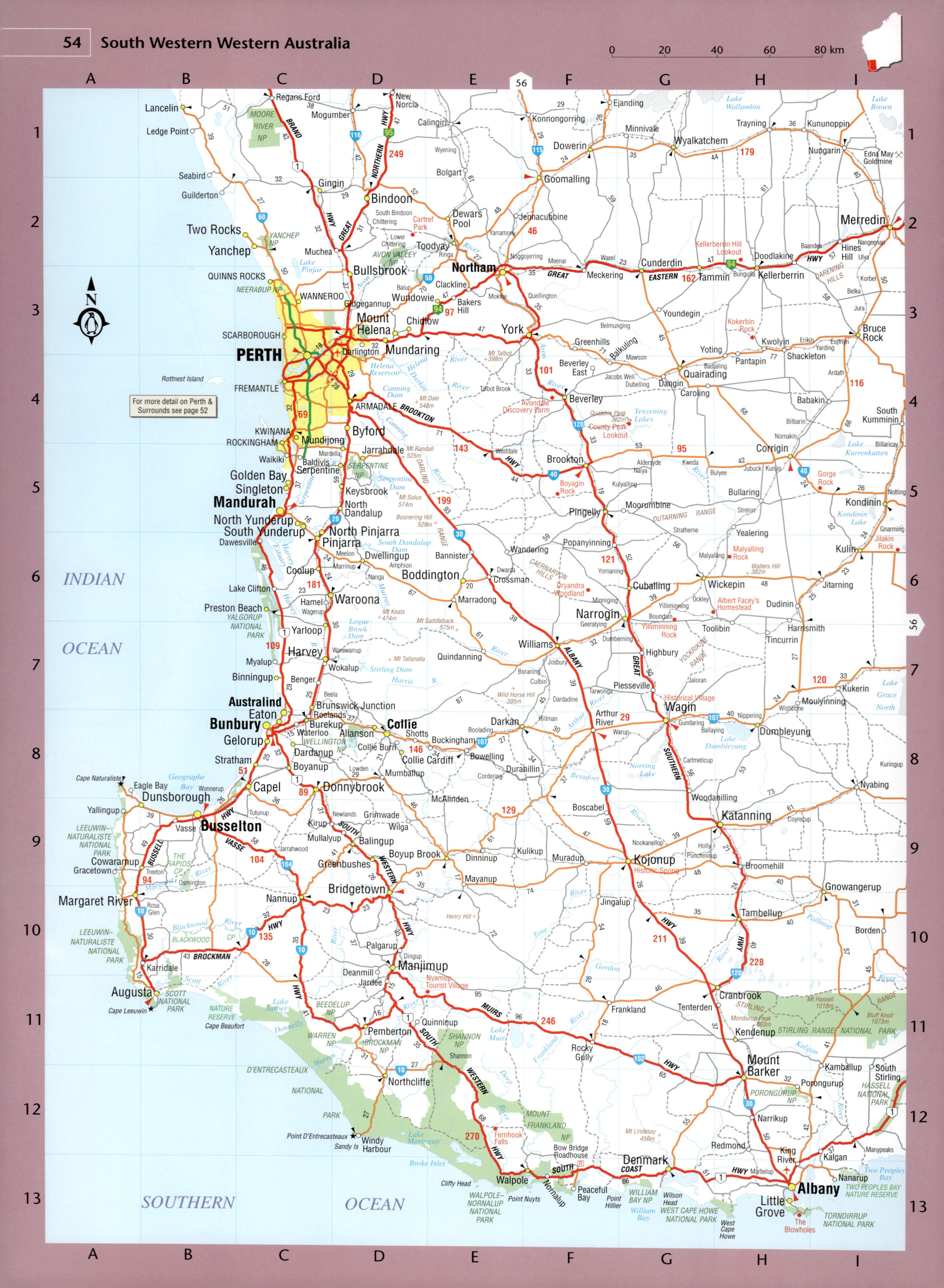

Central Western Western Australia

A
B
C
D
E
F
G
H
I
55
58
1
2
3
4
5
6
7
8
9
10
11
12
13
INDIAN
OCEAN
SOUTHERN
For more detail on South Western Western Australia see page 54
Kalbarri
Geraldton
Dongara
Port Denison
Northampton
Mullewa
Mingenew
Morawa
Perenjori
Three Springs
Carnamah
Coorow
Eneabba
Leeman
Green Head
Jurien Bay
Cervantes
The Pinnacles
Moora
Dalwallinu
Wongan Hills
Lancelin
Gingin
Bindoon
Toodyay
Two Rocks
Yanchep
Northam
York
PERTH
FREMANTLE
ROCKINGHAM
Mundaring
Mandurah
Pinjarra
Waroona
Harvey
Australind
Bunbury
Collie
Busselton
Dunsborough
Margaret River
Augusta
Bridgetown
Manjimup
Pemberton
Northcliffe
Walpole
Denmark
Albany
Mount Barker
Kojonup
Katanning
Wagin
Narrogin
Williams
Brookton
Beverley
Merredin
Kellerberrin
Southern Cross
Bruce Rock
Corrigin
Kondinin
Lake Grace
Ravensthorpe
Hopetoun
Jerramungup
Bremer Bay
Kalgoorlie–Boulder
Coolgardie
Leonora
Leinster
Menzies
Mount Magnet
Cue
Sandstone
Yalgoo
Paynes Find
GREAT NORTHERN HWY
GREAT EASTERN HWY
BRAND HWY
NORTH WEST COASTAL HWY
SOUTH COAST HWY
ALBANY HWY
BROOKTON HWY
GOLDFIELDS HWY
COOLGARDIE

57

Map: Southeastern Western Australia / Nullarbor Plain region

Scale: 0 – 50 – 100 – 150 – 200 km

Grid columns: J K L M N O P Q R
Grid rows: 1–13

Key places and features

Towns and roadhouses:
- Bandya
- Cosmo Newbery
- Tjukayirla Roadhouse
- Laverton
- Windarra
- Nambi
- Yerilla
- Edjudina
- Gindalbie
- Yindi
- Cundeelee
- Randell
- Karonie
- Chifley
- Zanthus
- Kitchener
- Naretha
- Rawlinna
- Haig
- Nurina
- Loongana
- Forrest
- Reid
- Deakin
- Kambalda
- Norseman
- Balladonia Roadhouse
- Balladonia
- Caiguna
- Cocklebiddy
- Madura Pass Oasis Motel & Roadhouse
- Mundrabilla Roadhouse
- Eucla
- Border Village
- Salmon Gums
- Grass Patch
- Scaddan
- Gibson
- Dalyup
- Condingup
- Esperance

Mountains / Hills:
- Mt Arthur 617m
- Mt Windarra 501m
- Admiral Hill 554m
- Mt Margaret 493m
- Mt Redcastle 500m
- Mt Weld 540m
- Mt Kilkenny 472m
- Mt East 565m
- Mt Sefton 529m
- Mt Collindie 511m
- Mt Kildara 451m
- Mt Remarkable
- Mt Percy 464m
- Mt Celia
- Faulkner Hill 536m
- Mt Agnes 671m
- Duplex Hill 425m
- Mt Monger
- Camilya Hill 416m
- Erayinia Hill 431m
- Coonanna Hill 415m
- Cowan Hill 384m
- Hayes Hill 348m
- Yalca Hill 425m
- Red Hill Lookout
- Mt Malcolm 455m
- Mt Coobaninya 243m
- Mt Buraninya 233m
- Mt Ragged 585m
- Beacon Hill Lookout
- Dundas Rocks
- Whistling Rock
- Binaronca Rock Nature Reserve

Lakes:
- Lake Throssel
- Yeo Lake
- Rason Lake
- Lake Carey
- Lake Minigwai
- Lake Raeside
- Lake Rebecca
- Lake Yindarlgooda
- Lake Roe
- Lake Rivers
- Harris Lake
- Lake Lefroy
- Lake Cowan
- Lake Dundas
- Lake Halbert
- Plumridge Lakes
- Lake Nyanga
- Jubilee Lake
- Carlisle Lakes
- Shell Lakes
- Lake Ilma
- Wanna Lakes
- Serpentine Lakes
- Forrest Lakes

Regions / Reserves:
- CENTRAL AUSTRALIA ABORIGINAL LAND TRUST
- LENNIS HILLS
- YEO LAKE NATURE RESERVE
- COSMO NEWBERY ABORIGINAL LAND
- DUNGES TABLE
- GREAT VICTORIA DESERT
- GREAT VICTORIA DESERT NATURE RESERVE
- CONSERVATION PARK
- NULLARBOR PLAIN
- NULLARBOR REGIONAL RESERVE
- NULLARBOR NP
- EUCLA NP
- WILDLIFE SANCTUARY
- CUNDEELEE ABORIGINAL LAND
- NUYTSLAND NATURE RESERVE
- CAPE ARID NATIONAL PARK
- CAPE LE GRAND NATIONAL PARK
- ARCHIPELAGO OF THE RECHERCHE

Highways/Routes:
- GREAT CENTRAL RD
- OUTBACK HWY
- CONNIE SUE HWY (4WD only)
- ANNE BEADELL HWY (4WD only)
- EYRE HWY (1)
- TRANS AUSTRALIA RAILWAY

Distances (km) shown in red:
- 203, 92, 105, 124, 20, 59, 22, 160, 65, 93, 116, 66, 13, 340, 373, 191, 206, 99, 65, 135, 26, 27, 30

Coastal features:
- Slessar Point
- Point Dover
- Sheer Cliffs
- Point Culver
- Wurrgoodyea Hills 90m
- Red Rocks Point
- Israelite Bay
- Point Dempster
- Cape Pasley
- Cape Arid

Water bodies:
- GREAT AUSTRALIAN BIGHT
- OCEAN (Southern Ocean)

Border: WESTERN AUSTRALIA / SOUTH AUSTRALIA

WARNINGS: In outback Australia, long distances separate some towns. Travellers should familiarise themselves with prevailing conditions before departure and take care to ensure their vehicle is roadworthy. Adequate supplies of petrol, water and food should be carried at all times.

In central Australia, rainfall can make some roads impassable. Full information on road conditions should be obtained from local authorities before departure.

If visitors intend diverting off public roads within Aboriginal Land areas, a permit is required from the relevant Aboriginal authority.

Cocklebiddy Cave • Eyre Bird Observatory • Numerous Old Mine Workings • Agricultural Check Point • Lookouts

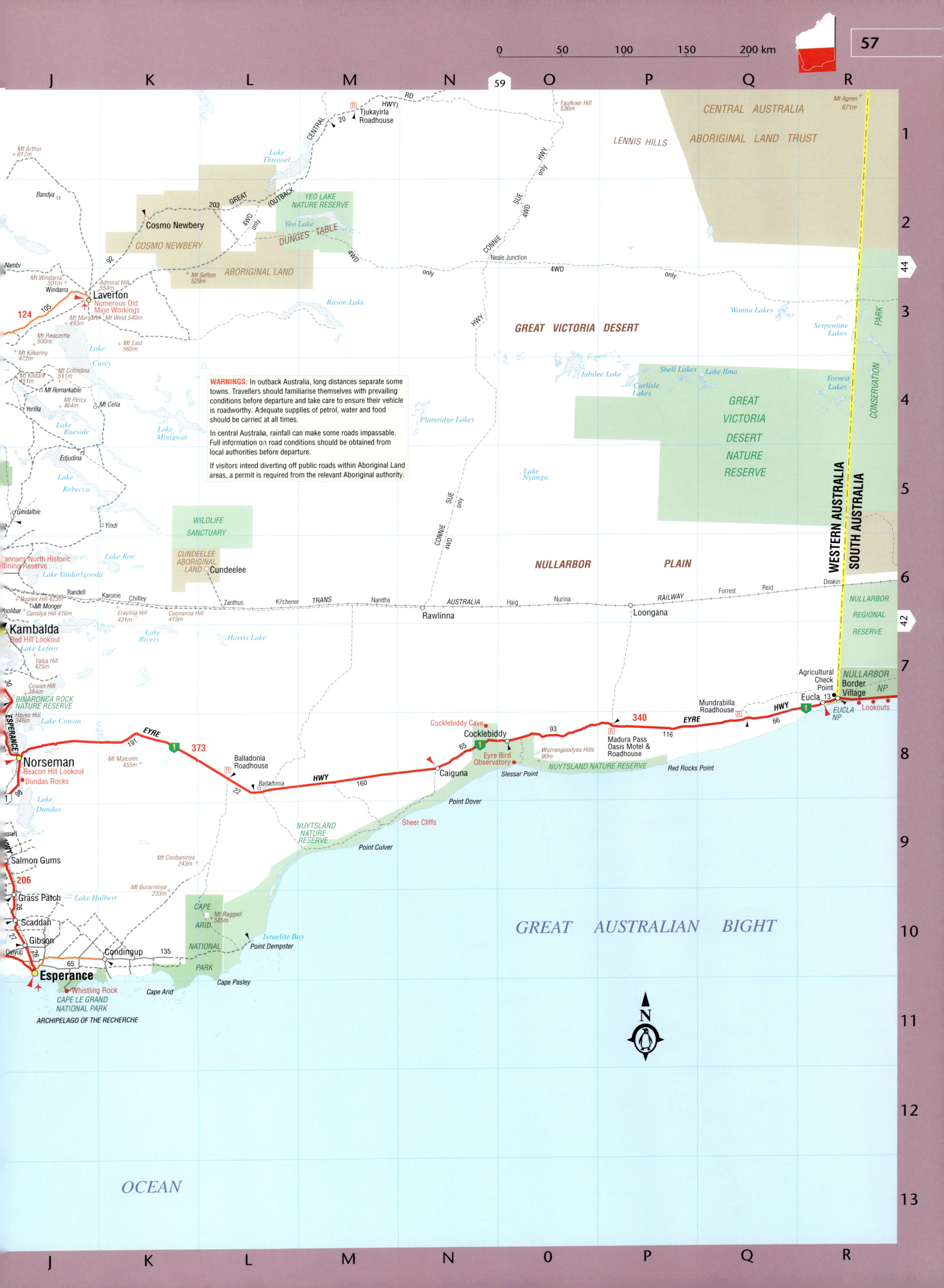

N (compass rose)

58 Central Western Australia

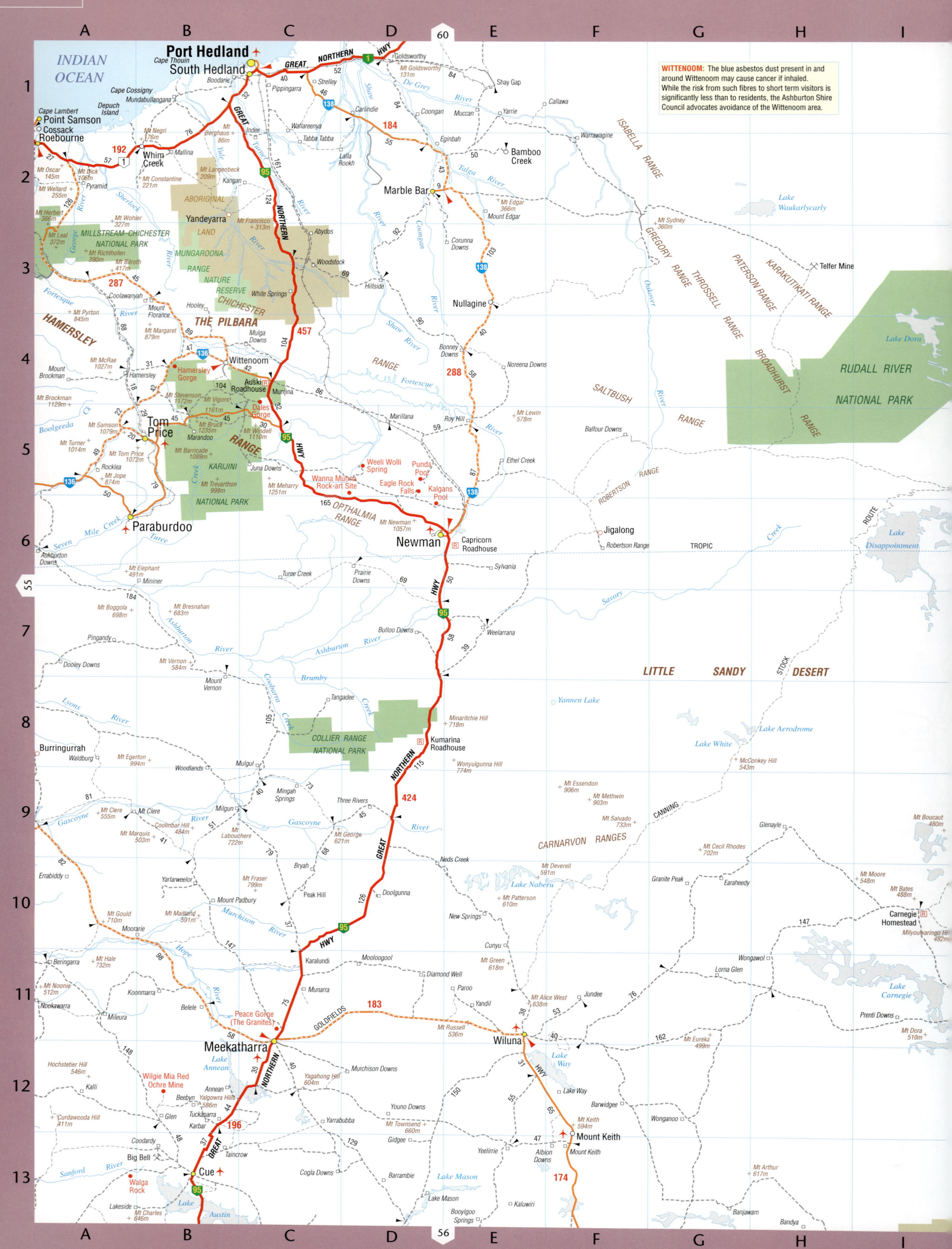

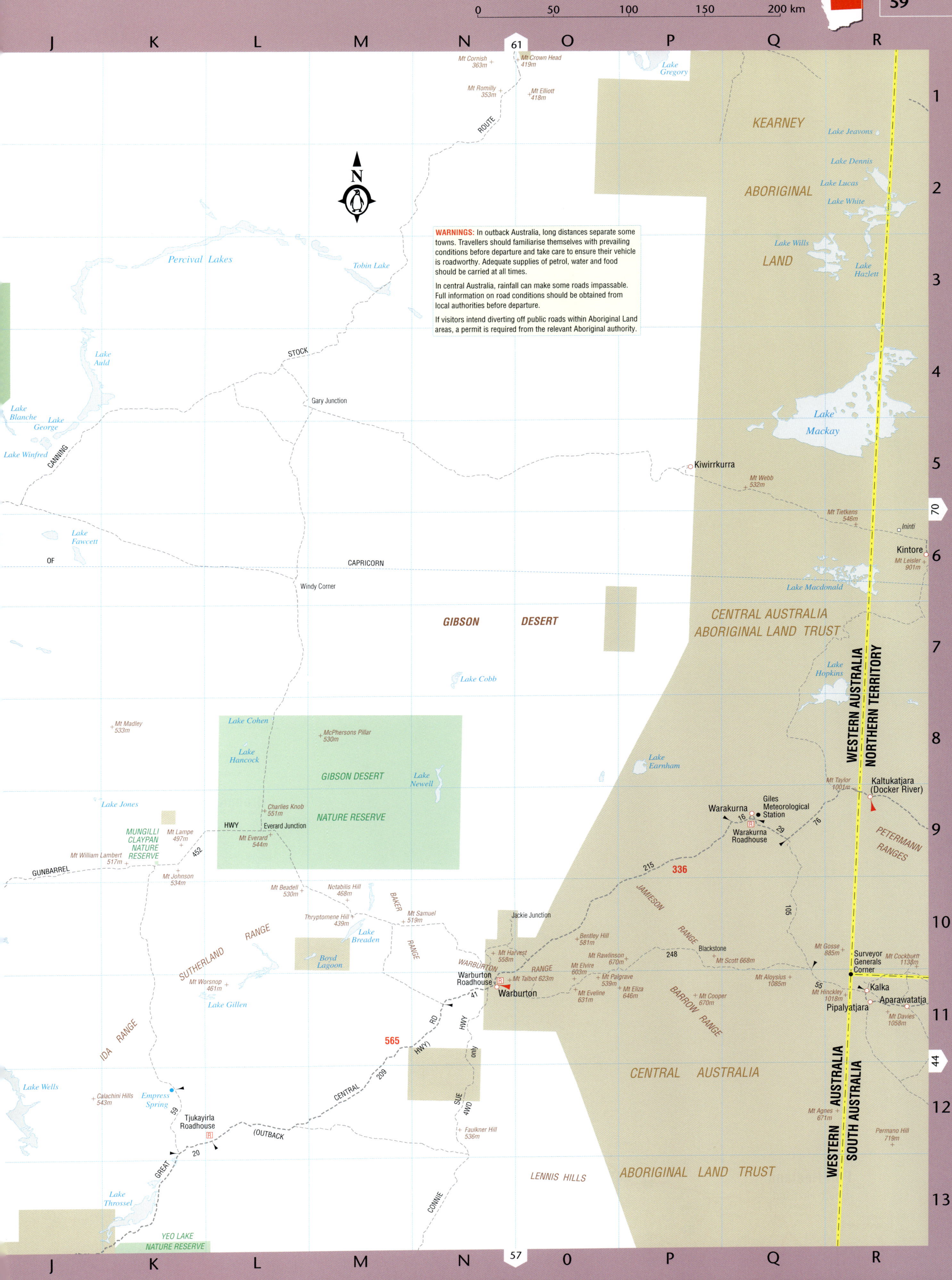

WARNINGS: In outback Australia, long distances separate some towns. Travellers should familiarise themselves with prevailing conditions before departure and take care to ensure their vehicle is roadworthy. Adequate supplies of petrol, water and food should be carried at all times.

In central Australia, rainfall can make some roads impassable. Full information on road conditions should be obtained from local authorities before departure.

If visitors intend diverting off public roads within Aboriginal Land areas, a permit is required from the relevant Aboriginal authority.

Northern Western Australia

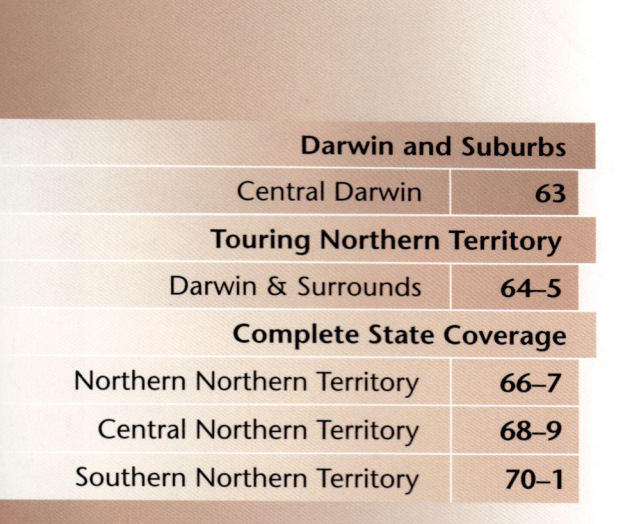

Northern Territory
Location Map

Darwin and Suburbs	
Central Darwin	63
Touring Northern Territory	
Darwin & Surrounds	64–5
Complete State Coverage	
Northern Northern Territory	66–7
Central Northern Territory	68–9
Southern Northern Territory	70–1

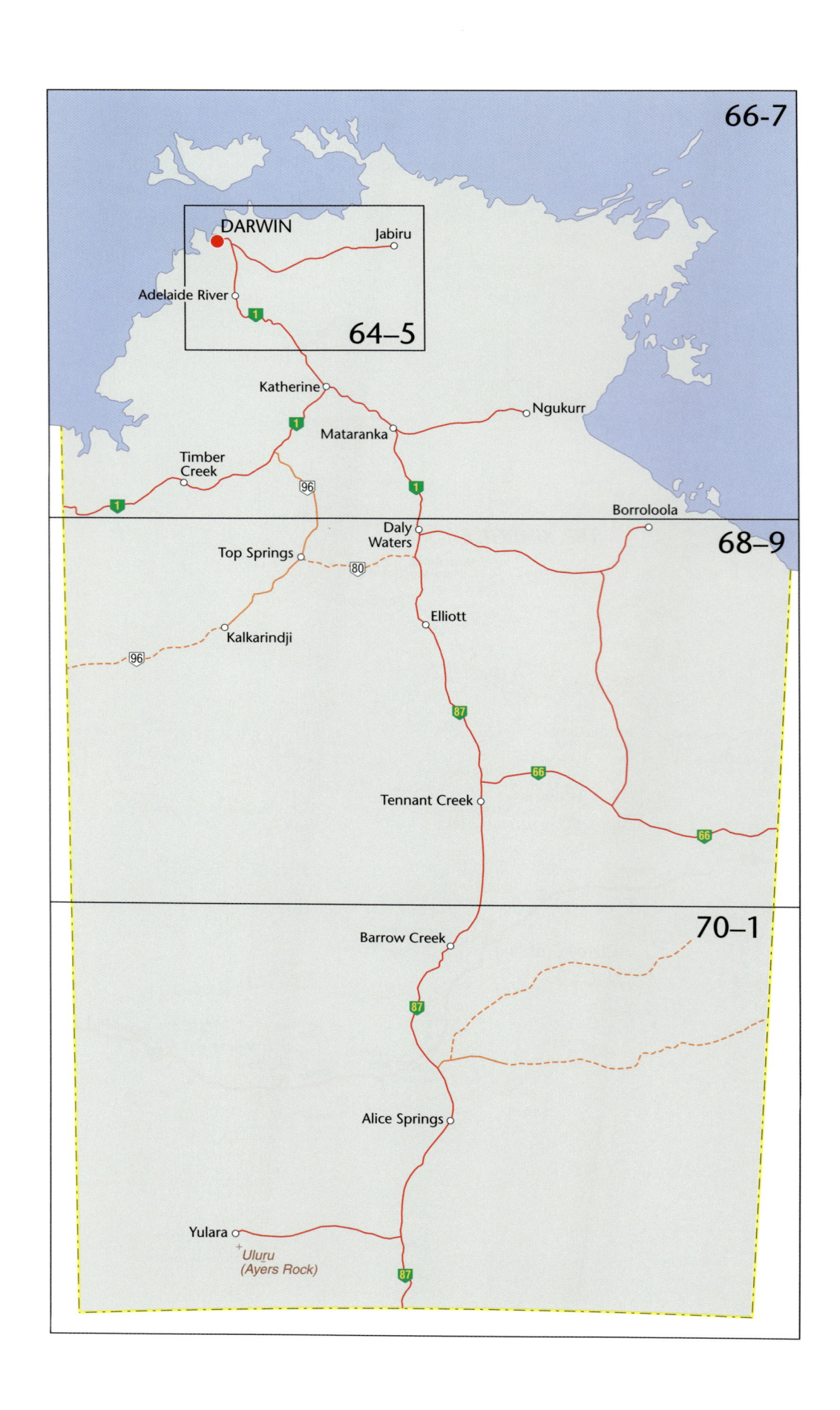

Central Darwin 63

Accommodation ◆
- Banyan View Lodge 1 C7
- Carlton Hotel Darwin 2 C8
- MGM Grand Darwin Hotel 3 A3
- Mirambeena Tourist Resort 4 E7
- Novotel Atrium Darwin 5 D9
- Poinciana Inn 6 D8
- Rydges Plaza Hotel 7 F9
- Top End Hotel 8 C7
- YHA Backpackers International 9 E9
- YMCA 10 B7

General Information ■
- Bus Terminal 11 G10
- Darwin Civic Centre & Library 12 G9
- Darwin Harbour seaplanes 13 H12
- Darwin Tourist Precinct / Greyhound Pioneer Coaches 14 E9
- Garuda Indonesia Airlines 15 F9
- General Post Office 16 F8
- McCafferty's Coaches 17 E8
- Motoring Organisation (AANT) 18 D8
- Police Station 19 F10
- Qantas Travel Centre 20 G9
- Visitor Information (Top End Tourism) 21 E9

Places of Interest ◆
- Aquascene 22 B7
- Australian Pearling Exhibition 23 I11
- Bicentennial Park 24 D9
- Brown's Mart 25 G10
- Burnett House 26 A4
- Chinese Temple 27 G9
- Christ Church Cathedral 28 G10
- Darwin Botanic Gardens 29 D1
- Darwin Entertainment Centre 30 D8
- Deckchair Cinema 31 I9
- Government House 32 F11
- Indo Pacific Marine 33 I11
- Lyons Cottage 34 E10
- MGM Grand Casino 35 A3
- Mindil Beach Sunset Market 36 B1
- Old Admiralty House 37 E10
- Old Police Station & Courthouse 38 G10
- Overland Telegraph Memorial 39 G11
- Palmerston (Darwin) Town Hall ruins 40 G10
- Parliament House & NT Library 41 F10
- Smith Street Mall 42 F9
- Stokes Hill Wharf 43 H12
- Supreme Court 44 F10
- Survivors Lookout 45 G11
- Tamarind Park 46 F9
- Tour Tub 46 F9
- Tree of Knowledge 47 G10
- Victoria Hotel 48 F9
- WW II Oil Storage Tunnels 49 G11

Accommodation Only a sample range is listed; inclusion is not necessarily a recommendation.

64 Darwin & Surrounds

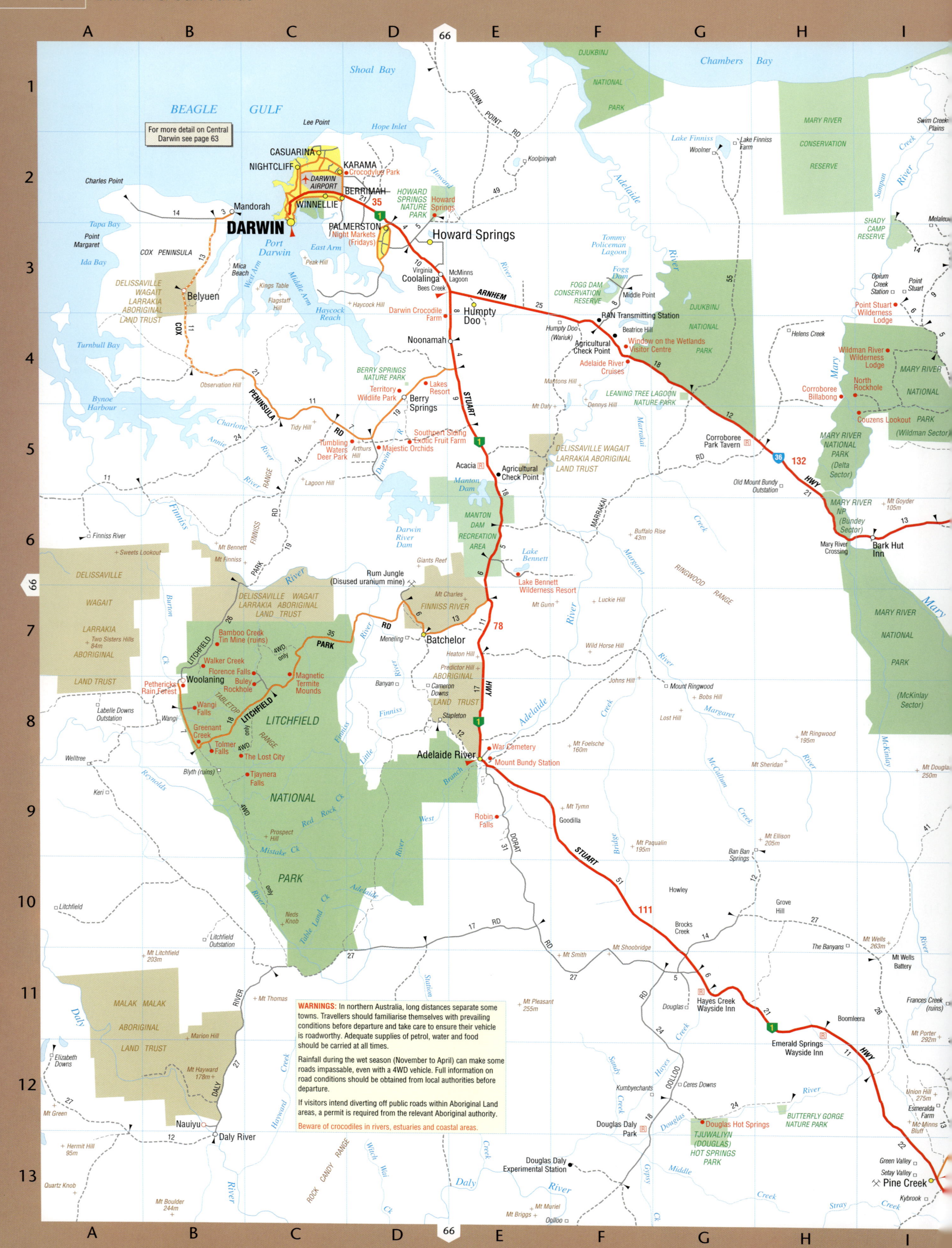

WARNINGS: In northern Australia, long distances separate some towns. Travellers should familiarise themselves with prevailing conditions before departure and take care to ensure their vehicle is roadworthy. Adequate supplies of petrol, water and food should be carried at all times.

Rainfall during the wet season (November to April) can make some roads impassable, even with a 4WD vehicle. Full information on road conditions should be obtained from local authorities before departure.

If visitors intend diverting off public roads within Aboriginal Land areas, a permit is required from the relevant Aboriginal authority.

Beware of crocodiles in rivers, estuaries and coastal areas.

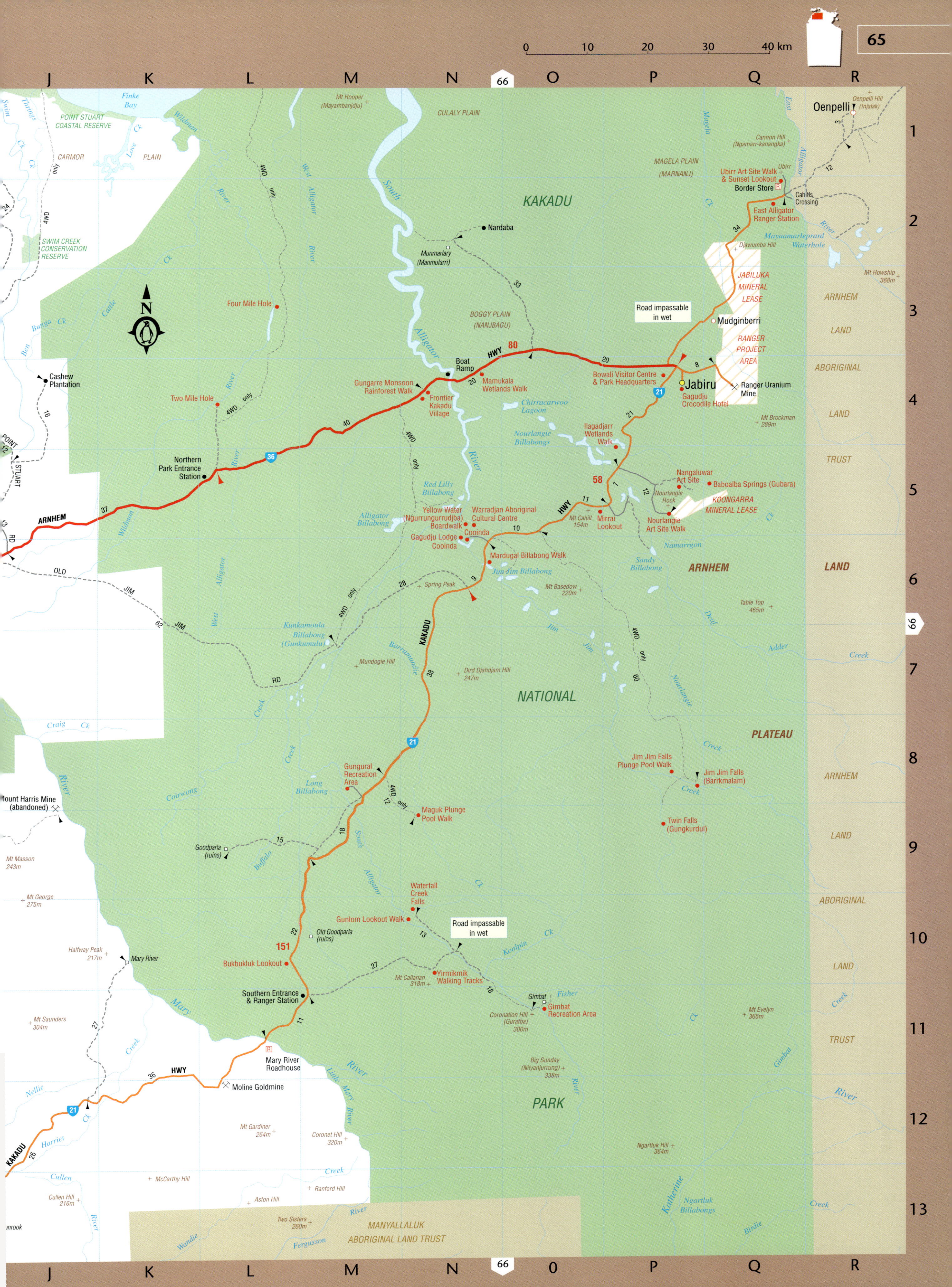
0 10 20 30 40 km
J K L M N 66 O P Q R
1 2 3 4 5 6 7 8 9 10 11 12 13
KAKADU
NATIONAL
PARK
Oenpelli
Oenpelli Hill (Injalak)
Cannon Hill (Ngamarr-kanangka)
MAGELA PLAIN (MARNANJ)
Ubirr Art Site Walk & Sunset Lookout
Border Store
Cahills Crossing
East Alligator Ranger Station
Mayaamarleprard Waterhole
Djawumba Hill
Mt Howship 368m
JABILUKA MINERAL LEASE
Road impassable in wet
Mudginberri
RANGER PROJECT AREA
Jabiru
Ranger Uranium Mine
Gagudju Crocodile Hotel
Bowali Visitor Centre & Park Headquarters
Mt Brockman 289m
ARNHEM LAND ABORIGINAL LAND TRUST
Mt Hooper (Mayambanjdju)
CULALY PLAIN
Nardaba
Munmarlary (Manmularri)
BOGGY PLAIN (NANJBAGU)
HWY 80
Boat Ramp
Gungarre Monsoon Rainforest Walk
Mamukala Wetlands Walk
Frontier Kakadu Village
Chirracarwoo Lagoon
Nourlangie Billabongs
Ilagadjarr Wetlands Walk
Nangaluwar Art Site
Baboalba Springs (Gubara)
Nourlangie Rock
KOONGARRA MINERAL LEASE
Nourlangie Art Site Walk
Mt Cahill 154m
Mirrai Lookout
Namarrgon
Sandy Billabong
ARNHEM LAND
Red Lilly Billabong
Yellow Water (Ngurrungurrudjba) Boardwalk
Warradjan Aboriginal Cultural Centre
Cooinda
Gagudju Lodge Cooinda
Alligator Billabong
Mardugal Billabong Walk
Jim Jim Billabong
Spring Peak
Mt Basedow 220m
Table Top 465m
Four Mile Hole
Two Mile Hole
Northern Park Entrance Station
ARNHEM
RD
OLD JIM JIM RD
POINT STUART COASTAL RESERVE
Finke Bay
CARMOR PLAIN
SWIM CREEK CONSERVATION RESERVE
Cashew Plantation
Kunkamoula Billabong (Gunkumulu)
Mundogie Hill
Dird Djahdjam Hill 247m
PLATEAU
Jim Jim Falls Plunge Pool Walk
Jim Jim Falls (Barrkmalam)
Twin Falls (Gungkurdul)
Gungural Recreation Area
Long Billabong
Maguk Plunge Pool Walk
Mount Harris Mine (abandoned)
Goodparla (ruins)
Mt Masson 243m
Mt George 275m
Waterfall Creek Falls
Gunlom Lookout Walk
Old Goodparla (ruins)
Halfway Peak 217m
Mary River
Bukbukluk Lookout
Yirmikmik Walking Tracks
Mt Callanan 318m
Southern Entrance & Ranger Station
Gimbat
Gimbat Recreation Area
Coronation Hill (Guratba) 300m
Mt Saunders 304m
Mt Evelyn 365m
Mary River Roadhouse
HWY
Moline Goldmine
Big Sunday (Nilyanjurrung) 338m
Mt Gardiner 264m
Coronet Hill 320m
Ngartluk Hill 364m
McCarthy Hill
Cullen Hill 216m
Ranford Hill
Aston Hill
Two Sisters 260m
MANYALLALUK ABORIGINAL LAND TRUST
Ngartluk Billabongs
KAKADU
4WD only
South Alligator River
West Alligator River
Wildman River
Magela Ck
East Alligator River
Jim Jim Creek
Barramundie Creek
Coirwong Creek
Koolpin Ck
Fisher Creek
Mary River
Katherine River
Gimbat Creek
Birdie Creek
Deaf Adder Creek
Nourlangie Creek
Fergusson River
Cullen Creek
Harriet Ck
Nellie Creek
Craig Ck

Northern Northern Territory

67

ARAFURA SEA

GULF OF CARPENTARIA

Cape Wessel
Marchinbar Island
WESSEL ISLANDS
Drysdale Island
Guluwuru Island
Elcho Island
GOULBURN ISLANDS
Braithwaite Point
Cape Stewart
Mooroongga Is
HOWARD ISLAND
Point Napier
Point Wilberforce
Bremer Island
Maningrida
Ji-Marda
Milingimbi
Galiwinku
Gunyangara
Nhulunbuy
Ngangalaia
Castlereagh Bay
Gapuwiyak Landing Ground
Rorruwuy
Yirrkala
Buku-Larrnggay Mulka (Aboriginal Art Museum)
Ramingining
Old Arafura
Gapuwiyak
GOVE PENINSULA
Cape Arnhem
Manmoyi
ARNHEM LAND ABORIGINAL
Mirrngadja Village
Gurrumuru
Garrthalala
Birany Birany
Point Alexander
LAND TRUST
ARNHEM CENTRAL
MITCHELL RANGE
FREDERICK HILLS
Cape Grey
Baniyala
Cape Shield
Bulman
Mt Marumba
Isle Woodah
Cape Barrow
Milyakburra
Bickerton Island
Alyangula
Umbakumba
Angurugu
GROOTE EYLANDT
Mountain Valley
Mainoru
Mt Furner 188m
Lake Allen
Roper Bar
Ngukurr
St Vidgeon (ruins)
Numbulwar
Tasman Point
Cape Beatrice
HWY
Roper Bar Store
Port Roper
Limmen Bight
Maria Island
Moroak
Roper Valley
Mt Harriet 187m
MARRA ABORIGINAL LAND TRUST
Miniyeri
HODGSON DOWNS LEASE
Limmen Bight River Fishing Camp
SIR EDWARD PELLEW GROUP
West Island
North Island
BARRANYI (NORTH ISLAND) NATIONAL PARK
Maryfield (ruins)
Hodgson River
ALAWA ABORIGINAL LAND TRUST
Lorella Springs
Bing Bong
WADA WADALLA LEASE
SW Is
Centre Island
Vanderlin Island
Nutwood Downs
Minamia
King Ash Bay
Manangoora
Garawa
NARWINBI ABORIGINAL LAND
Borroloola
Wandangula
Mara

WARNINGS: In northern Australia, long distances separate some towns. Travellers should familiarise themselves with prevailing conditions before departure and take care to ensure their vehicle is roadworthy. Adequate supplies of petrol, water and food should be carried at all times.
Rainfall during the wet season (November to April) can make some roads impassable, even with a 4WD vehicle. Full information on road conditions should be obtained from local authorities before departure.
If visitors intend diverting off public roads within Aboriginal Land areas, a permit is required from the relevant Aboriginal authority.
Beware of crocodiles in rivers, estuaries and coastal areas.

68 Central Northern Territory

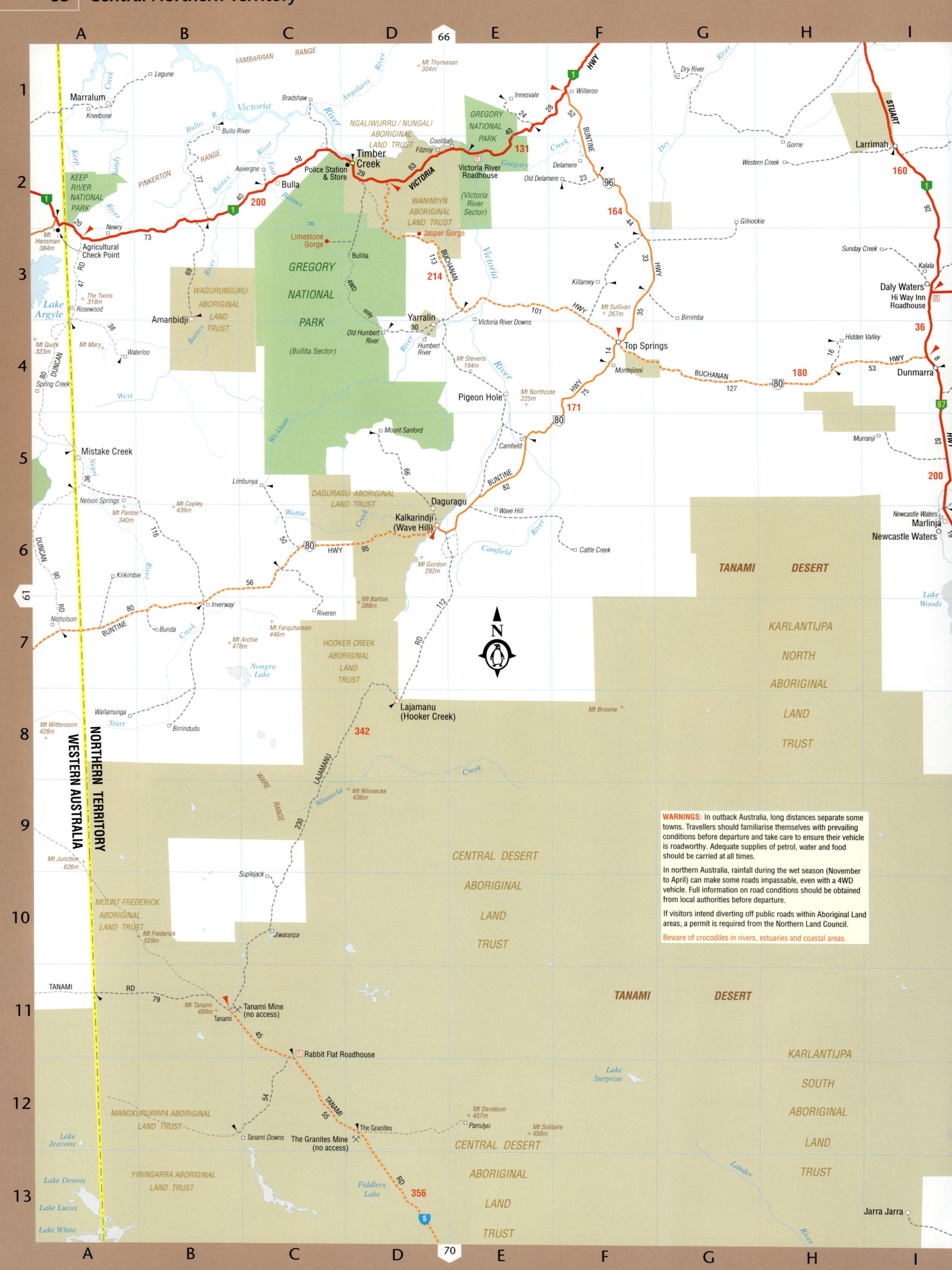

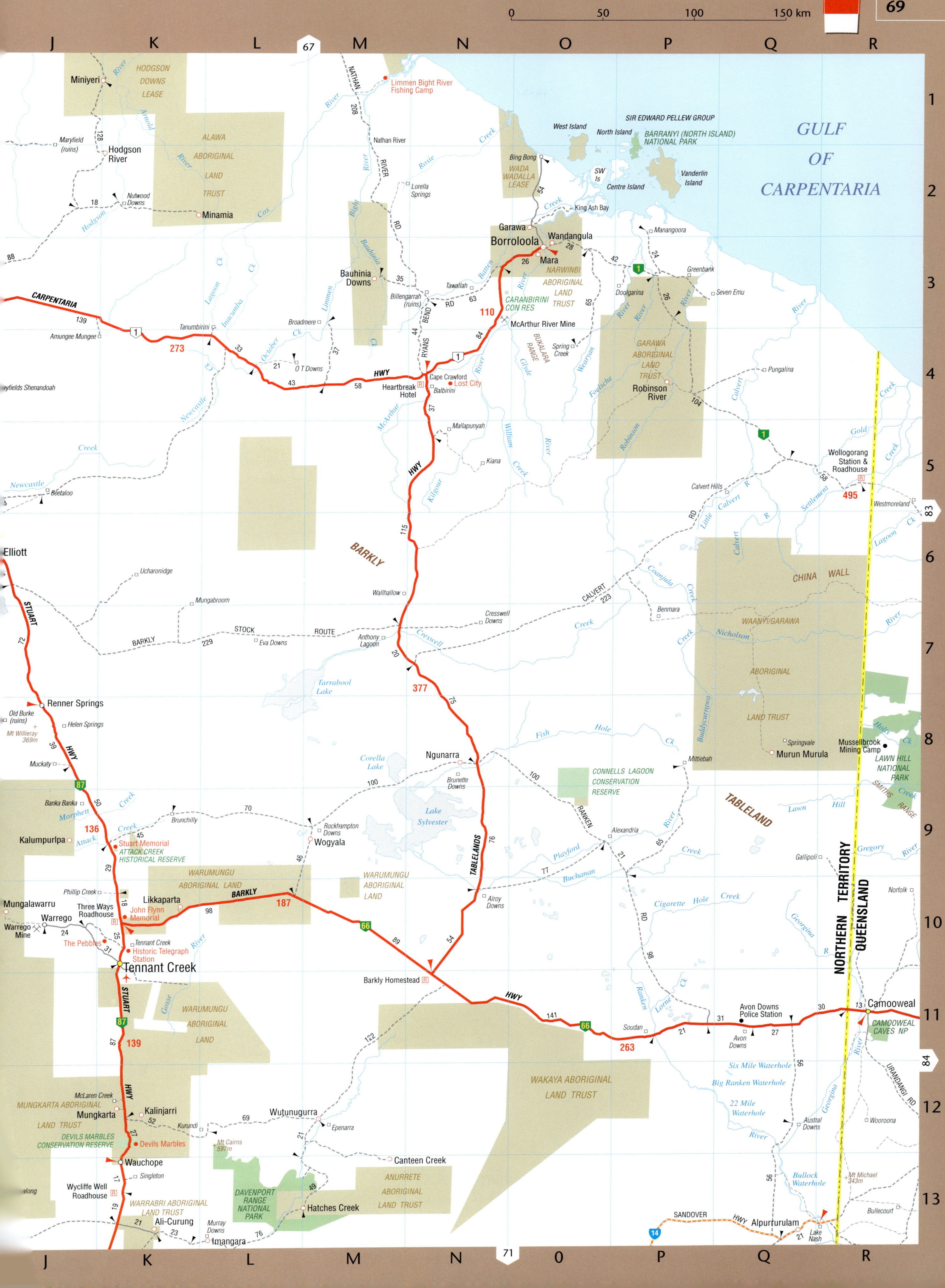

0
50
100
150 km
J
K
L
67
M
N
O
P
Q
R
1
2
3
4
5
6
7
8
9
10
11
12
13
GULF OF CARPENTARIA
SIR EDWARD PELLEW GROUP
West Island
North Island
BARRANYI (NORTH ISLAND) NATIONAL PARK
SW Is
Centre Island
Vanderlin Island
King Ash Bay
Bing Bong
WADA WADALLA LEASE
Limmen Bight River Fishing Camp
NATHAN 208 RIVER RD
Nathan River
Lorella Springs
Miniyeri
HODGSON DOWNS LEASE
Maryfield (ruins)
Hodgson River
Nutwood Downs
ALAWA ABORIGINAL LAND TRUST
Minamia
Garawa
Borroloola
Wandangula
Mara
NARWINBI ABORIGINAL LAND TRUST
CARANBIRINI CON RES
McArthur River Mine
BUKALARA RANGE
Spring Creek
Manangoora
Greenbank
Seven Emu
Doolgarina
GARAWA ABORIGINAL LAND TRUST
Robinson River
Pungalina
Bauhinia Downs
Tawallah
Billengarrah (ruins)
RYANS BEND RD
CARPENTARIA
Amungee Mungee
Tanumbirini
Broadmere
O T Downs
HWY
273
110
Cape Crawford
Lost City
Heartbreak Hotel
Balbirini
Mallapunyah
Kiana
Wollogorang Station & Roadhouse
Calvert Hills
495
Westmoreland
83
Shenandoah
Newcastle
Beetaloo
Elliott
Ucharonidge
Mungabroom
BARKLY
Wallhallow
CALVERT
Benmara
CHINA WALL
WAANYI/GARAWA ABORIGINAL LAND TRUST
Cresswell Downs
STOCK ROUTE
BARKLY 229
Eva Downs
Anthony Lagoon
Tarrabool Lake
377
STUART
Renner Springs
Old Burke (ruins)
Helen Springs
Mt Willieray 369m
Muckaty
Corella Lake
Ngunarra
Brunette Downs
Lake Sylvester
CONNELLS LAGOON CONSERVATION RESERVE
Mittiebah
Springvale
Murun Murula
Musselbrook Mining Camp
LAWN HILL NATIONAL PARK
SMITHS RANGE
TABLELAND
Banka Banka
Brunchilly
Rockhampton Downs
Wogyala
Kalumpurlpa
136
Stuart Memorial
ATTACK CREEK HISTORICAL RESERVE
Alexandria
TABLELANDS
RANKEN
Gallipoli
Norfolk
WARUMUNGU ABORIGINAL LAND
Phillip Creek
Likkaparta
John Flynn Memorial
187
Alroy Downs
NORTHERN TERRITORY
QUEENSLAND
Mungalawarru
Warrego
Warrego Mine
Three Ways Roadhouse
The Pebbles
Tennant Creek
Historic Telegraph Station
Barkly Homestead
Camooweal
CAMOOWEAL CAVES NP
Avon Downs Police Station
Avon Downs
Soudan
263
139
Six Mile Waterhole
Big Ranken Waterhole
22 Mile Waterhole
84
URANDANGI RD
WAKAYA ABORIGINAL LAND TRUST
McLaren Creek
Mungkarta
MUNGKARTA ABORIGINAL LAND TRUST
Kalinjarri
Kurundi
Wutunugurra
Epenarra
DEVILS MARBLES CONSERVATION RESERVE
Devils Marbles
Mt Cairns 597m
Wauchope
Canteen Creek
Austral Downs
Wooroona
Singleton
ANURRETE ABORIGINAL LAND TRUST
Bullock Waterhole
Mt Michael 243m
Wycliffe Well Roadhouse
WARRABRI ABORIGINAL LAND TRUST
DAVENPORT RANGE NATIONAL PARK
Hatches Creek
Bullecourt
Ali-Curung
Murray Downs
Imangara
SANDOVER HWY
Alpurrurulam
Lake Nash
71

Southern Northern Territory

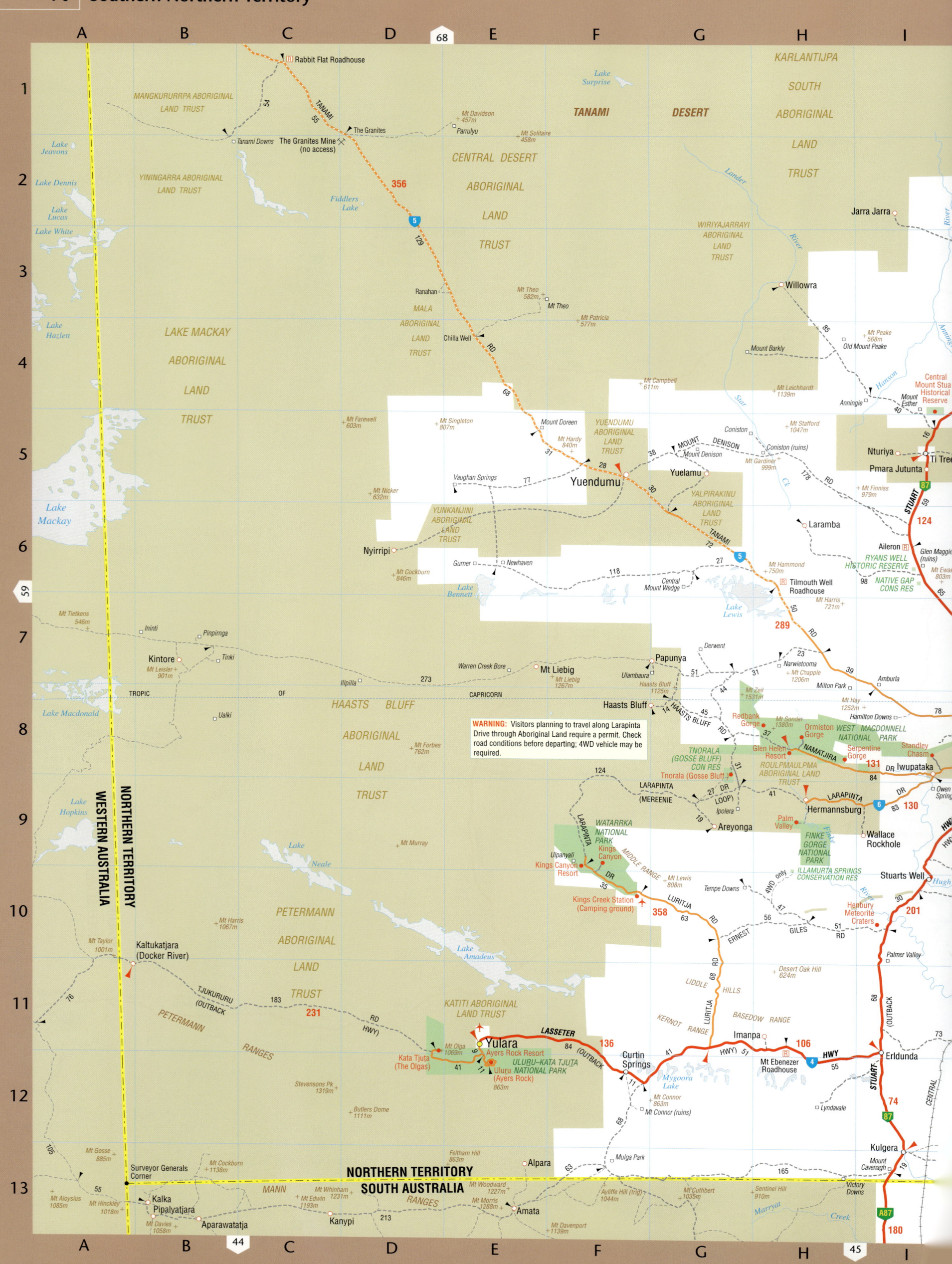

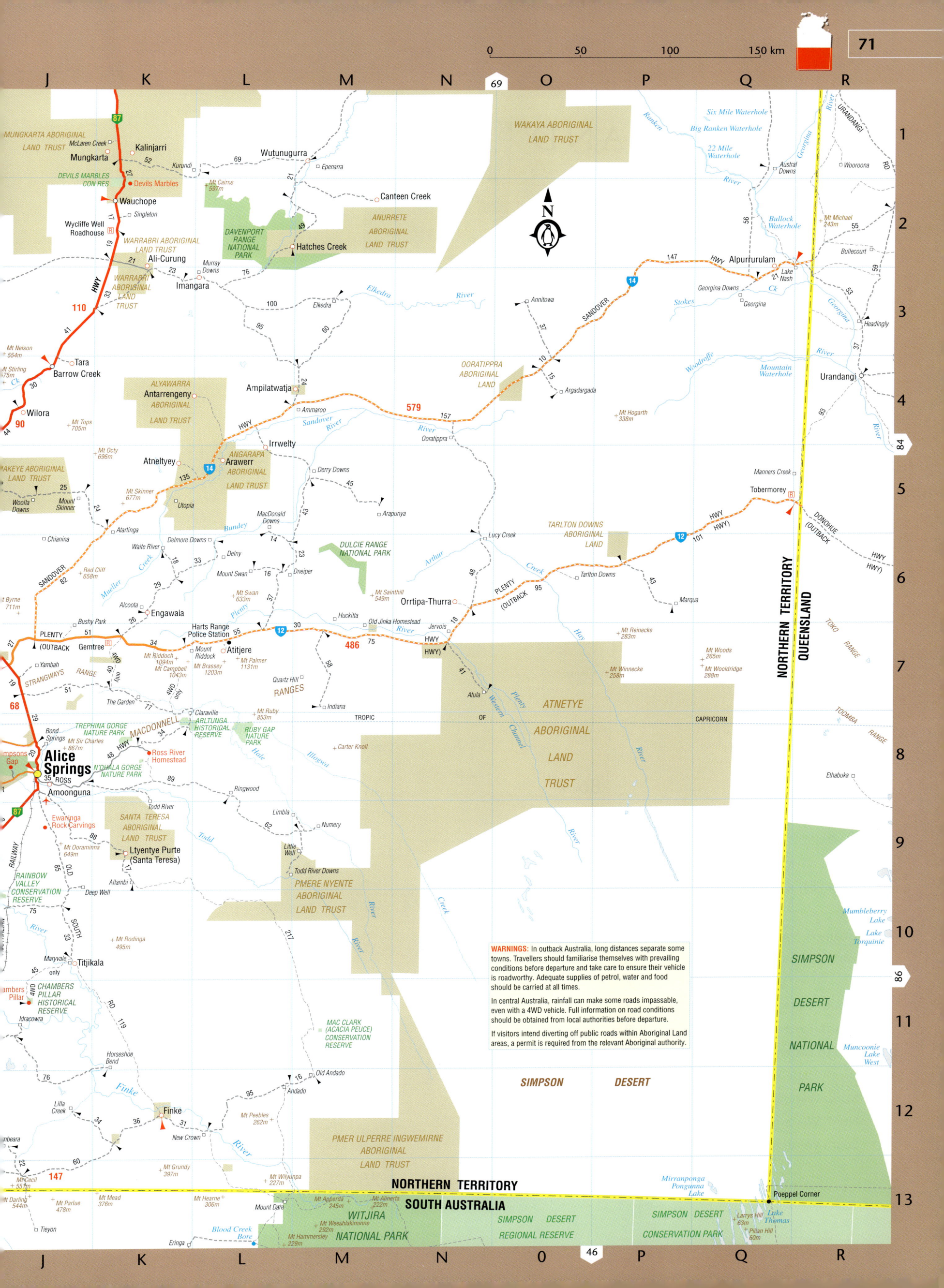

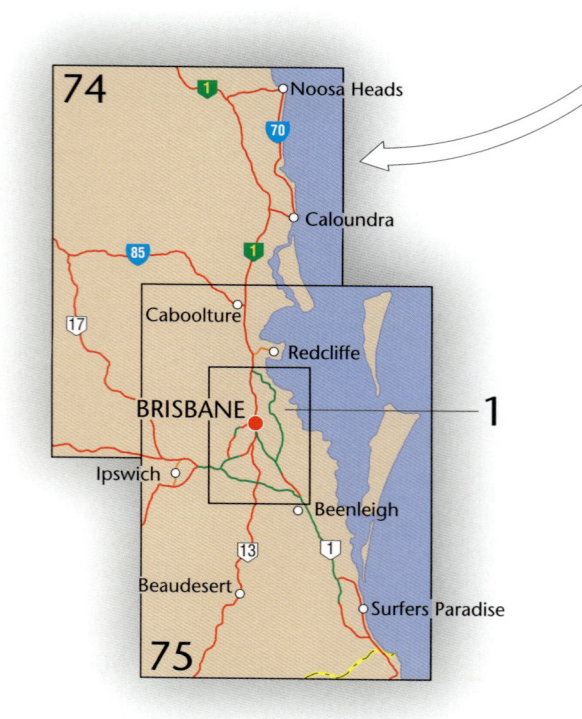

Queensland
Location Map

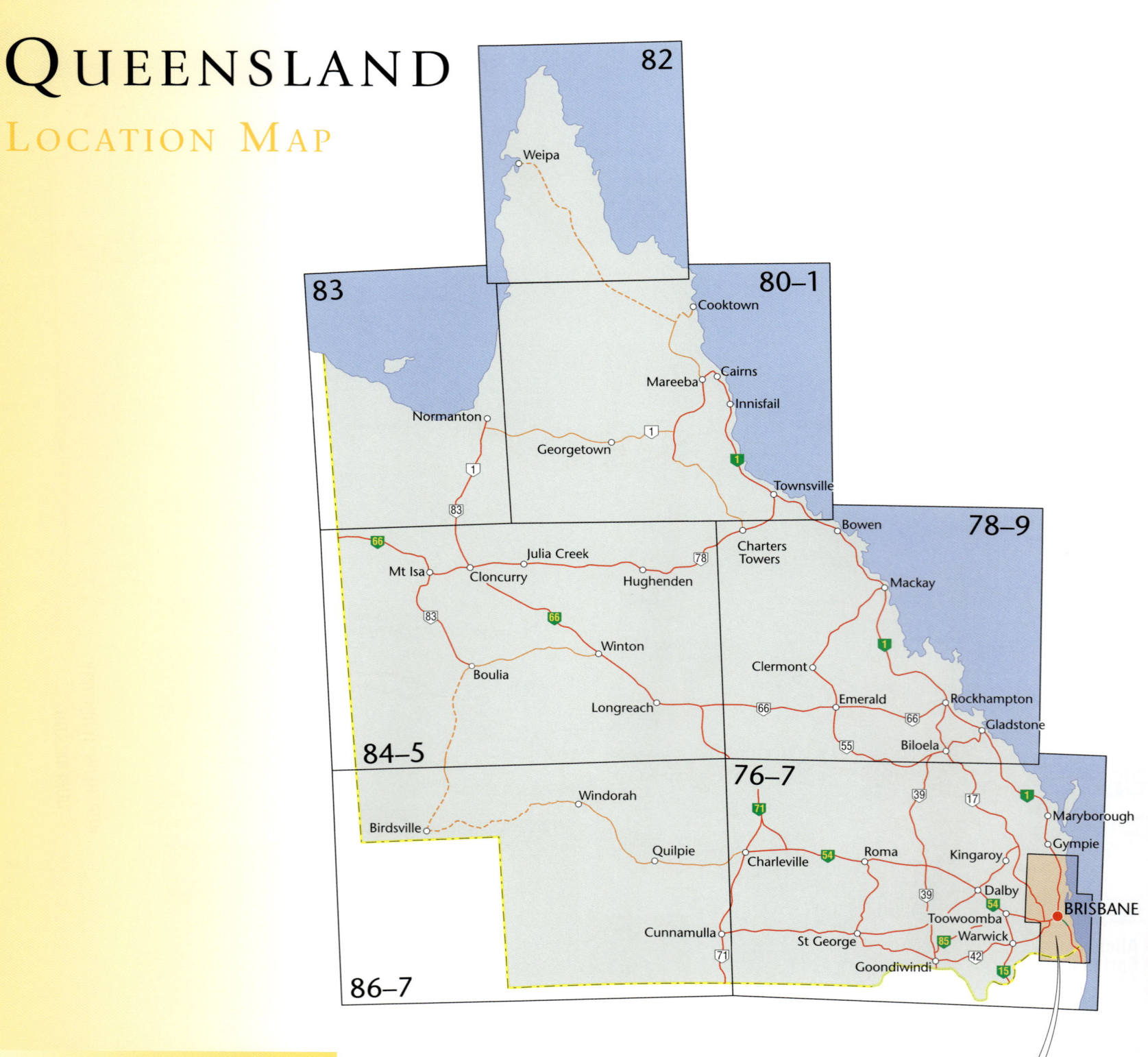

Brisbane and Suburbs	
Central Brisbane	73
Brisbane Approach & Bypass Routes	1
Touring Queensland	
Brisbane & Surrounds, North	74
Brisbane & Surrounds, South	75
Complete State Coverage	
South Eastern Queensland	76–7
North Eastern Queensland	78–9
Far North Eastern Queensland	80–1
Cape York Peninsula	82
Far North Western Queensland	83
North Western Queensland	84–5
South Western Queensland	86–7

Central Brisbane 73

Accommodation
- Brisbane City Travel Lodge 1 C5
- Brisbane International Hilton 2 E6
- Brisbane Marriott Hotel 3 G4
- Conrad International Hotel 4 D8
- Country Comfort Lennons Hotel 5 D7
- Gazebo Hotel 6 C4
- The Heritage Hotel 7 F7
- Hotel Grand Chancellor 8 D4
- Mercure Hotel Brisbane 9 C7
- North Quay Hotel 10 B5
- Novotel Brisbane 11 E4
- Palace Backpackers 12 E5
- Radisson Hotel and Suites Brisbane 13 G4
- Ridge Hotel 14 E4
- Rydges South Bank Hotel 15 C9
- Sheraton Brisbane Hotel 16 E5
- Story Bridge Motor Inn 17 H7

General Information
- Brisbane Transit Centre 18 C5
- Central Railway Station 19 E5
- City Police Station 20 F5
- General Post Office 21 F6
- Motoring Organisation (RACQ) 22 F6
- Qantas Travel Centre 23 F5
- Roma Street Station 24 C5
- Visitor Information 25 D10, E7

Places of Interest
- Brisbane City Hall 26 D6
- Brisbane Cricket Ground (The Gabba) 27 I13
- Brunswick Street Mall 28 H2
- Chinatown 29 H2
- City Botanic Gardens 30 F9
- Commissariat Stores 31 E8
- Conrad International Treasury Casino 32 D7
- Customs House 33 G5
- Eagle Street Pier 34 G6
- IMAX Theatre 35 C10
- Old Government House 36 F9
- Old Windmill 37 D5
- Parliament House 38 E9
- Pauls Breaka Beach 39 D10
- Queen Street Mall 40 E6
- Queensland Art Gallery 41 C8
- Queensland Maritime Museum 42 E11
- Queensland Museum 43 B8
- Queensland Performing Arts Complex 44 C8
- St John's Cathedral 45 F4
- St Stephen's Cathedral 46 F6
- Sciencentre 47 E8
- State Library of Queensland 48 B7

Accommodation
Only a sample range is listed; inclusion is not necessarily a recommendation.

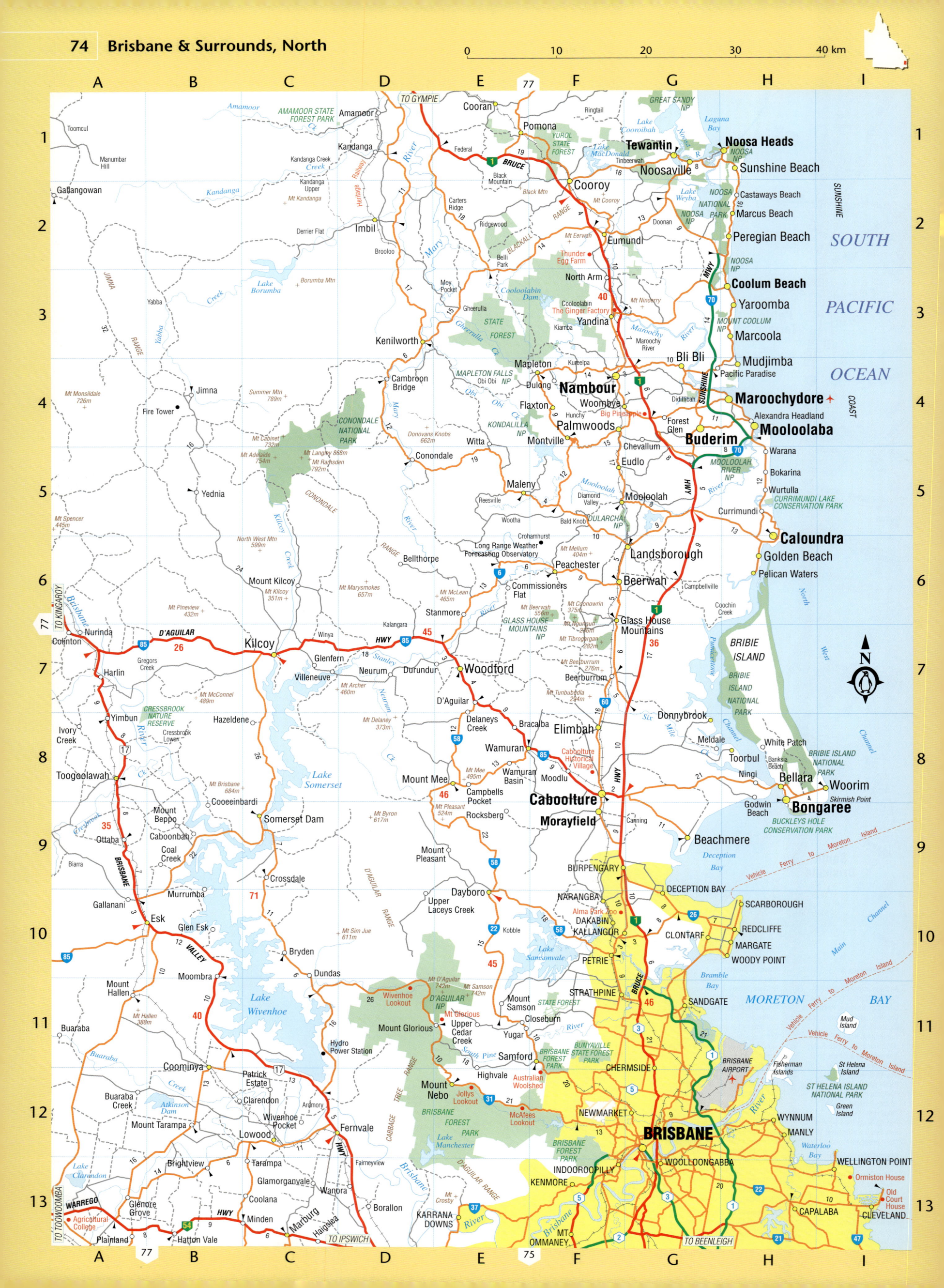

74 Brisbane & Surrounds, North

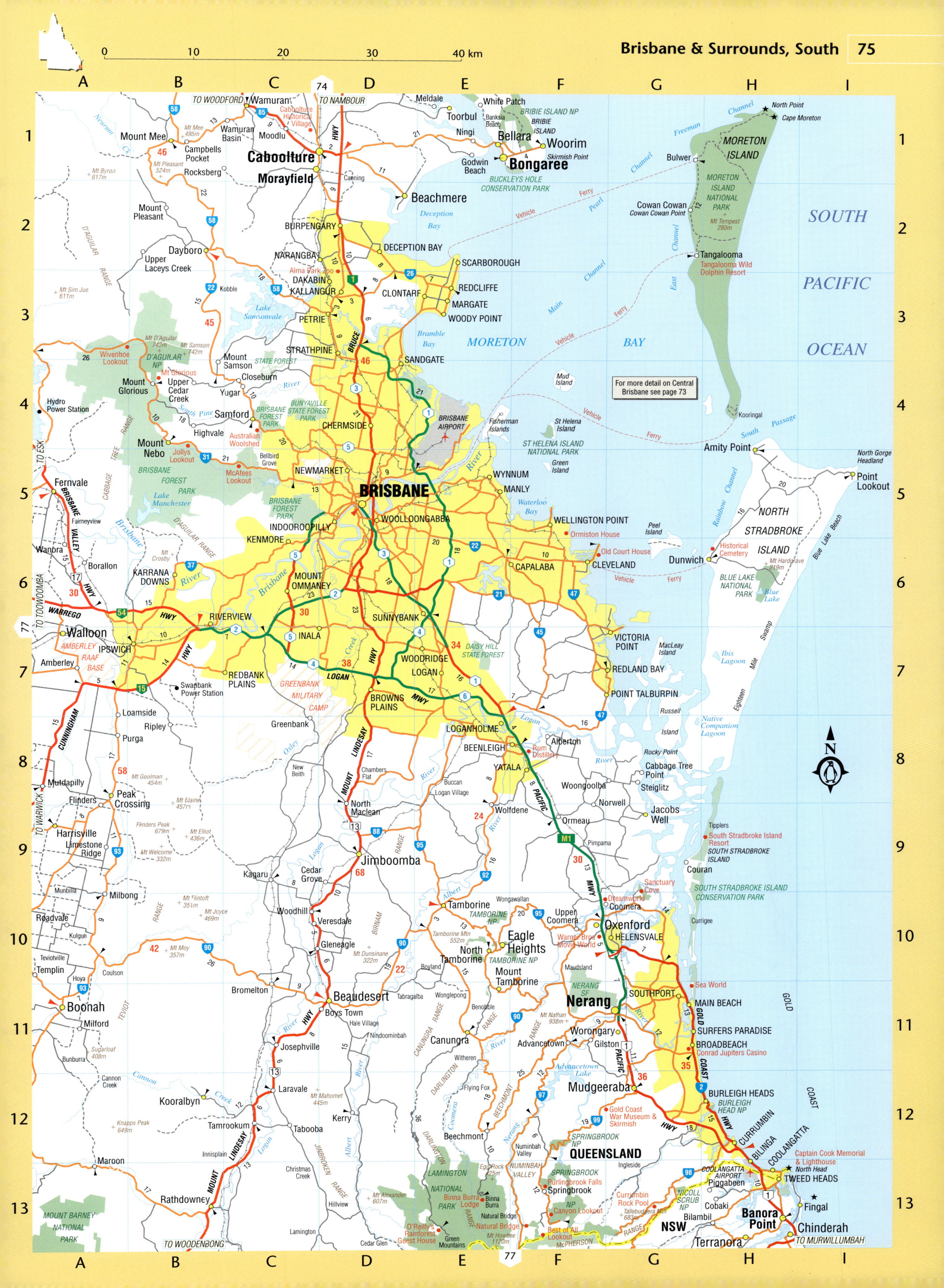

Brisbane & Surrounds, South 75

76 South Eastern Queensland

0 25 50 75 100 km

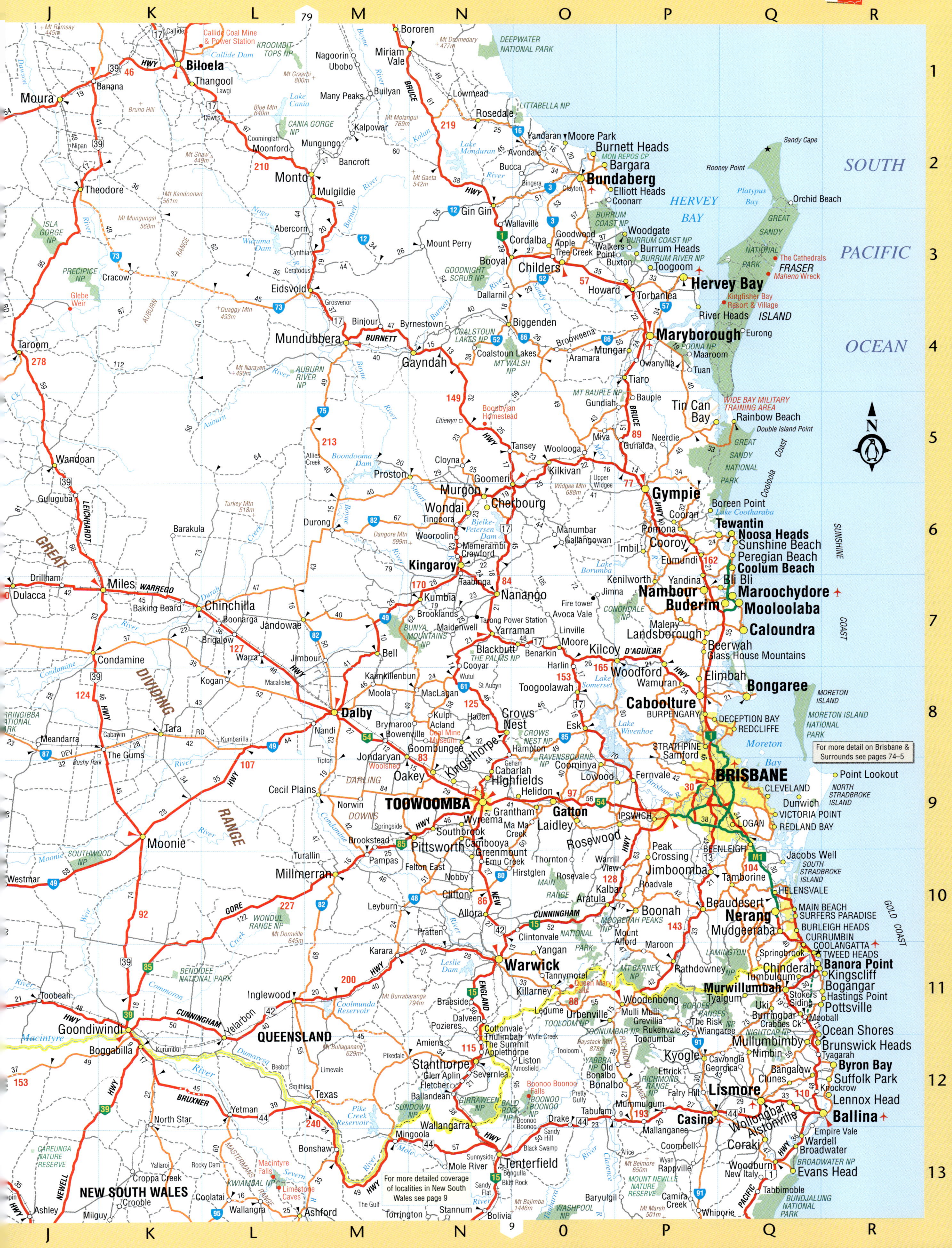

78 North Eastern Queensland

WARNINGS: In northern Australia, long distances separate some towns. Travellers should familiarise themselves with prevailing conditions before departure and take care to ensure their vehicle is roadworthy. Adequate supplies of petrol, water and food should be carried at all times.

Rainfall during the wet season (October to March) can make some roads impassable, even with a 4WD vehicle. Full information on road conditions should be obtained from local authorities before departure.

If visitors intend diverting off public roads within Aboriginal Land areas, a permit is required from the relevant Aboriginal authority.

Beware of crocodiles in rivers, estuaries and coastal areas.

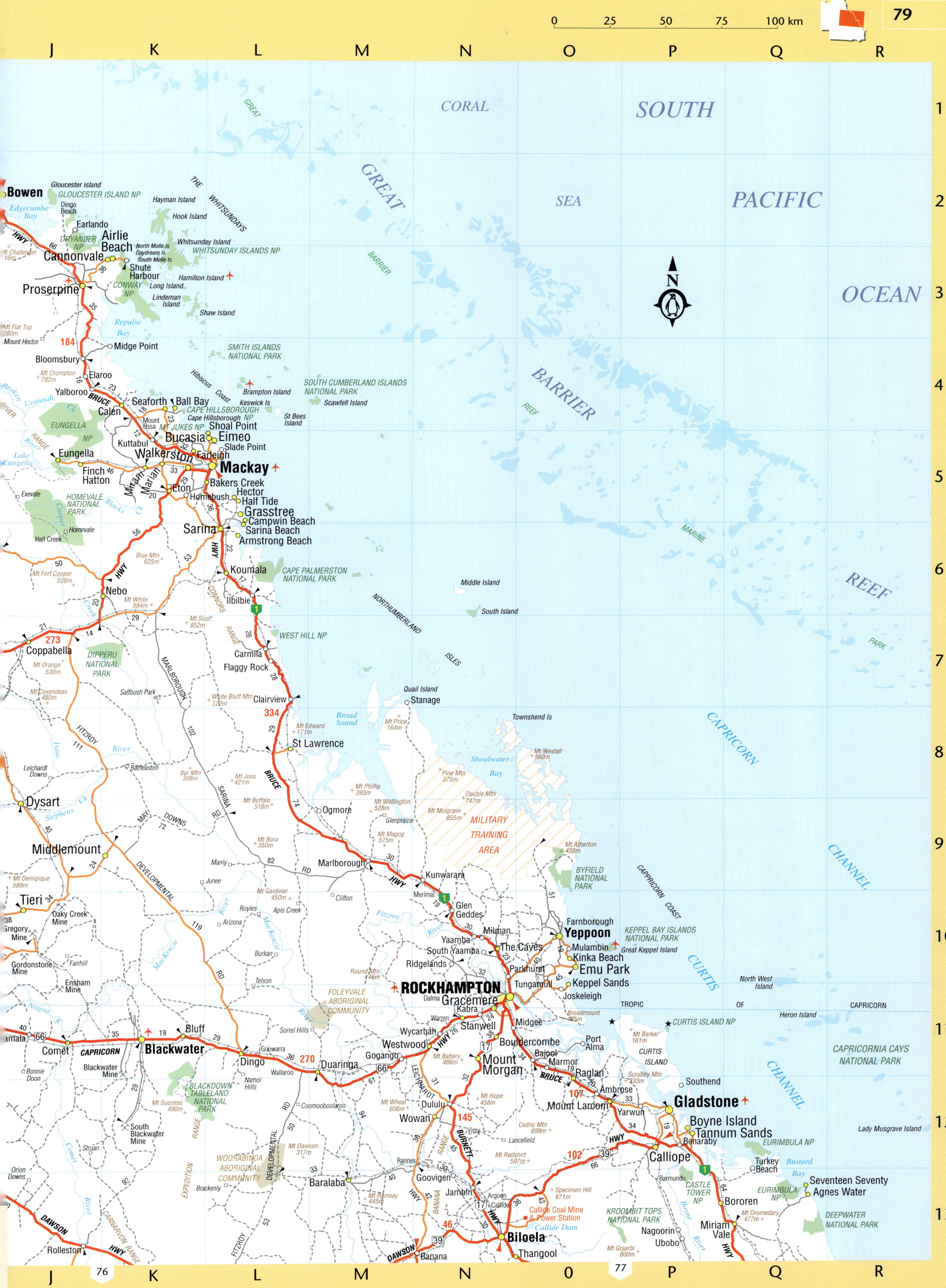
0 25 50 75 100 km
J K L M N O P Q R
1 2 3 4 5 6 7 8 9 10 11 12 13
CORAL
SEA
SOUTH
PACIFIC
OCEAN
GREAT
BARRIER
REEF
MARINE
PARK
N
CAPRICORN
CHANNEL
CURTIS
TROPIC OF CAPRICORN
Bowen
Gloucester Island
GLOUCESTER ISLAND NP
Edgecumbe Bay
Dingo Beach
Earlando
DRYANDER NP
Airlie Beach
Cannonvale
Shute Harbour
CONWAY NP
Proserpine
Hayman Island
Hook Island
THE WHITSUNDAYS
Whitsunday Island
WHITSUNDAY ISLANDS NP
North Molle Is
Daydream Is
South Molle Is
Hamilton Island
Long Island
Lindeman Island
Shaw Island
Repulse Bay
Midge Point
Mt Flat Top 580m
Mount Hector
Bloomsbury
Mt Crompton 792m
Elaroo
Yalboroo
SMITH ISLANDS NATIONAL PARK
Brampton Island
Keswick Is
SOUTH CUMBERLAND ISLANDS NATIONAL PARK
Scawfell Island
St Bees Island
Hibiscus Coast
Seaforth
Ball Bay
Calen
CAPE HILLSBOROUGH NP
Cape Hillsborough
Mount Ossa
MT JUKES NP
Shoal Point
EUNGELLA NP
Bucasia
Eimeo
Slade Point
Kuttabul
Eungella
Lake Eungella
Walkerston
Farleigh
Mackay
Finch Hatton
Mirani
Marian
Eton
Bakers Creek
Hector
Homebush
Half Tide
Grasstree
Campwin Beach
Sarina Beach
Armstrong Beach
Sarina
Exevale
HOMEVALE NATIONAL PARK
Homevale
Hail Creek
Blue Mtn 625m
Koumala
CAPE PALMERSTON NATIONAL PARK
Middle Island
South Island
NORTHUMBERLAND ISLES
Mt Fort Cooper 528m
Nebo
Mt White 594m
Ilbilbie
CONNORS RANGE
Mt Scott 852m
WEST HILL NP
Coppabella
DIPPERU NATIONAL PARK
Carmila
Flaggy Rock
Mt Orange 530m
Saltbush Park
MARLBOROUGH
Mt Coxendean 480m
White Bluff Mtn 522m
Clairview
Quail Island
Stanage
Broad Sound
Mt Price 164m
Townshend Is
Mt Edward 171m
St Lawrence
Shoalwater Bay
Mt Westall 550m
FITZROY
Isaac River
Leichhardt Downs
Bathleaston
Bar Mtn 308m
Mt Joss 421m
Pine Mtn 375m
Double Mtn 747m
Mt Phillip 393m
Dysart
Mt Buffalo 518m
Ogmore
Mt Wellington 528m
Glenprairie
Mt Mulgrave 655m
MILITARY TRAINING AREA
MAY DOWNS RD
Stephens Ck
Middlemount
Mt Bora 350m
Mt Magog 575m
Mt Atherton 438m
Marlborough
Kunwarara
BYFIELD NATIONAL PARK
Manly
Junee
Mt Demipique 589m
Tieri
Mt Gardiner 450m
Clifton
Merimal
Glen Geddes
CAPRICORN COAST
Oaky Creek Mine
Gregory Mine
Royles
Apis Creek
Arizona
Fitzroy River
Farnborough
Yeppoon
KEPPEL BAY ISLANDS NATIONAL PARK
Great Keppel Island
Milman
Yaamba
South Yaamba
The Caves
Mulambin
Kinka Beach
Emu Park
Gordonstone Mine
Fairhill
Burkan
Ridgelands
Parkhurst
Ensham Mine
Telson
Round Mtn 446m
ROCKHAMPTON
Tungamull
Keppel Sands
North West Island
Dalma
Gracemere
Joskeleigh
FOLEYVALE ABORIGINAL COMMUNITY
Kabra
Broadmount 205m
Heron Island
CURTIS ISLAND NP
Warren
Stanwell
Midgee
Mt Barker 161m
Sorrel Hills
Wycarbah
Comet
CAPRICORN
Blackwater
Bluff
Westwood
Bouldercombe
Port Alma
CAPRICORNIA CAYS NATIONAL PARK
Goowarra
Dingo
Duaringa
Gogango
Mt Battery 486m
Mount Morgan
Bajool
Marmor
CURTIS ISLAND
Bonnie Doon
Blackwater Mine
Wallaroo
Namoi Hills
Raglan
Scrubby Mtn 333m
Southend
BLACKDOWN TABLELAND NATIONAL PARK
Coomooboolaroo
Dululu
Mt Hope 458m
Ambrose
Mount Larcom
Gladstone
Mt Success 490m
South Blackwater Mine
Mt Wheal 606m
Wowan
Yarwun
Boyne Island
Tannum Sands
Benaraby
EURIMBULA NP
Lady Musgrave Island
Cedric Mtn 699m
Lancefield
Vimy
Mt Dawson 317m
Calliope
Turkey Beach
Bustard Bay
Struan
WOORABINDA ABORIGINAL COMMUNITY
Mt Redshirt 597m
Rannes
Orion Downs
Baralaba
Goovigen
Specimen Hill 671m
CASTLE TOWER NP
Seventeen Seventy
Agnes Water
Brackenly
Jambin
Argoon
Callide
Callide Coal Mine & Power Station
Callide Dam
KROOMBIT TOPS NATIONAL PARK
Bororen
EURIMBULA NP
Mt Ramsay 445m
Mt Dromedary 477m
DEEPWATER NATIONAL PARK
Nagoorin
Miriam Vale
Ubobo
Biloela
Mt Graarbi 800m
Rolleston
CARNARVON RANGE
DAWSON HWY
Banana
Thangool
BRUCE HWY
LEICHHARDT HWY
BURNETT HWY
DEVELOPMENTAL RD
EXPEDITION RANGE
76
77

80 Far North Eastern Queensland

0 25 50 75 100 km

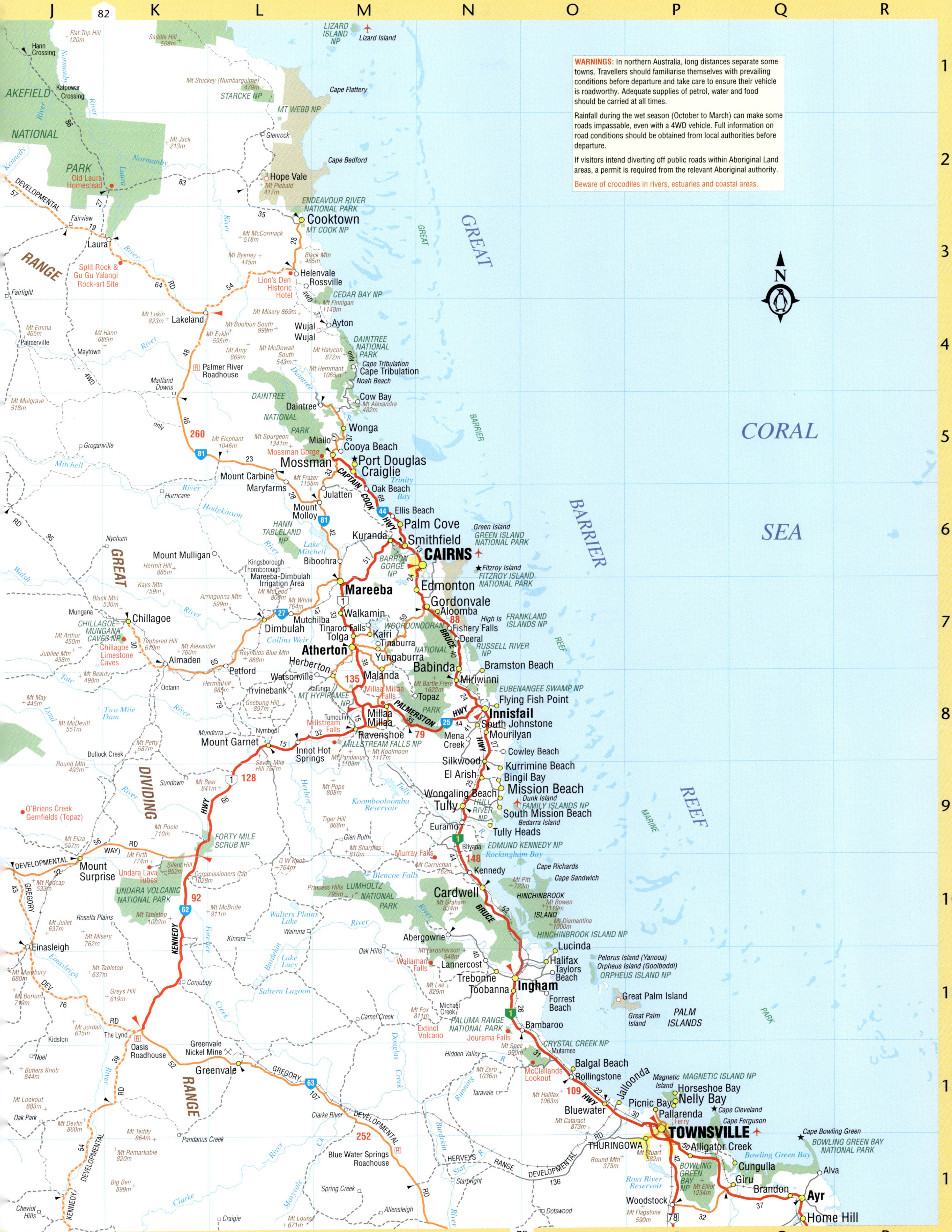

82 Cape York Peninsula

WARNINGS: In northern Australia, long distances separate some towns. Travellers should familiarise themselves with prevailing conditions before departure and take care to ensure their vehicle is roadworthy. Adequate supplies of petrol, water and food should be carried at all times.

Rainfall during the wet season (October to March) can make some roads impassable, even with a 4WD vehicle. Full information on road conditions should be obtained from local authorities before departure.

If visitors intend diverting off public roads within Aboriginal Land areas, a permit is required from the relevant Aboriginal authority.

Beware of crocodiles in rivers, estuaries and coastal areas.

Far North Western Queensland 83

GULF OF CARPENTARIA

WARNINGS: In northern Australia, long distances separate some towns. Travellers should familiarise themselves with prevailing conditions before departure and take care to ensure their vehicle is roadworthy. Adequate supplies of petrol, water and food should be carried at all times.

Rainfall during the wet season (October to March) can make some roads impassable, even with a 4WD vehicle. Full information on road conditions should be obtained from local authorities before departure.

If visitors intend diverting off public roads within Aboriginal Land areas, a permit is required from the relevant Aboriginal authority.

Beware of crocodiles in rivers, estuaries and coastal areas.

Key locations

- Birri Fishing Resort
- MORNINGTON ISLAND
- Gununa — Aboriginal Land
- WELLESLEY ISLANDS
- Bountiful Islands
- FORSYTH ISLANDS
- Bentinck Island
- SOUTH WELLESLEY ISLANDS
- Allen Island
- Sweers Island Resort / Sweers Island
- Point Burrowes
- Delta Downs
- Smithburne R
- Fitzmaurice Point
- Tarrant Point
- Pascoe Inlet
- Kangaroo Point
- Karumba Point / Karumba — Barge Service Karumba to Weipa
- Wollogorang Station & Roadhouse
- Westmoreland
- Hells Gate Roadhouse
- Buck Hill 258m
- Cliffdale
- Middle Point
- Normanton
- Mutton Hole
- Escott Barramundi Lodge
- Burketown — The Lake
- Timor Lagoon / Rocky Lake
- Dingo Dam / Manrika Lake / Morning Inlet
- Magowra / Shady Lagoon / Carron R
- Burke & Wills Cairn
- Twelve Mile Lagoon
- Glenore
- Doomadgee Aboriginal Land
- Doomadgee
- Inverleigh
- The Lakes
- Leichhardt Falls
- Wernadinga
- The Forty Mile Waterhole
- Mt Oscar 115m
- Almora
- Floraville
- Alexandra
- Macalister
- Bang Bang Jump Up Rock Formation
- Augustus Downs
- Neumayer Valley
- Bang Bang / Wondoola
- CHINA WALL
- WAANYI/GARAWA ABORIGINAL LAND TRUST
- Nicholson
- Springvale
- Bowthorn
- Musselbrook Mining Camp
- LAWN HILL NATIONAL PARK
- Lawn Hill
- Adels Grove
- Gregory Downs / Gregory
- Donors Hill
- Nardoo
- SMITHS RANGE / CONSTANCE RANGE
- Riversleigh Fossil Site
- Gallipoli
- Norfolk
- CAMOOWEAL
- Thorntonia
- Mammoth Mines
- Burke & Wills Roadhouse
- GULF SAVANNAH
- Iffley
- Muggera Lagoon
- Lyrian Waterhole
- Taldora
- Boomarra
- Canobie
- GREGORY DOWNS RD
- BURKE (MATILDA) HWY
- DEVELOPMENTAL RD
- WILLS DEVELOPMENTAL RD
- BURKETOWN RD
- NORTHERN TERRITORY / QUEENSLAND

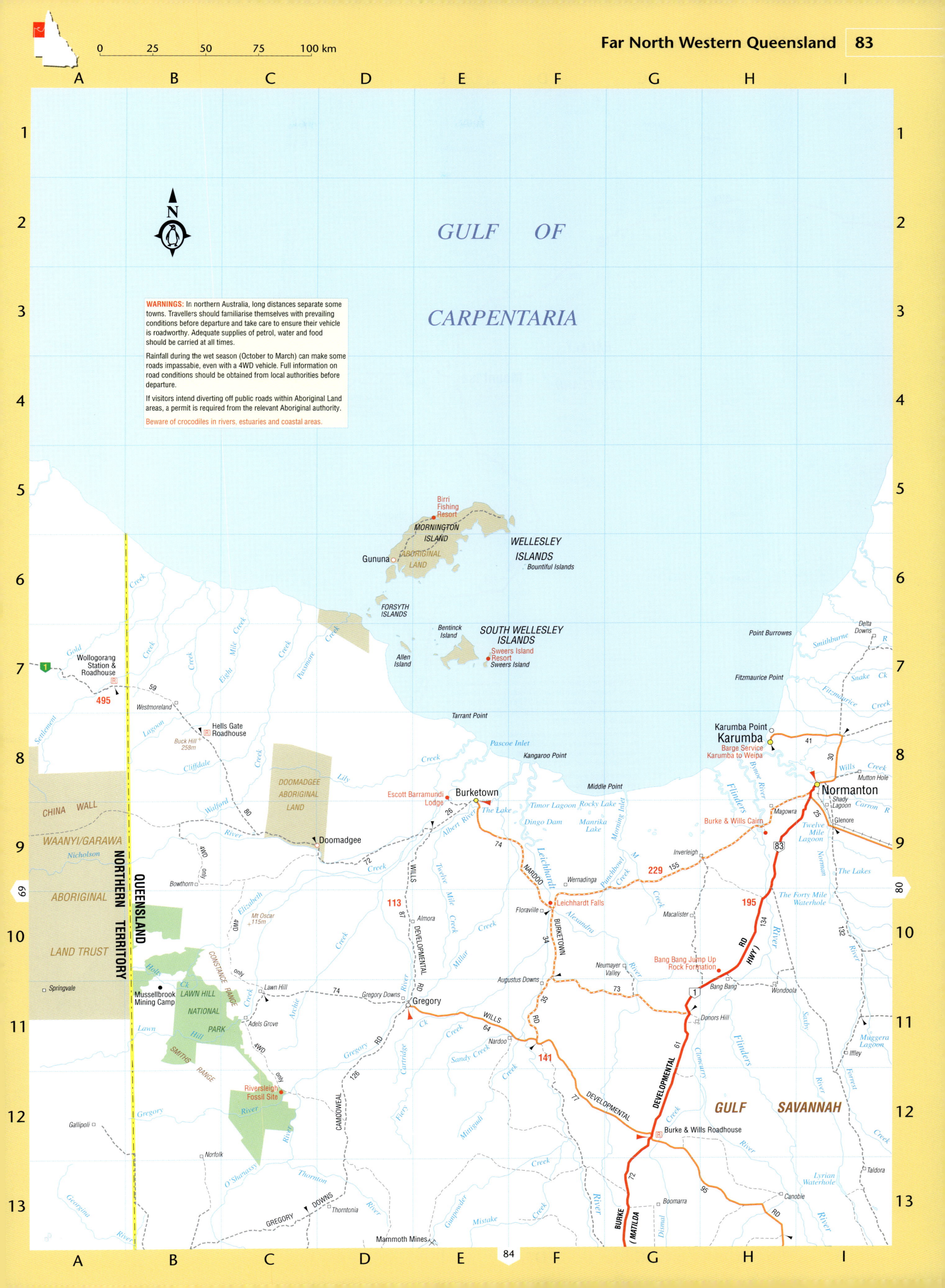

0 25 50 75 100 km

84 North Western Queensland

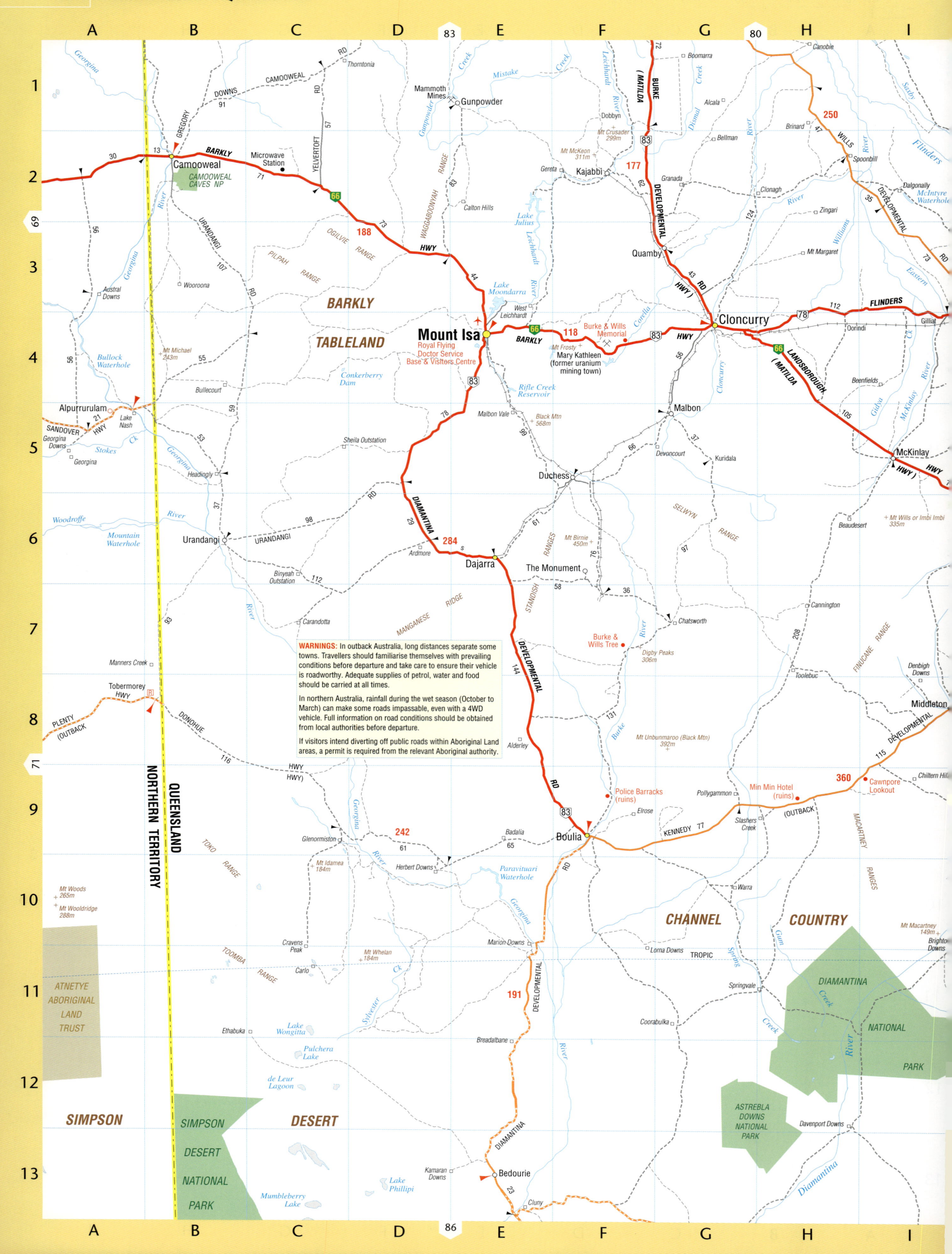

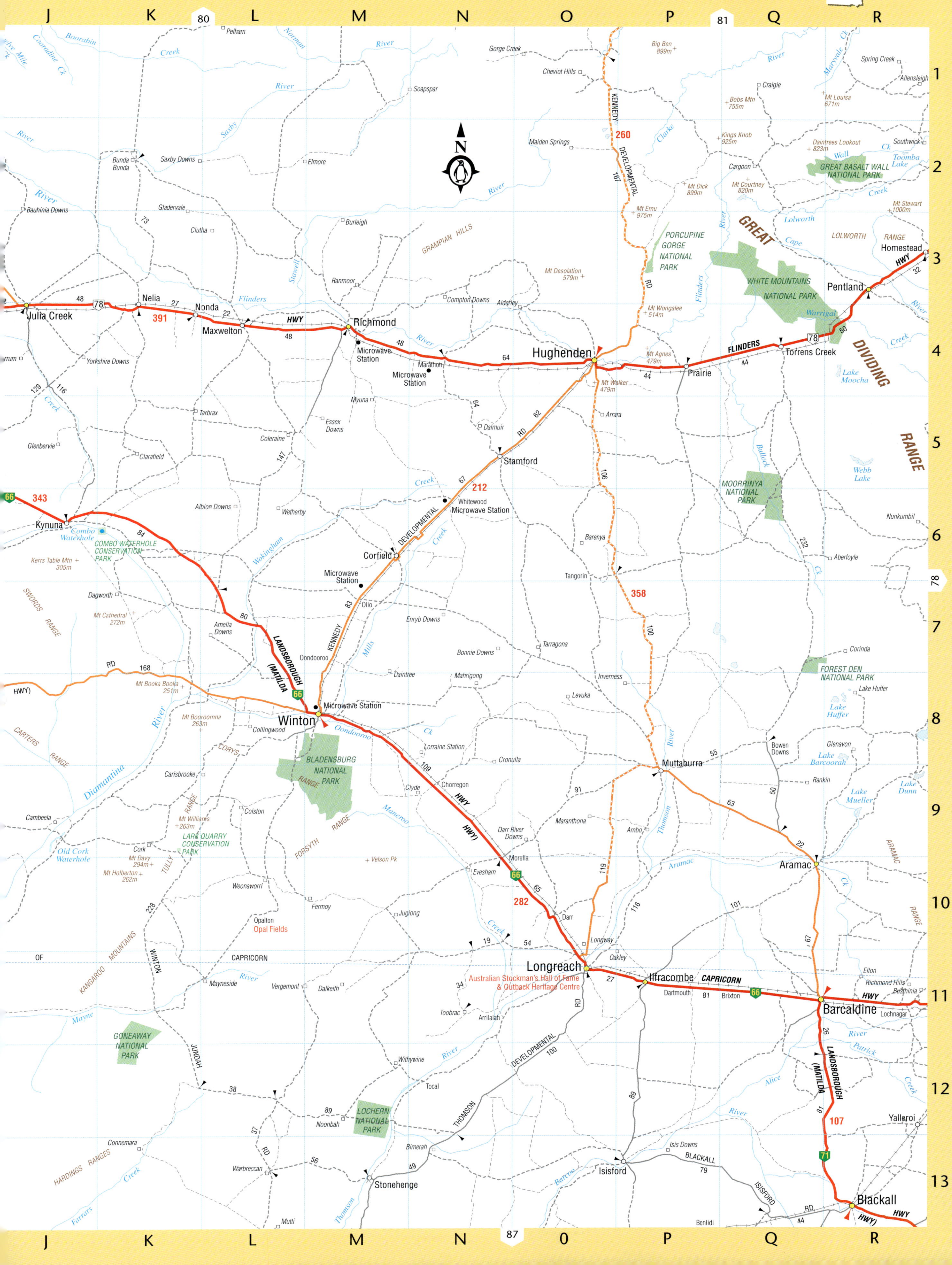
0 25 50 75 100 km
Julia Creek
Nelia
Nonda
Maxwelton
Richmond
Hughenden
Prairie
Torrens Creek
Pentland
Homestead
Kynuna
Corfield
Stamford
Winton
Muttaburra
Aramac
Longreach
Ilfracombe
Barcaldine
Isisford
Stonehenge
Blackall
Yalleroi
Lochnagar
Opalton
Opal Fields
Australian Stockman's Hall of Fame
& Outback Heritage Centre
PORCUPINE GORGE NATIONAL PARK
WHITE MOUNTAINS NATIONAL PARK
GREAT BASALT WALL NATIONAL PARK
MOORRINYA NATIONAL PARK
FOREST DEN NATIONAL PARK
BLADENSBURG NATIONAL PARK
LOCHERN NATIONAL PARK
GONEAWAY NATIONAL PARK
COMBO WATERHOLE CONSERVATION PARK
LARK QUARRY CONSERVATION PARK
GREAT DIVIDING RANGE
GRAMPIAN HILLS
FLINDERS HWY
LANDSBOROUGH (MATILDA) HWY
KENNEDY DEVELOPMENTAL RD
CAPRICORN HWY
THOMSON DEVELOPMENTAL RD
Flinders River
Thomson
Diamantina
Microwave Station
Whitewood Microwave Station
Mt Booka Booka 251m
Mt Cathedral 272m
Kerrs Table Mtn 305m
Mt Emu 975m
Mt Desolation 579m
Mt Wongalee 514m
Mt Agnes 479m
Mt Walker 479m
Big Ben 899m
Lake Huffer
Lake Barcoorah
Lake Mueller
Lake Dunn
Webb Lake
Lake Moocha
Toomba Lake
260
212
358
282
391
343
107
66
71
78
J K L M N O P Q R
1 2 3 4 5 6 7 8 9 10 11 12 13
80
81
87
78

86 South Western Queensland

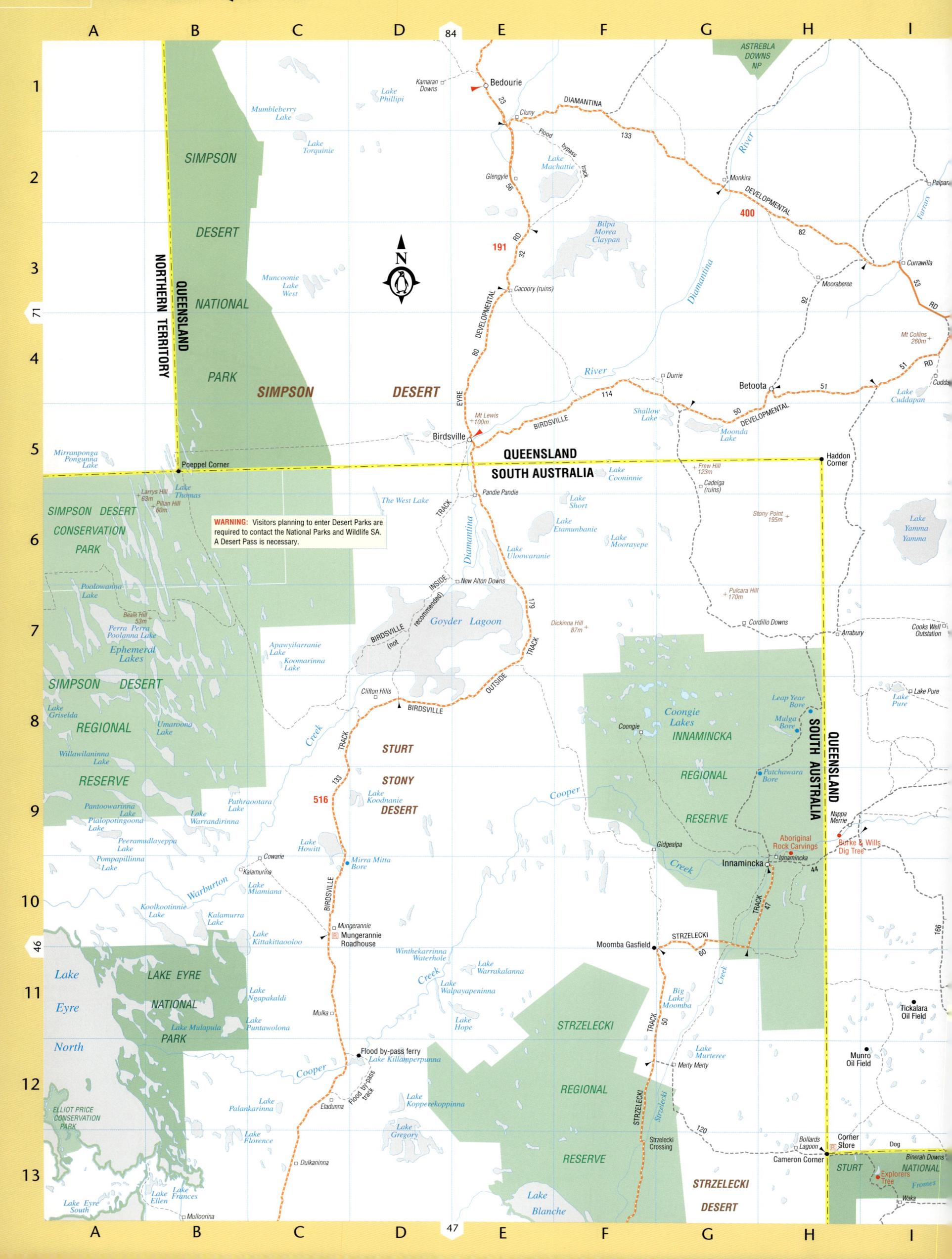

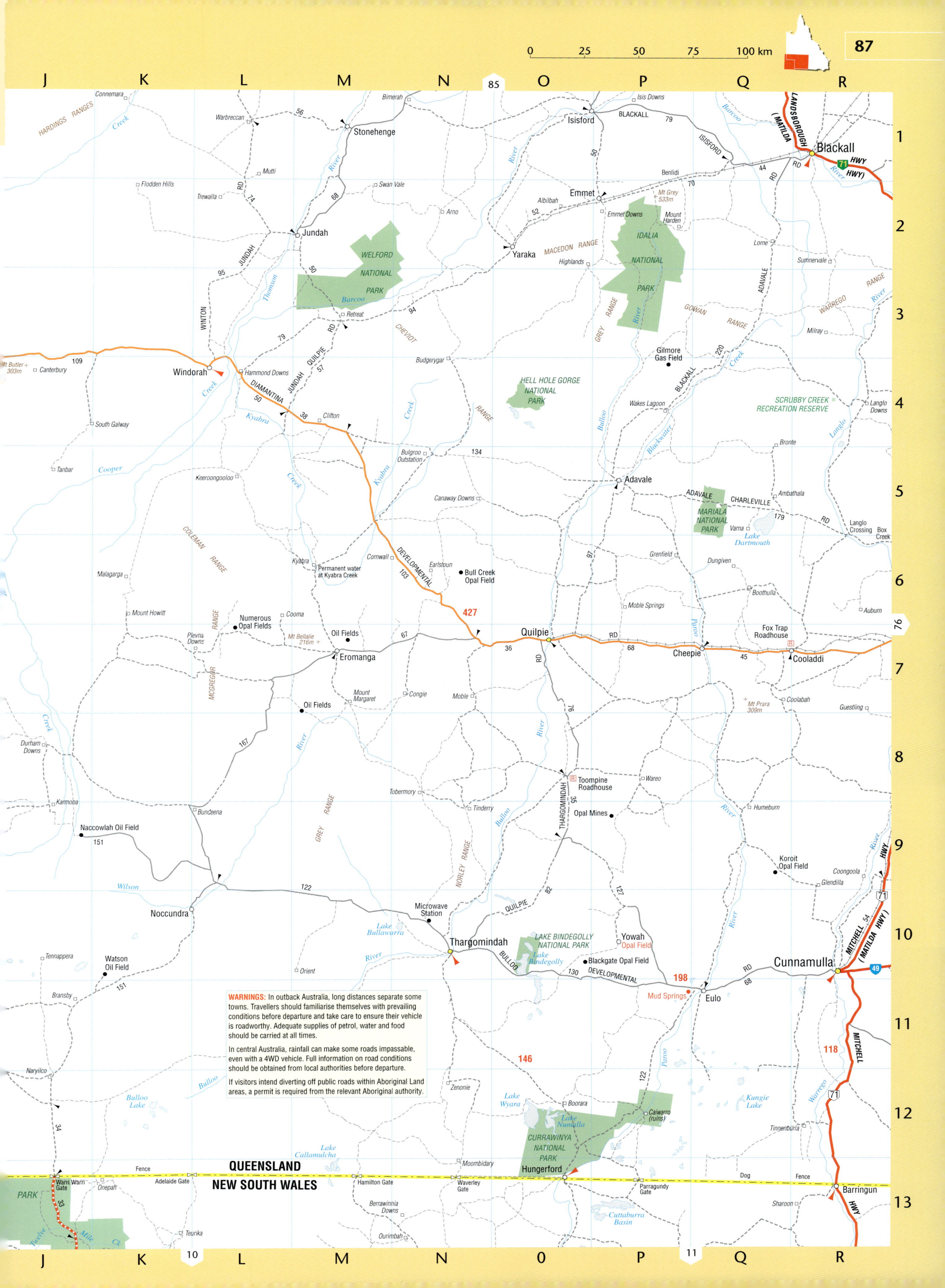

Tasmania
Location Map

Hobart and Suburbs	
Central Hobart	89
Touring Tasmania	
Hobart & Surrounds	90–1
Complete State Coverage	
Southern Tasmania	92–3
Northern Tasmania	94–5

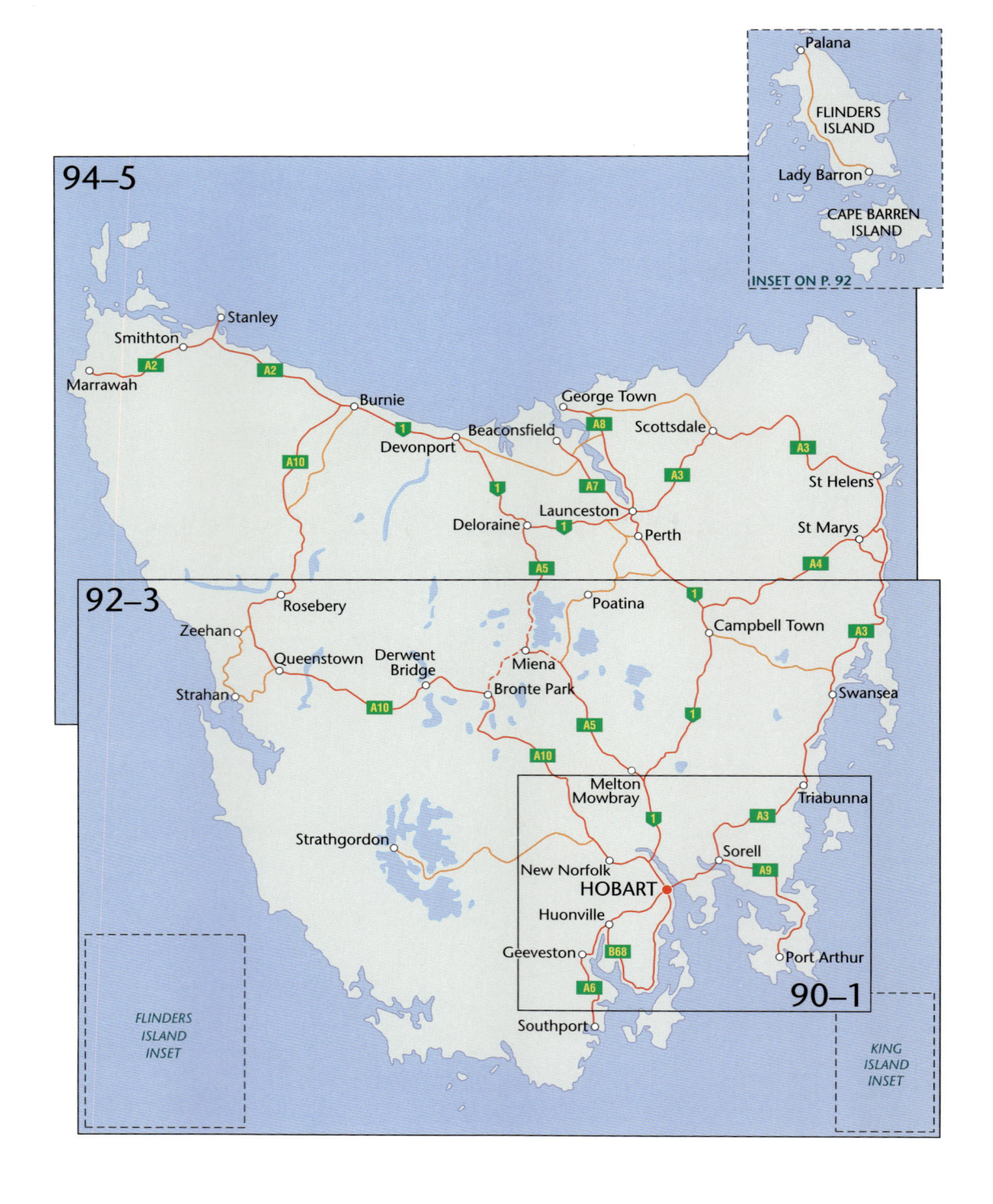

Central Hobart

Accommodation ■
- Barton Cottage 1 G9
- Colville Cottage 2 G10
- Country Comfort Hadleys Hotel 3 F8
- Hobart Macquarie 4 E8
- Hotel Grand Chancellor & Federation Concert Hall 5 G7
- Lenna of Hobart 6 G9
- Oakford on Elizabeth St Pier 7 G8
- The Old Woolstore 8 G6
- Salamanca Inn 9 F9

General Information ■
- Ferry/cruise departure point (incl. Cadbury cruises) 10 G8
- General Post Office 11 F7
- Hobart Transit Centre 12 E8
- Metro Tasmania Bus Terminal 13 F7
- Motoring Organisation (RACT) 14 D6
- Police Headquarters 15 F6
- Qantas Travel Centre 16 F7
- Tigerline Coach Terminal 17 F6
- Visitor Information 18 G7

Places of Interest ■
- Antarctic Adventure 19 G9
- Arthur Circus 20 G9
- Cat and Fiddle Arcade 21 F7
- Cenotaph 22 H6
- Constitution Dock 23 G7
- Elizabeth Street Mall 24 F7
- Franklin Square 25 F7
- Gasworks Shopping Village 26 G6
- Government House 27 G3
- Hope and Anchor Tavern 28 G7
- Ingle Hall 29 F7
- Kellys Steps 30 G9
- Maritime Museum of Tasmania 31 G7
- Parliament House 32 F8
- Penitentiary Chapel & Criminal Courts (National Trust HQ) 33 F6
- Queens Domain 34 F3
- Salamanca Arts Centre 35 G9
- Salamanca Place 36 G8
- Signalling Station 37 H9
- State Library / Allport Library & Museum of Fine Arts 38 E7
- Tasmanian Museum & Art Gallery 39 G7
- Theatre Royal 40 F6
- Town Hall 41 F7
- Van Diemen's Land Folk Museum (Narryna) 42 F9
- Victoria Dock 43 G7
- Wrest Point Hotel-Casino 44 H13

Accommodation: Only a sample range is listed; inclusion is not necessarily a recommendation.

90 Hobart & Surrounds

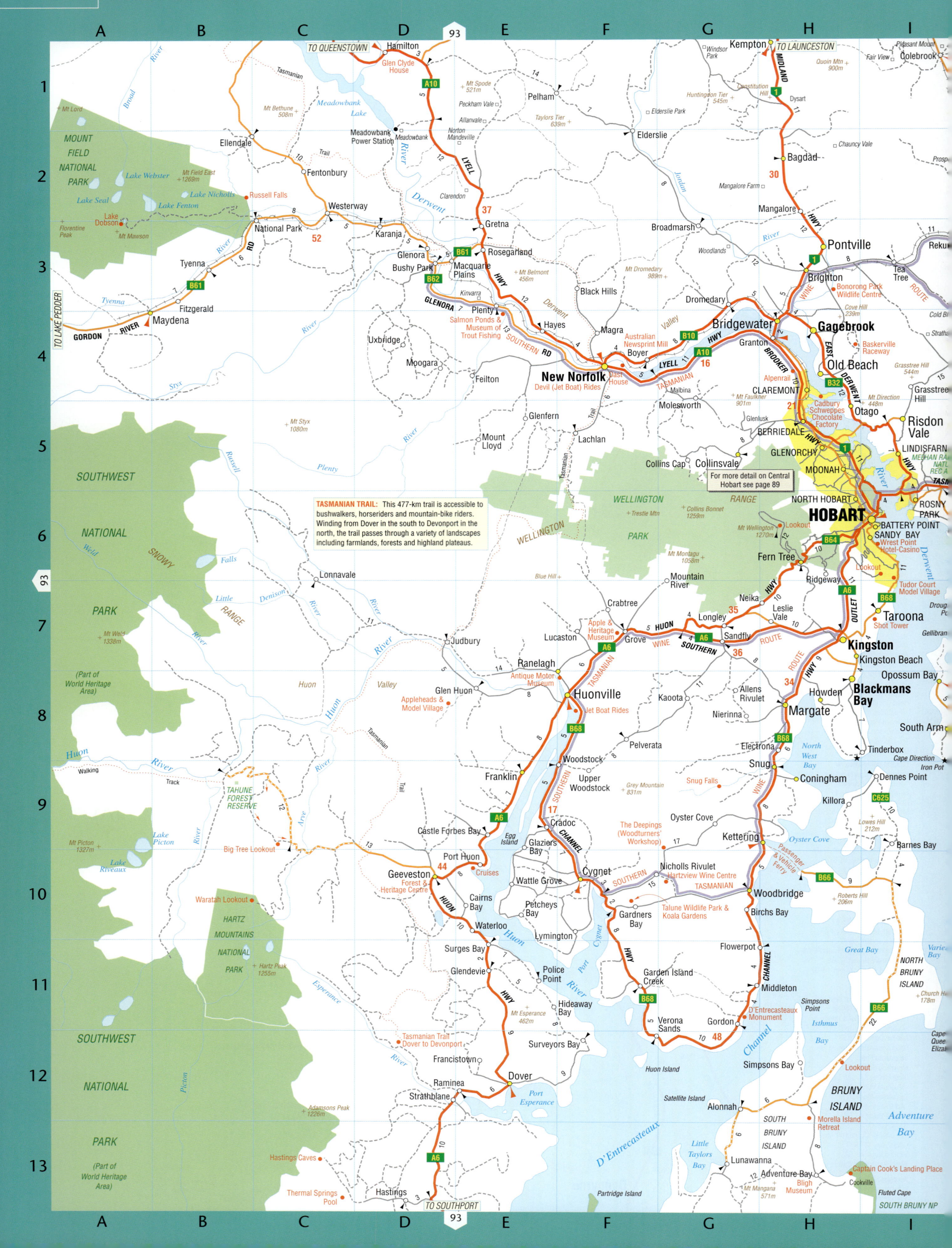

0 5 10 15 20 km
J K L M N O P Q R
93
1 2 3 4 5 6 7 8 9 10 11 12 13
MILITARY TRAINING AREA
TO SWANSEA
Triabunna
Woodstock
Okehampton
Cape Bougainville
Louisville
Eastcoaster Resort
Point Horne
Orford
Prosser Bay
Quarry Point
Shelly Beach
Spring Beach
Ferry
MARIA ISLAND NP MARINE EXTENSION
Isle du Nord
Cape Boullanger
Darlington
Historic Penal Settlement
Painted Cliffs
Bishop and Clerk
Mt Maria 709m
MARIA ISLAND NATIONAL PARK
Mistaken Cape
Johnsons Point
Rheban
Carrickfergus Bay
Passage
Lachlan Island
Ringrove
Earlham
Track
Point Des Galets
Shoal Bay
Cockle Bay
Riedle Bay
MARIA ISLAND
Cape Maurouard
Walking
Cape Bernier
Mercury
Cape Peron
Craigbourne Dam
Mt Bains 334m
Coal River
Mt Hobbs 823m
Levendale
Bluff River
Stonehurst
Brockley
Prosser River
Brown Mountain 792m
B31
54
Campania
Campania House
TASMAN
Whitemarsh
Runnymede
62
Buckland
Sally Peak
Historic Church
Court Farm
Three Thumbs 549m
HWY
Mt Morrison 469m
Byton Tops
A3
Prosser Sugarloaf 647m
Nugent
Richmond
Richmond Bridge (Australia's Oldest Bridge)
Park View
Orielton
Pawleena
Wattle Hill
Hillcrest
Mt Lord 279m
Penna
SOUTHERN
Sorell
Gordon SL 415m
Benders Hill 404m
Kellevie
Bream Creek
Milnathort
Pitt Water
Midway Point
Forcett
ARTHUR
TASMANIAN
HOBART AIRPORT
Cambridge
26
Lookout
Seven Mile Beach Protected Area
Lewisham
A9
Copping
Museum
WINE ROUTE
Marion Bay
Marion Bay
Mt Rumney 378m
Seven Mile Beach
Tiger Head
Dodges Ferry
Park Beach
Carlton
Carlton River
Rokeby
B33
Carlton Bluff
Connellys Marsh
Dunalley
Denison Canal
Blackman Bay
Cape Paul Lamanon
North Bay
Cape Frederick Hendrick
Ralphs Bay
Lauderdale
Frederick Henry Bay
Primrose Point
Primrose Sands
Fulham Island
Dunalley Bay
Mt Forestier 320m
FORESTIER PENINSULA
Humper Bluff
Sandford
Green Head
Lime Bay
Smooth Island
73
High Yellow Bluff
Cremorne
Sloping Island
LIME BAY NATURE RESERVE
Whitehouse Point
King George Island
Murdunna
Cape Surville
44
Cape Deslacs
Clifton Beach
Mt Stewart 130m
Norfolk Bay
Flinders Bay
FLINDERS BAY CONSERVATION AREA
Macgregor Peak 591m
North West Head
Coal Mines Historic Site
EAGLEHAWK BAY CONSERVATION AREA
Pirates Bay Lookout
Tessellated Pavement
Gwandalan
Cape Contrariety
Deer Point
Saltwater River
Premaydena Point
Eaglehawk Bay
Dart Island
Pirates Bay
Eaglehawk Neck
Penzance
Tasman Blowhole
Doo Town
Tasmans Arch
Devils Kitchen
Betsey Island
Outer North Head
Mt Communication 344m
Premaydena
B37
Tasmanian Devil Park
Taranna
Koonya
TASMAN NATIONAL PARK
Waterfall Bay
ROARING BEACH COASTAL RESERVE
O'Hara Bluff
Nubeena
Mt Koonya 488m
Storm Bay
Wedge Bay
White Beach
TASMAN
Oakwood
PENINSULA
Thumb Point
Wedge Island
STEWARTS BAY STATE RES
Bush Mill Steam Railway
Highcroft
Port Arthur
Port Arthur Historic Site
Mt Arthur
Fortescue Bay
Cape Hauy
Stormlea
Palmers Lookout
Port Arthur
TASMAN NATIONAL PARK
Salters Point
Remarkable Cave
Munro Bight
West Arthur Head
Raoul Bay
Maingon Bay
Black Head
Cape Pillar
Cape Raoul
Tasman Island
TASMAN SEA
N

92 Southern Tasmania

0 10 20 30 40 50 km
TASMAN
SEA
HOBART
Kingston
Blackmans Bay
Taroona
Rokeby
Lauderdale
Sorell
Midway Point
Dodges Ferry
Seven Mile Beach
Richmond
Bridgewater
Gagebrook
Old Beach
Risdon Vale
Brighton
Pontville
Bagdad
Kempton
New Norfolk
Huonville
Cygnet
Geeveston
Dover
Southport
Margate
Snug
Kettering
Woodbridge
Swansea
Bicheno
Triabunna
Orford
Buckland
Campania
Oatlands
Ross
Campbell Town
Fingal
Avoca
Bothwell
Hamilton
Dunalley
Eaglehawk Neck
Port Arthur
Nubeena
FREYCINET NATIONAL PARK
MARIA ISLAND NATIONAL PARK
TASMAN NATIONAL PARK
SOUTH BRUNY NATIONAL PARK
NORTH BRUNY ISLAND
BRUNY ISLAND
SOUTH BRUNY ISLAND
MARIA ISLAND
Great Oyster Bay
Storm Bay
Norfolk Bay
Frederick Henry Bay
Mercury Passage
D'Entrecasteaux Channel
For more detail on Hobart & Surrounds see pages 90–1
KING ISLAND
Currie
Grassy
Naracoopa
Egg Lagoon
BASS STRAIT
0 10 20 km

94 Northern Tasmania

0 10 20 30 40 50 km
J K L M N O P Q R
1 2 3 4 5 6 7 8 9 10 11 12 13
FLINDERS ISLAND
Ranga
Lady Barron
Loccota
Trousers Pt
STRZELECKI NATIONAL PARK
Adelaide Bay
Great Dog Is
Mt Chappell Is
FURNEAUX GROUP
Anderson Is
Vansittart Is
Badger Is
FRANKLIN SOUND
Puncheon Pt
Long Is
Cape Barren Island
Mt Munro 716m
CAPE BARREN ISLAND
Lesley Cove
Kent Bay
Mt Kerford 499m
Preservation Is
Sloping Pt
Passage Is
Clarke Island
Forsyth Is
Lookout Heads
Moriarty Point
STRAIT
Devil Cat Ferry George Town to Melbourne (December to April)
BANKS STRAIT
Cape Portland
Swan Island
Vinegar Hill 52m
Lyme Regis
Waterhouse Island
Waterhouse Point
Ninth Island
Petal Point
Cape Portland
Great Musselroe Bay
Croppies Point
Ringarooma Bay
Rushy Lagoon
Tomahawk
Musselroe Bay
Cape Naturaliste
Waterhouse
Boobyalla
WATERHOUSE CONSERVATION AREA
West Sandy Cape
East Sandy Cape
Anderson Bay
Bridport
Waterhouse
Stony Head
Noland Bay
Lulworth
Weymouth
Bellingham
Five Mile Bluff
Beechford
Low Head
West Head
Greens Beach
Badger Head
Low Head
George Town
Back Creek
Pipers River
Pipers Brook
Leura
Lefroy
Kelso
Clarence Point
NARAWNTAPU NATIONAL PARK
Port Sorell
Beauty Point
Bell Bay
Beaconsfield
Rowella
Kayena
The Glen
Glen
Retreat
Golconda
Lebrina
Nabowla
Lietinna
Scottsdale
Tunnel
Wyena
North Lilydale
Turners Marsh
Mount Direction
Bangor
Lilydale
Lisle
Springfield
West Scottsdale
Sidmouth
Deviot
Hillwood
Robigana
Flowery Gully
Holwell
Sassafras East
Stewarts Hill 419m
Gravelly Beach
Lower Turners Marsh
Karoola
Lalla
Mt Arthur 1187m
Underwood
Myrtle Bank
West Frankford
Winkleigh
Exeter
Lanena
Windermere
Dilston
Glengarry
Rosevears
Frankford
Notley Hills
Legana
Paterosnia
Targa
St Patricks River
Parkham
Birralee
Bridgenorth
ROCHERLEA
MOWBRAY
Rosevale
RIVERSIDE
TREVALLYN
Nunamara
Mt Barrow 1413m
Elizabeth Town
Reedy Marsh
Selbourne
LAUNCESTON
Weetah
Deloraine
Westwood
Hadspen
Hagley
Corra Linn
Relbia
White Hills
Exton
Westbury
Carrick
Red Hills
Needles
Osmaston
Glenore
Whitemore
Mt Arnon 314m
Breadalbane
Pateena
Perth
Western Junction
Evandale
Quamby Brook
Montana
Cluan
Bishopsbourne
Oaks
Toiberry
Longford
Golden Valley
Bracknell
Jackeys Marsh
Liffey
Liffey Falls
Cressy
Richmond Hill
Blackwood Creek
Kilrae
Symmons Plains Raceway
Powranna
Nile
Deddington
Hampden
GREAT WESTERN TIERS
Breona
Lake Augusta
Poatina
Poatina PS
Cramps
Talenty
Pisa
Parknook
Epping Forest
Cleveland
Conara
Brambletye
Esk Vale
Kelvin Grove
Ellerslie
Bona-vista Estate
Llewellyn Siding
Avoca
Great Lake
Liawenee
Tods Corner PS
Miena
Flintstone
Arthurs Lake
CONSERVATION AREA
Auburn
Goldsmith
Campbell Town
Front Rocky Hill 574m
Woodford
Wilburville
Shannon
Mt Penny West 1115m
St Patricks Plains
Mt Franklin 1102m
Ellinthorp
Ross
Female Factory Historic Site (Prison)
Lake Leake
Waddamana
Steppes
Woods Lake
Lake Sorell
Snobs Point 971m
Lake Echo
Interlaken
Lake Crescent
TURNBRIDGE TIER CONSERVATION AREA
Woodbury House
Tunbridge
Woodbury
Mount Morriston
Trefusis
Antill Ponds
Glengowan
Lake Echo PS
Shannon
Mt Hobgoblin 763m
Forester
Jetsonville
North Scottsdale
Mt Hadar 686m
Winnaleah
Warrentinna
Telita
Kamona
Derby
Mt Stronach 497m
Tonganah
Tulendeena
Branxholm
Cuckoo
Legerwood
Ringarooma
South Springfield
Cuckoo Hill 732m
SOUTH SPRINGFIELD FOREST PARK
Myrtle Grove
Mt Maurice 1120m
Talawa
Diddleum Plains
Trenah
Alberton
Tayene
Burns Creek
Musselboro
Upper Esk
Upper Blessington
ROSES TIER
Roses Tier
Whisloca
Blessington
Carr Villa
Alpine Village
Legges Tor 1575m
BEN LOMOND NATIONAL PARK
English Town
Mathinna
Tower Hill
Mt Victoria 1208m
St Columba Falls
Mt Young 903m
Mt Saddleback 1277m
Gladstone
Mt Cameron 551m
South Mount Cameron
Pioneer
Herrick
Moorina
Weldborough
Lottah
Goulds Country
Goshen
Priory
Pyengana
Mt Pearson 373m
Mt William 216m
MOUNT WILLIAM NATIONAL PARK
Eddystone Point
Eddystone Point
Ansons Bay
Ansons Bay
Bay of Fires
The Gardens
Sloop Lagoon
Grants Point
Binalong Bay
St Helens Point
St Helens
Akaroa
Stieglitz
Parkside
Parnella
ST HELENS POINT CONSERVATION AREA
St Helens Island
Dianas Basin
Beaumaris
Upper Scamander
Scamander
Henderson Lagoon
Falmouth
Mt Nicholas 869m
Cornwall
Four Mile Creek
St Marys
Gray
Storys Creek
Mangana
Rossarden
Fingal
FINGAL VALLEY
Rostrevor
Ormley
Break O'Day
TASMAN
Chain of Lagoons
DOUGLAS-APSLEY NATIONAL PARK
Lookout Hill
Seymour
Long Point
Royal George
Mt St John 777m
MacLean Bay
East Coast Birdlife & Animal Park
Lookout
Waubs Harbour
Governor Island
Ferndale
Bicheno
Greenlawn
Cape Lodi
Meetus Falls
Llandaff
Apslawn
Cygnet
Cranbrook
FREYCINET NATIONAL PARK
SEA
Moulting Lagoon
Freycinet Marine Farm
Mt Peter 280m
Swanwick
Cape Tourville
Swansea
The Swansea Bark Mill
Coles Bay
Sleepy Bay
Great Oyster Bay
The Hazards
Mayfield
BASS HWY
TASMAN HWY
MIDLAND HWY
LAKE HWY
EAST TAMAR HWY
WEST TAMAR HWY
ESK MAIN RD
93

Index of Place Names

A1 Mine Settlement Vic. 21 R4, 23 J2, 31 M13
Abbeyard Vic. 31 O9, 32 A7
Abbotsham Tas. 94 H7
Abercorn Qld 77 M3
Abercrombie River National Park NSW 4 C11, 6 H8, 14 F1
Aberdeen NSW 7 K2
Aberfeldy Vic. 23 J3
Abergowrie Qld 81 N10
Abermain NSW 7 M4
Acacia NT 64 E5
Acheron Vic. 21 O2, 31 J11
Acland Qld 77 N8
Acton ACT 15 A3
Acton Park WA 53 E8
Adaminaby NSW 14 D8, 16 E9, 33 L1
Adamsfield Tas. 92 H7
Adavale Qld 87 P5
Addington Vic. 20 B2
Adelaide SA 35, 36 B10, 39 K9, 48 B1
Adelaide Festival Centre SA 35 E7
Adelaide Hills SA 36 D10
Adelaide River NT 64 E8, 66 E7
Adelong NSW 6 D13, 14 B5
Adjungbilly NSW 6 E12, 14 C4
Advancetown Qld 75 F11
Adventure Bay Tas. 90 H13, 93 L11
Agery SA 38 I6
Agnes Vic. 23 J10
Agnes Banks NSW 5 K6
Agnes Water Qld 79 Q13
Agnew WA 56 H2
Aileron NT 70 I6
Ailsa Vic. 26 H7
Aireys Inlet Vic. 20 E12, 25 P10
Airlie Beach Qld 79 K3
Airly Vic. 23 N5
Akaroa Tas. 95 R8
Alawoona SA 39 Q8, 48 H1
Albacutya Vic. 26 F3
Albany WA 54 H13, 56 E12
Albert NSW 6 B3, 11 R13, 13 R1
Alberton Qld 75 F8
Alberton Tas. 95 O8
Alberton Vic. 23 L9
Alberton West Vic. 23 K9
Albury NSW 13 Q13, 31 P4, 32 C1
Alcomie Tas. 94 D5
Aldersyde WA 54 G5
Aldinga SA 36 A13, 37 F4
Aldinga Beach SA 37 E4, 39 K10, 48 B3
Alectown NSW 6 D4
Alexander Morrison National Park WA 56 B5
Alexandra Vic. 21 O1, 31 J11
Alexandra Headland Qld 74 H4
Alford SA 38 I5
Alfred National Park Vic. 14 F13, 33 O11
Alfred Town NSW 6 C12, 13 R10, 14 A5
Ali-Curung NT 69 K13, 71 K2
Alice NSW 9 O4, 77 P13
Alice Springs NT 71 J8
Allambee Vic. 21 Q11, 22 I7
Allambee South Vic. 21 Q12, 22 I8
Allanby Vic. 26 F6
Allans Flat Vic. 31 P5, 32 B3
Allansford Vic. 24 I9
Allanson WA 54 D8
Allawah NSW 13 M6
Alleena NSW 6 A9, 13 Q6
Allendale Vic. 25 P2, 27 P13
Allendale East SA 48 H12
Allendale North SA 36 E2, 39 L7
Allens Rivulet Tas. 90 G8
Allies Creek Qld 77 M5
Alligator Creek Qld 81 P13
Allora Qld 77 N10
Alma SA 36 B1, 39 L7
Alma Park NSW 13 P12, 31 O1
Almaden Qld 81 K7
Almonds Vic. 31 L5
Alonnah Tas. 90 G12, 93 L11
Aloomba Qld 81 N7
Alpara NT 44 G1, 70 E13
Alpha Qld 78 F11
Alphadale NSW 9 Q3
Alpine National Park Vic. 14 A10, 23 L1, 31 O12, 32 D6
Alpurrurulam NT 69 Q13, 71 Q2, 84 A5
Alstonville NSW 9 Q3, 77 Q12
Alton Qld 76 I10
Alton National Park Qld 76 I10
Altona Vic. 20 I7, 22 C4
Alva Qld 78 H1, 81 Q13
Alvie Vic. 20 A10, 25 N8
Alyangula NT 67 O9
Amamoor Qld 74 D1
Amanbidji NT 68 B3
Amata SA 44 G1, 70 E13
Amberley Qld 75 A7
Amboyne Crossing Vic. 14 D11, 33 K8
Ambrose Qld 79 O12
Amby Qld 76 F6
American Beach SA 38 I12
American River SA 38 I12
Amherst Vic. 20 B1, 25 N1, 27 N12
Amiens Qld 9 M2, 77 N12
Amity Point Qld 75 H5
Amoonguna NT 71 J8
Amosfield NSW 9 M2, 77 O12
Amphion WA 52 E11, 54 D6
Amphitheatre Vic. 25 M1, 27 M12
Ampilatwatja NT 71 M4
Anakie Qld 78 H11
Anakie Vic. 20 F7, 25 Q6
Anakie East Vic. 20 F7, 25 Q6
Anakie Junction Vic. 20 F7
Ancona Vic. 31 K10
Andamooka SA 40 G4
Anderson Vic. 21 M13, 22 F9
Ando NSW 14 E10, 33 N6
Andover Tas. 93 M5
Andrews SA 39 L4
Anembo NSW 14 F7, 16 I7
Angas Valley SA 36 I8
Angaston SA 36 G4, 39 M8, 49 I5
Angip Vic. 26 G5
Angle Vale SA 36 B6, 39 L8
Anglers Reach NSW 14 D8, 16 D9, 33 K1
Anglers Rest Vic. 14 A11, 32 E8
Anglesea Vic. 20 E12, 25 Q9
Angourie NSW 9 Q5
Angurugu NT 67 O9
Angus Place NSW 4 F3, 6 I6
Angustown Vic. 30 G8
Anna Bay NSW 7 N4
Annangrove NSW 5 M6
Annuello Vic. 29 J7
Ansons Bay Tas. 95 R6
Antarrengeny NT 71 L4
Antill Ponds Tas. 93 M4, 95 M13
Antwerp Vic. 26 F6
Apamurra SA 36 H9, 39 M9, 48 D1
Aparawatatja SA 44 B2, 59 R11, 70 B13
Apollo Bay Vic. 25 N12
Appila SA 39 K2, 41 J13
Appin NSW 5 L12, 7 K9
Appin Vic. 27 O4, 30 A3
Appin South Vic. 27 P4, 30 A3
Apple Tree Creek Qld 77 O3
Apple Tree Flat NSW 6 H4
Applethorpe Qld 9 M2, 77 N12
Apslawn Tas. 93 P3, 95 Q12
Apsley Tas. 93 L5
Apsley Vic. 26 B11, 48 I9
Arafura Sea 67 K2
Araluen NSW 14 G6, 17 L6
Araluen North NSW 17 L6
Aramac Qld 78 C10, 85 Q10
Aramara Qld 77 O4
Arapiles Vic. 26 F9
Ararat Vic. 25 K2, 27 K13
Aratula Qld 77 O10
Arawata Vic. 21 P12, 22 H8
Arawerr NT 71 L5
Arcadia Vic. 30 H7
Archdale Vic. 27 M10
Archer River Roadhouse Qld 82 D9
Archies Creek Vic. 21 N13, 22 G9
Archipelago of the Recherche WA 57 J11
Ardath WA 54 I4
Ardglen NSW 9 J13
Ardlethan NSW 6 A10, 13 Q7
Ardmona Vic. 30 H6
Ardmory Qld 74 C12
Ardno Vic. 24 A5, 48 I12
Ardrossan SA 39 J7
Areegra Vic. 26 I6
Areyonga NT 70 G9
Argalong NSW 16 B2
Argoon Qld 79 N13
Argyle Vic. 30 E9
Ariah Park NSW 6 B9, 13 Q7
Aringa Vic. 24 G9
Arkaroo Rock SA 41 K8
Arkaroola SA 41 M3
Arkona Vic. 26 F7
Armadale WA 52 D6, 54 D4, 56 C8
Armatree NSW 8 D12
Armidale NSW 9 L9
Armstrong Vic. 25 K1, 27 K12
Armstrong Beach Qld 79 L6
Armytage Vic. 20 C10
Arnhem Land NT 65 P6, 67 K6
Arno Bay SA 38 F5
Arnold Vic. 27 O9, 30 A8
Arnold West Vic. 27 O9, 30 A8
Arrawarra NSW 9 P7
Arrilalah Qld 85 N11
Arrino WA 56 C4
Arthur River Tas. 94 A5
Arthur River WA 54 F8
Arthurs Creek Vic. 21 L4
Arthurs Seat State Park Vic. 21 J11
Arthurton SA 38 I7
Arthurville NSW 6 F3
Ascot Vic. 20 C3
Ashbourne SA 37 H5, 39 L10, 48 C3
Ashens Vic. 26 I9
Ashford NSW 9 K4, 77 L13
Ashley NSW 8 G4, 77 J13
Ashton SA 36 C10, 37 H1
Ashville SA 39 M11, 48 D3
Astrebla Downs National Park Qld 84 G12, 86 G1
Atherton Qld 81 M7
Athlone Vic. 21 O10, 22 G7
Atitjere NT 71 L7
Atneltyey NT 71 K5
Attunga NSW 9 J10
Aubrey Vic. 26 G6
Auburn SA 39 L6
Auburn Tas. 93 L3, 95 M12
Auburn River National Park Qld 77 L4
Audley NSW 5 N10
Augathella Qld 76 C5
Augusta WA 53 C13, 54 B11, 56 B11
Aurukun Qld 82 A9
Auski Roadhouse WA 58 C4
Austinmer NSW 5 M13
Austral NSW 5 L9
Australia Plains SA 39 M6
Australian War Memorial ACT 15 H4
Australind WA 53 G4, 54 C8, 56 C10
Avalon NSW 5 P6
Avenel Vic. 30 H9
Avenue SA 48 G9
Avoca Tas. 93 N1, 95 O11
Avoca Vic. 27 M12
Avoca Beach NSW 5 Q4
Avoca Dell SA 36 I11
Avoca Vale Qld 77 O7
Avon SA 39 K7
Avon Plains Vic. 27 K8
Avon River WA 52 E1, 54 D3
Avon Valley National Park WA 52 E1, 54 D2, 56 C7
Avondale NSW 7 M5
Avondale Qld 77 O2
Avonmore Vic. 30 D7
Avonsleigh Vic. 21 M7, 22 F5
Awonga Vic. 26 C11
Axe Creek Vic. 27 R10, 30 D9
Axedale Vic. 30 D8
Ayers Rock Resort *see* **Yulara**
Ayers Rock *see* **Uluru**
Ayr Qld 78 H1, 81 Q13
Ayrford Vic. 25 J10
Ayton Qld 81 M4
Baan Baa NSW 8 H9
Baandee WA 54 H2
Baarmutha Vic. 31 O6, 32 A4
Babakin WA 54 I4
Babinda Qld 81 N7
Bacchus Marsh Vic. 20 G5, 22 A3, 25 R4
Back Creek Tas. 95 L6
Back Creek Vic. 31 P5, 32 B3
Back Valley SA 37 F8
Backwater NSW 9 M7
Baddaginnie Vic. 31 K7
Baden Tas. 93 M6
Badgerys Creek NSW 5 K9
Badgingarra WA 56 B6
Badgingarra National Park WA 56 B6
Badja Mill NSW 17 J9, 33 P1
Badjaling WA 54 G4
Bael Bael Vic. 27 O2, 29 O13
Baerami NSW 7 J3
Bagdad Tas. 90 H2, 93 L7
Bagnoo NSW 9 N12
Bagot Well SA 36 F2, 39 M7
Bagshot Vic. 27 R9, 30 D8
Bailieston Vic. 30 G8
Baird Bay SA 43 P13
Bairnsdale Vic. 23 P4, 32 F13
Bajool Qld 79 O11
Bakara SA 39 O8
Baker Vic. 26 D5
Bakers Creek Qld 79 L5
Bakers Hill WA 52 G3, 54 E3
Bakers Swamp NSW 6 F4
Baking Board Qld 77 K7
Balaklava SA 39 K6
Bald Knob Qld 74 F5
Bald Nob NSW 9 M6
Bald Rock Vic. 27 Q5, 30 B3
Bald Rock National Park NSW 9 M3, 77 N12
Baldivis WA 52 B8, 54 C5
Baldry NSW 6 E4
Balfes Creek Qld 78 D2
Balfour Tas. 94 B7
Balgal Beach Qld 81 O12
Balgo Hills WA 61 P12
Balgowan SA 38 H7
Balgowlah NSW 5 O8
Balhannah SA 36 D10, 37 I1, 39 L9, 48 C2
Balingup WA 53 I8, 54 D9, 56 C11
Balintore Vic. 20 B11
Balkuling WA 54 F4
Ball Bay Qld 79 K4
Balladonia Roadhouse WA 57 L8
Balladoran NSW 6 E1, 8 D13
Ballalaba NSW 6 H13, 14 F6, 17 K5
Ballan Vic. 20 F4, 25 Q4, 30 C13
Ballan North Vic. 20 F4
Ballandean Qld 9 M3, 77 N12
Ballangeich Vic. 24 I8
Ballapur Vic. 27 J4
Ballarat Vic. 20 C4, 25 O3, 30 A13
Ballark Vic. 20 D5
Ballaying WA 54 G8
Ballbank NSW 12 I11, 27 P1, 29 P11
Balldale NSW 13 P12, 31 N2
Ballendella Vic. 30 E5
Balliang Vic. 20 F6, 25 R5
Balliang East Vic. 20 G6, 22 A4, 25 R5
Ballidu WA 56 D6
Ballimore NSW 6 F2
Ballina NSW 9 Q3, 77 R12
Balmain NSW 5 O8
Balmattum Vic. 31 J8
Balmoral NSW 5 J13
Balmoral Vic. 24 E2, 26 F13
Balnarring Vic. 21 K11, 22 D8
Balook Vic. 23 K8
Balranald NSW 12 H8, 29 N6
Balrootan North Vic. 26 E6
Balumbah SA 38 F3, 40 E13
Balup WA 52 F2, 54 D3
Bamaga Qld 82 C3
Bamawm Vic. 30 D5
Bamawm Extension Vic. 30 E5
Bambaroo Qld 81 O11
Bambill Vic. 12 B8, 28 D5
Bambill South Vic. 28 D5
Bamboo Creek WA 58 E2
Bambra Vic. 20 D11, 25 P9
Bamganie Vic. 20 D7, 25 P6
Banana Qld 77 J1, 79 N13
Bancroft Qld 77 M2
Bandiana Vic. 13 Q13, 31 P4, 32 C2
Bandon NSW 6 E6
Bandon Grove NSW 7 M2
Banealla SA 39 P13, 48 G5
Bangalow NSW 9 Q2, 77 Q12
Bangerang Vic. 26 I6
Bangham SA 26 A8, 48 I7
Bangor Tas. 95 L7
Baniyala NT 67 O7
Banksia Beach Qld 74 H8, 75 E1
Bankstown NSW 5 M9
Bannaby NSW 6 I10, 14 G2
Bannerton Vic. 12 F9, 29 J6
Bannister NSW 6 H10, 14 F3
Bannister WA 52 G11, 54 E6
Bannockburn Vic. 20 E8, 25 Q7
Banora Point NSW 9 Q1, 75 H13, 77 Q11
Banyan Vic. 27 J2, 29 J13
Banyena Vic. 27 J8
Banyenong Vic. 27 L6
Barabba SA 36 B2
Baradine NSW 8 E10
Barakula Qld 77 K6
Baralaba Qld 79 M13
Baranduda Vic. 31 P4, 32 C2
Barcaldine Qld 78 C11, 85 Q11
Barellan NSW 13 P7
Barfold Vic. 25 R1, 27 R12, 30 D10
Bargara Qld 77 O2
Bargo NSW 5 J13, 7 J9, 14 I2
Barham NSW 12 I12, 27 Q2, 29 Q13, 30 B1
Baring Vic. 26 G1, 28 G11
Baringhup Vic. 27 P11, 30 B10
Barjarg Vic. 31 L10
Bark Hut Inn NT 64 I6, 66 F6
Barkers Creek Vic. 27 Q11, 30 C10
Barkly Vic. 27 L11
Barkly Homestead NT 69 N11
Barkly Tableland NT & Qld 69 M6, 84 C3
Barkstead Vic. 20 E3
Barmah Vic. 13 K13, 30 F3
Barmah State Park Vic. 30 G2
Barmedman NSW 6 B9, 13 R7
Barmera SA 39 P7
Barmundu Qld 79 P13
Barnadown Vic. 30 D8
Barnawartha Vic. 13 P13, 31 O4, 32 A2
Barnawartha North Vic. 31 O4, 32 B1
Barnes NSW 13 K13, 30 E3
Barnes Bay Tas. 90 I9, 93 L10
Barongarook Vic. 20 B12
Barongarook West Vic. 20 A12, 25 N9
Barooga NSW 13 M13, 31 J3
Baroota SA 39 J2, 40 I12
Barossa Valley SA 36 E4, 49
Barpinba Vic. 20 B9, 25 N7
Barraba NSW 8 I8
Barrakee Vic. 27 M6
Barramunga Vic. 20 B13
Barranyi (North Island) National Park NT 67 P12, 69 P1
Barraport Vic. 12 H13, 27 N5
Barringo Vic. 20 H3
Barrington NSW 7 N1
Barrington Tas. 94 I7
Barrington Tops National Park NSW 7 M1
Barringun NSW 11 N1, 76 A13, 87 R13
Barrogan NSW 6 F6
Barron Gorge National Park Qld 81 M6
Barrow Creek NT 71 J4
Barry NSW 6 G7, 9 K12
Barrys Reef Vic. 20 F3
Barton ACT 15 D10
Barton SA 43 K4
Barunga NT 66 H10
Barunga Gap SA 39 J5
Barwidgee Creek Vic. 31 O7, 32 B5
Barwo Vic. 30 G3
Barwon Downs Vic. 20 C12, 25 O10
Barwon Heads Vic. 20 G10, 22 A7, 25 R8
Baryulgil NSW 9 O4, 77 P13
Basin View NSW 17 Q2
Bass Vic. 21 M13, 22 F9
Bass Strait 22 D12, 94 G3
Batchelor NT 64 D7, 66 E7
Batchica Vic. 26 H6
Bateau Bay NSW 5 Q3
Batehaven NSW 17 N7
Batemans Bay NSW 14 H7, 17 N7
Bates SA 43 K4
Batesford Vic. 20 F9, 25 Q7
Bathumi Vic. 31 L4
Bathurst NSW 4 B4, 6 H6
Bathurst Island NT 66 C3
Batlow NSW 6 D13, 14 B6, 16 A4
Battery Point Tas. 89 G9, 90 I6
Bauhinia Qld 76 I1
Bauhinia Downs NT 69 M3
Baulkamaugh Vic. 30 H3
Bauple Qld 77 P5
Baw Baw National Park Vic. 21 R6, 23 J5
Bawley Point NSW 7 J13, 14 H6, 17 P5
Baxter Vic. 21 K10, 22 D7
Bayles Vic. 21 N10, 22 G7
Baynton Vic. 20 H1
Beachmere Qld 74 G9, 75 D2
Beachport SA 48 F11
Beacon WA 56 E6
Beaconsfield Tas. 95 K7
Beaconsfield Vic. 21 M8, 22 E6
Beagle Bay WA 60 H7
Bealiba Vic. 27 N10
Bearbung NSW 8 E12
Beardmore Vic. 23 K4
Beargamil NSW 6 D5
Bearii Vic. 13 L13, 30 H3
Bears Lagoon Vic. 27 P7, 30 A6
Beatrice Hill NT 64 F4
Beauchamp Vic. 27 N2, 29 N12
Beaudesert Qld 75 D11, 77 P10
Beaufort SA 39 J6
Beaufort Vic. 25 M3
Beaumaris Tas. 95 Q9
Beauty Point Tas. 95 K6
Beazleys Bridge Vic. 27 L9
Beckom NSW 6 A9, 13 Q7
Bedarra Island Qld 81 O9
Bedgerebong NSW 6 C6
Bedourie Qld 84 E13, 86 E1
Beeac Vic. 20 B10, 25 N8
Beebo Qld 9 J2, 77 L12
Beech Forest Vic. 25 N11
Beechford Tas. 95 L6
Beechmont Qld 75 E12
Beechwood NSW 9 O12
Beechworth Vic. 31 O6, 32 A3
Beedelup National Park WA 53 H13, 54 C11
Beela WA 53 H3, 54 C7
Beelbangera NSW 13 N7
Beenleigh Qld 75 F8, 77 Q9
Beerburrum Qld 74 F7
Beerwah Qld 74 F6, 77 P7
Bees Creek NT 64 D3
Bega NSW 14 G10, 33 Q6
Beggan Beggan NSW 6 D10, 14 C3
Beilpajah NSW 12 I2
Belair National Park SA 36 B11, 37 G1, 39 L9, 48 B2
Belalie North SA 39 L3, 41 K13
Belbora NSW 7 O1
Belconnen ACT 16 G2
Belfield NSW 5 N9
Belgrave Vic. 21 M7, 22 E5
Belka WA 54 I3
Bell NSW 4 H5
Bell Qld 77 M7
Bell Bay Tas. 95 K6
Bellara Qld 74 H8, 75 E1
Bellarine Vic. 20 H9, 22 B6
Bellarine Peninsula Vic. 22 B7
Bellarwi NSW 6 B9, 13 Q7
Bellata NSW 8 G7
Bellbird NSW 7 L4
Bellbird Creek Vic. 33 L12
Bellbrae Vic. 20 F11, 25 Q9
Bellbridge Vic. 13 Q13, 31 Q4, 32 C2
Bellbrook NSW 9 N10
Bellellen Vic. 25 J1, 27 J12
Belli Park Qld 74 E2
Bellingen NSW 9 P8
Bellinger River National Park NSW 9 O8
Bellingham Tas. 95 M6
Bellmount Forest NSW 6 G11, 14 E4
Bells Beach Vic. 20 F11
Bellthorpe Qld 74 D6
Belltrees NSW 7 L1
Belmont Vic. 20 F9
Belmunging WA 54 F3
Beloka NSW 14 D10, 33 L5
Belowra NSW 14 G8, 17 K11, 33 P2
Beltana SA 41 J5
Beltana Roadhouse SA 41 J5
Belton SA 41 K10
Belvidere SA 39 L10, 48 C3
Belyando Crossing Qld 78 F6
Belyuen NT 64 B3, 66 D6
Bemboka NSW 14 F10, 33 P5
Bemm River Vic. 33 M13
Ben Boyd National Park NSW 14 G12, 33 R9
Ben Bullen NSW 4 F2, 6 I5
Ben Halls Gap National Park NSW 9 K12
Ben Lomond NSW 9 L7
Ben Lomond National Park Tas. 95 O9
Bena NSW 6 A7, 13 Q4
Bena Vic. 21 O12, 22 G8
Benalla Vic. 31 K7
Benambra Vic. 14 A11, 32 F7
Benandarah NSW 17 N6
Benaraby Qld 79 P12
Benarkin Qld 77 O7
Benayeo Vic. 26 B11
Bencubbin WA 56 E6
Bendalong NSW 14 I5, 17 Q3
Bendemeer NSW 9 K10
Bendick Murrell NSW 6 E9, 14 C1
Bendidee National Park Qld 8 I1, 77 K11
Bendigo Vic. 27 Q10, 30 C8
Bendoc Vic. 14 D12, 33 L9
Bendolba NSW 7 M2
Benetook Vic. 28 F4
Benger WA 53 H3, 54 C7
Bengworden Vic. 23 P5
Beni NSW 6 F2
Benjeroop Vic. 27 O1, 29 O12
Benlidi Qld 85 P13, 87 P1
Benobble Qld 75 E11
Bentley NSW 9 P3
Benwerrin Vic. 20 D12, 25 P10
Beremboke Vic. 20 F6
Berendebba NSW 6 C8, 14 A1
Beresfield NSW 7 M4
Bergalia NSW 14 G8, 17 M9, 33 R1
Bermagui NSW 14 H9, 17 M13, 33 R4
Bermagui South NSW 14 H9, 17 M13, 33 R4
Berowra NSW 5 N6
Berrara NSW 14 I5, 17 Q3
Berri SA 39 Q7
Berridale NSW 14 D9, 16 E12, 33 L4
Berriedale Tas. 90 H5, 93 L8
Berrigan NSW 13 N12, 31 K1
Berrima NSW 7 J10, 14 H3
Berrimah NT 64 C2
Berrimal Vic. 27 M8
Berringa Vic. 20 B6, 25 O5
Berringama Vic. 14 A9, 32 F3
Berriwillock Vic. 12 F12, 27 K2, 29 K13
Berrook Vic. 28 A8, 39 R9, 48 I1
Berry NSW 7 K11, 14 I4
Berry Springs NT 64 D4
Berry Springs Nature Park NT 64 D4
Berrybank Vic. 20 A8, 25 M6
Berwick Vic. 21 M8, 22 E5
Bessiebelle Vic. 24 F8
Beswick NT 66 I10
Bet Bet Vic. 27 O11
Beta Qld 78 E11
Bete Bolong Vic. 33 J12
Bethanga Vic. 13 Q13, 31 Q4, 32 C2
Bethany SA 36 F5, 49 F6
Bethel SA 36 E2
Bethungra NSW 6 C11, 14 B4
Betoota Qld 86 H4
Beulah Tas. 94 I8
Beulah Vic. 12 E13, 26 H4
Beulah East Vic. 26 I4
Beulah West Vic. 26 H4
Bevendale NSW 6 F10, 14 E3
Beverford Vic. 12 H10, 29 N10
Beveridge Vic. 21 J3, 22 D1, 30 G12
Beverley WA 54 F4, 56 D8
Beverley East WA 54 F4
Bexhill NSW 9 Q3
Bexley NSW 5 N9
Beyal Vic. 27 J5
Biala NSW 6 G10, 14 E3
Biamanga National Park NSW 14 G10, 33 Q5
Biarra Qld 74 A9
Bibbenluke NSW 14 E11, 33 N7
Biboohra Qld 81 M6
Bicheno Tas. 93 Q2, 95 Q12
Bickley WA 52 D5
Biddon NSW 8 D12
Bidyadanga WA 60 G10
Big Desert Vic. 12 B11, 26 C1, 28 C11
Big Pats Creek Vic. 21 O6
Big Pineapple, The Qld 74 G4
Bigga NSW 6 G8, 14 E1
Biggara Vic. 14 B9, 32 H3
Biggenden Qld 77 N4
Bilambil NSW 75 H13
Bilbarin WA 54 H4
Bilbul NSW 13 O7
Bilinga Qld 75 H13
Billabong Vic. 12 D7, 28 G3
Billabong Roadhouse WA 55 C12, 56 A1
Billaricay WA 54 I5
Billilingra Siding NSW 16 G9
Billimari NSW 6 E7
Billinudgel NSW 9 Q2
Billys Creek NSW 9 O7
Biloela Qld 77 K1, 79 N13
Bilpin NSW 5 J5, 7 J6
Bilyana Qld 81 N9
Bimbaya NSW 14 F10, 33 P6
Bimbi NSW 6 D8, 14 B1
Bimbimbie NSW 17 N8
Binalong NSW 6 E10, 14 D3
Binalong Bay Tas. 95 R8
Binbee Qld 78 I3
Binda NSW 4 A13, 6 G9, 14 F2
Bindarri National Park NSW 9 P8
Bindi Vic. 14 B12, 32 G8
Bindi Bindi WA 56 D6
Bindle Qld 76 G9
Bindoon WA 54 D2, 56 C7
Bingara NSW 8 I6
Bingera Qld 77 O2
Bingil Bay Qld 81 N9
Binginwarri Vic. 23 K9
Biniguy NSW 8 H5
Binjour Qld 77 M4
Binna Burra Qld 75 E13
Binnaway NSW 8 F12
Binningup WA 53 G3, 54 C7
Binnu WA 56 A2
Binnum SA 26 A10, 48 H8
Binya NSW 13 O7
Birany Birany NT 67 O6
Birchip Vic. 12 F13, 27 K4
Birchs Bay Tas. 90 G10, 93 L10
Birdsville Qld 86 E5
Birdsville Track SA 47 K7, 86 C10
Birdwood NSW 9 N11
Birdwood SA 36 F8, 39 L9, 48 C1
Birdwoodton Vic. 12 D7, 28 G3
Birralee Tas. 95 K8
Birrego NSW 13 O10
Birregurra Vic. 20 C11, 25 O9
Birriwa NSW 6 G2
Bishopsbourne Tas. 95 L9
Bittern Vic. 21 K11, 22 E8
Black Bobs Tas. 92 I5
Black Hill SA 39 N8, 48 E1
Black Hills Tas. 90 F3, 93 K7
Black Mountain NSW 9 L8
Black Mountain Qld 74 E1
Black River Tas. 94 D4
Black Rock SA 39 L2, 41 K12
Black Springs NSW 4 D8, 6 H8
Black Springs SA 39 L5
Black Swamp NSW 9 N4, 77 O13
Blackall Qld 76 A1, 78 D13, 85 R13, 87 R1
Blackbutt Qld 77 O7
Blackdown Tableland National Park Qld 79 K12
Blackfellow Caves SA 48 G12
Blackheath NSW 4 H6, 7 J7
Blackheath Vic. 26 H7
Blackmans Bay Tas. 90 H8, 93 L9
Blackstone WA 59 P10
Blacktown NSW 5 M7
Blackville NSW 8 H12
Blackwarry Vic. 23 L8
Blackwater Qld 79 K11
Blackwood Vic. 20 F3, 25 Q3, 30 C13
Blackwood Creek Tas. 93 K1, 95 K10
Blackwood National Park Qld 78 F5
Blackwood River WA 53 D11
Bladensburg National Park Qld 85 M8
Blair Athol Qld 78 H9
Blairgowrie Vic. 20 I11
Blakehurst NSW 5 N10
Blakeville Vic. 20 F3, 25 Q3, 30 C13
Blampied Vic. 20 D2
Blanchetown SA 39 N7
Bland NSW 6 B8, 13 R6, 14 A1
Blandford NSW 9 J13
Blanket Flat NSW 6 G9, 14 E1
Blaxland NSW 5 J7, 7 K7
Blaxlands Ridge NSW 5 K5
Blayney NSW 6 G6
Bleak House Vic. 26 D6
Blessington Tas. 95 N9
Bletchley SA 36 F13
Bli Bli Qld 74 G4, 77 Q7
Blighty NSW 13 L12, 30 H1
Blinman SA 41 K6
Bloomsbury Qld 79 J4
Blow Clear NSW 6 B7, 13 Q5
Blowclear NSW 6 C5
Blue Lake SA 48 H12
Blue Lake National Park Qld 75 H6
Blue Mountains National Park NSW 4 G8, 6 I8, 7 J7, 14 G1
Blue Mountains Scenic World NSW 4 H7
Blue Water Springs Roadhouse Qld 81 M13
Bluewater Qld 81 O12
Blueys Beach NSW 7 P2
Bluff Qld 79 K11
Bluff Beach SA 38 H8
Bluff Rock NSW 9 M4, 77 N13
Blyth SA 39 K5
Boambee NSW 9 P8
Boat Harbour Tas. 94 F5
Boat Harbour Beach Tas. 94 F5
Boatswain Point SA 48 F9
Bobadah NSW 11 P13
Bobin NSW 9 N13
Bobinawarrah Vic. 31 N7, 32 A5
Bobs Creek Vic. 31 M10
Bochara Vic. 24 F5
Bodalla NSW 14 H8, 17 M10, 33 R2
Bodallin WA 56 F7
Boddington WA 52 G12, 54 E6, 56 D9
Bogan Gate NSW 6 C5
Bogangar NSW 9 Q1, 77 R11
Bogantungan Qld 78 H11
Boggabilla NSW 8 I2, 77 K12
Boggabri NSW 8 H9
Bogolong NSW 6 D8
Bogong Vic. 31 Q9, 32 D6
Bogong High Plains Vic. 31 Q9
Boho Vic. 31 J8
Boho South Vic. 31 K8
Boigbeat Vic. 27 K2, 29 K12
Boinka Vic. 12 C10, 28 D10
Boisdale Vic. 23 M5
Bokarina Qld 74 H5
Bolgart WA 54 E1
Bolinda Vic. 20 I3
Bolivia NSW 9 M4, 77 N13
Bollon Qld 76 E10
Bolton Vic. 29 K8
Boltons Bore Vic. 28 A9, 39 R10, 48 I2
Bolwarra Vic. 24 D9
Bolwarrah Vic. 20 E4, 25 P3, 30 B13
Bomaderry NSW 7 K11, 14 I4
Bombala NSW 14 E11, 33 N7
Bomera NSW 8 G12
Bonalbo NSW 9 O3, 77 P12
Bonang Vic. 14 D12, 33 L9
Bonang West Vic. 14 D12, 33 K9
Bondi NSW 5 O9
Bondi Gulf National Park NSW 14 E12, 33 N8
Bondo NSW 6 E12, 14 C5, 16 C1
Bonegilla Vic. 13 Q13, 31 Q4, 32 C2
Boneo Vic. 21 J12

Bongaree–Claremont 97

Bongaree Qld 74 H8, 75 E1, 77 Q8
Bongil Bongil National Park NSW 9 P8
Bonnie Doon Vic. 31 K10
Bonnie Rock WA 56 F6
Bonny Hills NSW 9 O12
Bonshaw NSW 9 K4, 77 M13
Bonville NSW 9 P8
Booborowie SA 39 L4
Boobyalla Tas. 95 P5
Booderee National Park JBT 7 K12, 17 R3
Bookaar Vic. 25 L7
Bookabie SA 43 L8
Bookham NSW 6 E11, 14 D4
Bool Lagoon SA 48 H9
Bool Lagoon Game Reserve SA 48 H9
Boolading WA 54 E8
Boolarra Vic. 21 R12, 23 J8
Boolba Qld 76 F10
Booleroo SA 39 K1, 41 J12
Booleroo Centre SA 39 K2, 41 J12
Boolgun SA 39 O7
Booligal NSW 13 K6
Boolite Vic. 27 J7
Boomahnoomoonah Vic. 31 L4
Boomerang Beach NSW 7 P2
Boomi NSW 8 G2, 76 I12
Boomleera NT 64 H11
Boonah Qld 75 A11, 77 P10
Boonah Vic. 20 D12, 25 P10
Boonarga Qld 77 L7
Boonoo Boonoo NSW 9 N3, 77 O12
Boonoo Boonoo National Park NSW 9 N3, 77 O12
Boonoonar Vic. 28 G5
Boorabbin National Park WA 56 H7
Booral NSW 7 N3
Boorcan Vic. 25 K8
Boorhaman Vic. 31 M5
Boorindal NSW 11 O6
Boorolite Vic. 21 R1
Boorongie Vic. 28 I9
Boorongie North Vic. 28 H9
Booroopki Vic. 26 C10
Booroorban NSW 13 K9
Boorowa NSW 6 F10, 14 D2
Boort Vic. 12 H13, 27 O5
Boosey Vic. 31 J4
Booti Booti National Park NSW 7 P2
Booyal Qld 77 N3
Boppy Mount NSW 11 O10
Borallon Qld 74 D13, 75 A6
Boralma Vic. 31 M5
Borambil NSW 6 I1
Boraning WA 54 E7
Boranup WA 53 B12
Borden WA 54 I10
Border Ranges National Park NSW 9 O1, 77 P11
Border Store NT 65 C2, 66 H5
Border Village SA 42 B8, 57 R7
Bordertown SA 48 H6
Boree NSW 6 F6
Boree Creek NSW 13 P10
Boreen Point Qld 77 P6
Borenore NSW 6 F6
Boro NSW 6 H12, 14 G5, 17 K1
Bororen Qld 77 M1, 79 P13
Borrika SA 39 O9, 48 F2
Borroloola NT 67 O13, 69 O3
Borung Vic. 27 O6
Boscabel WA 54 F9, 56 E10
Bostobrick NSW 9 O8
Boston Island SA 38 D8
Botany NSW 5 O9
Botany Bay NSW 5 O10
Botany Bay National Park NSW 5 O10
Bothwell Tas. 93 K5
Bouddi National Park NSW 5 P5
Bouldercombe Qld 79 N11
Boulia Qld 84 F9
Boulka Vic. 28 H9
Boundain WA 54 G6
Boundary Bend Vic. 12 G9, 29 L7
Bourke NSW 11 N5
Bournda National Park NSW 14 G10, 33 R6
Bow NSW 7 J2
Bow Bridge Roadhouse WA 54 F13
Bowan Park NSW 6 F6
Bowden SA 35 A3
Bowelling WA 54 E8
Bowen Qld 79 J2
Bowen Mountain NSW 5 J5
Bowenfels NSW 4 F4
Bowenvale Vic. 27 O11
Bowenville Qld 77 M8
Bower SA 39 N6
Boweya Vic. 31 L5
Bowhill SA 39 N9, 48 E1
Bowling Alley Point NSW 9 K12
Bowling Green Bay National Park Qld 78 F1, 81 P13
Bowmans SA 39 K6
Bowna NSW 13 Q13, 31 Q3, 32 D1
Bowning NSW 6 F11, 14 D4
Bowral NSW 7 J10, 14 I3
Bowraville NSW 9 O9
Bowser Vic. 31 M5
Box Creek Qld 76 A5, 87 R5
Box Hill Vic. 21 K6, 22 D4
Box Tank NSW 10 D12
Boxwood Vic. 31 K5
Boxwood Hill WA 56 F11
Boyanup WA 53 G6, 54 C8
Boydtown NSW 33 Q8
Boyeo Vic. 26 D6
Boyer Tas. 90 F4, 93 K8
Boyland Qld 75 E10
Boyne Island Qld 79 P12
Boys Town Qld 75 D11
Boyup Brook WA 54 E9, 56 D11
Bracalba Qld 74 E8
Brackendale NSW 9 L11
Bracknell Tas. 95 K10
Braddon ACT 15 E2
Bradford Vic. 27 P10, 30 B9
Bradvale Vic. 20 A6, 25 M5
Brady Creek SA 39 M6
Braefield NSW 9 J12
Braemar Bay NSW 16 D10
Braeside Qld 9 M1, 77 N11
Braidwood NSW 6 H13, 14 G6, 17 L4
Bramfield SA 38 B5
Bramley WA 53 B9
Brampton Island Qld 79 L4
Bramston Beach Qld 81 N8
Brandon Qld 78 H1, 81 Q13
Brandy Creek Vic. 21 P9, 22 H6
Branxholm Tas. 95 O7
Branxholme Vic. 24 E6
Branxton NSW 7 M3
Brawlin NSW 6 D11, 14 B3
Bray Junction SA 48 F10
Breadalbane NSW 6 H11, 14 F4
Breadalbane Tas. 95 M9
Break O Day Vic. 21 M2, 22 E1, 30 H12
Breakfast Creek NSW 6 I3
Breakfast Creek NSW 6 E8, 14 D1
Bream Creek Tas. 91 N5, 93 O8
Breamlea Vic. 20 G11, 22 A7, 25 R8
Brecon SA 48 G6
Bredbo NSW 14 E8, 16 G8, 33 N1
Breelong NSW 6 F1, 8 D13
Breeza NSW 8 I11
Bremer Bay WA 56 G11
Brentwood SA 38 H9
Brentwood Vic. 26 G4
Breona Tas. 93 J1, 95 J10
Bretti NSW 9 M13
Brewarrina NSW 11 Q5
Brewongle NSW 4 C5
Brewster Vic. 20 A3, 25 N3
Briagolong Vic. 23 N4, 32 C13
Bribbaree NSW 6 C9, 14 B1
Bribie Island Qld 75 F1
Bribie Island National Park Qld 74 H7, 75 F1
Bridge Inn Vic. 27 J11
Bridgenorth Tas. 95 L8
Bridgetown WA 54 D10, 56 D11
Bridgewater SA 36 D11, 37 H1
Bridgewater Tas. 90 H4, 93 L7
Bridgewater on Loddon Vic. 27 P9, 30 A7
Bridport Tas. 95 N6
Brigalow Qld 77 L7
Bright Vic. 31 P8, 32 C6
Brighton SA 36 A11, 37 F2
Brighton Tas. 90 H3, 93 L7
Brighton Vic. 21 J7, 22 D5
Brighton Le Sands NSW 5 N9
Brightview Qld 74 B13
Brightwaters NSW 5 Q1
Brim Vic. 12 E13, 26 H5
Brimbago SA 39 P13, 48 H6
Brimboal Vic. 24 C3
Brimin Vic. 13 O13, 31 M4
Brimpaen Vic. 26 G11
Brindabella National Park NSW 6 F12, 14 D5, 16 E1
Bringagee NSW 13 M8
Bringalbert Vic. 26 B10, 48 I8
Bringelly NSW 5 K9
Bringenbrong Bridge NSW 14 B8, 32 H2
Brinkley SA 36 H13
Brinkworth SA 39 K5
Brisbane Qld 73, 74 G12, 75 D5, 77 P9
Brisbane Forest Park Qld 74 D12
Brisbane Ranges National Park Vic. 20 F5, 25 Q5
Brisbane River Qld 75 C6
Brisbane Water National Park NSW 5 O4, 5 O4
Brit Brit Vic. 24 E3
Brittons Swamp Tas. 94 C4
Brixton Qld 78 B11, 85 Q11
Broad Arrow WA 56 I5
Broadbeach Qld 75 G11
Broadford Vic. 21 K1, 30 G11
Broadmarsh Tas. 90 G3, 93 L7
Broadwater NSW 9 Q3, 77 Q13
Broadwater Vic. 24 F7
Broadwater National Park NSW 9 Q4, 77 Q13
Broadway NSW 3 A13
Brocklehurst NSW 6 E2
Brocklesby NSW 13 P12, 31 O2
Brockman National Park WA 54 D11
Brocks Creek NT 64 G10
Brodies Plains NSW 9 K6
Brodribb River Vic. 33 K12
Brogo NSW 14 G10, 33 Q5
Broke NSW 7 L4
Broken Hill NSW 10 B12
Bromelton Qld 75 C11
Brompton SA 35 A2
Bronte Park Tas. 92 I3, 94 I13
Bronzewing Vic. 28 H10
Brooker SA 38 D6
Brooklands Qld 77 N7
Brooklyn NSW 5 O5
Brookstead Qld 77 M9
Brookton WA 54 F5, 56 D8
Brookville Vic. 14 A12, 23 Q1, 32 F10
Brooloo Qld 74 D2
Broome WA 60 G9
Broomehill WA 54 H9, 56 E11
Broomfield Vic. 20 D2, 25 O2, 27 O13, 30 A12
Brooms Head NSW 9 Q6
Brooweena Qld 77 O4
Broughton Vic. 26 C6
Broughton Island NSW 7 O3
Broula NSW 6 E8, 14 D1
Broulee NSW 14 H7, 17 N8
Brownlow SA 36 I1, 39 M7
Brownlow Hill NSW 5 K10
Browns Plains Qld 75 D7
Browns Plains Vic. 31 O3, 32 A1
Bruarong Vic. 31 P6, 32 B4
Bruce SA 41 J11
Bruce Rock WA 54 I3, 56 F8
Brucefield SA 38 I5
Brucknell Vic. 25 K10
Brukunga SA 36 E10
Brungle NSW 6 D12, 14 C5, 16 A1
Brunswick Heads NSW 9 Q2, 77 Q12
Brunswick Junction WA 53 H4, 54 C7
Bruny Island Tas. 90 H12, 93 M11
Brushgrove NSW 9 P5
Bruthen Vic. 23 Q3, 32 G12
Bryden Qld 74 C10
Brymaroo Qld 77 N8
Buangor Vic. 25 L2, 27 L13
Buaraba Qld 74 A11
Buaraba Creek Qld 74 A12
Bucasia Qld 79 L5
Bucca Qld 77 O2
Buccan Qld 75 E8
Buccaneer Archipelago WA 60 I5
Buccarumbi NSW 9 N6
Buccleuch SA 39 O10, 48 F3
Buchan Vic. 14 B13, 32 I11
Buchan South Vic. 14 B13, 32 H11
Bucheen Creek Vic. 14 A9, 32 F4
Buckenderra NSW 14 D8, 16 D10, 33 L2
Bucketty NSW 5 N1, 7 L5
Buckingham SA 48 H6
Buckingham WA 54 E8
Buckland Tas. 91 M2, 93 N7
Buckland Vic. 31 P9, 32 B7
Buckleboo SA 38 E2, 40 D12
Buckley Vic. 20 E10
Buckleys Swamp Vic. 24 G6
Buckrabanyule Vic. 27 N6
Budawang National Park NSW 6 I13, 14 H6, 17 N3
Buddabaddah NSW 6 A1, 11 R11
Buddigower NSW 6 A8, 13 Q6
Buderim Qld 74 G4, 77 Q7
Budgee Budgee NSW 6 H3
Budgeree Vic. 23 J8
Budgeree East Vic. 23 J8
Budgerum Vic. 27 N3, 29 N13
Budgewoi NSW 5 Q2
Buffalo Vic. 22 I10
Bugaldie NSW 8 E11
Bugilbone NSW 8 D7
Builyan Qld 77 M1
Bukalong NSW 14 E11, 33 N6
Bukkulla NSW 9 K5
Bulahdelah NSW 7 O3
Bulart Vic. 24 F4
Buldah Vic. 14 E12, 33 M9
Bulga NSW 7 L3, 9 N12
Bulgandramine NSW 6 D3
Bulgandry NSW 13 P12, 31 O1
Bulgobac Tas. 94 E9
Bull Creek SA 36 D13, 37 H4
Bull Island SA 48 G8
Bulla NT 66 C13, 68 C2
Bulla Vic. 20 I5, 22 C3
Bullaburra NSW 4 I7
Bullarah NSW 8 F5
Bullaring WA 54 H5
Bullarook Vic. 20 D4, 25 P3, 30 B13
Bullarto Vic. 20 F3, 25 Q2, 27 Q13, 30 C12
Bullarto South Vic. 20 F3
Bullengarook Vic. 20 G4
Bullengarook East Vic. 20 G3, 22 A2, 25 R3, 30 D13
Bulleringa National Park Qld 80 I8
Bullfinch WA 56 G6
Bullhead Creek Vic. 31 R6, 32 D3
Bulli NSW 5 M13
Bullio NSW 4 G13, 6 I9, 14 H2
Bullioh Vic. 31 R5, 32 E2
Bullita NT 68 D3
Bullock Creek Qld 81 J8
Bullocks Flat NSW 16 B13
Bullsbrook WA 52 D2, 54 D3
Bullumwaal Vic. 14 A13, 23 P3, 32 F12
Bulman NT 67 K8
Buln Buln Vic. 21 P9, 22 H6
Buln Buln East Vic. 21 Q9, 22 I6
Bulwer Qld 75 G1
Bulyee WA 54 G5
Bumbaldry NSW 6 E8, 14 C1
Bumberry NSW 6 E6
Bumbunga SA 39 K5
Bunbartha Vic. 30 H5
Bunburra Qld 75 A11
Bunbury WA 53 F4, 54 C8, 56 C10
Bundaberg Qld 77 O2
Bundaburrah NSW 6 C7
Bundalaguah Vic. 23 M6
Bundaleer SA 39 K3
Bundalong Vic. 13 O13, 31 L3
Bundalong South Vic. 13 O13, 31 L4
Bundanoon NSW 7 J10, 14 H3
Bundarra NSW 9 K7
Bundeena NSW 5 N11
Bundella NSW 8 H12
Bunding Vic. 20 E4, 25 Q3, 30 C13
Bundjalung National Park NSW 9 Q4, 77 Q13
Bundook NSW 7 N1, 9 M13
Bundure NSW 13 N10
Bunga NSW 14 G10, 33 R5
Bungal Vic. 20 E5, 25 P4
Bungarby NSW 14 E10, 33 M6
Bungaree Vic. 20 D4, 25 P3, 30 B13
Bungawalbin National Park NSW 9 P4
Bungeet Vic. 31 L5
Bungendore NSW 6 H12, 14 F5, 17 J2
Bungil Vic. 31 R3, 32 E1
Bungle Bungle National Park *see* Purnululu National Park
Bungonia NSW 6 I11, 14 G4
Bungowannah NSW 13 P13, 31 O3, 32 B1
Bungulla NSW 9 M4, 77 N13
Bungulla WA 54 H3
Bunguluke Vic. 27 M5
Bungunya Qld 8 G1, 76 I11
Bungwahl NSW 7 O3
Buninyong Vic. 20 C5, 25 O4
Bunnaloo NSW 13 K12, 30 E2
Bunnan NSW 7 K1
Buntine WA 56 D5
Bunya Mountains National Park Qld 77 M7
Bunyah NSW 7 O2
Bunyan NSW 14 E8, 16 G10, 33 N2
Bunyip Vic. 21 O9, 22 G6
Buraja NSW 13 O12, 31 M2
Burbong ACT 16 I2
Burcher NSW 6 B7, 13 R5
Burekup WA 53 H4, 54 C8
Burgooney NSW 13 P4
Burke & Wills Roadhouse Qld 80 B12, 83 G12
Burkes Flat Vic. 27 N9
Burketown Qld 83 E8
Burleigh Head National Park Qld 75 H12
Burleigh Heads Qld 75 H12, 77 Q10
Burnbank Vic. 20 A1
Burnett Heads Qld 77 O2
Burnie Tas. 94 G6
Burns Beach WA 52 B3
Burns Creek Tas. 95 N9
Burnt Yards NSW 6 F7
Buronga NSW 12 D7, 28 G3
Burpengary Qld 74 F9, 75 D2, 77 P8
Burra SA 39 L5
Burraboi NSW 13 J11, 27 R1, 29 R11
Burracoppin WA 56 F7
Burraga NSW 4 B9, 6 H8, 14 F1
Burragate NSW 14 F11, 33 P8
Burramine Vic. 31 K3
Burramine South Vic. 31 K4
Burrandana NSW 6 B13, 13 R11
Burrawang NSW 7 J10, 14 I3
Burraway NSW 6 D1
Burrell Creek NSW 7 O1, 9 N13
Burren Junction NSW 8 E7
Burrereo Vic. 27 J8
Burrill Lake NSW 7 J13, 14 I6, 17 P4
Burringbar NSW 9 Q2, 77 Q11
Burringurrah WA 55 G8, 58 A8
Burrinjuck NSW 6 E11, 14 D4
Burroin Vic. 26 H2, 28 H13
Burrowa–Pine Mountain National Park Vic. 14 A8, 32 F2
Burrowye Vic. 13 R13, 14 A8, 32 F1
Burrum Vic. 27 J9
Burrum Coast National Park Qld 77 P3
Burrum Heads Qld 77 P3
Burrum River National Park Qld 77 P3
Burrumbeet Vic. 20 B3, 25 N3
Burrumboot Vic. 30 F7
Burrumbuttock NSW 13 P12, 31 P2
Bushfield Vic. 24 I9
Bushy Park Tas. 90 D3, 93 J7
Bushy Park Vic. 23 M5
Busselton WA 53 D7, 54 B9, 56 C10
Butchers Ridge Vic. 14 C12, 32 I9
Bute SA 39 J5
Butler Tanks SA 38 E6
Butlers Gorge Tas. 92 H4, 94 H13
Butmaroo NSW 17 J2
Butterleaf National Park NSW 9 M5
Buxton NSW 5 J12, 7 J9, 14 I2
Buxton Qld 77 P3
Buxton Vic. 21 O3, 22 G1, 31 J12
Byabarra NSW 9 O12
Byaduk Vic. 24 F6
Byaduk North Vic. 24 F6
Byawatha Vic. 31 N5
Byfield National Park Qld 79 O9
Byford WA 52 D7, 54 D4
Bylands Vic. 21 J2, 22 C1, 30 F12
Bylong NSW 6 I3
Bymount Qld 76 G5
Byrneside Vic. 30 G6
Byrnestown Qld 77 N4
Byrneville Vic. 26 H8
Byrock NSW 11 P7
Byron Bay NSW 9 R2, 77 R12
Cabarita Vic. 12 D7, 28 G3
Cabarlah Qld 77 N9
Cabawin Qld 77 K8
Cabbage Tree Creek Vic. 33 K12
Cabbage Tree Point Qld 75 G8
Caboolture Qld 74 F8, 75 C1, 77 P8
Caboonbah Qld 74 B9
Cabramatta NSW 5 M9
Cabramurra NSW 14 C8, 16 B8, 33 J1
Cactus Beach SA 43 L9
Cadbury Schweppes Chocolate Factory Tas. 90 H4
Caddens Flat Vic. 24 F2, 26 F13
Cadell SA 39 O6
Cadney Homestead SA 45 P8
Cadoux WA 56 D6
Cahills Crossing NT 65 Q2, 66 H5
Caiguna WA 57 N8
Cairns Qld 81 N6
Cairns Bay Tas. 90 E10, 93 K10
Calca SA 43 P13
Calder Tas. 94 F6
Caldwell NSW 13 J12, 30 D1
Calen Qld 79 K4
Calga NSW 5 O4
Calingiri WA 54 E1, 56 D7
Caliph SA 39 P8
Calivil Vic. 27 Q6, 30 B5
Callala Bay NSW 7 K11, 14 I4, 17 R1
Callawadda Vic. 27 J10
Calleen NSW 6 A7, 13 Q5
Callide Qld 77 K1, 79 N13
Callignee Vic. 23 K8
Callignee North Vic. 23 L8
Callington SA 36 F12, 39 M10, 48 D2
Calliope Qld 79 P12
Caloona NSW 8 G2, 76 I12
Caloote SA 36 I10
Caloundra Qld 74 H6, 77 Q7
Caltowie SA 39 K3, 41 K13
Calulu Vic. 23 P4, 32 E13
Calvert Vic. 25 J3
Camballin WA 61 J9
Cambarville Vic. 21 P4
Camberwell NSW 7 L3
Cambewarra NSW 7 J11, 14 I4
Cambooya Qld 77 N9
Cambrai SA 36 I6, 39 M8, 48 D1
Cambrian Hill Vic. 20 C4
Cambridge Tas. 91 J5, 93 M8
Cambroon Bridge Qld 74 D4
Camdale Tas. 94 G5
Camden NSW 5 K10, 7 K8, 14 I1
Camena Tas. 94 G6
Cameron Corner 10 A2, 86 H13
Camira Creek NSW 9 P4, 77 P13
Camooweal Qld 69 R11, 84 B2
Camooweal Caves National Park Qld 69 R11, 84 B2
Camp Coorong SA 39 M12, 48 D4
Campania Tas. 91 J3, 93 M7
Campbell ACT 15 H6
Campbell Town Tas. 93 M2, 95 N12
Campbells Bridge Vic. 27 J11
Campbells Creek Vic. 27 Q12, 30 C10
Campbells Forest Vic. 27 Q9, 30 B7
Campbells Pocket Qld 74 E8, 75 B1
Campbells River NSW 4 C9
Campbelltown NSW 5 L11, 7 K8
Campbelltown Vic. 20 D1, 25 P1, 27 P12, 30 A11
Campbellville Qld 74 G6
Camperdown Vic. 25 L8
Campwin Beach Qld 79 L5
Camurra NSW 8 H5
Canary Island Vic. 27 P4, 30 A3
Canary Island South Vic. 27 O5, 30 A3
Canbelego NSW 11 O10
Canberra ACT 6 G12, 14 E5, 15, 16 G2
Candelo NSW 14 G10, 33 P6
Cangai NSW 9 O5
Cania Gorge National Park Qld 77 L2
Caniambo Vic. 31 J6
Canimble NSW 6 E7
Cann River Vic. 14 E13, 33 N11
Canna WA 56 C4
Cannawigara SA 48 H6
Cannie Vic. 27 M3, 29 M13
Canning Qld 74 G9, 75 D1
Canning Stock Route WA 58 G9, 61 N12
Cannington WA 52 C5
Cannon Creek Qld 75 A12
Cannons Creek Vic. 21 L10
Cannonvale Qld 79 K3
Cannum Vic. 26 G6
Canomodine NSW 6 F6
Canonba NSW 8 A12, 11 R9
Canowie SA 39 L4
Canowindra NSW 6 E7
Canteen Creek NT 69 M13, 71 M2
Canunda National Park SA 48 G11
Canungra Qld 75 E11
Capalaba Qld 74 H13, 75 F6
Caparra NSW 9 N13
Cape Arid National Park WA 57 K10
Cape Barren Island Tas. 92 B12, 95 Q2
Cape Borda SA 38 F12
Cape Bridgewater Vic. 24 C9
Cape Byron NSW 9 R2
Cape Clear Vic. 20 B6, 25 N5
Cape Crawford NT 69 N4
Cape Gantheaume Conservation Park SA 38 H12
Cape Gantheaume Wilderness Protection Area SA 38 H13
Cape Hillsborough National Park Qld 79 K4
Cape Jervis SA 37 B9, 39 J11, 48 A4
Cape Le Grand National Park WA 57 J11
Cape Leeuwin WA 53 C13, 333, 335
Cape Melville National Park Qld 82 H12
Cape Naturaliste WA 53 B6
Cape Palmerston National Park Qld 79 L6
Cape Paterson Vic. 22 G10
Cape Range National Park WA 55 B3
Cape Tribulation Qld 81 M4
Cape Upstart National Park Qld 78 I1
Cape Vlamingh WA 54 B4
Cape Woolamai Vic. 21 L13, 22 E9
Cape York Peninsula Qld 80 G2, 82 C10
Capel WA 53 F6, 54 C8, 56 C10
Capella Qld 78 I10
Capels Crossing Vic. 27 P2, 29 P13, 30 A1
Capertee NSW 4 E1, 6 I5
Capietha SA 38 A1, 43 Q11
Capricorn Region Qld 78 E11
Capricorn Roadhouse WA 58 E6
Capricornia Cays National Park Qld 79 R11
Captain Billy Landing Qld 82 D5
Captains Flat NSW 6 H13, 14 F6, 16 I5
Carabost NSW 14 A6
Caragabal NSW 6 C8
Caralue SA 38 E4
Caralulup Vic. 20 B1
Caramut Vic. 24 I6
Carapooee Vic. 27 M9
Carapook Vic. 24 D4
Carawa SA 43 P10
Carboor Vic. 31 N7, 32 A5
Carbunup River WA 53 C8
Carcoar NSW 6 G7
Carcuma SA 39 O12, 48 F4
Cardigan Village Vic. 20 B3, 25 O3
Cardinia Vic. 21 M9, 22 F6
Cardross Vic. 12 D7, 28 G4
Cardwell Qld 81 N10
Cargerie Vic. 20 D6, 25 P5
Cargo NSW 6 F6
Carinda NSW 8 A8
Carisbrook Vic. 27 O11, 30 A10
Carlisle River Vic. 20 A13, 25 M10
Carlsruhe Vic. 20 G2, 25 R2, 27 R13, 30 D11
Carlton Tas. 91 L6, 93 N8
Carlton Vic. 19 E3
Carlwood NSW 4 E6
Carmila Qld 79 L7
Carnamah WA 56 C5
Carnarvon WA 55 B8
Carnarvon National Park Qld 76 D2, 78 I13
Carnegie Homestead WA 58 I10
Carngham Vic. 20 B4
Caroda NSW 8 I7
Caroline SA 24 A6, 48 I12
Caroling WA 54 G4
Caroona NSW 8 I12
Carpa SA 38 F5
Carpendeit Vic. 25 L9
Carpenter Rocks SA 48 G12
Carrabin WA 56 F7
Carrajung Vic. 23 L8
Carrajung South Vic. 23 L8
Carranballac Vic. 25 L4
Carraragarmungee Vic. 31 N5
Carrathool NSW 13 M7
Carrick Tas. 95 L9
Carrickalinga SA 37 D6
Carrieton SA 41 K10
Carroll NSW 8 I10
Carroll Gap NSW 8 I10
Carron Vic. 27 J7
Carrow Brook NSW 7 L2
Carrowidgin NSW 14 D11, 33 L8
Carrum Downs Vic. 21 L9
Carters Ridge Qld 74 E2
Cartmeticup WA 54 G8
Carwarp Vic. 12 D8, 28 G5
Cascade WA 56 I10
Cascade National Park NSW 9 O8
Cashmore Vic. 24 D9
Casino NSW 9 P3, 77 P12
Cassilis NSW 6 I1
Cassilis Vic. 14 A12, 32 F9
Castambul SA 36 C9
Castaways Beach Qld 74 H2
Castella Vic. 21 M4
Casterton Vic. 24 C4
Castle Forbes Bay Tas. 90 E9, 93 K10
Castle Hill NSW 5 M7
Castle Tower National Park Qld 79 P13
Castleburn Vic. 23 N3, 32 D11
Castlemaine Vic. 27 Q11, 30 C10
Casuarina NT 64 C2
Cataby Roadhouse WA 56 B6
Catamaran Tas. 93 J13
Catani Vic. 21 N10
Cathcart NSW 14 F11, 33 O7
Cathedral Rock National Park NSW 9 N8
Catherine Field NSW 5 K10
Catherine Hill Bay NSW 5 R1, 7 M5
Cathkin Vic. 21 N1
Cathundral NSW 6 C1, 8 B13
Cattai NSW 5 M5
Cattai National Park NSW 5 L5
Catumnal Vic. 27 N5
Caulfield Vic. 21 K7
Cavan NSW 6 F11, 14 D4
Caveat Vic. 30 I10
Cavendish Vic. 24 F4
Caveside Tas. 94 I9
Cawdor NSW 5 K11
Cawongla NSW 9 P2, 77 Q12
Cecil Park NSW 5 L8
Cecil Plains Qld 77 M9
Cedar Bay National Park Qld 81 M3
Cedar Brush NSW 5 O1
Cedar Brush Creek NSW 5 O1
Cedar Glen Qld 75 D13
Cedar Grove Qld 75 D9
Cedar Party Creek NSW 9 N13
Ceduna SA 43 N9
Cement Creek Vic. 21 O5, 22 G3
Central Castra Tas. 94 H7
Central Coast NSW 5 Q5, 7 M7
Central Colo NSW 5 K4
Central Mangrove NSW 5 O2
Central McDonald NSW 5 M3
Central Tilba NSW 14 H9, 17 M12, 33 R3
Ceratodus Qld 77 L3
Ceres NSW 6 D2
Ceres Vic. 20 F9, 25 Q8
Cervantes WA 56 B6
Cessnock NSW 7 M4
Chaelundi National Park NSW 9 N7
Chain of Ponds SA 36 D8
Chakola NSW 16 G10
Challambra Vic. 26 I6
Chambers Flat Qld 75 D8
Chambers Pillar Historical Reserve NT 71 J11
Chambigne NSW 9 O6
Chandada SA 38 A1, 43 Q12
Chandler SA 45 N4
Chandlers Creek Vic. 14 E12, 33 M10
Channel Country Qld 84 G10
Chapman River SA 37 A11
Chapple Vale Vic. 25 L11
Charam Vic. 26 D11
Charleston SA 36 E9
Charlestown NSW 7 M5
Charleville Qld 76 B6
Charley Creek Vic. 20 A13
Charleyong NSW 6 I12, 14 G5, 17 M2
Charlotte Pass NSW 14 C9, 16 A13, 33 J4
Charlton NSW 11 Q5
Charlton Vic. 27 M6
Charters Towers Qld 78 E2
Chasm Creek Tas. 94 G6
Chatsbury NSW 6 I10, 14 G3
Chatswood NSW 5 O8
Chatsworth NSW 9 Q5
Chatsworth Vic. 24 I6
Cheepie Qld 87 Q7
Cheesemans Creek NSW 6 F5
Chelsea Vic. 21 K8
Chepstowe Vic. 20 A4
Cherbourg Qld 77 N6
Chermside Qld 74 G11, 75 D4
Cherokee Vic. 20 H2
Cheshunt Vic. 31 N9
Chesney Vale Vic. 31 L6
Chesterton Range National Park Qld 76 E6
Chetwynd Vic. 24 C2, 26 C13
Chevallum Qld 74 G4
Chevoit Vic. 21 M1
Chewton Vic. 27 Q11, 30 C10
Chidlow WA 52 F4, 54 D3
Chifley WA 57 K6
Childers Qld 77 O3
Childers Vic. 21 Q11, 22 I7
Chilla Well NT 70 E4
Chillagoe Qld 81 K7
Chillagoe–Mungana Caves National Park Qld 81 K7
Chillingham NSW 9 Q1
Chillingollah Vic. 12 G10, 29 L10
Chilpanunda SA 43 Q11
Chiltern Vic. 13 P13, 31 O4, 32 A2
Chiltern Box–Ironbark National Park Vic. 31 O4, 32 A2
Chiltern Valley Vic. 31 N4, 32 A2
Chinaman Wells SA 48 F10
Chinbingina SA 43 P10
Chinchilla Qld 77 K7
Chinderah NSW 9 Q1, 75 H13, 77 Q11
Chinkapook Vic. 12 F10, 29 K10
Chintin Vic. 20 I3
Chittering WA 54 D2
Chorregon Qld 85 N9
Christmas Creek Qld 75 C13
Christmas Hills Tas. 94 C4
Christmas Hills Vic. 21 L5
Chudleigh Tas. 94 I9
Churchill Vic. 23 K8
Churchill Island Vic. 21 M13, 22 E9
Churchill National Park Vic. 21 L7, 22 E5
Chute Vic. 25 M2, 27 M13
City Beach WA 52 B4
Clackline WA 54 G2, 54 E3
Clairview Qld 79 L7
Clandulla NSW 6 I4
Clare Qld 78 G1
Clare SA 39 L5
Clare Valley SA 39 K5
Claremont Tas. 90 H4, 93 L8

98 Clarence–East Kurrajong

Clarence NSW 4 G4
Clarence Point Tas. 95 K6
Clarence Town NSW 7 N3
Clarendon NSW 5 K6
Clarendon Qld 74 B12
Clarendon SA 36 B12, 37 G3, 39 K10, 48 B2
Clarendon Vic. 20 D5, 25 P4
Clarkefield Vic. 20 I3, 22 B2, 30 E13
Clarkes Hill Vic. 20 D3
Claude Road Tas. 94 H8
Clay Wells SA 48 G10
Claypans SA 39 N9, 48 E1
Clayton Qld 77 O2
Clear Lake Vic. 26 F11
Clear Ridge NSW 6 B7, 13 R5
Cleaverville WA 55 G1
Cleland Conservation Park SA 36 C10, 37 G1
Clematis Vic. 21 M7
Clements Gap SA 39 J4
Clermont Qld 78 H9
Cleve SA 38 F5
Cleveland Qld 74 I13, 75 F6, 77 Q9
Cleveland Tas. 93 M1, 95 M11
Clifton NSW 5 M12
Clifton Qld 77 N10
Clifton Beach Tas. 91 J8, 93 M9
Clifton Creek Vic. 23 Q3, 32 F12
Clifton Springs Vic. 20 H9, 22 A6
Clinton Centre SA 39 J7
Clintonvale Qld 77 O10
Clonbinane Vic. 21 K2
Cloncurry Qld 84 G4
Clontarf Qld 74 G10, 75 E3
Closeburn Qld 74 E11, 75 C4
Clouds Creek NSW 9 O7
Cloven Hills Vic. 25 L7
Cloyna Qld 77 N5
Cluan Tas. 95 K9
Club Terrace Vic. 14 D13, 33 M11
Clunes NSW 9 Q3, 77 Q12
Clunes Vic. 20 C2, 25 Q2, 27 O13, 30 A11
Clybucca NSW 9 O10
Clyde Vic. 21 L9
Clydebank Vic. 23 N6
Clydesdale Vic. 20 E1
Coal Creek Qld 74 B9
Coalcliff NSW 5 M12, 7 K9
Coaldale NSW 9 O5
Coalstoun Lakes Qld 77 N4
Coalstoun Lakes National Park Qld 77 N4
Coalville Vic. 21 R10
Cobains Vic. 23 N6
Cobaki NSW 75 H13
Cobar NSW 11 N10
Cobargo NSW 14 G9, 17 L13, 33 Q4
Cobark NSW 7 M1, 9 L13
Cobaw Vic. 20 H2
Cobbadah NSW 8 I8
Cobbannah Vic. 23 N3, 32 D12
Cobbitty NSW 5 K10, 7 K8, 14 I1
Cobbora NSW 6 G1
Cobden Vic. 25 K9
Cobdogla SA 39 P7
Cobera SA 39 P8, 48 G1
Cobram Vic. 13 M13, 31 J3
Cobrico Vic. 25 K9
Cobungra Vic. 31 R11, 32 E8
Coburg Vic. 21 J6, 22 D3
Cocamba Vic. 29 K9
Cochranes Creek Vic. 27 N9
Cockaleechie SA 38 D7
Cockatoo Vic. 21 M7, 22 F5
Cockatoo Valley SA 36 D6, 49 A9
Cockburn SA 10 A12, 41 Q9
Cockle Creek Tas. 93 J13
Cocklebiddy WA 57 O8
Cocoparra National Park NSW 13 O6
Codrington Vic. 24 F9
Coen Qld 82 E11
Coffin Bay SA 38 C8
Coffin Bay National Park SA 38 B8
Coffs Harbour NSW 9 P8
Coghills Creek Vic. 20 C2, 25 Q2, 27 O13, 30 A12
Cohuna Vic. 13 J12, 27 Q3, 30 C2
Coimadai Vic. 20 G4
Colac Vic. 20 B11, 25 N9
Colac Colac Vic. 14 A9, 32 G3
Colbinabbin Vic. 30 F7
Colbinabbin West Vic. 30 E7
Coldstream Vic. 21 M5, 22 E3
Cole Crossing SA 37 H5
Coleambally NSW 13 N9
Colebrook Tas. 90 I1, 93 M6
Coledale NSW 5 M13
Coleraine Vic. 24 E4
Coles Bay Tas. 93 Q4, 95 Q13
Colignan Vic. 12 E8, 28 H5
Colinroobie NSW 13 P8
Colinton NSW 16 G7
Colinton Qld 74 A7
Collarenebri NSW 8 D5
Collaroy NSW 5 P7, 6 I2
Collector NSW 6 H11, 14 F4
College Park SA 35 H5
Collerina NSW 11 P4
Colley SA 38 A3, 43 Q13
Collie NSW 8 C13
Collie WA 54 D8, 56 C10
Collie Burn WA 54 D8
Collie Cardiff WA 54 D8
Collier Range National Park WA 58 C8
Collingullie NSW 6 A12, 13 Q10
Collins Cap Tas. 90 G5
Collinsfield SA 39 K4
Collinsvale Tas. 90 G5, 93 L8
Collinsville Qld 78 I3
Collombatti Rail NSW 9 O10
Colly Blue NSW 8 H12
Colo NSW 5 L4
Colo Heights NSW 5 K3, 7 K6
Colo Vale NSW 7 J9, 14 I2
Colquhoun Vic. 23 R4, 32 H13
Colton SA 38 B4
Comara NSW 9 N9
Comaum SA 24 A2, 26 A13, 48 I10
Combara NSW 8 C11
Combienbar Vic. 14 E13, 33 M10
Comboyne NSW 9 N12
Come-by-Chance NSW 8 D8
Comet Qld 79 J11
Comleroy Road NSW 5 K5
Commissioners Flat Qld 74 E6
Compton Downs NSW 11 P6
Conara Tas. 93 M2, 95 N11
Conargo NSW 13 L11
Concordia SA 36 D5
Condah Vic. 24 E6
Condamine Qld 77 J7
Condingup WA 57 K10
Condobolin NSW 6 A5, 13 Q3
Condong NSW 9 Q1
Condoulpe NSW 12 G9, 29 N7
Condowie SA 39 K5
Congo NSW 14 H8, 17 N9
Congupna Vic. 30 I5
Conimbla National Park NSW 6 E7
Coningham Tas. 90 H9, 93 L10
Conjola NSW 7 J12, 14 I5, 17 P3
Conjola National Park NSW 17 P3
Conmurra SA 48 G9
Connangorach Vic. 26 F11
Connellys Marsh Tas. 91 M6
Connemarra NSW 8 G12
Connewarre Vic. 20 G10
Connewirricoo Vic. 24 D1, 26 D12
Conondale Qld 74 D5
Conondale National Park Qld 74 D4, 77 O7
Conway National Park Qld 79 K3
Coober Pedy SA 45 R11
Coobowie SA 38 I10
Coochin Creek Qld 74 G6
Cooee Tas. 94 G5
Cooeeinbardi Qld 74 B9
Coogee NSW 5 O9
Coojar Vic. 24 E2, 26 E13
Cook SA 42 E4
Cookamidgera NSW 6 D5
Cookardinia NSW 13 Q12
Cooke Plains SA 39 N11, 48 E3
Cooks Gap NSW 6 H2
Cooktown Qld 81 L3
Cookville Tas. 90 H13, 93 L12
Coolabah NSW 11 P8
Coolac NSW 6 D11, 14 B4
Cooladdi Qld 76 A7, 87 R7
Coolah NSW 6 H1, 8 G13
Coolah Tops National Park NSW 6 I1, 8 H13
Coolalie NSW 6 F11, 14 E3
Coolalinga NT 64 D3
Coolamon NSW 6 B11, 13 Q9
Coolana Qld 74 C13
Coolangatta Qld 9 Q1, 75 H13, 77 Q11
Coolatai NSW 9 J4, 77 L13
Coolcha SA 39 N9, 48 E1
Coolgardie WA 56 I6
Coolimba WA 56 B5
Coolongolook NSW 7 O2
Cooloolabin Qld 74 F3
Cooltong SA 39 Q6
Coolum Beach Qld 74 H3, 77 Q6
Coolup WA 52 C11, 54 C6
Cooma NSW 14 E9, 16 G11, 33 M3
Cooma Vic. 30 G6
Cooma West NSW 14 E9, 16 F11, 33 M3
Coomalbidgup WA 56 I10
Coomandook SA 39 N11, 48 E3
Coomba NSW 7 P2
Coombah Roadhouse NSW 12 C3
Coombe SA 39 P13, 48 G5
Coombell NSW 9 P3, 77 P13
Coomberdale WA 56 C6
Coombogolong NSW 8 B8
Coomera Qld 75 G10
Coominglah Qld 77 L2
Coominya Qld 74 B11, 77 O9
Coomoora Vic. 20 E2
Coonabarabran NSW 8 F11
Coonalpyn SA 39 O12, 48 F4
Coonamble NSW 8 C10
Coonarr Qld 77 O2
Coonawarra SA 24 A2, 26 A13, 48 H10
Coonerang NSW 16 G13
Coongie Lakes SA 47 P5
Coongulla Vic. 23 L5
Coongulmerang Vic. 23 O4, 32 E13
Coonong NSW 13 O10
Coonooer Bridge Vic. 27 M8
Cooper Creek SA 47 N6
Coopernook NSW 7 P1, 9 O13
Coopers Creek Vic. 23 K5
Cooplacurripa NSW 9 M12
Coopracambra National Park Vic. 14 E12, 33 N10
Coorabie SA 43 K9
Cooran Qld 74 E1, 77 P6
Cooranbong NSW 7 M5
Coorong National Park SA 39 M12, 48 D5
Coorow WA 56 C5
Cooroy Qld 74 F2, 77 P6
Cootamundra NSW 6 D10, 14 B3
Cooya Beach Qld 81 M5
Cooyal NSW 6 H3
Cooyar Qld 77 N7
Cope Cope Vic. 27 L7
Copeland NSW 7 N1
Copeville SA 39 O9, 48 F1
Copi Hollow NSW 10 E13
Copley SA 41 J4
Copmanhurst NSW 9 O5
Coppabella Qld 79 J7
Copping Tas. 91 N5, 93 N8
Cora Lynn Vic. 21 N9, 22 G6
Corack Vic. 27 K6
Corack East Vic. 27 K6
Coradgery NSW 6 C4
Coragulac Vic. 20 A10, 25 N8
Coraki NSW 9 Q3, 77 Q13
Coral Bank Vic. 31 Q7, 32 C5
Coral Bay WA 55 B5
Coral Sea 79 N1, 82 H3
Coralville NSW 7 P1, 9 O13
Coramba NSW 9 P8
Corang NSW 6 I12, 14 G5, 17 N2
Corattum SA 48 H12
Cordalba Qld 77 O3
Cordering WA 54 E8
Coree South NSW 13 M11
Coreen NSW 13 O12, 31 M2
Corfield Qld 85 M6
Corindhap Vic. 20 C7, 25 O5
Corindi NSW 9 P7
Corinella Vic. 21 M12, 22 F8
Corinna Tas. 94 C9
Corio Vic. 20 F8, 22 A6, 25 R7
Cornella Vic. 30 E8
Corner Store Qld 10 A1, 47 R11, 86 H13
Cornwall Tas. 95 Q10
Corny Point SA 38 G9
Corobimilla NSW 13 O9
Coromby Vic. 26 I8
Coronation Beach WA 56 A3
Coronet Bay Vic. 21 M12, 22 F8
Corop Vic. 30 F6
Cororooke Vic. 20 A11, 25 N8
Corowa NSW 13 O13, 31 M3
Corra Linn Tas. 95 M9
Corrigin WA 54 H5, 56 E8
Corrimal NSW 5 M13, 7 K9
Corringle NSW 6 B7, 13 R5
Corringle Vic. 33 J13
Corroboree Park Tavern NT 64 G5
Corryong Vic. 14 B8, 32 G2
Corunna NSW 17 M12
Cosgrove Vic. 31 J5
Cosmo Newbery WA 57 K2
Cossack WA 55 G1, 58 A1
Costerfield Vic. 30 F9
Cottan–Bimbang National Park NSW 9 M12
Cottesloe WA 52 B5
Cottles Bridge Vic. 21 L4, 22 E2, 30 H13
Cottonvale Qld 9 M2, 77 N11
Couangalt Vic. 20 H4
Cougal NSW 9 P1
Coulson Qld 75 A10
Coulta SA 38 C7
Countegany NSW 16 I11
Courada NSW 8 H7
Couran Qld 75 G9
Couridjah NSW 5 J12
Couta Rocks Tas. 94 B6
Coutts Crossing NSW 9 P6
Cow Bay Qld 81 M5
Cow Flat NSW 4 B6
Cowabbie West NSW 6 A10, 13 Q8
Cowan NSW 5 N5
Cowan Cowan Qld 75 G2
Cowangie Vic. 12 B10, 28 C10
Cowaramup WA 53 C9, 54 B9
Cowell SA 38 G5
Cowes Vic. 21 L12, 22 E9
Cowled Landing SA 38 H3, 40 G13
Cowley Beach Qld 81 N8
Cowper NSW 9 P5
Cowra NSW 6 F8
Cowwarr Vic. 23 L6
Coyrecup WA 54 H9
Crabbes Creek NSW 9 Q2, 77 Q11
Crabtree Tas. 90 F7, 93 K9
Cracow Qld 77 K3
Cradle Mountain Tas. 94 G10
Cradle Mountain–Lake St Clair National Park Tas. 92 F1, 94 F10
Cradle Valley Tas. 94 G9
Cradoc Tas. 90 E9, 93 K10
Cradock SA 41 K9
Crafers SA 36 C10, 37 H1
Craigie NSW 14 E12, 33 M8
Craigieburn Vic. 21 J4, 22 C2, 30 F13
Craiglie Qld 81 M5
Cramenton Vic. 28 H7
Cramps Tas. 93 J2, 95 K11
Cranbourne Vic. 21 L9, 22 E6
Cranbourne South Vic. 21 L9, 22 E6
Cranbrook Tas. 93 P3, 95 P12
Cranbrook WA 54 H11, 56 E11
Craven NSW 7 N2
Cravensville Vic. 14 A9, 32 F4
Crawford Qld 77 N6
Crayfish Creek Tas. 94 E4
Crayford SA 49 E6
Creek Junction Vic. 31 K9
Creek View Vic. 30 E7
Creighton Vic. 30 I8
Creighton Creek Vic. 30 I9
Cremorne Tas. 91 K7, 93 M9
Crescent Head NSW 9 P11
Cressbrook Lower Qld 74 B8
Cressy Tas. 93 L1, 95 L10
Cressy Vic. 20 B8, 25 N6
Creswick Vic. 20 C3, 25 Q2, 27 O13, 30 A12
Crib Point Vic. 21 L11, 22 E8
Croajingolong National Park Vic. 14 F13, 33 M13
Crohamhurst Qld 74 E6
Cronulla NSW 5 N10
Crooble NSW 8 H4, 77 K13
Crooked River Vic. 23 N2, 31 Q13, 32 C10
Crookwell NSW 6 H10, 14 F2
Croppa Creek NSW 8 I4, 77 K13
Crossdale Qld 74 C9
Crossley Vic. 24 H9
Crossman WA 52 H12, 54 E6
Crossover Vic. 21 P9, 22 H6
Crow Mountain NSW 9 J8
Crowdy Bay National Park NSW 7 P1, 9 O13
Crower SA 48 G9
Crowlands Vic. 25 L1, 27 L12
Crows Nest Qld 77 N8
Crows Nest National Park Qld 77 O8
Crowther NSW 6 E9, 14 C1
Croxton East Vic. 24 G5
Croydon Qld 80 F10
Croydon Vic. 21 L6
Crymelon Vic. 26 H6
Cryon NSW 8 D7
Crystal Brook SA 39 J4
Crystal Creek National Park Qld 81 O12
Cuballing WA 54 G6, 56 E9
Cubbaroo NSW 8 E7
Cuckoo Tas. 95 N7
Cudal NSW 6 F6
Cuddell NSW 13 O9
Cudgee Vic. 24 I9
Cudgen NSW 9 Q1
Cudgewa Vic. 14 A8, 32 G2
Cudgewa North Vic. 14 B8, 32 G2
Cudlee Creek SA 36 D9
Cudmirrah NSW 14 I5, 17 Q3
Cudmirrah National Park NSW 7 J12, 17 P2
Cudmore National Park Qld 78 E9
Cue WA 55 H13, 56 E1, 58 B13
Culbin WA 54 F7
Culburra NSW 7 K11
Culburra SA 39 O12, 48 F5
Culcairn NSW 13 Q12, 31 Q1
Culfearne Vic. 27 P2, 29 Q13, 30 B1
Culgoa Vic. 12 G12, 27 L3, 29 L13
Culgoa Floodplain National Park Qld 11 Q1, 76 D12
Culgoa National Park NSW 11 Q2, 76 D13
Culla Vic. 24 D2, 26 E13
Cullen Bullen NSW 4 F3, 6 I6
Cullendulla NSW 14 H7, 17 O6
Culler NSW 6 G11, 14 F3
Culloden Vic. 23 N4, 32 D13
Cullulleraine Vic. 12 C7, 28 D4
Cumborah NSW 8 B6
Cummins SA 38 D7
Cumnock NSW 6 F4
Cundare Vic. 20 A9
Cundeelee WA 57 L6
Cunderdin WA 54 G3, 56 E7
Cungena SA 38 A1, 43 Q11
Cungulla Qld 81 Q13
Cunjurong NSW 17 Q3
Cunliffe SA 38 I6
Cunnamulla Qld 76 A10, 87 R10
Cunningar NSW 6 E10, 14 C3
Cunningham SA 38 I7
Cunninyeuk NSW 12 H10, 29 O10
Cuprona Tas. 94 G6
Curara WA 56 C3
Curban NSW 8 D12
Curdie Vale Vic. 25 J10
Curlewis NSW 8 H11
Curlwaa NSW 12 D6, 28 F2
Currabubula NSW 9 J11
Curramulka SA 38 I8
Currarong NSW 7 K12
Currawang NSW 6 H11, 14 F4
Currawarna NSW 6 A12, 13 Q10
Currawinya National Park Qld 11 J1, 87 O12
Currency Creek SA 37 H7
Currie Tas. 93 Q12
Currigee Qld 75 G10
Currimundi Qld 74 H5
Currowan Corner Upper NSW 6 I13, 14 H6, 17 M5
Currumbin Qld 75 H12, 77 Q11
Curtin Springs NT 70 F12
Curtinye SA 38 F3, 40 E13
Curtis Island Qld 79 P11
Curtis Island National Park Qld 79 P11
Curyo Vic. 12 F13, 27 J4
Custon SA 26 A7, 48 I7
Cuttabri NSW 8 F8
Cygnet Tas. 90 F10, 93 K10
Cygnet River SA 38 I12
Cynthia Qld 77 L3
D'Aguilar Qld 74 E7
D'Aguilar National Park Qld 74 D11, 75 B4
D'Entrecasteaux Channel Tas. 90 F13, 93 K12
D'Entrecasteaux National Park WA 53 F13, 54 C12, 56 C12
Dadswells Bridge Vic. 26 I11
Daguragu NT 68 D6
Dahlen Vic. 26 G9
Dahwilly NSW 13 K11
Daintree Qld 81 M5
Daintree National Park Qld 81 M4, 81 M4
Daisy Dell Tas. 94 H9
Daisy Hill Vic. 25 O1, 27 O12
Daisy Hill State Forest Qld 75 E7
Dajarra Qld 84 E6
Dakabin Qld 74 F10, 75 D3
Dalbeg Qld 78 G3
Dalby Qld 77 M8
Dales Gorge WA 55 I4, 58 C4, 337
Dalgety NSW 14 D10, 16 E13, 33 L5
Dalhousie Springs SA 46 B2
Dallarnil Qld 77 N3
Dalma Qld 79 N11
Dalmalee Vic. 26 G5
Dalmeny NSW 14 H8, 17 N11, 33 R2
Dalmorton NSW 9 N6
Dalton NSW 6 G11, 14 E3
Dalveen Qld 9 M2, 77 N11
Dalwallinu WA 56 D5
Daly River NT 64 B13, 66 D8
Daly Waters NT 68 I3
Dalyston Vic. 21 N13, 22 F9
Dalyup WA 57 J10
Dampier WA 55 G1
Dandaloo NSW 6 C2
Dandaragan WA 56 C6
Dandenong Vic. 21 L8, 22 E5
Dandenong Ranges National Park Vic. 21 L6, 22 E4
Dandongadale Vic. 31 N8, 32 A6
Dangarfield NSW 7 L2
Dangarsleigh NSW 9 L9
Dangin WA 54 G4
Danyo Vic. 28 C10
Darby Falls NSW 6 F8, 14 D1
Darbyshire Vic. 32 E2
Dardadine WA 54 F7
Dardanup WA 53 G5, 54 C8
Dareton NSW 12 D6, 28 F2
Dargo Vic. 23 O2, 31 R13, 32 D11
Dargo High Plains Vic. 31 Q11
Dark Corner NSW 4 E3, 6 I6
Darkan WA 54 E8
Darke Peak SA 38 E4
Darkwood NSW 9 O8
Darley Vic. 20 G5
Darling Downs Qld 77 M9
Darling Harbour NSW 3 B10
Darling Range WA 52 D3, 54 D5
Darling River NSW 10 F12, 12 D5
Darlinghurst NSW 3 H10
Darlington Tas. 91 P2, 93 P7
Darlington Vic. 25 K7
Darlington WA 52 D4, 54 D3
Darlington Point NSW 13 N8
Darnick NSW 12 H2
Darnum Vic. 21 Q10, 22 I7
Daroobalgie NSW 6 D6
Darr Qld 78 A10, 85 O10
Darraweit Guim Vic. 21 J3, 22 C1, 30 F12
Darriman Vic. 23 M9
Dart Dart Vic. 26 G7
Dartmoor Vic. 24 C6
Dartmouth Qld 78 B11, 85 P11
Dartmouth Vic. 14 A10, 32 E5
Darwin NT 63, 64 C2, 66 D5
Darwin Crocodile Farm NT 64 D4
Dattuck Vic. 26 H2, 28 H12
Davenport Range National Park NT 69 L13, 71 L2
Daveyston SA 36 E4, 49 C4
Davis Creek NSW 7 L2
Dawes Qld 77 L2
Dawes Point NSW 3 D2
Dawesville WA 52 A10, 54 C6
Dawson SA 39 M2, 41 L12
Dawson Vic. 23 L5
Dawsons Hill NSW 7 L2
Dayboro Qld 74 E10, 75 B2
Daydream Island Qld 79 K3
Daylesford Vic. 20 E2, 25 Q2, 27 Q13, 30 B12
Daymar Qld 8 E2, 76 H12
Daysdale NSW 13 O12, 31 M1
Daytrap Vic. 29 J10
Daytrap Corner Vic. 29 J10
Dead Horse Gap NSW 16 A13
Deakin ACT 15 A13
Deakin WA 42 A5, 57 R6
Dean Vic. 20 D3, 25 P3, 30 B12
Deanmill WA 54 D10
Deans Marsh Vic. 20 D12, 25 O9
Deception Bay Qld 74 G10, 75 D2, 77 P8
Deddick Vic. 14 C11, 33 J8
Deddington Tas. 95 N10
Dederang Vic. 31 Q6, 32 C4
Dee Lagoon Tas. 92 I4
Dee Why NSW 5 O7
Deep Creek Vic. 14 A11, 32 F7
Deep Lead Vic. 27 J11
Deepwater NSW 9 M5
Deepwater National Park Qld 77 N1, 79 Q13
Deeral Qld 81 N7
Delamere SA 37 C8
Delaneys Creek Qld 74 E7
Delatite Vic. 21 R1, 31 L11
Delburn Vic. 21 R11, 23 J8
Delegate NSW 14 E11, 33 M8
Delegate River Vic. 14 D11, 33 L8
Dellicknora Vic. 14 D12, 33 K8
Deloraine Tas. 95 J9
Delta Qld 78 I2
Delungra NSW 9 J6
Delvine Vic. 23 O5
Denham WA 55 B10
Deniliquin NSW 13 L11
Denison Vic. 23 M5
Denman NSW 7 K3
Denman SA 42 D4
Denmark WA 54 G13, 56 E12
Dennes Point Tas. 90 I9, 93 L10
Dennington Vic. 24 H9
Denver Vic. 20 F2, 25 Q2, 27 Q13, 30 C11
Depot Beach NSW 17 O6
Deptford Vic. 14 A13, 23 Q3, 32 F12
Derby Tas. 95 O7
Derby Vic. 27 P9, 30 B8
Derby WA 61 J7
Dereel Vic. 20 C6, 25 O5
Dergholm Vic. 24 B3
Dering Vic. 28 G11
Deringulla NSW 8 F12
Derrier Flat Qld 74 C2
Derrinal Vic. 30 E9
Derrinallum Vic. 25 L6
Derriwong NSW 6 B5, 13 R3
Derwent Bridge Tas. 92 H3, 94 H13
Derwent Valley Tas. 90 E3
Detention River Tas. 94 E4
Detpa Vic. 26 F5
Deua National Park NSW 14 G7, 17 K8, 33 P1
Devenish Vic. 31 K5
Devils Kitchen Tas. 91 O9
Devils Marbles NT 69 K12, 71 K2
Devils Marbles Conservation Reserve NT 69 J12
Deviot Tas. 95 L7
Devlins Bridge Vic. 21 M3
Devon North Vic. 23 L9
Devonian Reef National Parks WA 61 L8
Devonport Tas. 94 I6
Dewars Pool WA 54 E2
Dharug National Park NSW 5 N3, 7 L6
Dhulura NSW 6 B12, 13 Q10
Dhuragoon NSW 13 J10, 29 Q10
Dhurringile Vic. 30 H7
Diamantina National Park Qld 84 H11
Diamond Beach NSW 7 P1
Diamond Valley Qld 74 F5
Diapur Vic. 26 D7
Diddleum Plains Tas. 95 N8
Didillibah Qld 74 G4
Digby Vic. 24 D5
Diggers Rest Vic. 20 I4, 22 B3
Diggora Vic. 30 E6
Dilkoon NSW 9 P5
Dilston Tas. 95 L8
Dimboola Vic. 26 F7
Dimbulah Qld 81 L7
Dingabledinga SA 37 G4
Dingee Vic. 27 Q7, 30 C6
Dingo Qld 79 L11
Dingo Beach Qld 79 J2
Dingup WA 54 D10
Dingwall Vic. 27 O3, 30 A2
Dinmont Vic. 25 N11
Dinner Plain Vic. 31 R10, 32 D8
Dinninup WA 54 E9
Dinoga NSW 8 I7
Dinyarrak Vic. 26 B7, 48 I6
Dipperu National Park Qld 79 J7
Dirk Hartog Island WA 55 A10
Dirranbandi Qld 8 C2, 76 G12
Discovery Bay Coastal Park Vic. 24 B7
Dixie Vic. 25 K9
Dixons Creek Vic. 21 M4, 22 F2, 30 I13
Djilkminggan NT 66 I11
Djukbinj National Park NT 64 F1
Dobbyn Qld 84 F1
Docker Vic. 31 M7
Docklands Vic. 19 A9
Doctors Flat Vic. 14 A12, 23 Q1, 32 F10
Dodges Ferry Tas. 91 L6, 93 N8
Don Tas. 94 I6
Don Valley Vic. 21 N6
Donald Vic. 27 K7
Dongara WA 56 B4
Donnybrook Qld 74 G8
Donnybrook Vic. 21 J4, 22 C2, 30 F13
Donnybrook WA 54 C8, 56 C10
Donovans Landing SA 24 A7, 48 I12
Doo Town Tas. 91 O9
Dooboobetic Vic. 27 L7
Doodlakine WA 54 H2
Dooen Vic. 26 H9
Dookie Vic. 31 J5
Doomadgee Qld 83 D9
Doonan Qld 74 G2
Dooralong NSW 5 P1
Dopewora Vic. 26 C10
Doreen NSW 8 F7
Dorodong Vic. 24 B2, 26 B13, 48 I10
Dorrien SA 49 F5
Dorrigo NSW 9 O8
Dorrigo National Park NSW 9 O8
Doughboy NSW 6 H12, 14 G5, 17 K2
Douglas Vic. 26 E11
Douglas–Apsley National Park Tas. 93 P1, 95 Q11
Douglas Daly Park NT 64 F12, 66 E8
Douglas Park NSW 5 K12
Dover Tas. 90 E12, 93 K11
Dover Heights NSW 5 O8
Dowerin WA 54 F1
Dowlingville SA 39 J7
Downside NSW 6 B12, 13 R10
Doyalson NSW 5 Q1, 7 M5
Drake NSW 9 N3, 77 O12
Dreamworld Qld 75 G10
Dreeite Vic. 20 A10, 25 N8
Drik Drik Vic. 24 C7
Drillham Qld 77 J7
Dripstone NSW 6 F4
Dromana Vic. 21 J11, 22 D8
Dromedary Tas. 90 G3, 93 L7
Dropmore Vic. 30 I10
Drouin Vic. 21 P9, 22 H6
Drouin South Vic. 21 P10, 22 H7
Drouin West Vic. 21 P9, 22 H6
Drumborg Vic. 24 D7
Drummartin Vic. 27 R7, 30 D6
Drummond Vic. 20 F1, 25 Q1, 27 Q12, 30 C11
Drummond Cove WA 56 A3
Drung Drung Vic. 26 H9
Drung Drung South Vic. 26 H10
Dry Creek Vic. 31 K10
Dryander National Park Qld 79 J2
Drysdale Vic. 20 H9, 22 B6
Drysdale River National Park WA 61 O3
Duaringa Qld 79 M11
Dubbo NSW 6 E2
Dubelling WA 54 G4
Dublin SA 39 K7
Duchess Qld 84 F5
Duckmaloi NSW 4 E7
Duddo Vic. 28 C10
Dudinin WA 54 H6, 56 E9
Dudley Vic. 22 G10
Dulacca Qld 77 J7
Dularcha National Park Qld 74 F5
Dullah NSW 6 A11, 13 Q9
Dulong Qld 74 F4
Dululu Qld 79 N12
Dumbalk Vic. 21 Q13, 22 I9
Dumberning WA 54 F7
Dumbleyung WA 54 H8, 56 E10
Dumosa Vic. 12 G13, 27 L4
Dunach Vic. 20 B1, 25 O1, 27 O12
Dunalley Tas. 91 M6, 93 N9
Dunbogan NSW 9 O12
Dundas Qld 74 C10
Dundas Tas. 92 D1, 94 E11
Dundee NSW 9 M5
Dundee Beach NT 66 C6
Dundonnell Vic. 25 K6
Dundurrabin NSW 9 O7
Dunedoo NSW 6 G1
Dunggir National Park NSW 9 O9
Dungog NSW 7 N3
Dungowan NSW 9 K11
Dunk Island Qld 81 O9
Dunkeld NSW 4 B4, 6 H6
Dunkeld Vic. 24 H4
Dunmarra NT 68 I4
Dunmore NSW 6 C4
Dunmore Vic. 24 G7
Dunneworthy Vic. 25 K1, 27 K12
Dunnstown Vic. 20 D4, 25 P3, 30 B13
Dunolly Vic. 27 O10
Dunoon NSW 9 Q2
Dunorlan Tas. 95 J8
Dunrobin Vic. 24 C4
Dunsborough WA 53 C7, 54 B9, 56 B10
Dunwich Qld 75 H6, 77 Q9
Duranillin WA 54 F8, 56 D10
Durdidwarrah Vic. 20 E6, 25 Q5
Durham Lead Vic. 20 C5, 25 O4
Durham Ox Vic. 12 I13, 27 P5, 30 A4
Duri NSW 9 J11
Durong Qld 77 M6
Durran Durra NSW 6 I12, 14 G5, 17 L3
Durras NSW 14 H7, 17 O6
Durundur Qld 74 E7
Dutson Vic. 23 N7
Dutton SA 36 H3, 39 M7
Duverney Vic. 20 A8, 25 N6
Dwarda WA 52 H11, 54 E6
Dwellingup WA 52 D11, 54 D6, 56 C9
Dwyers NSW 11 O6
Dynnyrne Tas. 89 D13
Dysart Qld 79 J9
Dysart Tas. 90 H1, 93 L6
Eagle Bay WA 53 B6, 54 A8
Eagle Heights Qld 75 E10
Eagle Point Vic. 23 Q5
Eaglehawk Vic. 27 Q9, 30 C8
Eaglehawk Neck Tas. 91 N8, 93 O9
Earlando Qld 79 J2
Earlston Vic. 31 J7
East Bairnsdale Vic. 23 Q4, 32 F13
East Boyd NSW 14 G12, 33 Q8
East Gresford NSW 7 M3
East Jindabyne NSW 16 D12, 33 K4
East Kurrajong NSW 5 L5

East Lynne–Gumly Gumly 99

East Lynne NSW 14 H6, 17 O6
East Melbourne Vic. 19 H6
East Perth WA 51 H5
East Yolla Tas. 94 F6
Eastern Creek NSW 5 L8
Eastern View Vic. 20 E12, 25 P10
Eastville Vic. 27 P10, 30 B9
Eastwood SA 35 I13
Eaton WA 53 G4, 54 C8
Eatonsville NSW 9 O6
Eba SA 39 N6
Ebden Vic. 31 Q4, 32 C2
Ebenezer NSW 5 L5
Ebor NSW 9 N8
Eccleston NSW 7 M2
Echuca Vic. 13 K13, 30 E4
Echuca Village Vic. 13 K13, 30 F4
Echunga SA 36 D12, 37 I3
Ecklin South Vic. 25 K9
Eddington Vic. 27 O10, 30 A9
Eddystone Point Tas. 95 R6
Eden NSW 14 G11, 33 Q8
Eden Park Vic. 21 K3
Eden Valley SA 36 G6, 39 M8
Edenhope Vic. 26 C11
Edgcumbe Beach Tas. 94 E4
Edgecombe Vic. 20 G1
Edgeroi NSW 8 G7
Edi Vic. 31 N7
Edi Upper Vic. 31 N8
Edillilie SA 38 D7
Edith NSW 4 E8, 6 I7
Edith Creek Tas. 94 C5
Edith River NT 66 F9
Edithburgh SA 38 I10
Edmonton Qld 81 N7
Edmund Kennedy National Park Qld 81 N9
Egg Lagoon Tas. 93 Q11
Eidsvold Qld 77 M3
Eildon Vic. 21 P2, 31 K11
Eimeo Qld 79 L5
Einasleigh Qld 81 J10
Ejanding WA 54 F1
El Arish Qld 81 N9
Elaine Vic. 20 D6, 25 P5
Elands NSW 9 N12
Elanora Heights NSW 5 O7
Elaroo Qld 79 J4
Elbow Hill SA 38 G5
Elcombe NSW 8 I6
Elderslie Tas. 90 F2, 93 K7
Eldon Tas. 93 M6
Eldorado Vic. 31 N5, 32 A3
Electrona Tas. 90 H8
Elimbah Qld 74 F8, 77 P8
Elizabeth SA 36 C7, 39 L8, 48 C1
Elizabeth Beach NSW 7 P2
Elizabeth Town Tas. 95 J8
Ellalong NSW 7 L4
Ellam Vic. 12 D13, 26 F5
Ellenborough NSW 9 N12
Ellendale Tas. 90 B2, 93 J7
Ellerslie Vic. 25 J8
Ellerston NSW 7 L1, 9 K13
Elliminyt Vic. 20 B11, 25 N9
Ellinbank Vic. 21 P10, 22 H7
Elliott NT 69 J6
Elliott Tas. 94 F6
Elliott Heads Qld 77 O2
Ellis Beach Qld 81 M6
Elliston SA 38 A5
Elmhurst Vic. 25 L1, 27 L12
Elmore Vic. 30 E6
Elong Elong NSW 6 F2
Elphinstone Vic. 27 R12, 30 C10
Elsey National Park NT 66 I11
Elsinore NSW 11 L10
Elsmore NSW 9 K6
Eltham NSW 9 Q3
Elwomple SA 39 N10, 48 E3
Emerald Qld 78 I11
Emerald Vic. 21 M7, 22 F5
Emerald Beach NSW 9 P7
Emerald Hill NSW 8 H10
Emerald Springs Wayside Inn NT 64 H11, 66 F8
Emita Tas. 92 B10
Emmaville NSW 9 L5
Emmdale Roadhouse NSW 11 J10
Emmet Qld 87 P2
Empire Vale NSW 9 Q3, 77 Q12
Emu Vic. 27 M9
Emu Bay SA 38 H11
Emu Creek Qld 77 N10
Emu Downs SA 39 M5
Emu Junction SA 45 J10
Emu Park Qld 79 O10
Endeavour Hills Vic. 21 L8
Endeavour River National Park Qld 81 L2
Eneabba WA 56 B5
Enfield SA 36 B9
Enfield Vic. 20 C6, 25 O5
Engawala NT 71 K6
Englefield Vic. 24 E2, 26 E13
English Town Tas. 95 N9
Enmore NSW 9 M9
Enngonia NSW 11 N2
Enoch Point Vic. 21 Q3
Ensay Vic. 14 B12, 23 R1, 32 G10
Ensay North Vic. 23 R1, 32 G10
Ensay South Vic. 14 A13, 23 Q1, 32 G10
Eppalock Vic. 27 R10, 30 D9
Epping Forest Tas. 93 M1, 95 M11
Epsom Vic. 27 R9, 30 C8
Ercildoun Vic. 20 B3
Erica Vic. 23 J5
Erigolia NSW 13 O6
Erikin WA 54 H3
Erina NSW 5 P4
Erith SA 39 K7
Erldunda NT 70 I11
Eromanga Qld 87 M7
Erowal Bay NSW 17 R2
Erriba Tas. 94 H8
Erringibba National Park Qld 77 J8
Errinundra Vic. 14 D12, 33 L10
Errinundra National Park Vic. 14 D12, 33 L10
Erskine Park NSW 5 L8
Esk Qld 74 B10, 77 O8
Eskdale Vic. 31 R6, 32 D4
Esmond Vic. 13 C13, 31 L4
Esperance WA 57 J10
Essington NSW 4 C7
Etmilyn WA 52 D11
Eton Qld 79 K5
Ettalong NSW 5 P5
Ettamogah NSW 13 Q13, 31 P3, 32 C1
Ettrick NSW 9 P2, 77 P12
Euabalong NSW 13 P3
Euabalong West NSW 13 O3
Eubenangee Swamp National Park Qld 81 N8
Euchareena NSW 6 G4
Eucla WA 42 A8, 57 R7
Eucla National Park WA 42 A8, 57 R8
Eucumbene NSW 14 D8, 16 D10, 33 K2
Eudlo Qld 74 F5
Eudunda SA 39 M6
Eugowra NSW 6 E6
Eujinyn WA 54 I3
Eulo Qld 87 Q11
Eumundi Qld 74 F2, 77 P6
Eumungerie NSW 6 E1
Eungai Creek NSW 9 O10
Eungella NSW 9 P1
Eungella Qld 79 J5
Eungella National Park Qld 79 J4
Eurack Vic. 20 B9, 25 O7
Euramo Qld 81 N9
Euratha NSW 13 P6
Eurelia SA 39 K1, 41 K11
Euri Creek Qld 78 I2
Eurimbula National Park Qld 79 Q13
Euroa Vic. 30 I8
Eurobin Vic. 31 P7, 32 B5
Eurobodalla NSW 14 G8, 17 M11, 33 R2
Eurobodalla National Park NSW 14 H8, 17 N9
Eurong Qld 77 Q4
Eurongilly NSW 6 C11, 14 A4
Euston NSW 12 F8, 29 J6
Eva Valley NT 66 H9
Evandale Tas. 95 M9
Evans Head NSW 9 Q4, 77 Q13
Evans Plains NSW 4 B4
Evansford Vic. 20 B2, 25 N1, 27 N12
Everard Junction WA 59 L9
Eversley Vic. 25 L1, 27 L12
Everton Vic. 31 N6, 32 A4
Ewens Ponds SA 48 H13
Exeter Tas. 95 L7
Exford Vic. 20 H5, 22 B3
Exmouth WA 55 C3
Expedition National Park Qld 76 H3
Exton Tas. 95 K9
Eyre Peninsula SA 38 C6
Fairfield NSW 5 M8
Fairhaven Vic. 14 G13, 33 Q11
Fairhaven Vic. 20 E12, 25 P10
Fairhaven Vic. 21 L11
Fairholme NSW 6 B6, 13 R4
Fairley Vic. 27 O2, 29 O13, 30 A1
Fairneyview Qld 74 D13, 75 A5
Fairview Vic. 27 M5
Fairy Dell Vic. 30 E6
Fairy Hill NSW 9 P3, 77 P12
Falls Creek NSW 7 K11, 14 I4
Falls Creek Vic. 31 R9, 32 D7
Falmouth Tas. 95 Q9
Family Islands National Park Qld 81 O9
Faraday Vic. 27 Q11, 30 C10
Farleigh Qld 79 K5
Farnborough Qld 79 O10
Farnham NSW 6 G4
Farrell Flat SA 39 L5
Faulconbridge NSW 5 J7
Fawcett Vic. 21 O1
Fawkner Vic. 21 J5
Federal Qld 74 E1
Feilton Tas. 90 E4, 93 K8
Felton East Qld 77 N10
Fentonbury Tas. 90 C2, 93 J7
Fentons Creek Vic. 27 N8
Fern Hill Vic. 20 G2
Fern Tree Tas. 90 H6, 93 L9
Fernbank Vic. 23 O5, 32 E13
Ferndale NSW 13 P11
Ferndene Tas. 94 H6
Fernihurst Vic. 27 O6, 30 A5
Fernlees Qld 78 I12
Ferntree Gully Vic. 21 L7
Fernvale Qld 74 C12, 75 A5, 77 P9
Fields Find WA 56 D4
Fiery Flat Vic. 27 O7, 30 A6
Fifield NSW 6 B4, 13 R2
Finch Hatton Qld 79 J5
Fine Flower Creek NSW 9 O5
Fingal NSW 9 Q1, 75 I13
Fingal Tas. 93 P1, 95 P10
Finke NT 71 K12
Finke Gorge National Park NT 70 H9
Finley NSW 13 M12, 30 I1
Finniss SA 37 I6, 39 L11, 48 C3
Fish Creek Vic. 22 I10
Fish Point Vic. 27 O1, 29 O11
Fisher SA 42 G4
Fishermans Paradise NSW 17 P3
Fishery Falls Qld 81 N7
Fiskville Vic. 20 F5, 25 Q4
Fitzgerald Tas. 90 B3, 92 I7
Fitzgerald River National Park WA 56 G11
Fitzroy SA 35 D2
Fitzroy Crossing WA 61 M9
Fitzroy Island Qld 81 N6
Fitzroy Island National Park Qld 81 N7
Fitzroy River WA 61 M9
Five Ways NSW 6 A2, 11 Q12
Flaggy Rock Qld 79 L7
Flamingo Beach Vic. 23 O7
Flaxley SA 36 D12, 37 I3
Flaxton Qld 74 F4
Fletcher Qld 77 N12
Fleurieu Peninsula SA 37 E7, 39 K12, 48 A4
Flinders Qld 75 A8
Flinders Vic. 21 J12, 22 D9
Flinders Bay WA 53 C13
Flinders Chase National Park SA 38 F13
Flinders Group National Park Qld 82 G11
Flinders Island Tas. 92 C9, 95 R1
Flinders Ranges SA 41 K8
Flinders Ranges National Park SA 41 K7
Flinton Qld 76 I10
Flintstone Tas. 93 J2, 95 K12
Flora River Nature Park NT 66 F10
Florida NSW 11 O10
Florida WA 52 A10
Florieton SA 39 N5
Flowerdale Tas. 94 F5
Flowerdale Vic. 21 L2, 22 E1, 30 H12
Flowerpot Tas. 90 H11, 93 L10
Flowery Gully Tas. 95 K7
Flying Fish Point Qld 81 N8
Flying Fox Qld 75 E12
Flynn Vic. 23 L7
Flynns Creek Vic. 23 K7
Fogg Dam NT 64 F3
Foleyvale Aboriginal Community Qld 79 M11
Footscray Vic. 21 J6, 22 C4
Forbes NSW 6 D6
Forcett Tas. 91 L5
Fords SA 36 E3
Fords Bridge NSW 11 M4
Fordwich NSW 7 L4
Forest Tas. 94 D4
Forest Den National Park Qld 78 C7, 85 Q7
Forest Glen Qld 74 G4
Forest Hill NSW 6 B12, 13 R10, 14 A5
Forest Range SA 36 D10, 37 I1
Forest Reefs NSW 6 G6
Forester Tas. 95 O6
Forestier Peninsula Tas. 91 O7, 93 O9
Forge Creek Vic. 23 P5
Forrest ACT 15 C12
Forrest Vic. 20 B13, 25 O10
Forrest WA 57 Q6
Forrest Beach Qld 81 O11
Forresters Beach NSW 5 Q4
Forreston SA 36 E8
Forsayth Qld 80 I11
Forster SA 39 N8, 48 E1
Forster–Tuncurry NSW 7 P2
Fortescue Roadhouse WA 55 F2
Forth Tas. 94 I7
Fortis Creek National Park NSW 9 O5
Fortitude Valley Qld 73 H1
Forty Mile Scrub National Park Qld 81 L9
Foster Vic. 23 J10
Fosterville Vic. 27 R9, 30 D8
Four Mile Creek Tas. 95 Q10
Fowlers Bay SA 43 K9
Fox Ground NSW 7 K11
Fox Trap Roadhouse Qld 76 A7, 87 Q7
Framlingham Vic. 25 J8
Framlingham East Vic. 25 J8
Frampton NSW 6 C11, 14 B3
Frances SA 26 A9, 48 I8
Francistown Tas. 90 E12, 93 K11
Francois Peron National Park WA 55 B9
Frank Hann National Park WA 56 H9
Frankford Tas. 95 K8
Frankland WA 54 F11, 56 E11
Frankland Islands National Park Qld 81 N7
Franklin Tas. 90 E9, 93 K10
Franklin–Gordon Wild Rivers National Park Tas. 92 F4, 94 F13
Franklin River Tas. 92 E6, 94 F13
Franklinford Vic. 20 E1
Frankston Vic. 21 K9, 22 D6
Frankton SA 36 H2, 39 M7
Fraser Island Qld 77 Q3
Frederickton NSW 9 O10
Freeburgh Vic. 31 Q8, 32 C6
Freeling SA 36 D4, 39 L7, 49 A3
Freemans Reach NSW 5 L5, 7 K7
Freemans Waterhole NSW 7 M5
Fregon SA 45 J3
Fremantle WA 52 B5, 54 C4, 56 C8
French Island Vic. 21 L11, 22 E8
French Island National Park Vic. 21 M11, 22 E8
Frenchmans Cap Tas. 92 F4, 94 F13
Frenchs Forest NSW 5 O7
Freshwater Creek Vic. 20 F10, 25 Q8
Freycinet National Park Tas. 93 Q4, 95 Q12
Freycinet Peninsula Tas. 93 Q5
Frogmore NSW 6 F9, 14 D2
Fryerstown Vic. 20 F1
Fulham Vic. 23 M6
Fullerton NSW 4 C12, 6 H9, 14 F2
Fumina Vic. 21 Q7
Furneaux Group Tas. 92 C11
Furner SA 48 G10
Furnissdale WA 52 B10
Furracabad NSW 9 L6
Fyansford Vic. 20 F9, 25 Q7
Gadara NSW 16 A2
Gaffneys Creek Vic. 21 R4, 23 J2, 31 M13
Gagebrook Tas. 90 H4, 93 L7
Galah Vic. 28 G9
Galaquil Vic. 26 H4
Galaquil East Vic. 26 I4
Galga SA 39 O8, 48 F1
Galiwinku NT 67 M5
Gallanani Qld 74 A10
Gallangowan Qld 74 A2, 77 O6
Galong NSW 6 E10, 14 D3
Galston NSW 5 N6, 7 L7
Gama Vic. 26 I1, 28 I12
Gammon Ranges National Park SA 41 L4
Ganmain NSW 6 A11, 13 Q9
Gannawarra Vic. 27 Q3, 29 Q13, 30 B2
Gapsted Vic. 31 O7, 32 A4
Gapuwiyak NT 67 N5
Garah NSW 8 G4, 76 I13
Garawa NT 67 O13, 69 O2
Garden Island WA 52 A7
Garden Island Creek Tas. 90 F11, 93 K11
Gardens of Stone National Park NSW 4 F1, 6 I5
Gardners Bay Tas. 90 F10, 93 K10
Garema NSW 6 D7
Garfield Vic. 21 O9, 22 G6
Garfield North Vic. 21 O8
Garibaldi Vic. 20 C5, 25 O4
Garland NSW 6 F7
Garra NSW 6 F5
Garrawilla NSW 8 G11
Garrthalala NT 67 O6
Garvoc Vic. 25 J9
Gary Junction WA 59 M4
Gascoyne Junction WA 55 D8
Gatton Qld 77 O9
Gatum Vic. 24 F3
Gawler SA 36 D5, 39 L8
Gawler Tas. 94 H6
Gawler Ranges National Park SA 40 B11
Gayndah Qld 77 N4
Gazette Vic. 24 G6
Geelong Vic. 20 F9, 22 A6, 25 R7
Geeralying WA 54 F7
Geeveston Tas. 90 D10, 93 K10
Geham Qld 77 N9
Geikie Gorge National Park WA 61 M9
Gelantipy Vic. 14 C12, 32 I9
Gellibrand Vic. 20 A13, 25 N10
Gelliondale Vic. 23 L10
Gelorup WA 53 F5, 54 C8
Gembrook Vic. 21 N8, 22 F5
Gemtree NT 71 K7
Genoa Vic. 14 F13, 33 P11
Geographe Bay WA 53 D6, 331
George Camp NT 66 G10
George Town Tas. 95 K6
Georges Creek Vic. 31 R4, 32 D2
Georges Plains NSW 4 B5, 6 H6
Georges River National Park NSW 5 M9
Georgetown Qld 80 I10
Georgetown SA 39 K4
Georgica NSW 9 P2, 77 Q12
Geraldton WA 56 A3
Gerang Gerung Vic. 26 F7
Gerangamete Vic. 20 B12, 25 O10
Geranium SA 39 P11, 48 G3
Geranium Plain SA 39 M6
Gerogery NSW 13 Q12, 31 P2
Gerogery West NSW 13 Q13, 31 P2
Gerringong NSW 7 K11
Geurie NSW 6 F3
Gheerulla Qld 74 E3
Gheringhap Vic. 20 F8
Ghin Ghin Vic. 21 M1
Gibraltar Range National Park NSW 9 N5
Gibson WA 57 J10
Gibson Desert WA 59 N7
Gibsonvale NSW 13 P5
Gidgegannup WA 52 E3, 54 D3
Gidginbung NSW 6 B9, 13 R7, 14 A2
Giffard Vic. 23 N8
Gilbert River Qld 80 G10
Gilberton SA 35 G3
Gilberts SA 37 I6
Giles Corner SA 36 C1, 39 L7
Gilgai NSW 9 K6
Gilgandra NSW 8 D13
Gilgooma NSW 8 D9
Gilgunnia NSW 11 N13, 13 N1
Gillenbah NSW 13 P9
Gilliat Qld 84 I4
Gillieston Vic. 30 G5
Gillingarra WA 56 C6
Gilmore NSW 16 A2
Gilston Qld 75 F11
Gin Gin NSW 6 D1, 8 C13
Gin Gin Qld 77 N2
Gindie Qld 78 I11
Gingin WA 54 C2, 56 C7
Ginquam Vic. 28 G5
Gippsland Vic. 21 P12
Gippsland Lakes Vic. 23 Q5
Gipsy Point Vic. 14 G13, 33 P11
Girgarre Vic. 30 F6
Girilambone NSW 11 Q9
Girral NSW 6 A7, 13 Q5
Girraween National Park Qld 9 M3, 77 N12
Giru Qld 78 G1, 81 Q13
Gisborne Vic. 20 H3, 22 B2, 30 E13
Gladesville NSW 5 N8
Gladfield Vic. 27 P5, 30 A4
Gladstone NSW 9 P10
Gladstone Qld 79 P12
Gladstone SA 39 K3, 41 J13
Gladstone Tas. 95 P6
Gladstone WA 55 C10
Gladysdale Vic. 21 N6, 22 G4
Glamis NSW 9 M12
Glamorganvale Qld 74 C13
Glanmire NSW 4 C4
Glass House Mountains Qld 74 F6, 77 P7
Glass House Mountains National Park Qld 74 E6
Glaziers Bay Tas. 90 E9
Glebe Tas. 89 E4
Glen Tas. 95 L7
Glen Alice NSW 7 J5
Glen Aplin Qld 9 M3, 77 N12
Glen Creek Vic. 31 P6, 32 C4
Glen Davis NSW 4 H1, 7 J5
Glen Elgin NSW 9 M5
Glen Esk Qld 74 B10
Glen Forbes Vic. 21 N12, 22 F9
Glen Geddes Qld 79 N10
Glen Helen Resort NT 70 H8
Glen Huon Tas. 90 E8, 93 K9
Glen Innes NSW 9 L6
Glen Waverley Vic. 21 K7
Glen Wills Vic. 14 A11, 32 F7
Glenaire Vic. 25 M12
Glenaladale Vic. 23 O4, 32 D13
Glenalbyn Vic. 27 O8, 30 A7
Glenariff NSW 11 P8
Glenaroua Vic. 21 J1
Glenbrae Vic. 20 A2
Glenbrook NSW 5 J7, 7 K7
Glenburn Vic. 21 M3, 22 F1, 30 I12
Glenburnie SA 24 A6, 48 I12
Glencoe NSW 9 L7
Glencoe SA 48 H11
Glencoe West SA 48 H11
Glendambo SA 40 C5
Glendaruel Vic. 20 B2, 25 N2, 27 N13
Glenden Qld 78 I5
Glendevie Tas. 90 E11, 93 K10
Glendinning Vic. 24 F2, 26 F13
Glendon Brook NSW 7 L3
Gleneagle Qld 75 C10
Glenelg SA 36 A10, 37 F1, 39 K9, 48 B2
Glenfern Qld 74 C7
Glenfern Tas. 90 E5, 93 K8
Glenfyne Vic. 25 K9
Glengarry NSW 8 A6
Glengarry Tas. 95 K8
Glengarry Vic. 23 K6
Glengower Vic. 20 C1, 25 O1, 27 O12, 30 A11
Glenhaven NSW 5 M7
Glenhope Vic. 30 D10
Glenisla Vic. 24 G2, 26 G13
Glenlee Vic. 26 F6
Glenlofty Vic. 25 L1, 27 L12
Glenloth Vic. 12 G13, 27 M5
Glenluce Vic. 20 F1, 25 Q1, 27 Q12, 30 C11
Glenlusk Tas. 90 G5
Glenlyon Vic. 20 F2, 25 Q2, 27 Q13, 30 C11
Glenmaggie Vic. 23 L5
Glenmore NSW 5 J10
Glenmore Vic. 20 F5, 25 Q4
Glenmorgan Qld 76 I8
Glenora Tas. 90 D3, 93 J7
Glenorchy Tas. 90 H5, 93 L8
Glenorchy Vic. 27 J11
Glenore Qld 83 I9
Glenore Tas. 95 K9
Glenore Crossing Qld 80 C9
Glenore Grove Qld 74 A13
Glenorie NSW 5 M6
Glenormiston Vic. 25 K8
Glenormiston North Vic. 25 K8
Glenreagh NSW 9 P7
Glenrowan Vic. 31 M6
Glenroy NSW 4 G5
Glenroy SA 48 H10
Glenthompson Vic. 24 I4
Glenvale Vic. 21 K3, 22 D2, 30 G13
Glenworth Valley NSW 5 O4
Glossodia NSW 5 L5
Glossop SA 39 Q7
Gloucester NSW 7 N1
Gloucester Island Qld 79 J2
Gloucester Island National Park Qld 79 J2
Gnarming WA 54 I5
Gnarpurt Vic. 25 M6
Gnarwarre Vic. 20 E9, 25 Q8
Gnotuk Vic. 25 L8
Gnowangerup WA 54 I10, 56 F11
Goangra NSW 8 C7
Gobarralong NSW 6 D12, 14 C4
Gobondery NSW 6 C4
Gobur Vic. 31 J10
Gocup NSW 16 A1
Godfreys Creek NSW 6 F9, 14 D1
Godwin Beach Qld 74 H8, 75 E1
Gogango Qld 79 M11
Gol Gol NSW 12 D7, 28 G3
Golconda Tas. 95 M7
Gold Coast Qld 75 H11, 77 R10
Gold Coast Hinterland Qld 75 E13, 77 P10
Golden Bay WA 52 B9, 54 C5
Golden Beach Qld 74 H6
Golden Beach Vic. 23 O7
Golden Grove SA 36 C8
Golden Valley Tas. 95 J9
Goldfields Woodlands National Park WA 56 H6
Goldsborough Vic. 27 N10
Goldsmith Tas. 93 L3, 95 M12
Goldsworthy WA 58 D1, 60 C13
Gollan NSW 6 G2
Golspie NSW 4 D13, 6 H9, 14 G2
Gomersal SA 49 C6
Goneaway National Park Qld 85 K11
Gongolgon NSW 11 Q6
Gonn Crossing Vic. 12 I11, 27 P1, 29 P12
Goobang National Park NSW 6 E5
Goobarragandra NSW 6 E13, 14 C6, 16 C3
Good Hope NSW 6 F11, 14 D4
Goodilla NT 64 F9
Goodmans Ford NSW 4 F13
Goodnight NSW 12 G9, 29 M8
Goodooga NSW 8 A4, 11 R2, 76 E13
Goodwood Qld 77 O3
Goolgowi NSW 13 M6
Goolma NSW 6 G3
Goolmangar NSW 9 Q3
Gooloogong NSW 6 E7
Goolwa SA 37 I7, 39 L11, 48 C3
Goomalibee Vic. 31 K6
Goomalling WA 54 F1, 56 D7
Goombungee Qld 77 N8
Goomeri Qld 77 O6
Goon Nure Vic. 23 P5
Goondah NSW 6 F11, 14 D3
Goondiwindi Qld 8 H2, 77 K11
Goondooloo SA 39 O9, 48 F1
Goongarrie WA 56 I5
Goongarrie National Park WA 56 I5
Goongee Vic. 28 B9, 39 R10
Goongerah Vic. 14 D12, 33 K10
Goonumbla NSW 6 D5
Gooram Vic. 31 J9
Goorambat Vic. 31 K6
Goorawin NSW 13 M5
Goornong Vic. 30 D7
Gooroc Vic. 27 L8
Gooseberry Hill National Park WA 52 D4
Goovigen Qld 79 N13
Goowarra Qld 79 L11
Gorae Vic. 24 D8
Gorae West Vic. 24 D8
Gordon SA 41 J9
Gordon Tas. 90 G11, 93 L11
Gordon Vic. 20 E4, 25 Q3, 30 B13
Gordon River Tas. 92 E5
Gordonvale Qld 81 N7
Gormandale Vic. 23 L7
Gormanston Tas. 92 E3, 94 E12
Gorokan NSW 5 Q2
Goroke Vic. 26 D9
Goschen Vic. 27 M1, 29 N12
Gosford NSW 5 P4, 7 L6
Goshen Tas. 95 Q8
Gosse SA 38 G12
Goughs Bay Vic. 21 Q1, 31 L11
Goulburn NSW 6 H11, 14 G3
Goulburn River Vic. 30 G4
Goulburn River National Park NSW 6 H2
Goulburn Weir Vic. 30 G8
Goulds Country Tas. 95 P7
Gove Peninsula NT 67 O5
Gowanford Vic. 27 L1, 29 L11
Gowangardie Vic. 31 J6
Gowar East Vic. 27 M8
Gowrie Park Tas. 94 H8
Goyura Vic. 26 H3
Grabben Gullen NSW 6 G10, 14 F3
Grabine NSW 6 F8, 14 E1
Gracemere Qld 79 N11
Gracetown WA 53 B9, 54 A9, 56 B11
Gradgery NSW 8 B11
Gradule Qld 8 E2, 76 H11
Grafton NSW 9 P6
Graham NSW 6 F9, 14 D1
Graman NSW 9 J5
Grampians, The Vic. 24 H2, 26 H13
Grampians National Park Vic. 24 H1, 26 H12
Granite Island SA 37 G8
Grantham Qld 77 O9
Granton Tas. 90 H4, 93 L7
Granton Vic. 21 O4, 22 G2, 31 J13
Grantville Vic. 21 N12, 22 F8
Granville Harbour Tas. 92 B1, 94 C10
Granya Vic. 13 R13, 31 R4, 32 E2
Grasmere NSW 5 K10
Grass Flat Vic. 26 F9
Grass Patch WA 57 J10
Grassdale Vic. 24 E5
Grassmere Vic. 24 I9
Grassmere Junction Vic. 24 I9
Grasstree Qld 79 L5
Grasstree Hill Tas. 90 I4
Grassy Tas. 93 R13
Gravelly Beach Tas. 95 L7
Gravesend NSW 8 I5
Grawin NSW 8 A6
Grawlin Plains NSW 6 D6
Gray Tas. 93 Q1, 95 Q10
Graytown Vic. 30 F9
Gre Gre Vic. 27 K9
Great Australian Bight 42 C10, 57 O10
Great Australian Bight Marine Park SA 42 G8
Great Barrier Reef Qld 79 M2, 81 N3, 82 E3
Great Basalt Wall National Park Qld 78 C2, 85 Q2
Great Dividing Range NSW, Qld & Vic. 9 K13, 14 C8, 22 H4, 32 A8, 77 J6, 80 H1
Great Keppel Island Qld 79 O10
Great Lake Tas. 93 J2, 95 J11
Great Northern Vic. 31 N3, 32 A1
Great Ocean Road Vic. 20 D13, 25 N12
Great Palm Island Qld 81 O11
Great Sandy Desert WA 60 G12
Great Sandy National Park Qld 77 Q3
Great Victoria Desert WA 57 O3
Great Western Vic. 25 J1, 27 J12
Gredgwin Vic. 12 H13, 27 N4
Green Head WA 56 B5
Green Hill NSW 9 O10
Green Hill Creek Vic. 20 A1
Green Hills SA 36 D12, 37 I3
Green Island Qld 81 N6
Green Island National Park Qld 81 N6
Green Lake Vic. 27 J2, 29 K12
Green Lake Vic. 26 H10
Green Mountains Qld 75 E13
Green Patch JBT 17 R2
Green Point NSW 7 P2
Greenbank Qld 75 C8
Greenbushes WA 54 D9
Greendale Vic. 20 F4, 25 Q3, 30 C13
Greenhills WA 54 F3
Greenmantle NSW 6 G8, 14 E1
Greenmount Qld 77 N10
Greenmount Vic. 23 L9
Greenmount WA 52 D4
Greenmount National Park WA 52 D4
Greenock SA 36 E4, 39 L7, 49 E3
Greenough WA 56 A3
Greenpatch SA 38 D8
Greens Beach Tas. 95 K6
Greensborough Vic. 21 K5
Greenthorpe NSW 6 E8, 14 C1
Greenvale Qld 81 L12
Greenwald Vic. 24 C7
Greenways SA 48 G10
Greenwell Point NSW 7 K11
Greg Greg NSW 14 B8, 32 H1
Gregors Creek Qld 74 A7
Gregory Qld 83 D11
Gregory WA 56 A3
Gregory National Park NT 66 E12, 68 C3
Grenfell NSW 6 D8, 14 B1
Grenville Vic. 20 C6, 25 O5
Gresford NSW 7 M3
Greta Vic. 31 M7
Greta West Vic. 31 M7
Gretna Tas. 90 E3, 93 K7
Grevillia NSW 9 O2, 77 P11
Griffith NSW 13 N7
Griffiths Island Vic. 24 G9
Grimwade WA 53 I7, 54 D9
Gringegalgona Vic. 24 E3
Gritjurk Vic. 24 E4
Grogan NSW 6 C9, 14 A2
Grong Grong NSW 6 A11, 13 P9
Grose Vale NSW 5 J6
Grosvenor Qld 77 M4
Grove Tas. 90 F7, 93 K9
Grove Hill NT 64 H10
Grovedale Vic. 20 F10
Gruyere Vic. 21 M5
Gubbata NSW 13 P5
Guilderton WA 54 B2, 56 C7
Guildford Tas. 94 F8
Guildford Vic. 20 E1, 25 Q1, 27 Q12, 30 B11
Guildford WA 52 D4
Gul Gul NT 66 G2
Gular NSW 8 C11
Gulargambone NSW 8 D11
Gulf Creek NSW 9 J7
Gulf of Carpentaria 82 A3, 83 E2
Gulf St Vincent 37 C4, 39 J8
Gulf Savannah Qld 80 C12, 83 H12
Gulflander Train, The Qld 80 D9
Gulgong NSW 6 H3
Gullewa WA 56 C3
Gulnare SA 39 K4
Gulpa NSW 13 K12, 30 F1
Guluguba Qld 77 J6
Gum Creek SA 39 L5
Gum Lake NSW 12 F2
Gumble NSW 6 E5
Gumbowie SA 39 L2, 41 L13
Gumeracha SA 36 E8, 39 L9, 48 C1
Gumlu Qld 78 H2
Gumly Gumly NSW 6 B12, 13 R10

100 Gunalda–Koolunga

Gunalda Qld 77 P5
Gunbar NSW 13 M6
Gunbar South NSW 13 M6
Gunbower Vic. 13 J13, 27 R4, 30 C3
Gundabooka National Park NSW 11 M6
Gundagai NSW 6 D12, 14 B5
Gundaring WA 54 G8
Gundaroo NSW 6 G11, 14 E4
Gundary NSW 17 M8
Gunderman NSW 5 N4
Gundiah Qld 77 P5
Gundillion NSW 14 F7, 17 K7
Gundowring Vic. 31 Q6, 32 C4
Gundowring North Vic. 31 Q6, 32 C3
Gundy NSW 7 L1
Gunebang NSW 13 P3
Gungahlin ACT 16 G1
Gungal NSW 7 J2
Gunnary NSW 6 F9, 14 D2
Gunnedah NSW 8 H10
Gunner Vic. 28 F10
Gunnewin Qld 76 G5
Gunning NSW 6 G11, 14 E4
Gunning Grach NSW 14 E10, 33 M6
Gunningbland NSW 6 C5
Gunns Plains Tas. 94 H7
Gunpowder Qld 84 E1
Gununa Qld 83 D6
Gunyah Vic. 23 J9
Gunyangara NT 67 P5
Gurig National Park NT 66 G3
Gurig Store NT 66 G2
Gurley NSW 8 G6
Gurrai SA 39 Q10, 48 H2
Gurrumuru NT 67 O6
Gurrundah NSW 6 G10, 14 F3
Guthalungra Qld 78 I2
Guthega NSW 14 C9, 16 B12, 33 J4
Guy Fawkes River National Park NSW 9 N7
Guyong NSW 6 G6
Guyra NSW 9 L8
Guys Forest Vic. 14 A8, 32 F2
Gwabegar NSW 8 E9
Gwalia WA 56 I3
Gwandalan NSW 5 R1
Gwandalan Tas. 91 K8, 93 N9
Gymbowen Vic. 26 D9
Gympie Qld 77 P6
Gypsum Vic. 28 H10
Haasts Bluff NT 70 G8
Hackham SA 36 A12, 37 F3
Hackney SA 35 H6
Haddon Vic. 20 B4, 25 O3
Haden Qld 77 N8
Hadspen Tas. 95 L9
Hagley Tas. 95 K9
Hahndorf SA 36 D11, 37 I2, 39 L9, 48 C2
Haig WA 57 O6
Haigslea Qld 74 C13
Hail Creek Qld 79 J6
Halbury SA 39 K6
Hale Village Qld 75 D11
Half Tide Qld 79 L5
Halfway Creek NSW 9 P7
Halfway Mill Roadhouse WA 56 B5
Halidon SA 39 P9, 48 G1
Halifax Qld 81 O11
Hall ACT 16 G1
Hallett SA 39 L4
Hallett Cove SA 36 A11, 37 F2
Hallidays Point NSW 7 P2
Halls Creek WA 61 P9
Halls Gap Vic. 24 I1, 26 I12
Halls Head WA 52 B9
Hallston Vic. 21 Q12, 22 I8
Halton NSW 7 M2
Hamel WA 52 C12, 54 C6
Hamelin Bay WA 53 B12
Hamersley Range WA 55 G3, 58 A4
Hamilton SA 36 E1, 39 L7
Hamilton Tas. 90 D1, 93 J6
Hamilton Vic. 24 F5
Hamilton Island Qld 79 K3
Hamley Bridge SA 36 C2, 39 L7
Hammond SA 39 K1, 41 J11
Hampden SA 39 M6
Hampshire Tas. 94 F7
Hampton NSW 4 F6, 6 I7
Hampton Qld 77 N8
Hanging Rock Vic. 20 H2
Hann Crossing Qld 81 J1, 82 G13
Hann River Roadhouse Qld 80 I2
Hann Tableland National Park Qld 81 L6
Hannahs Bridge NSW 6 H1
Hannan NSW 13 O5
Hansborough SA 36 G1, 39 M7
Hanson SA 39 L5
Hanwood NSW 13 N7
Happy Valley Vic. 20 B5, 25 N4, 29 J6
Harcourt Vic. 27 Q11, 30 C10
Harcourt North Vic. 27 Q11, 30 C10
Harden NSW 6 E10, 14 C3
Hardwicke Bay SA 38 H9
Harefield NSW 6 C12, 13 R10, 14 A4
Harford Tas. 95 J7
Hargraves NSW 6 H4
Harkaway Vic. 21 M8
Harlin Qld 74 A7, 77 O7
Harrietville Vic. 31 Q9, 32 C7
Harrington NSW 7 P1, 9 O13
Harrismith WA 54 H6
Harrisville Qld 75 A9
Harrogate SA 36 F10
Harrow Vic. 24 D1, 26 D12
Harrys Creek Vic. 31 J8
Harston Vic. 30 G6
Hart SA 39 K5
Hartley NSW 4 G5, 6 I6
Hartley SA 36 F13
Hartley Vale NSW 4 G5
Hartz Mountains National Park Tas. 90 B10, 93 J10
Harvey WA 53 H2, 54 C7, 56 C10
Harwood NSW 9 Q5
Haslam SA 43 P11
Hassell National Park WA 54 I12, 56 F12
Hastings Tas. 90 D13, 93 J12
Hastings Vic. 21 L11, 22 E7
Hastings Caves Tas. 90 C13
Hastings Point NSW 9 Q1, 77 R11
Hat Head NSW 9 P10
Hat Head National Park NSW 9 P10
Hatches Creek NT 69 M13, 71 L2
Hatfield NSW 12 H6, 29 O1
Hatherleigh SA 48 G11
Hattah Vic. 12 E9, 28 H7
Hattah–Kulkyne National Park Vic. 12 D8, 28 H6
Hatton Vale Qld 74 B13
Havelock Vic. 27 O11
Haven Vic. 26 G10
Havilah Vic. 31 P7, 32 B5
Hawker SA 41 J9
Hawkesbury Heights NSW 5 K6
Hawkesbury River NSW 5 L5
Hawkesdale Vic. 24 H7
Hawks Nest NSW 7 O4
Hawley Beach Tas. 95 J6
Hay NSW 13 K8
Haydens Bog Vic. 14 D12, 33 L8
Hayes Tas. 90 E4, 93 K7
Hayes Creek Wayside Inn NT 64 G11, 66 E8
Hayman Island Qld 79 K2
Haymarket NSW 3 C12
Haysdale Vic. 29 L8
Hazel Park Vic. 23 J10
Hazelbrook NSW 4 I7
Hazeldene Qld 74 C8
Hazeldene Vic. 21 L2, 22 E1, 30 H12
Hazelgrove NSW 4 E6
Hazelwood Vic. 23 J7
Head of Bight SA 42 G7
Healesville Vic. 21 N5, 22 F3
Healesville Sanctuary Vic. 21 N5
Heartbreak Hotel NT 69 N4
Heath Hill Vic. 21 O10, 22 G7
Heathcote NSW 5 M11, 7 L8
Heathcote Vic. 30 E9
Heathcote Junction Vic. 21 K2, 22 D1, 30 G12
Heathcote National Park NSW 5 M11
Heathfield Vic. 24 B4, 48 I11
Heathmere Vic. 24 D8
Heathvale Vic. 26 H11
Hebden NSW 7 L3
Hebel Qld 8 B3, 76 F13
Hector Qld 79 L5
Hedley Vic. 23 K10
Heidelberg Vic. 21 K6
Heka Tas. 94 G7
Helensburgh NSW 5 M12, 7 L9
Helensvale Qld 75 G10, 77 Q10
Helenvale Qld 81 L3
Helidon Qld 77 O9
Hell Hole Gorge National Park Qld 87 O4
Helling NT 66 G10
Hells Gate Roadhouse Qld 83 B8
Hellyer Tas. 94 E4
Henley Beach SA 36 A9
Henrietta Tas. 94 F6
Hensley Park Vic. 24 G4
Henty NSW 6 A13, 13 Q11
Henty Vic. 24 D5
Hepburn Springs Vic. 20 E2, 25 Q2, 27 Q13, 30 B12
Herberton Qld 81 M8
Hermannsburg NT 70 H9
Hermidale NSW 11 P10
Hernani NSW 9 N8
Heron Island Qld 79 Q11
Herons Creek NSW 9 O12
Herrick Tas. 95 P6
Hervey Bay Qld 77 P3
Hesket Vic. 20 H2
Hesso SA 40 H9
Hewetsons Mill NSW 9 N2
Hexham NSW 7 M4
Hexham Vic. 25 J7
Heybridge Tas. 94 G6
Heyfield Vic. 23 L5
Heywood Vic. 24 D8
Hi Way Inn Roadhouse NT 68 I3
Hiamdale Vic. 23 L7
Hiawatha Vic. 23 K9
Hideaway Bay Tas. 90 E11
High Camp Vic. 20 I1, 30 F11
High Range NSW 4 H13, 7 J9, 14 H2
Highbury WA 54 G7
Highclere Tas. 94 G6
Highcroft Tas. 91 M10, 93 N10
Higher McDonald NSW 5 M2
Highfields Qld 77 N9
Highgate WA 51 F2
Highgate Hill Qld 73 C13
Highlands Vic. 21 M1, 30 H10
Highvale Qld 74 E11, 75 B4
Hilgay Vic. 24 D4
Hill End NSW 4 A1, 6 G5
Hill End Vic. 21 R8, 22 I5
Hillarys WA 52 B3
Hillcrest Vic. 20 B4
Hillgrove NSW 9 M9
Hillman WA 54 F8
Hillside Vic. 23 P4, 32 F13
Hillston NSW 13 M4
Hilltop NSW 5 J13, 7 J9, 14 I2
Hilltown SA 39 L5
Hillview Qld 75 D13
Hillwood Tas. 95 L7
Hinchinbrook Island Qld 81 N10
Hinchinbrook Island National Park Qld 81 O10
Hindmarsh Island SA 37 I8, 48 C4
Hindmarsh Valley SA 37 G7
Hines Hill WA 54 I2
Hinnomunjie Vic. 14 A11, 32 F8
Hirstglen Qld 77 N10
Hobart Tas. 89, 90 I6, 93 L8
Hobbys Yards NSW 4 A7, 6 G7
Hoddle Vic. 22 I10
Hoddles Creek Vic. 21 N6, 22 F4
Hodgson River NT 67 K12, 69 K2
Holbrook NSW 13 R12, 31 R1
Hollow Tree Tas. 93 K6
Holly WA 54 G9
Hollydeen NSW 7 K2
Holmwood NSW 6 F7
Holwell Tas. 95 K7
Home Hill Qld 78 H1, 81 Q13
Homebush NSW 7 L8
Homebush Qld 79 K5
Homebush Bay NSW 5 N8
Homecroft Vic. 26 I6
Homerton Vic. 24 E8
Homestead Qld 78 D3, 85 R3
Homevale National Park Qld 79 J5
Homewood Vic. 21 M1
Honiton SA 38 I10
Hook Island Qld 79 K2
Hope Forest SA 37 G5
Hope Vale Qld 81 L2
Hopetoun Vic. 12 E12, 26 H3, 28 H13
Hopetoun WA 56 H11
Hopetoun West Vic. 26 G2, 28 G13
Hopevale Vic. 26 G3
Hoppers Crossing Vic. 20 H7
Hordern Vale Vic. 25 M12
Horn Island Qld 82 C2
Hornsby NSW 5 N7
Hornsdale SA 39 K2, 41 K13
Horrocks WA 56 A3
Horse Lake NSW 10 D12
Horseshoe Bay Qld 81 P12
Horsham SA 36 C13, 37 H4
Horsham Vic. 26 G9
Horsley Park NSW 5 L8
Hoskinstown NSW 6 H13, 14 F6, 17 J3
Hotham Heights Vic. 31 Q10, 32 D8
Hotspur Vic. 24 D6
Houghton SA 36 D8
Houtman Abrolhos Islands WA 56 A4
Howard Qld 77 P3
Howard Springs NT 64 D3, 66 E5
Howard Springs Nature Park NT 64 D2
Howden Tas. 90 H8, 93 L9
Howes Valley NSW 7 K4
Howley NT 64 G10
Howlong NSW 13 P13, 31 O3, 32 A1
Howqua Vic. 21 R2, 31 L11
Howrah Tas. 93 M8
Howth Tas. 94 G6
Hoya Qld 75 A10
Hoyleton SA 39 K6
Huddleston SA 39 K3
Hughenden Qld 78 A4, 85 O4
Hughes SA 42 C5
Hull River National Park Qld 81 N9
Hume ACT 16 H3
Hume Park NSW 6 F11, 14 D4
Humevale Vic. 21 K3
Humpty Doo NT 64 E3, 66 E6
Humula NSW 6 C13, 14 A6
Hunchy Qld 74 F4
Hungerford Qld 11 J1, 87 O13
Hunter Vic. 30 D6
Hunterston Vic. 23 M9
Huntly Vic. 27 R9, 30 C8
Huon Vic. 31 Q5, 32 C2
Huon Valley Tas. 90 C8
Huonville Tas. 90 F8, 93 K9
Hurdle Flat Vic. 31 O6, 32 A4
Hurstbridge Vic. 21 L5, 22 E3
Hurstville NSW 5 N9
Huskisson NSW 7 K12, 14 I4, 17 R1
Hutt WA 56 A2
Hyams Beach NSW 17 R2
Hyden WA 56 F8
Hyland Park NSW 9 P9
Hynam SA 26 A11, 48 I9
Icy Creek Vic. 21 Q7, 22 I4
Ida Bay Tas. 93 J12
Idalia National Park Qld 87 P2
Iguana Creek Vic. 23 O4, 32 E13
Ilbilbie Qld 79 L6
Ilford NSW 6 I5
Ilfracombe Qld 78 A11, 85 P11
Illabarook Vic. 20 B6, 25 N5
Illabo NSW 6 C11, 14 A4
Illalong Creek NSW 6 E11, 14 D3
Illawarra Vic. 27 J11
Illawarra Coast NSW 7 K13, 14 I7, 17 Q6
Illawong WA 56 B5
Illowa Vic. 24 H9
Iluka NSW 9 Q5
Imangara NT 69 L13, 71 L3
Imanpa NT 70 H11
Imbil Qld 74 D2, 77 P6
Impimi NSW 12 H9, 29 O7
Inala Qld 75 D7
Indented Head Vic. 20 I9, 22 B6
Indian Ocean 54 A6, 60 C4
Indigo Vic. 31 N4, 32 A2
Indigo Upper Vic. 31 O5, 32 B3
Indooroopilly Qld 74 F13, 75 D5
Ingebyra NSW 14 C10, 33 J6
Ingham Qld 81 N11
Inglegar NSW 8 B12
Ingleside Qld 75 G13
Inglewood Qld 9 K1, 77 L11
Inglewood SA 36 D8
Inglewood Tas. 93 M5
Inglewood Vic. 27 O8, 30 A7
Ingliston Vic. 20 F5
Injinoo Qld 82 C3
Injune Qld 76 G5
Inkerman Qld 78 H1
Inkerman SA 39 J7
Inman Valley SA 37 E7
Innamincka SA 47 Q7, 86 H10
Innamincka Regional Reserve SA 47 P5, 86 G8
Innes National Park SA 38 G10
Inneston SA 38 G10
Innisfail Qld 81 N8
Innisplain Qld 75 B12
Innot Hot Springs Qld 81 L8
Interlaken Tas. 93 L4, 95 L13
Inverell NSW 9 K6
Invergordon Vic. 13 M13, 30 I4
Inverleigh Vic. 20 E9, 25 P7
Inverloch Vic. 22 G10
Iona Vic. 21 O9
Ipswich Qld 75 B7, 77 P9
Iraak Vic. 12 E8, 28 H5
Irishtown Tas. 94 D4
Iron Baron SA 38 H2, 40 G13
Iron Knob SA 38 H1, 40 G12
Iron Range Qld 82 E8
Iron Range National Park Qld 82 E7
Irrewarra Vic. 20 B11
Irrewillipe Vic. 20 A12, 25 M9
Irrwelty NT 71 L5
Irvinebank Qld 81 L8
Irymple Vic. 12 D7, 28 G3
Isabella NSW 4 C9, 6 H8, 14 F1
Isisford Qld 78 A13, 85 P13, 87 O1
Isla Gorge National Park Qld 77 J3
Island Bend NSW 16 C11
Isles of St Francis SA 43 M11
Ivanhoe NSW 13 J2
Ivory Creek Qld 74 A8
Iwantja (Indulkana) SA 45 N4
Iwupataka NT 70 I8
Jabiru NT 65 P4, 66 H6
Jabuk SA 39 O11, 48 F3
Jack River Vic. 23 K9
Jackadgery NSW 9 O5
Jackeys Marsh Tas. 95 J10
Jackie Junction WA 59 N10
Jackson Qld 76 I7
Jacobs Well Qld 75 G9, 77 Q10
Jacobs Well WA 54 F4
Jalloonda Qld 81 O12
Jallumba Vic. 26 F11
Jaloran WA 54 G7
Jamberoo NSW 7 K10
Jambin Qld 79 N13
Jamestown SA 39 L3, 41 K13
Jamieson Vic. 21 R2, 22 I1, 31 L12
Jan Juc Vic. 20 F11
Jancourt East Vic. 25 L9
Jandakot WA 52 C6
Jandowae Qld 77 L7
Jardee WA 54 D11
Jardine River National Park Qld 82 C4
Jarklin Vic. 27 P6, 30 A5
Jarra Jarra NT 68 I13, 70 I2
Jarrahdale WA 52 D8, 54 D5
Jarrahmond Vic. 33 J12
Jarrahwood WA 53 G8, 54 C9
Jarvis Creek Vic. 31 R4, 32 D2
Jaurdi WA 56 H6
Jeeralang North Vic. 23 K8
Jeffcott Vic. 27 L7
Jeffcott North Vic. 27 L6
Jemalong NSW 6 C6
Jennacubbine WA 54 E2
Jenolan Caves NSW 4 F8, 6 I7
Jeogla NSW 9 M9
Jeparit Vic. 26 F6
Jerangle NSW 14 F7, 16 I8
Jericho Qld 78 E11
Jericho Tas. 93 L5
Jericho Vic. 21 R5, 23 J3
Jerilderie NSW 13 M11
Jerramungup WA 56 G11
Jerrawa NSW 6 G11, 14 E4
Jerrys Plains NSW 7 K3
Jerseyville NSW 9 P10
Jervis Bay JBT 7 K12, 14 I5, 17 R2
Jervois SA 39 N10, 48 E3
Jetsonville Tas. 95 N6
Ji-Marda NT 67 L5
Jigalong WA 58 F6
Jil Jil Vic. 27 K3
Jilliby NSW 5 P2, 7 M6
Jimaringle NSW 13 J11, 29 R10
Jimboomba Qld 75 D9, 77 P10
Jimbour Qld 77 M7
Jimenbuen NSW 14 D10, 33 L6
Jimna Qld 74 B4, 77 O7
Jindabyne NSW 14 D9, 16 C12, 33 K4
Jindera NSW 13 P13, 31 P3, 32 B1
Jindivick Vic. 21 P8, 22 H5
Jindong WA 53 D8
Jingalup WA 54 F10
Jingellic NSW 14 A8, 32 F1
Jitarning WA 54 I6, 56 E9
Joadja NSW 7 J10, 14 H2
Joanna SA 24 A1, 26 A12, 48 I9
Joel Joel Vic. 27 K11
Johanna Vic. 25 M12
John Forrest National Park WA 52 D4
Johnburgh SA 41 K11
Johns River NSW 9 O13
Johnsonville Vic. 23 Q4, 32 G13
Jondaryan Qld 77 M8
Joondalup WA 52 B3
Josbury WA 54 F7
Josephville Qld 75 C11
Joskeleigh Qld 79 O11
Jubuck WA 54 H5
Judbury Tas. 90 D7, 93 K9
Jugiong NSW 6 E11, 14 C4
Julatten Qld 81 M6
Julia SA 39 M6
Julia Creek Qld 85 J4
Jumbuk Vic. 23 K8
Jumbunna Vic. 21 O12, 22 H9
Junction Hill NSW 9 P6
Jundah Qld 87 M2
Junee NSW 6 C11, 13 R9, 14 A4
Junee Reefs NSW 6 C11, 14 A3
Jung Vic. 26 H8
Junortoun Vic. 27 R10, 30 C8
Jupiter Creek SA 36 C12, 37 H3
Jura WA 54 I3
Jurien Bay WA 56 B6
Jurunjung Vic. 20 H4
Kaarimba Vic. 30 H4
Kabra Qld 79 N11
Kadina SA 38 I6
Kadnook Vic. 24 C1, 26 C12
Kadungle NSW 6 C4
Kagaru Qld 75 C9
Kaglan WA 54 I12
Kaimkillenbun Qld 77 M8
Kain NSW 14 F7, 17 J6
Kainton SA 39 J6
Kairi Qld 81 M7
Kajabbi Qld 84 F2
Kakadu National Park NT 65 O2, 66 G5
Kalamunda WA 52 D5
Kalamunda National Park WA 52 D5
Kalangadoo SA 48 H11
Kalangara Qld 74 D7
Kalannie WA 56 D6
Kalaru NSW 14 G10, 33 Q6
Kalbar Qld 77 P10
Kalbarri WA 55 C13, 56 A2
Kalbarri National Park WA 55 C13, 56 A1
Kaleentha Loop NSW 12 F1
Kalgoorlie–Boulder WA 56 I6
Kalimna Vic. 23 R5, 32 H13
Kalimna West Vic. 23 R4, 32 G13
Kalinjarri NT 69 K12, 71 K1
Kalka SA 44 A1, 59 R11, 70 B13
Kalkallo Vic. 21 J4, 22 C2, 30 F13
Kalkarindji NT 68 D6
Kalkee Vic. 26 G8
Kalkite NSW 16 D12
Kallangur Qld 74 F10, 75 D3
Kalpienung Vic. 27 M3
Kalpowar Qld 77 M2
Kalpowar Crossing Qld 81 J1, 82 G13
Kaltukatjara (Docker River) NT 59 R9, 70 A11
Kalumburu WA 61 N2
Kalumpurlpa NT 69 J9
Kalunga Qld 81 L8
Kalyan SA 39 O9, 48 F1
Kamarah NSW 6 A9, 13 P7
Kamarooka Vic. 27 R8, 30 D7
Kambalda WA 57 J7
Kamballup WA 54 I11
Kamber NSW 8 D12
Kameruka NSW 14 G10, 33 P6
Kamona Tas. 95 O7
Kanangra–Boyd National Park NSW 4 F8, 6 I8, 14 H1
Kanawalla Vic. 24 G5
Kancoona Vic. 31 P7, 32 C5
Kandanga Qld 74 D1
Kandanga Creek Qld 74 C1
Kandanga Upper Qld 74 C2
Kandiwal WA 61 M3
Kandos NSW 6 I4
Kangarilla SA 36 C12, 37 G3, 39 L10, 48 B2
Kangaroo Flat NSW 9 M11
Kangaroo Flat SA 36 C5
Kangaroo Island SA 37 A11, 38 F11
Kangaroo Point Qld 73 I7
Kangaroo Valley NSW 7 J11, 14 I3
Kangarooby NSW 6 E7
Kangawall Vic. 26 D10
Kangiara NSW 6 F10, 14 D3
Kaniva Vic. 26 C7
Kanmantoo SA 36 F11
Kanumbra Vic. 31 J10
Kanya Vic. 27 K10
Kanyapella Vic. 13 K13, 30 F4
Kanypi SA 44 D2, 70 C13
Kaoota Tas. 90 G8, 93 L9
Kapinnie SA 38 C6
Kapooka NSW 6 B12, 13 R10
Kapunda SA 36 E3, 39 L7
Karabeal Vic. 24 G4
Karadoc Vic. 12 E7, 28 H4
Karalundi WA 58 C11
Karama NT 64 C2
Karanja Tas. 90 D3
Karara Qld 9 L1, 77 M11
Karatta SA 38 G13
Karawinna Vic. 12 C8, 28 E4
Kariah Vic. 25 L8
Karijini National Park WA 55 I5, 58 B5
Karkoo SA 38 D6
Karlgarin WA 56 F9
Karlo Creek Vic. 14 F13, 33 O11
Karn Vic. 31 L7
Karnak Vic. 26 D10
Karnup WA 52 B8
Karonie WA 57 K6
Karoola Tas. 95 M7
Karoonda SA 39 O10, 48 F2
Karoonda Roadhouse Vic. 14 C12, 32 I9
Karrana Downs Qld 74 E13, 75 B6
Karratha WA 55 G1
Karratha Roadhouse WA 55 G1
Karridale WA 53 C12, 54 B10
Kars Springs NSW 7 J1, 8 I13
Karte SA 39 Q10, 48 H2
Karuah NSW 7 N3
Karumba Qld 80 B8, 83 H8
Karumba Point Qld 80 B8, 83 H8
Karween Vic. 12 B8, 28 C4
Karyrie Vic. 27 K4
Kata Tjuṯa NT 70 D12
Katamatite Vic. 13 M13, 31 J4
Katandra Vic. 30 I5
Katandra West Vic. 30 I5
Katanning WA 54 H9, 56 E10
Katherine NT 66 G10
Katoomba NSW 4 H7, 7 J7
Kattyong Vic. 28 F9
Katunga Vic. 13 M13, 30 I3
Katyil Vic. 26 G7
Kawarren Vic. 20 B12, 25 N10
Kayena Tas. 95 K7
Keep River National Park NT 61 R5, 66 A13, 68 A2
Keera NSW 9 J7
Keilor Vic. 20 I5, 22 C3
Keith SA 39 P13, 48 G6
Kellalac Vic. 26 H7
Kellatier Tas. 94 F6
Kellerberrin WA 54 H3, 56 E7
Kellevie Tas. 91 N5, 93 N8
Kelmscott WA 52 D6
Kelso NSW 4 B4
Kelso Tas. 95 K6
Kelvin NSW 8 I10
Kelvin View Vic. 31 J9
Kempsey NSW 9 O11
Kempton Tas. 90 H1, 93 L6
Kendall NSW 9 O12
Kendenup WA 54 H11
Kenebri NSW 8 E9
Kenilworth Qld 74 D3, 77 P7
Kenley Vic. 29 M7
Kenmare Vic. 12 D13, 26 G4
Kenmore NSW 6 H11, 14 G3
Kenmore Qld 74 F13, 75 C6
Kennedy Qld 81 N10
Kennedy Range National Park WA 55 D8
Kennedys Creek Vic. 25 L11
Kennett River Vic. 25 O11
Kennys Creek NSW 6 F10, 14 D2
Kent Town SA 35 H8
Kentbruck Vic. 24 C8
Kenthurst NSW 5 M6
Kentucky NSW 9 L9
Keppel Bay Islands National Park Qld 79 P10
Keppel Sands Qld 79 O11
Keppoch SA 48 H8
Kerang Vic. 12 I12, 27 P3, 29 P13, 30 A2
Kerang East Vic. 27 P3, 30 B2
Kerang South Vic. 12 I13, 27 P3, 30 A2
Kergunyah Vic. 31 Q5, 32 C3
Kergunyah South Vic. 31 P6, 32 C4
Kernot Vic. 21 N12, 22 G8
Kerrabee NSW 7 J3
Kerrie Vic. 20 H2
Kerrisdale Vic. 21 L1, 30 H11
Kerrs Creek NSW 6 G5
Kerry Qld 75 D12
Kersbrook SA 36 E8, 39 L9, 48 C1
Keswick SA 35 A13
Kettering Tas. 90 H9, 93 L10
Kevington Vic. 21 R3, 22 I1, 31 L12
Kew NSW 9 O12
Kew Vic. 21 K6
Kewell Vic. 26 H8
Keyneton SA 36 H5, 39 M8
Keysbrook WA 52 D9, 54 D5
Khancoban NSW 14 B9, 32 H3
Ki Ki SA 39 O11, 48 F4
Kiah NSW 14 G12, 33 Q9
Kialla NSW 6 H10, 14 F3
Kialla Vic. 30 I6
Kialla West Vic. 30 H6
Kiama NSW 7 K10
Kiamba Qld 74 F3
Kiamil Vic. 12 E10, 28 H8
Kiana SA 38 C6
Kiandra NSW 14 C7, 16 C7
Kianga NSW 17 N11
Kiata Vic. 26 E7
Kidston Qld 81 J11
Kielpa SA 38 E4
Kies Hill SA 49 C10
Kiewa Vic. 31 Q5, 32 C3
Kikoira NSW 13 P5
Kilcoy Qld 74 C7, 77 P8
Kilcunda Vic. 21 M13, 22 F9
Kilkerran SA 38 I7
Kilkivan Qld 77 O5
Killabakh NSW 9 N13
Killarney Qld 9 N1, 77 O11
Killarney Vic. 24 H9
Killawarra Vic. 31 L5
Killcare NSW 5 P5
Killiecrankie Tas. 92 A10
Killora Tas. 90 H9, 93 L10
Kilmany Vic. 23 M6
Kilmany South Vic. 23 M6
Kilmore Vic. 21 J2, 30 F11
Kilpalie SA 39 O9, 48 G2
Kimba SA 38 F3, 40 E13
Kimberley, The WA 60 L6
Kimbriki NSW 7 O1, 9 N13
Kinalung NSW 10 D12
Kinchega National Park NSW 10 D13, 12 D1
Kinchela NSW 9 P10
Kincumber NSW 5 P4, 7 M6
Kindred Tas. 94 H7
King Ash Bay NT 67 O13, 69 O2
King Island Tas. 93 R10
King River WA 54 H13
King Valley Vic. 31 N8
Kingaroy Qld 77 N6
Kinglake Vic. 21 M4, 22 E2, 30 H13
Kinglake Central Vic. 21 L3
Kinglake East Vic. 21 M4
Kinglake National Park Vic. 21 M3, 22 E1, 30 H13
Kinglake West Vic. 21 L3, 22 E2, 30 H13
Kingoonya SA 40 B5
Kingower Vic. 27 O9
Kings Camp SA 48 E9
Kings Canyon NT 70 F9
Kings Canyon Resort NT 70 F9
Kings Cross NSW 3 I9
Kings Plains National Park NSW 9 K5
Kings Point NSW 7 J13, 14 I6, 17 P4
Kingsborough Qld 81 L6
Kingscliff NSW 9 Q1, 77 R11
Kingscote SA 38 I12
Kingsdale NSW 6 H10, 14 G3
Kingsford NSW 5 O9
Kingsthorpe Qld 77 N9
Kingston ACT 15 G13
Kingston Tas. 90 H7, 93 L9
Kingston Vic. 20 D2, 25 P2, 27 P13, 30 B12
Kingston Beach Tas. 90 H7
Kingston S.E. SA 48 F8
Kingston-on-Murray SA 39 P7
Kingstown NSW 9 K8
Kingsvale NSW 6 E10, 14 C2
Kingswood NSW 5 K7
Kingswood SA 41 J10
Kinimakatka Vic. 26 D7
Kinka Beach Qld 79 O10
Kinnabulla Vic. 27 J4
Kintore NT 59 R6, 70 B7
Kioloa NSW 7 J13, 14 H6, 17 P6
Kiora NSW 17 M9
Kirkstall Vic. 24 H9
Kirup WA 53 H7, 54 C9
Kitchener WA 57 L6
Kithbrook Vic. 31 J9
Kiwirrkurra WA 59 P5
Knebsworth Vic. 24 F7
Knockrow NSW 9 Q3, 77 Q12
Knockwood Vic. 21 R3
Knorrit Flat NSW 7 O1, 9 M13
Knowsley Vic. 30 E9
Koallah Vic. 25 L9
Kobble Qld 74 E10, 75 B3
Kobyboyn Vic. 30 H10
Koetong Vic. 14 A8, 32 E2
Kogan Qld 77 L8
Koimbo Vic. 29 K8
Kojonup WA 54 G9, 56 E11
Koloona NSW 9 J6
Kolora Vic. 25 K8
Komungla NSW 6 H11, 14 G4
Konagaderra Vic. 20 I4
Kondalilla National Park Qld 74 E4
Kondinin WA 54 I5, 56 F9
Kongal SA 48 H6
Kongorong SA 48 H12
Kongwak Vic. 21 O13, 22 G9
Konnongorring WA 54 F1
Konong Wootong Vic. 24 D3
Konong Wootong North Vic. 24 D3
Koo-wee-rup Vic. 21 M10, 22 F7
Kookaburra NSW 9 N10
Kookynie WA 56 I4
Koolan WA 61 J5
Kooloonong Vic. 12 G9, 29 L8
Koolunga SA 39 K4

Koolyanobbing–Melrose 101

Koolyanobbing WA 56 G6
Koolywurtie SA 38 I8
Koonda Vic. 28 D9, 31 J7
Koondrook Vic. 12 I12, 27 Q2, 29 Q13, 30 B1
Koongawa SA 38 D3, 40 C13
Koonibba SA 43 N9
Kooninderie SA 36 G1
Koonoomoo Vic. 30 I2
Koonunga SA 36 F3, 49 G1
Koonwarra Vic. 21 P13, 22 H9
Koonya Tas. 91 M9, 93 N10
Koorack Koorack Vic. 27 N3, 29 N13
Kooralbyn Qld 75 B12
Koorawatha NSW 6 E8, 14 C1
Koorda WA 56 E6
Kooreh Vic. 27 M9
Kooringal Qld 75 H4
Koorkab Vic. 29 L7
Koorlong Vic. 12 D7, 28 G4
Kootingal NSW 9 K10
Koppamurra SA 26 A11, 48 I9
Koppio SA 38 D7
Korbel WA 54 I3
Koriella Vic. 21 O1
Korobeit Vic. 20 F4
Koroit Vic. 24 H9
Korong Vale Vic. 27 O7
Koroop Vic. 27 Q3, 30 B2
Korora NSW 9 P8
Korumburra Vic. 21 O12, 22 H8
Korweinguboora Vic. 20 E3
Kosciuszko National Park NSW 6 E13, 14 C8, 16 C4, 33 J1
Kotta Vic. 30 D5
Kotupna Vic. 13 L13, 30 G4
Koumala Qld 79 L6
Kowanyama Qld 80 D3
Kowat Vic. 14 E12, 33 N10
Koyuga Vic. 30 F5
Krambach NSW 7 O1
Kringin SA 39 Q9, 48 H2
Kroemers Crossing SA 49 F5
Krongart SA 48 H11
Kroombit Tops National Park Qld 77 L1, 79 O13
Krowera Vic. 21 O12
Ku-ring-gai Chase National Park NSW 5 O6, 7 L7
Kudardup WA 53 C12
Kuitpo SA 36 C13, 37 G4
Kuitpo Colony SA 37 H5
Kukerin WA 54 I7, 56 F10
Kulgera NT 70 I13
Kulgun Qld 75 A10
Kulikup WA 54 E9
Kulin WA 54 I6, 56 F9
Kulkami SA 39 P10, 48 G2
Kulkyne Vic. 28 H6
Kulnine Vic. 28 D3
Kulnine East Vic. 12 C7, 28 D3
Kulnura NSW 5 O2, 7 L5
Kulpara SA 39 J6
Kulpi Qld 77 N8
Kulwin Vic. 28 I9
Kulyalling WA 54 F5
Kumarina Roadhouse WA 58 D8
Kumarl WA 57 J9
Kumbarilla Qld 77 L8
Kumbatine National Park NSW 9 O11
Kumbia Qld 77 N7
Kumorna SA 39 P13, 48 G5
Kunama NSW 14 B6
Kunat Vic. 27 N1, 29 N12
Kundabung NSW 9 O11
Kungala NSW 9 P7
Kunghur NSW 9 P2
Kunjin WA 54 H5
Kunlara SA 39 O8, 48 F1
Kununoppin WA 54 H1
Kununurra WA 61 Q5
Kunwarara Qld 79 N9
Kupingarri WA 61 M7
Kuranda Qld 81 M6
Kureelpa Qld 74 F4
Kuridala Qld 84 G5
Kuringup WA 54 I8
Kurmond NSW 5 K5
Kurnbrunin Vic. 26 E4
Kurnell NSW 5 O10
Kurnwill Vic. 12 B8, 28 C5
Kurraca Vic. 27 N8
Kurraca West Vic. 27 N8
Kurrajong NSW 5 K5
Kurrajong Heights NSW 5 J5, 7 K6
Kurri Kurri NSW 7 M4
Kurrimine Beach Qld 81 N9
Kurting Vic. 27 O8, 30 A7
Kurumbul Qld 8 I2, 77 K12
Kuttabul Qld 79 K5
Kweda WA 54 G5
Kwiambal National Park NSW 9 J4
Kwinana WA 52 B7, 54 C4, 56 C8
Kwolyin WA 54 H3
Kyabram Vic. 30 G5
Kyalite NSW 12 H9, 29 N8
Kyancutta SA 38 C3, 40 C13
Kybunga SA 39 K5
Kybybolite SA 26 A10, 48 I8
Kyeamba NSW 6 C13, 13 R11, 14 A6
Kyndalyn Vic. 12 F9, 29 K7
Kyneton Vic. 20 G1, 25 R1, 27 R12, 30 D11
Kynuna Qld 85 J6
Kyogle NSW 9 P2, 77 P12
Kyotmunga WA 52 E1
Kyup Vic. 24 F4
Kyvalley Vic. 30 G5
Kywong NSW 13 P10
La Perouse NSW 5 O10
Laanecoorie Vic. 27 P10, 30 A9
Laang Vic. 25 J9
Labertouche Vic. 21 O9, 22 G6
Lachlan Tas. 90 F5, 93 K8
Lacmalac NSW 16 B2
Lady Barron Tas. 92 B11, 95 R1
Lady Bay Tas. 93 K12
Lady Julia Percy Island Vic. 24 F9
Lady Musgrave Island Qld 79 R12
Ladys Pass Vic. 30 E9
Ladysmith NSW 6 C12, 13 R10, 14 A5
Laen Vic. 27 J7
Laen North Vic. 27 J7
Laggan NSW 6 H9, 14 F2
Lah Vic. 26 H5
Laharum Vic. 26 H11
Laheys Creek NSW 6 G2
Laidley Qld 77 O9
Lajamanu (Hooker Creek) NT 68 D8
Lake Alexandrina SA 48 D3
Lake Argyle WA 61 Q6
Lake Barrington Tas. 94 H8
Lake Bathurst NSW 6 H11, 14 F4
Lake Biddy WA 56 G9
Lake Bindegolly National Park Qld 87 O10
Lake Boga Vic. 12 H11, 27 N1, 29 N11
Lake Bolac Vic. 25 J5
Lake Boort Vic. 27 N5
Lake Buloke Vic. 27 K7
Lake Burley Griffin ACT 15 C7
Lake Cargelligo NSW 13 O4
Lake Cathie NSW 9 O12
Lake Charm Vic. 12 H12, 27 O2, 29 O13, 30 A1
Lake Clifton WA 52 B12, 54 C6
Lake Condah Vic. 24 E7
Lake Conjola NSW 7 J12, 14 I5, 17 Q3
Lake Cowal NSW 6 B7, 13 R5
Lake Eildon Vic. 21 P1, 31 K10
Lake Eildon National Park Vic. 21 P1, 22 H1, 31 K11
Lake Eppalock Vic. 30 D9
Lake Eyre SA 46 G8
Lake Eyre National Park SA 46 G10, 86 B11
Lake Gairdner National Park SA 40 D8, 43 R7
Lake Gilles Conservation Park SA 38 F2
Lake Gordon Tas. 92 G7
Lake Grace WA 56 F9
Lake Hindmarsh Vic. 26 E5
Lake Hume NSW 13 Q13, 31 Q3
Lake King WA 56 G9
Lake Leake Tas. 93 O3, 95 O12
Lake Margaret Tas. 92 E2, 94 E11
Lake Marmal Vic. 27 N6
Lake Meering Vic. 27 O4
Lake Mountain Vic. 21 P4, 22 H2, 31 K13
Lake Mundi Vic. 24 B4, 48 I11
Lake Munmorah NSW 5 R1, 7 M5
Lake Pedder Tas. 92 H8
Lake Poomaho NSW 12 H10, 29 N9
Lake Powell Junction Vic. 29 K6
Lake Rowan Vic. 31 K5
Lake St Clair Tas. 92 H3, 94 H12
Lake Tabourie NSW 14 H6, 17 P5
Lake Torrens National Park SA 40 I5
Lake Tyers Vic. 32 H13
Lake View SA 39 K4
Lakefield National Park Qld 81 J1, 82 G13
Lakeland Qld 81 K4
Lakes Entrance Vic. 23 R5, 32 H13
Lakesland NSW 5 J12
Lal Lal Vic. 20 D5, 25 P4
Lalbert Vic. 12 G12, 27 M2, 29 M13
Lalbert Road Vic. 27 M1, 29 M12
Lalla Tas. 95 M7
Lallat Vic. 27 J9
Lallat North Vic. 27 J8
Lameroo SA 39 Q11, 48 H3
Lamington Qld 75 C13
Lamington National Park Qld 9 P1, 75 E13, 77 P11
Lamplough Vic. 20 A1, 25 M1, 27 N12
Lancaster Vic. 30 G5
Lancefield Vic. 20 I2, 30 E11
Lancelin WA 54 B1, 56 B7
Landsborough Qld 74 G6, 77 P7
Landsborough Vic. 27 L11
Lane Cove NSW 5 N8
Lane Cove National Park NSW 5 N7
Lanena Tas. 95 L7
Lang Lang Vic. 21 N10, 22 F7
Langhorne Creek SA 39 M10, 48 D3
Langi Kal Kal Vic. 20 A3, 25 N2, 27 N13
Langi Logan Vic. 25 K2, 27 K13
Langkoop Vic. 24 B1, 26 B12, 48 I9
Langley Vic. 20 G1, 25 R1, 27 R12, 30 D11
Langlo Crossing Qld 76 A5, 87 R5
Langloh Tas. 93 J6
Langsborough Vic. 23 L10
Langtree NSW 13 M5
Langville Vic. 27 O4, 30 A2
Lankeys Creek NSW 13 R12, 14 A7
Lannercost Qld 81 N11
Lansdowne NSW 7 P1, 9 N13
Lapoinya Tas. 94 E5
Lara Vic. 20 G8, 22 A5, 25 R7
Lara Lake Vic. 20 F8
Laramba NT 70 H6
Laravale Qld 75 C12
Larpent Vic. 20 A11, 25 N9
Larras Lee NSW 6 F5
Larrimah NT 66 I12, 68 I2
Lascelles Vic. 12 E12, 26 I2, 28 I12
Latham WA 56 D5
Latrobe Tas. 94 I7
Lauderdale Tas. 91 J6, 93 M9
Laughtondale NSW 5 M4
Launceston Tas. 95 L8
Launching Place Vic. 21 N6, 22 F4
Laura Qld 81 K3
Laura SA 39 K3, 41 J13
Laurel Hill NSW 14 B7
Laurieton NSW 9 O12
Lauriston Vic. 20 F1, 25 R1, 27 R12, 30 C11
Lavers Hill Vic. 25 M11
Laverton WA 57 J3
Lawgi Qld 77 L1
Lawler Vic. 27 J7
Lawley River National Park WA 61 M3
Lawloit Vic. 26 D7
Lawn Hill National Park Qld 69 R8, 83 B11
Lawrence NSW 9 P5
Lawrence Vic. 20 C2, 25 O2, 27 O13, 30 A12
Lawrence Road NSW 9 P5
Lawrenny Tas. 93 J6
Lawson NSW 4 I7, 7 J7
Le Roy Vic. 23 K8
Leadville NSW 6 H1
Leaghur Vic. 27 O4, 30 A3
Learmonth Vic. 20 B3, 25 O2, 27 O13
Learmonth WA 55 B4
Leasingham SA 39 L6
Lebrina Tas. 95 M7
Leda WA 52 B7
Ledge Point WA 54 B1
Leeman WA 56 B5
Leeor Vic. 26 B7
Leeton NSW 13 O8
Leets Vale NSW 5 M4
Leeuwin–Naturaliste National Park WA 53 A8, 54 A9, 56 A11
Leeville NSW 9 P3
Lefroy Tas. 95 L6
Legana Tas. 95 L8
Legerwood Tas. 95 O7
Legume NSW 9 N1, 77 O11
Leichardt Vic. 27 P9, 30 B8
Leichhardt River Qld 83 F9, 84 E3
Leigh Creek SA 41 J4
Leigh Creek Vic. 20 D4, 25 P3, 30 A13
Leighton SA 39 L5
Leinster WA 56 H2
Leitchville Vic. 13 J13, 27 R4, 30 C3
Lemana Tas. 95 J9
Lemnos Vic. 30 I5
Lemon Springs Vic. 26 C9
Lemon Tree Passage NSW 7 N4
Lemont Tas. 93 N5
Leneva Vic. 31 P5, 32 B2
Lennox Head NSW 9 R3, 77 R12
Lenswood SA 36 D10
Leonards Hill Vic. 20 E3
Leongatha Vic. 21 P13, 22 H9
Leongatha South Vic. 21 P13, 22 H9
Leonora WA 56 I3
Leopold Vic. 20 G10, 22 A7, 25 R8
Leppington NSW 5 L9
Leschenault WA 53 G3
Leslie Vale Tas. 90 H7, 93 L9
Lesmurdie Falls National Park WA 52 D5
Lesueur National Park WA 56 B5
Lethbridge Vic. 20 E7, 25 Q6
Leumeah NSW 5 L10
Leura NSW 4 H7
Levendale Tas. 91 K1, 93 M6
Lewis Ponds NSW 6 G6
Lewisham Tas. 91 L5, 93 N8
Lewiston SA 36 B5
Lexton Vic. 20 A2, 25 N2, 27 N13
Leyburn Qld 77 M10
Liawenee Tas. 93 J2, 95 J11
Licola Vic. 23 L3, 32 A12
Liddell NSW 7 L3
Lidsdale NSW 4 F4, 6 I6
Liena Tas. 94 H9
Lietinna Tas. 95 N7
Lietpar Vic. 28 I9
Liffey Tas. 93 K1, 95 K10
Light Pass SA 49 G4
Lightning Ridge NSW 8 B5
Likkaparta NT 69 K10
Lileah Tas. 94 D5
Lillicur Vic. 20 A1
Lillimur Vic. 26 B7
Lillimur South Vic. 26 B8, 48 I7
Lilydale Tas. 95 M7
Lilydale Vic. 21 M6, 22 E3
Lima Vic. 31 K8
Limeburners Creek NSW 7 N3
Limekilns NSW 4 D2, 6 H5
Limerick NSW 4 A11, 6 G8, 14 F1
Limestone Vic. 21 N2, 30 I11
Limestone Ridge Qld 75 A9
Limevale Qld 9 K2, 77 M12
Lincoln National Park SA 38 E9
Lincolnfields SA 39 J5
Lind National Park Vic. 14 E13, 33 M11
Linda Tas. 92 E3, 94 E12
Lindeman Island Qld 79 K3
Linden NSW 5 J7
Lindenow Vic. 23 P4, 32 E13
Lindenow South Vic. 23 P4, 32 E13
Lindisfarne Tas. 90 I5, 93 L8
Lindsay Vic. 24 A4, 48 I11
Lindsay Point Vic. 12 A7, 28 A3, 39 R6
Linga Vic. 12 C10, 28 E10
Linton Vic. 20 B5, 25 N4
Linville Qld 77 O7
Linwood SA 36 D3
Lipson SA 38 E7
Lisarow NSW 5 P3
Lisle Tas. 95 M7
Lismore NSW 9 Q3, 77 Q12
Lismore Vic. 25 M6
Liston NSW 9 M2, 77 O12
Litchfield Vic. 27 J6
Litchfield National Park NT 64 C8, 66 D7
Lithgow NSW 4 G5, 6 I6
Littabella National Park Qld 77 O1
Little Billabong NSW 13 R12, 14 A6
Little Desert National Park Vic. 26 B8, 48 I7
Little Grove WA 54 H13, 56 E12
Little Hampton Vic. 20 F2, 25 Q2, 27 Q13, 30 C12
Little Hard Hills Vic. 20 C6
Little Hartley NSW 4 G5
Little Jilliby NSW 5 P2
Little River Vic. 20 G7, 22 A5, 25 R6
Little Sandy Desert WA 58 F7
Little Snowy Creek Vic. 31 R7, 32 D4
Little Swanport Tas. 93 O5
Little Topar Roadhouse NSW 10 D11
Littlehampton SA 36 E11, 37 I2
Liverpool NSW 5 M9, 7 K8
Lizard Island Qld 81 M1
Lizard Island National Park Qld 81 M1
Llandaff Tas. 93 Q3, 95 Q12
Llandeilo Vic. 20 E4
Llanelly Vic. 27 O9, 30 A8
Llangothlin NSW 9 L7
Llewellyn Siding Tas. 93 N2, 95 N11
Llowalong Vic. 23 M5
Loamside Qld 75 A7
Lobethal SA 36 E9, 39 L9, 48 C1
Loccota Tas. 92 B11, 95 Q1
Loch Vic. 21 O12, 22 G8
Loch Ard Gorge Vic. 25 K11
Loch Sport Vic. 23 P6
Loch Valley Vic. 21 Q6
Lochaber SA 48 H8
Lochern National Park Qld 85 M12
Lochiel SA 39 J6
Lochinvar NSW 7 M4
Lochnagar Qld 78 D11, 85 R11
Lock SA 38 D4
Lockhart NSW 13 P10
Lockhart River Qld 82 E8
Lockington Qld 78 H12
Lockington Vic. 30 D5
Locksley NSW 4 D5, 6 H6
Locksley Vic. 30 H9
Lockwood Vic. 27 Q10, 30 B9
Lockwood South Vic. 27 Q10, 30 B9
Loddon Vale Vic. 27 P5, 30 A3
Logan Qld 75 E7, 77 Q9
Logan Vic. 27 N9
Logan Village Qld 75 E8
Loganholme Qld 75 E8
Logie Brae NSW 13 M11
Lombadina–Djarindjin WA 60 H6
London Bridge Vic. 25 K11
Londonderry NSW 5 K6
Londrigan Vic. 31 N5
Long Beach NSW 14 H7, 17 O7
Long Flat NSW 9 N12
Long Island Qld 79 K3
Long Jetty NSW 5 Q3
Long Plains SA 39 K7
Long Plains Vic. 27 K1, 29 K11
Longerenong Vic. 26 H9
Longford Tas. 95 L9
Longford Vic. 23 N7
Longlea Vic. 27 R10, 30 D8
Longley Tas. 90 G7, 93 L9
Longreach Qld 78 A11, 85 O11
Longwarry Vic. 21 O9, 22 G6
Longwood Vic. 30 I9
Longwood East Vic. 30 I9
Lonnavale Tas. 90 C6, 93 J9
Looma WA 61 J9
Loongana Tas. 94 G8
Loongana WA 57 P6
Loorana Tas. 93 Q12
Lorinna Tas. 94 H9
Lorne NSW 9 O13
Lorne Vic. 20 D13, 25 P10
Lorquon Vic. 26 E6
Lorquon West Vic. 26 E5
Lostock NSW 7 M2
Lottah Tas. 95 P7
Louisville Tas. 91 O1, 93 O6
Louth NSW 11 L7
Louth Bay SA 38 D8
Loveday SA 39 P7
Low Head Tas. 95 K6
Lowaldie SA 39 O10, 48 F2
Lowan Vale SA 48 H6
Lowanna NSW 9 P8
Lowbank SA 39 P6
Lowden WA 53 I6, 54 D8
Lowdina Tas. 91 J2, 93 M7
Lower Acacia Creek NSW 9 N2
Lower Barrington Tas. 94 I7
Lower Beulah Tas. 94 I8
Lower Boro NSW 17 L1
Lower Bucca NSW 9 P7
Lower Chittering WA 54 D2
Lower Creek NSW 9 N9
Lower Glenelg National Park Vic. 24 B7
Lower Light SA 39 K8
Lower Mangrove NSW 5 N4
Lower Marshes Tas. 93 L5
Lower Mookerawa NSW 6 G4
Lower Mount Hicks Tas. 94 F5
Lower Norton Vic. 26 G10
Lower Quipolly NSW 8 I12
Lower Turners Marsh Tas. 95 L7
Lower Wilmot Tas. 94 H7
Lowes Mount NSW 4 D6
Lowesdale NSW 13 O12, 31 M2
Lowlands NSW 13 M3
Lowmead Qld 77 N1
Lowood Qld 74 C12, 77 P9
Lowther NSW 4 F6
Loxton SA 39 Q7
Loxton North SA 39 Q7
Loy Yang Vic. 23 K7
Loyetea Tas. 94 G7
Ltyentye Purte (Santa Teresa) NT 71 K9
Lubeck Vic. 26 I9
Lucaston Tas. 90 F7, 93 K9
Lucinda Qld 81 O11
Lucindale SA 48 G9
Lucknow NSW 6 G6
Lucknow Vic. 23 Q4, 32 F13
Lucky Bay SA 38 G5
Lucyvale Vic. 14 A9, 32 F3
Luddenham NSW 5 K8
Ludlow WA 53 E7
Lue NSW 6 I3
Lughrata Tas. 92 B10
Luina Tas. 94 E8
Lulworth Tas. 95 L5
Lumholtz National Park Qld 81 M10
Lunawanna Tas. 90 G13, 93 L11
Lune River Tas. 93 J12
Lurg Vic. 31 L7
Lyal Vic. 27 R11, 30 D10
Lyme Regis Tas. 95 Q4
Lymington Tas. 90 F10, 93 K10
Lymwood Tas. 93 Q12
Lynchford Tas. 92 E3, 94 E12
Lynchs Creek NSW 9 P2
Lyndhurst NSW 6 F7
Lyndhurst SA 41 J3
Lyndhurst Vic. 21 L8, 22 E5
Lyndoch SA 36 E6, 39 L8, 49 C9
Lyons Vic. 24 D7
Lyonville Vic. 20 F3
Lyrup SA 39 Q7
Lysterfield Vic. 21 L7
Ma Ma Creek Qld 77 O9
Maaoope SA 48 H10
Maaroom Qld 77 P4
McAlinden WA 54 E8
Macalister Qld 77 L8
McAllister NSW 6 H10, 14 F3
Macarthur Vic. 24 F7
Macclesfield SA 36 D12, 37 I3, 39 L10, 48 C2
Macclesfield Vic. 21 M7, 22 F4
McCrae Vic. 21 J11
McCullys Gap NSW 7 L2
MacDonnell Ranges NT 71 K8
Macedon Vic. 20 H3, 22 A1, 30 D12
McGillivray SA 38 H12
McGraths Hill NSW 5 L6
McHarg Creek SA 37 H5
McIntyre Vic. 27 O9
Mackay Qld 79 L5
McKees Hill NSW 9 Q3
McKenzie Creek Vic. 26 G10
McKinlay Qld 84 I5
Macks Creek Vic. 23 L9
Macksville NSW 9 P9
MacLagan Qld 77 N8
McLaren Flat SA 36 B13, 37 F4
McLaren Vale SA 36 A13, 37 F4, 39 K10, 48 B2
Maclean NSW 9 P5
McLoughlins Beach Vic. 23 M9
McMahons Creek Vic. 21 P5, 22 H3
McMahons Reef NSW 6 E11, 14 C3
MacMasters Beach NSW 5 P4
McMillans Vic. 12 I12, 27 Q3, 30 B2
McMinns Lagoon NT 64 E3
Macorna Vic. 12 I13, 27 P4, 30 B3
McPhail NSW 6 D3
Macquarie Fields NSW 5 L10
Macquarie Plains Tas. 90 D3
Macquarie River Tas. 93 L1, 95 M11
Macrossan Qld 78 F2
Macs Cove Vic. 21 R1, 31 L11
Madalya Vic. 23 K9
Maddington WA 52 D5
Madora WA 52 B9
Madura Roadhouse WA 57 P8
Mafeking Vic. 24 I3
Maffra NSW 14 D10, 33 M5
Maffra Vic. 23 M5
Maffra West Upper Vic. 23 M5
Maggea SA 39 O7
Magill SA 36 C9
Magnetic Island Qld 81 P12
Magnetic Island National Park Qld 81 P12
Magpie Vic. 20 C4
Magra Tas. 90 F4, 93 K7
Magrath Flat SA 39 N12, 48 E5
Maharatta NSW 14 E11, 33 N8
Mahogany Creek WA 52 E4
Maianbar NSW 5 N10
Maiden Gully Vic. 27 Q9, 30 C8
Maidenwell Qld 77 N7
Mailors Flat Vic. 24 I9
Maimuru NSW 6 D9, 14 C2
Main Beach Qld 75 G11, 77 Q10
Main Range National Park Qld 9 N1, 77 O10
Maindample Vic. 31 K10
Maitland NSW 7 M4
Maitland SA 38 I7
Major Plains Vic. 31 K6
Majorca Vic. 20 C1, 25 O1, 27 O12, 30 A10
Majors Creek NSW 6 H13, 14 G6, 17 K5
Majors Creek Vic. 30 F9
Malanda Qld 81 M7
Malbina Tas. 90 G4
Malbon Qld 84 G5
Malcolm WA 56 I3
Maldon NSW 5 K12
Maldon Vic. 27 P11, 30 B10
Maleny Qld 74 E5, 77 P7
Malinong SA 39 N11, 48 E3
Mallacoota Vic. 14 G13, 33 Q11
Mallala SA 36 A3, 39 K7
Mallan NSW 12 I10, 29 O9
Mallanganee NSW 9 O3, 77 P12
Mallanganee National Park NSW 9 O3
Mallee Vic. 12 D10, 28 H10
Mallee Cliffs National Park NSW 12 E7, 28 I3
Malmsbury Vic. 20 F1, 25 R1, 27 R12, 30 C11
Malpas SA 39 Q8, 48 H1
Malua Bay NSW 14 H7, 17 O7
Malyalling WA 54 G6
Mambray Creek SA 39 J2, 40 I12
Manangatang Vic. 12 F10, 29 K9
Manara NSW 12 G2
Mandagery NSW 6 D6
Mandalong NSW 5 P1
Mandorah NT 64 B2, 66 D5
Mandurah WA 52 B9, 54 C5, 56 C9
Mandurama NSW 6 G7
Mandurang Vic. 27 R10, 30 C9
Mangalo SA 38 F4
Mangalore NSW 11 P11
Mangalore Tas. 90 H2, 93 L7
Mangalore Vic. 30 G9
Mangana Tas. 95 P10
Mangoplah NSW 6 B13, 13 Q11
Mangrove Creek NSW 5 N3
Mangrove Mountain NSW 5 O3
Manguri SA 45 Q11
Manildra NSW 6 F5
Manilla NSW 9 J9
Maningrida NT 67 K5
Manjimup WA 54 D10, 56 D11
Manly NSW 5 O8, 7 L7
Manly Qld 74 H12, 75 E5
Manmanning WA 56 D6
Manmoyi NT 67 K6
Mannahill SA 41 O11
Mannanarie SA 39 L2, 41 K13
Mannerim Vic. 20 H10
Mannering Park NSW 5 Q1, 7 M5
Mannibadar Vic. 20 A6, 25 N5
Manns Beach Vic. 23 L10
Mannum SA 39 M9, 48 D1
Manoora SA 39 L6
Mansfield Vic. 31 L10
Mantung SA 39 P8
Manumbar Qld 77 O6
Manumbar Hill Qld 74 A1
Many Peaks Qld 77 M1
Manya Vic. 28 A9, 39 R10, 48 I2
Manyallaluk NT 66 H9
Manyana NSW 17 Q3
Manypeaks WA 54 I12
Mapleton Qld 74 F4
Mapleton Falls National Park Qld 74 E4
Mapoon Qld 82 B6
Mara NT 67 O13, 69 O3
Maralinga SA 42 H3
Marama SA 39 P10, 48 G2
Marananga SA 49 E4
Maranboy NT 66 H10
Marathon Qld 85 H4
Maraylya NSW 5 M6
Marbelup WA 54 H13
Marble Bar WA 58 D2
Marburg Qld 74 C13
Marchagee WA 56 C5
Marcoola Qld 74 H3
Marcus Beach Qld 74 H2
Marcus Hill Vic. 20 H10, 22 B7
Mardella WA 52 C8, 54 C5
Mareeba Qld 81 M7
Marengo NSW 9 N7
Marengo Vic. 25 N12
Margaret River WA 53 C10, 54 A10, 56 B11
Margate Qld 74 H10, 75 E3
Margate Tas. 90 H8, 93 L9
Margooya Vic. 29 J7
Maria Island Tas. 91 P4, 93 P7
Maria Island National Park Tas. 91 Q3, 93 P7
Mariala National Park Qld 87 Q5
Marian Qld 79 K5
Marion SA 36 B10, 37 F1
Marion Bay SA 38 G10
Marion Bay Tas. 91 N5, 93 O8
Markdale NSW 6 G9, 14 E2
Markwell NSW 7 O2
Markwood Vic. 31 N6, 32 A4
Marla SA 45 N5
Marlbed Vic. 27 K4
Marlborough Qld 79 M9
Marlee NSW 7 O1, 9 N13
Marlinja NT 68 I6
Marlo Vic. 33 J13
Marma Vic. 26 I9
Marmor Qld 79 O11
Marnoo Vic. 27 K9
Marnoo West Vic. 27 J9
Marong Vic. 27 Q9, 30 B8
Maroochy River Qld 74 G3
Maroochydore Qld 74 H4, 77 Q7
Maroon Qld 9 O1, 75 A13, 77 P11
Maroona Vic. 25 J3
Maroota NSW 5 M4
Maroubra NSW 5 O9
Marp Vic. 24 B6
Marrabel SA 39 L6
Marradong WA 52 G12, 54 E6
Marralum NT 61 R4, 66 A12, 68 A1
Marramarra National Park NSW 5 N5, 7 L6
Marrangaroo NSW 4 F4
Marrar NSW 6 B11, 13 R9
Marrawah Tas. 94 B4
Marraweeny Vic. 31 J8
Marree SA 40 I1, 46 I13
Marrickville NSW 5 N9
Marrinup WA 52 D11, 54 D6
Marsden NSW 6 B7, 13 R5
Marsden Park NSW 5 L7
Marshall Vic. 20 F10, 22 A7, 25 R8
Martindale NSW 7 K3
Martins Creek Vic. 14 C13, 33 K10
Marulan NSW 6 I11, 14 G3
Marulan South NSW 6 I11, 14 H4
Marungi Vic. 30 I4
Marvel Loch WA 56 G7
Mary River Crossing NT 64 H6
Mary River National Park NT 64 I4, 66 F7
Mary River Roadhouse NT 65 L11, 66 G8
Maryborough Qld 77 P4
Maryborough Vic. 27 O11
Marybrook WA 53 C7
Maryfarms Qld 81 L5
Maryknoll Vic. 21 N8
Marysville Vic. 21 O4, 22 G2, 31 J13
Maryvale NSW 6 F3
Maslin Beach SA 36 A13, 37 E4
Massey Vic. 27 K6
Matakana NSW 13 N3
Mataranka NT 66 I11
Matcham NSW 5 P4
Matheson NSW 9 L6
Mathiesons Vic. 30 F7
Mathinna Tas. 95 P9
Mathoura NSW 13 K12, 30 F2
Matlock Vic. 21 R5, 23 J3
Matong NSW 6 A11, 13 Q9
Maude NSW 13 J8, 29 R5
Maude Vic. 20 E7, 25 Q6
Maudsland Qld 75 F10
Mawbanna Tas. 94 E5
Mawson WA 54 G4
Maxwelton Qld 85 L4
May Reef Vic. 27 R8, 30 D7
Mayanup WA 54 E9
Mayberry Tas. 94 I9
Maydena Tas. 90 A4, 92 I7
Mayfield Tas. 93 P4, 95 P13
Mayrung NSW 13 L11
Maytown Qld 81 J4
Mazeppa National Park Qld 78 G7
Mead Vic. 27 Q3, 30 B2
Meadow Creek Vic. 31 N7
Meadow Flat NSW 4 E4
Meadows SA 36 D13, 37 H3, 39 L10, 48 C2
Meandarra Qld 77 J8
Meander Tas. 95 J10
Meatian Vic. 27 M2, 29 M12
Meckering WA 54 F3, 56 D7
Medindie SA 35 E2
Medlow Bath NSW 4 H6
Meekatharra WA 55 I11, 58 C11
Meelon WA 52 C11, 54 D6
Meelup WA 53 B6
Meenar WA 54 F2
Meeniyan Vic. 22 I10
Meerlieu Vic. 23 O5
Meerschaum Vale NSW 9 Q3
Megalong NSW 4 H7
Megan NSW 9 O8
Melaleuca Tas. 92 G11
Melba Flats Tas. 92 D1, 94 D10
Melba Gully State Park Vic. 25 L11
Melbourne Vic. 19, 21 J6, 22 D4
Meldale Qld 74 G8, 75 E1
Mella Tas. 94 C4
Mellis Vic. 26 I6
Melros WA 52 A10
Melrose NSW 6 A4, 13 Q2

102 Melrose–Nelson

Melrose SA 39 J2, 41 J12
Melrose Tas. 94 I7
Melton SA 39 J6
Melton Vic. 20 H5, 22 B3
Melton Mowbray Tas. 93 L6
Melton South Vic. 20 H5
Melville Forest Vic. 24 F3
Melville Island NT 66 D3
Memana Tas. 92 B10
Memerambi Qld 77 N6
Mena Creek Qld 81 N8
Mena Park Vic. 20 A4
Menangle NSW 5 K11
Menangle Park NSW 5 K11
Mendooran NSW 6 G1, 8 E13
Mengha Tas. 94 D4
Menindee NSW 10 E13, 12 E1
Meningie SA 39 M12, 48 D4
Menzies WA 56 I4
Menzies Creek Vic. 21 M7
Mepunga East Vic. 25 J10
Mepunga West Vic. 24 I10
Merah North NSW 8 F7
Merbein Vic. 12 D7, 28 G3
Merbein South Vic. 12 D7, 28 F3
Merbein West Vic. 12 D7, 28 F3
Mercunda SA 39 O8
Merebene NSW 8 E9
Meredith Vic. 20 E6, 25 P5
Meribah SA 12 A9, 28 A6, 39 R8, 48 I1
Merildin SA 39 L5
Merimal Qld 79 N10
Merimbula NSW 14 G11, 33 Q7
Merinda Qld 78 I2
Meringo NSW 14 H8, 17 N9
Meringur Vic. 12 B8, 28 C4
Meringur North Vic. 12 B7, 28 C4
Merino Vic. 24 D5
Mernda Vic. 21 K4, 22 D2, 30 G13
Merredin WA 54 I2, 56 F7
Merriang Vic. 21 K3, 22 D2, 30 G13, 31 O7, 32 A5
Merriang Vic. 21 K3, 22 D2, 30 G13
Merricks Vic. 21 K10
Merrigum Vic. 30 G6
Merrijig Vic. 31 M10
Merrinee Vic. 12 C8, 28 E4
Merrinee North Vic. 28 E4
Merriton SA 39 J4
Merriwa NSW 7 J2
Merriwagga NSW 13 M5
Merrygoen NSW 6 G1, 8 F13
Merrylands NSW 5 M8
Merrywinbone NSW 8 D6
Merseylea Tas. 94 I8
Merton Vic. 31 J10
Metcalfe Vic. 27 R11, 30 D10
Methul NSW 6 A10, 13 Q8
Metricup WA 53 C8
Metung Vic. 23 R5, 32 G13
Meunna Tas. 94 E6
Mia Mia Vic. 30 D10
Miallo Qld 81 M5
Miami WA 52 A10
Miandetta NSW 11 Q10
Michael Creek Qld 81 N11
Michelago NSW 14 E7, 16 G6
Mickleham Vic. 21 J4, 22 C2, 30 F13
Middle Creek Vic. 25 L2
Middle Indigo Vic. 31 O4, 32 A2
Middle Island Qld 79 N6
Middle Point NT 64 F3
Middle River SA 38 G12
Middle Tarwin Vic. 22 H10
Middlemount Qld 79 K9
Middleton Qld 84 I8
Middleton SA 37 H7
Middleton Tas. 90 G11, 93 L11
Middlingbank NSW 16 E11
Midge Point Qld 79 K4
Midgee Qld 79 N11
Midgee SA 38 H4
Midland WA 52 D4
Midway Point Tas. 91 K5, 93 M8
Miena Tas. 93 J2, 95 J12
Miepoll Vic. 30 I7
Miga Lake Vic. 26 E11
Mil Lel SA 24 A5, 48 I12
Mila NSW 14 E12, 33 N8
Milabena Tas. 94 E5
Milang SA 39 L11, 48 C3
Milawa Vic. 31 N6
Milbong Qld 75 A10
Milbrulong NSW 6 A13, 13 P10
Milchomi NSW 8 D8
Mildura Vic. 12 D7, 28 G3
Miles Qld 77 K7
Milford Qld 75 A11
Milguy NSW 8 H5, 77 K13
Milikapiti NT 66 D3
Miling WA 56 C6
Milingimbi NT 67 L5
Millaa Millaa Qld 81 M8
Millaroo Qld 78 G2
Millbrook Vic. 20 E4, 25 P3, 30 B13
Millers Point NSW 3 B4
Millfield NSW 7 L4
Millgrove Vic. 21 N6, 22 G3
Millicent SA 48 G11
Millie NSW 8 F6
Millmerran Qld 77 M10
Milloo Vic. 27 R7, 30 C5
Millstream–Chichester National Park WA 55 H2, 58 A3
Millstream Falls National Park Qld 81 M8
Millthorpe NSW 6 G6
Milltown Vic. 24 E7
Millwood NSW 6 A12, 13 Q9
Milman Qld 79 N10
Milparinka NSW 10 C4
Milperra NSW 5 M9
Miltalie SA 38 G4
Milton NSW 7 J13, 14 I5, 17 P4
Milvale NSW 6 D9, 14 B2
Milyakburra NT 67 O8
Mimili SA 45 L4
Mimmindie Vic. 12 H13, 27 O5
Mimosa NSW 6 B10, 13 R8
Mimosa Rocks National Park NSW 14 G10, 33 R5
Minamia NT 67 K13, 69 K2
Minbrie SA 38 G4
Mincha Vic. 12 I13, 27 P4, 30 B3
Mindarie SA 39 P9, 48 G1
Minden Qld 74 C13
Mindibungu WA 61 P11
Mindil Beach NT 63 A2
Mindiyarra SA 39 O9, 48 F2
Miners Rest Vic. 20 C3, 25 O3, 30 A13
Minerva Hills National Park Qld 78 I12
Minetta SA 37 F5
Mingary SA 41 Q10
Mingay Vic. 25 L5
Mingela Qld 78 F2
Mingenew WA 56 B4
Mingoola NSW 9 L3, 77 M13
Minhamite Vic. 24 H7
Minilya Roadhouse WA 55 B6
Minimay Vic. 26 B9, 48 I8
Mininera Vic. 25 K4
Miniyeri NT 67 J12, 69 K1
Minjilang NT 66 H2
Minlaton SA 38 I9
Minmi NSW 7 M4
Minnie Water NSW 9 Q6
Minniging WA 54 F6
Minnipa SA 38 B2, 40 A12, 43 R12
Minnivale WA 54 G1
Minore NSW 6 E2
Mintabie SA 45 N5
Mintaro SA 39 L5
Minto NSW 5 L10
Minvalara SA 39 L2, 41 K12
Minyip Vic. 26 I8
Miowera NSW 8 A12, 11 R10
Miralie Vic. 29 M9
Miram Vic. 26 C7
Miram South Vic. 26 C8
Miranda NSW 5 N10
Mirani Qld 79 K5
Mirannie NSW 7 M2
Mirboo Vic. 21 R13, 23 J9
Mirboo North Vic. 21 R12, 22 I8
Miriam Vale Qld 77 M1, 79 Q13
Mirima National Park WA 61 R5
Mirimbah Vic. 31 N11
Miriwinni Qld 81 N8
Mirrabooka WA 52 C4
Mirranatwa Vic. 24 H3
Mirrngadja Village NT 67 M6
Mirrool NSW 6 A9, 13 Q7
Missabotti NSW 9 O9
Mission Beach Qld 81 N9
Mistake Creek NT 61 R7, 68 A5
Mitcham SA 36 B10, 37 G1
Mitchell Qld 76 F6
Mitchell–Alice Rivers National Park Qld 80 E3
Mitchell River National Park Vic. 23 O3, 32 E12
Mitchell River National Park WA 61 M4
Mitchells Hill Vic. 27 K9
Mitchellstown Vic. 30 F9
Mitchellville SA 38 H4
Mitiamo Vic. 27 Q6, 30 C5
Mitre Vic. 26 E9
Mitta Mitta Vic. 31 R7, 32 E5
Mittagong NSW 7 J10, 14 I2
Mittons Bridge Vic. 21 L4
Mittyack Vic. 12 E10, 29 J9
Miva Qld 77 O5
Moama NSW 13 K13, 30 E4
Moana SA 36 A13, 37 E4, 39 K10, 48 B2
Mockinya Vic. 26 G11
Moculta SA 36 G4
Modanville NSW 9 Q3
Modbury SA 36 C8
Modella Vic. 21 O10, 22 G7
Modewarre Vic. 20 E10, 25 Q8
Moe Vic. 21 R10, 23 J7
Mogendoura NSW 17 M8
Mogil Mogil NSW 8 D5
Moglonemby Vic. 30 I7
Mogo NSW 14 H7, 17 N7
Mogriguy NSW 6 E2
Mogumber WA 54 D1
Moina Tas. 94 H8
Moira NSW 13 K13, 30 F3
Mokepilly Vic. 24 I1, 27 J12
Mokine WA 52 H3, 54 E3
Mole Creek Tas. 94 I9
Mole Creek Karst National Park Tas. 94 I9
Mole River NSW 9 M4, 77 N13
Molesworth Tas. 90 G4
Molesworth Vic. 21 N1, 30 I11
Moliagul Vic. 27 N10
Molka Vic. 30 I8
Mollongghip Vic. 20 D3
Mollymook NSW 17 P4
Mologa Vic. 27 Q6, 30 B4
Molong NSW 6 F5
Moltema Tas. 95 J8
Molyullah Vic. 31 L7
Mon Repos Conservation Park Qld 77 O2
Mona SA 39 J6
Mona Vale NSW 5 P6
Monak NSW 28 H4
Monarto SA 36 G11
Monarto South SA 36 G12, 39 M10, 48 D2
Monash SA 39 Q7
Monbulk Vic. 21 M7, 22 F4
Monea Vic. 30 H9
Monegeetta Vic. 20 I3, 22 B1, 30 E12
Monga NSW 17 M5
Mongarlowe NSW 6 I13, 14 G6, 17 M4
Monkey Mia WA 55 B10
Monomeith Vic. 21 N10
Montagu Tas. 94 C4
Montague Island NSW 14 H9
Montague Island Nature Reserve NSW 14 H9, 17 N12
Montana Tas. 95 J9
Monteagle NSW 6 E9, 14 C1
Montebello Islands WA 55 E1
Montezuma Falls Tas. 92 D1, 94 E10
Montgomery Vic. 23 N6
Monto Qld 77 M2
Montumana Tas. 94 E5
Montville Qld 74 F4
Mooball NSW 9 Q2, 77 Q11
Moockra SA 41 J11
Moodlu Qld 74 F8, 75 C1
Moogara Tas. 90 D4, 93 J8
Moogerah Peaks National Park Qld 77 O10
Moola Qld 77 M8
Moolerr Vic. 27 L9
Mooloolaba Qld 74 H4, 77 Q7
Mooloolah Qld 74 F5
Mooloolah River National Park Qld 74 H5
Moolpa NSW 12 H9, 29 O8
Moombooldool NSW 13 P7
Moombra Qld 74 B10
Moona Plains NSW 9 M10
Moonah Tas. 90 H5
Moonambel Vic. 27 M11
Moonan Flat NSW 7 L1, 9 K13
Moonbah NSW 16 C13
Moonbi NSW 9 K10
Moondarra Vic. 23 J6
Moonee Beach NSW 9 P8
Mooney Mooney NSW 5 O5
Moonford Qld 77 L2
Moonie Qld 77 K9
Moonlight Flat SA 38 B2, 40 A13, 43 R12
Moonta SA 38 I6
Moonta Bay SA 38 I6
Moora WA 56 C6
Mooralla Vic. 24 G3
Moore Qld 77 O7
Moore Creek NSW 9 J10
Moore Park Qld 77 O2
Moore River National Park WA 54 C1, 56 C7
Mooreville Tas. 94 G6
Moorilda NSW 4 A6, 6 G7
Moorilim Vic. 30 H7
Moorina Tas. 95 P7
Moorine Rock WA 56 G7
Moorland NSW 7 P1, 9 O13
Moorlands SA 39 N10, 48 E3
Moorleah Tas. 94 F5
Moormbool Vic. 30 F8
Moorngag Vic. 31 L8
Moorooduc Vic. 21 K10
Moorook SA 39 P7
Moorookyle Vic. 20 D2
Mooroopna Vic. 30 H6
Moorooroo SA 49 E7
Moorowie SA 38 H10
Moorrinya National Park Qld 78 B6, 85 Q5
Moorumbine WA 54 G5
Moppin NSW 8 G4, 77 J13
Moranbah Qld 78 I7
Morangarell NSW 6 C9, 14 A1
Morawa WA 56 C4
Morayfield Qld 74 F9, 75 C1
Morchard SA 39 K1, 41 K12
Mordialloc Vic. 21 K8
Morea Vic. 26 C10
Moree NSW 8 G5
Moree Vic. 24 D2, 26 D13
Morella Qld 85 N10
Moreton Island Qld 77 Q8
Moreton Island National Park Qld 75 H1, 77 Q8
Morgan SA 39 N6
Morgans Crossing NSW 14 F10, 33 P6
Moriac Vic. 20 E10, 25 Q8
Moriarty Tas. 95 J7
Morisset NSW 5 Q1, 7 M5
Morkalla Vic. 12 B7, 28 B4, 39 R7
Mornington Vic. 21 K10, 22 D7
Mornington Island Qld 83 E5
Mornington Peninsula Vic. 21 J12, 22 C8
Mornington Peninsula National Park Vic. 20 H11, 21 J12, 22 B8
Morongla NSW 6 F8, 14 D1
Morpeth NSW 7 M4
Morphett Vale SA 36 A12, 37 F3
Morri Morri Vic. 27 K10
Morrisons Vic. 20 E6
Mortat Vic. 26 C9
Mortchup Vic. 20 A5, 25 M4
Mortlake Vic. 25 J7
Morton National Park NSW 7 J11, 14 H4, 17 O1
Morton Plains Vic. 27 K5
Morundah NSW 13 O9
Moruya NSW 14 H7, 17 M8
Moruya Heads NSW 14 H7, 17 N8
Morven NSW 13 Q12, 31 Q1
Morven Qld 76 D6
Morwell Vic. 23 J7
Morwell National Park Vic. 23 J8
Mosman NSW 5 O8
Mosquito Creek NSW 8 I5
Mosquito Flat SA 37 H6
Moss Tas. 93 J13
Moss Vale NSW 7 J10, 14 I3
Mossgiel NSW 13 J3
Mossiface Vic. 23 Q4, 32 G13
Mossman Qld 81 M5
Mossy Point NSW 14 H7, 17 N8
Moulamein NSW 12 I10, 29 P9
Moulyinning WA 54 H7
Mount Aberdeen National Park Qld 78 H2
Mount Adrah NSW 6 C12, 14 B5
Mount Alford Qld 77 P10
Mount Alfred Vic. 14 A8, 32 F1
Mount Arapiles Vic. 26 E9
Mount Augustus National Park WA 55 F7
Mount Barker SA 36 E11, 37 I2, 39 L10, 48 C2
Mount Barker WA 54 H12, 56 E12
Mount Barnett Roadhouse WA 61 M6
Mount Barney National Park Qld 9 O1, 75 A13, 77 P11
Mount Bartle Frere Qld 81 N8
Mount Bauple National Park Qld 77 O5
Mount Baw Baw Vic. 21 R7, 23 J4
Mount Beauty Vic. 31 Q8, 32 D6
Mount Beckworth Vic. 20 B2
Mount Benson SA 48 F9
Mount Beppo Qld 74 B9
Mount Best Vic. 23 J9
Mount Bogong Vic. 32 D6
Mount Bruce SA 48 G10
Mount Bruce WA 55 I4, 58 B5, 337
Mount Bryan SA 39 L4
Mount Bryan East SA 39 M4
Mount Buffalo Chalet Vic. 31 P8, 32 B6
Mount Buffalo National Park Vic. 31 O7, 32 B5
Mount Buller Vic. 31 N11
Mount Burr SA 48 G11
Mount Bute Vic. 20 A7, 25 M5
Mount Camel Vic. 30 E8
Mount Carbine Qld 81 L5
Mount Christie SA 43 M4
Mount Compass SA 37 G5, 39 K10, 48 B3
Mount Cook National Park Qld 81 L3
Mount Coolon Qld 78 H5
Mount Coolum National Park Qld 74 G3
Mount Cooper SA 38 A3, 43 Q13
Mount Cottrell Vic. 20 H6
Mount Damper SA 38 B3, 40 A13, 43 R13
Mount David NSW 4 C8, 6 H7
Mount Direction Tas. 95 L7
Mount Donna Buang Vic. 21 O5, 22 G3
Mount Doran Vic. 20 D5, 25 P4
Mount Druitt NSW 5 L8
Mount Drysdale NSW 11 N9
Mount Duneed Vic. 20 F10
Mount Ebenezer Roadhouse NT 70 H11
Mount Eccles Vic. 21 P12, 22 H8
Mount Eccles National Park Vic. 24 F7
Mount Egerton Vic. 20 E5, 25 Q4
Mount Eliza Vic. 21 K10
Mount Emu Vic. 20 A5, 25 M4
Mount Fairy NSW 17 K1
Mount Feathertop Vic. 32 D7
Mount Field National Park Tas. 90 A2, 92 I7
Mount Frankland National Park WA 54 F12, 56 D12
Mount Franklin Vic. 20 E2
Mount Gambier SA 48 H12
Mount Garnet Qld 81 L8
Mount George NSW 7 O1, 9 N13
Mount Glorious Qld 74 E11, 75 B4
Mount Hallen Qld 74 A11
Mount Helen Vic. 20 C4, 25 O4
Mount Helena WA 52 E4, 54 D3
Mount Hope NSW 13 N2
Mount Hope SA 38 C6
Mount Horeb NSW 6 D12, 14 B5
Mount Hotham Vic. 31 Q10, 32 D8
Mount Hunter NSW 5 K10
Mount Hypipamee National Park Qld 81 M8
Mount Imlay National Park NSW 14 F12, 33 P9
Mount Irvine NSW 4 I4
Mount Isa Qld 84 E4
Mount Jukes National Park Qld 79 K5
Mount Kaputar National Park NSW 8 H7
Mount Keith WA 56 H1, 58 F12
Mount Kilcoy Qld 74 C6
Mount Kosciuszko NSW 14 C9, 16 A13, 32 I4
Mount Lambie NSW 4 E4
Mount Larcom Qld 79 O12
Mount Liebig NT 70 E7
Mount Lloyd Tas. 90 E5, 93 K8
Mount Lofty SA 36 C10
Mount Lonarch Vic. 25 M1, 27 M13
Mount Macedon Vic. 20 H3, 22 B1, 30 E12
Mount McIntyre SA 48 H11
Mount Magnet WA 56 E2
Mount Martha Vic. 21 J10, 22 D7
Mount Mary SA 39 N6
Mount Mee Qld 74 E8, 75 B1
Mount Meharry WA 55 I5, 58 C5
Mount Mercer Vic. 20 C6, 25 O5
Mount Molloy Qld 81 M6
Mount Morgan Qld 79 N11
Mount Moriac Vic. 20 E10, 25 Q8
Mount Muirhead SA 48 G11
Mount Mulligan Qld 81 L6
Mount Nebo Qld 74 E12, 75 B4
Mount Olive NSW 7 L3
Mount Ommaney Qld 74 F13, 75 C6
Mount Ossa Qld 79 K4
Mount Ossa Tas. 92 G1, 94 G11
Mount Perry Qld 77 N3
Mount Peter Tas. 93 Q3, 95 Q13
Mount Pleasant Qld 74 E9, 75 B2
Mount Pleasant SA 36 G8, 39 M9, 48 D1
Mount Rat SA 38 I8
Mount Remarkable National Park SA 39 J1, 40 I12
Mount Richmond Vic. 24 C8
Mount Richmond National Park Vic. 24 C8
Mount Rowan Vic. 20 C3
Mount St Gwinear Vic. 23 J4
Mount Samson Qld 74 E11, 75 B4
Mount Schank SA 48 H12
Mount Seaview NSW 9 M12
Mount Selwyn NSW 14 C7, 16 C8
Mount Seymour Tas. 93 M5
Mount Slide Vic. 21 M4
Mount Stirling Vic. 31 N11, 32 A9
Mount Surprise Qld 81 J10
Mount Tamborine Qld 75 E11
Mount Tarampa Qld 74 B12
Mount Taylor Vic. 23 P4, 32 F12
Mount Templeton SA 39 K6
Mount Thorley NSW 7 L3
Mount Tomah NSW 4 I5
Mount Torrens SA 36 F9
Mount Victoria NSW 4 H6, 7 J7
Mount Walker WA 56 F8
Mount Wallace Vic. 20 F5, 25 Q4
Mount Walsh National Park Qld 77 N4
Mount Warning National Park NSW 9 P1
Mount Webb National Park Qld 81 L2
Mount Wedge SA 38 B4
Mount Wellington Tas. 90 H6, 93 L8
Mount Wells Battery NT 64 I11
Mount White NSW 5 O4, 7 L6
Mount William National Park Tas. 95 Q5
Mount Wilson NSW 4 H5
Mountain River Tas. 90 G7, 93 K9
Moura Qld 77 J1
Mourilyan Qld 81 N8
Moutajup Vic. 24 G4
Mowbray Tas. 95 L8
Mowbray Park NSW 5 J11
Mowen WA 53 C10
Moy Pocket Qld 74 E3
Moyhu Vic. 31 M7
Moyreisk Vic. 27 M10
Moyston Vic. 25 J2, 27 J13
Muchea WA 52 D1, 54 D2
Muckadilla Qld 76 G6
Mudamuckla SA 43 O10
Mudgee NSW 6 H3
Mudgeeraba Qld 75 G12, 77 Q10
Mudgegonga Vic. 31 P6, 32 B4
Mudginberri NT 65 Q3
Mudjimba Qld 74 H4
Muggleton Qld 76 H6
Mukinbudin WA 56 F6
Mulambin Qld 79 O10
Mulcra Vic. 28 B10, 39 R10, 48 I2
Mulgildie Qld 77 M2
Mulgoa NSW 5 K8, 7 K8
Mullaley NSW 8 G11
Mullaloo WA 52 B3
Mullalyup WA 53 I8, 54 D9
Mullaway NSW 9 P7
Mullengandra Village NSW 13 Q13, 31 Q3
Mullengudgery NSW 8 A13, 11 R11
Mullewa WA 56 B3
Mulli Mulli NSW 9 O2, 77 P11
Mullindolingong Vic. 31 Q8, 32 C5
Mullion Creek NSW 6 G5
Mullumbimby NSW 9 Q2, 77 Q12
Mulpata SA 39 P10, 48 G2
Mulwala NSW 13 N13, 31 L3
Mumballup WA 54 D8
Mumbannar Vic. 24 B6, 48 I12
Mumbel Vic. 27 M2, 29 M12
Mumbil NSW 6 F4
Mumblin Vic. 25 K9
Mummel Gulf National Park NSW 9 L11
Mummulgum NSW 9 O3, 77 P12
Munbilla Qld 75 A9
Mundaring WA 52 E4, 54 D3, 56 C8
Mundaring Weir WA 52 E4
Mundijong WA 52 D7, 54 D5
Mundoona Vic. 30 H4
Mundoora SA 39 J4
Mundrabilla Roadhouse WA 57 Q8
Mundubbera Qld 77 M4
Mundulla SA 48 H7
Mungala SA 43 L4
Mungalawarru NT 69 J10
Mungallala Qld 76 E6
Mungana Qld 81 J7
Mungar Qld 77 P4
Mungerannie Roadhouse SA 47 K8, 86 C10
Mungeribar NSW 6 D2
Mungery NSW 6 C3
Mungindi NSW 8 E3, 76 H13
Mungkan Kandju National Park Qld 82 D10
Mungkarta NT 69 K12, 71 K1
Munglinup WA 56 I10
Mungo National Park NSW 12 G5
Mungungo Qld 77 M2
Munjina WA 58 C4
Munro Vic. 23 N5
Munster WA 52 B6
Muntadgin WA 56 F7
Muradup WA 54 F9
Murchison Vic. 30 H7
Murchison WA 55 E12, 56 C1
Murchison East Vic. 30 H7
Murdinga SA 38 D5
Murdunna Tas. 91 N7, 93 O9
Murga NSW 6 E6
Murgenella NT 66 H3
Murgheboluc Vic. 20 E9, 25 Q7
Murgon Qld 77 N6
Murmungee Vic. 31 O6
Murninnie Beach SA 38 H3
Murphys Creek Vic. 27 O9
Murra Warra Vic. 26 G7
Murrabit Vic. 12 I11, 27 P1, 29 P12
Murramarang National Park NSW 14 H7, 17 O7
Murrami NSW 13 O8
Murrawal NSW 8 F12
Murray Bridge SA 36 I12, 39 M10, 48 D2
Murray River NSW & SA 12 A6, 13 J12, 14 B9, 28 B2, 30 C1, 39 N7
Murray River National Park SA 12 A7, 39 Q7
Murray–Sunset National Park Vic. 12 B9, 28 C7, 39 R8, 48 I1
Murray Town SA 39 K2, 41 J12
Murrays Run NSW 7 L5
Murrayville Vic. 12 B11, 28 B10, 39 R10
Murrindal Vic. 14 C13, 32 I10
Murrindindi Vic. 21 N2, 22 F1, 30 I12
Murringo NSW 6 E9, 14 C2
Murroon Vic. 20 C12, 25 O10
Murrumba Qld 74 B10
Murrumbateman NSW 6 F11, 14 E4
Murrumbidgee River ACT & NSW 13 J8, 29 N5
Murrumburrah NSW 6 E10, 14 C3
Murrungowar Vic. 14 D13, 33 K12
Murrurundi NSW 9 J13
Murtoa Vic. 26 I9
Murun Murula NT 69 Q8
Murwillumbah NSW 9 Q1, 77 Q11
Musgrave Roadhouse Qld 80 H1, 82 F13
Musk Vic. 20 E2
Musk Vale Vic. 20 E2
Muskerry East Vic. 30 D8
Musselboro Tas. 95 N9
Musselroe Bay Tas. 95 Q5
Muston SA 38 I12
Muswellbrook NSW 7 K2
Mutarnee Qld 81 O12
Mutawintji National Park NSW 10 E8
Mutchilba Qld 81 L7
Mutdapilly Qld 75 A8
Muttaburra Qld 78 B9, 85 P9
Muttama NSW 6 D11, 14 B4
Muttonbird Island Nature Reserve NSW 9 P8
Myall Vic. 27 P2, 29 P12
Myall Lakes National Park NSW 7 O3
Myall Mundi NSW 6 C1
Myall Plains NSW 13 N11
Myalla Tas. 94 E5
Myalup WA 53 G2, 54 C7
Myamyn Vic. 24 E7
Myaring Vic. 24 B5
Mylestom NSW 9 P8
Mylor SA 36 D11, 37 H2
Myola Vic. 30 E8
Mypolonga SA 39 N9, 48 D2
Myponga SA 37 E6, 39 K11, 48 B3
Myponga Beach SA 37 D6
Myrla SA 39 P7
Myrniong Vic. 20 F4, 25 R4, 30 C13
Myrrhee Vic. 31 M8
Myrtle Bank Tas. 95 M7
Myrtle Creek Vic. 27 R11, 30 D10
Myrtle Scrub NSW 9 M11
Myrtleford Vic. 31 O7, 32 B5
Myrtleville NSW 6 I10, 14 G3
Mysia Vic. 27 O6
Mystic Park Vic. 12 H11, 27 O2, 29 O12
Mywee Vic. 30 I2
Nabageena Tas. 94 C5
Nabawa WA 56 B3
Nabiac NSW 7 O2
Nabowla Tas. 95 N7
Nackara SA 39 M2, 41 M12
Nadda SA 12 A8, 39 Q8
Nagambie Vic. 30 G8
Nagoorin Qld 77 M1, 79 P13
Nairne SA 36 E11, 39 L9, 48 C2
Nala Tas. 93 M5
Nalinga Vic. 31 J6
Nalya WA 54 G5
Namadgi National Park ACT 6 F13, 14 D6, 16 E4
Nambour Qld 74 F4, 77 P7
Nambrok Vic. 23 M6
Nambucca Heads NSW 9 P9
Nambung National Park WA 56 B6
Nana Glen NSW 9 P7
Nanango Qld 77 N7
Nanarup WA 54 I13
Nandaly Vic. 12 F11, 29 J10
Nandi Qld 77 M8
Nanga WA 52 D12, 54 D6
Nanga Bay Resort WA 55 B11
Nangana Vic. 21 N7, 22 F4
Nangar National Park NSW 6 E6
Nangari SA 12 A8, 28 A5, 39 R8
Nangeenan WA 54 I2
Nangiloc Vic. 12 E8, 28 H5
Nangkita SA 37 H5, 39 L10, 48 C3
Nangus NSW 6 C12, 14 B5
Nangwarry SA 48 H11
Nanneella Vic. 30 F5
Nannup WA 53 H10, 54 C10, 56 C11
Nanson WA 56 A3
Nantabibbie SA 39 M2, 41 L12
Nantawarra SA 39 K6
Nanutarra Roadhouse WA 55 E4
Napoleons Vic. 20 C5, 25 O4
Napperby SA 39 J3, 41 J13
Napranum Qld 82 B8
Nar Nar Goon Vic. 21 N9, 22 F6
Naracoopa Tas. 93 R12
Naracoorte SA 48 H9
Naracoorte Caves Conservation Park SA 48 H9
Naradhan NSW 13 O5
Naraling WA 56 B3
Narangba Qld 74 F10, 75 C2
Narara NSW 5 P3
Narawntapu National Park Tas. 95 J6
Narbethong Vic. 21 N4, 22 G2, 31 J13
Nareen Vic. 24 D3
Narellan NSW 5 K10
Narembeen WA 56 F8
Naretha WA 57 M6
Nariel Vic. 14 B9, 32 G4
Naringal Vic. 25 J9
Narioka Vic. 30 G4
Narnu Bay SA 37 I8
Narooma NSW 14 H9, 17 N11, 33 R3
Narrabarba NSW 14 G12, 33 P10
Narrabeen NSW 5 P7
Narrabri NSW 8 G8
Narrabri West NSW 8 G8
Narracan Vic. 21 R11, 23 J7
Narrandera NSW 13 P9
Narraport Vic. 27 K5
Narrawa NSW 6 G10, 14 E2
Narrawa Tas. 94 H8
Narrawallee NSW 17 P3
Narrawong Vic. 24 E8
Narre Warren Vic. 21 L8
Narrewillock Vic. 27 M5
Narridy SA 39 K4
Narrien Range National Park Qld 78 G9
Narrikup WA 54 H12
Narrogin WA 54 G6, 56 E9
Narromine NSW 6 D2
Narrung SA 39 M11, 48 D3
Narrung Vic. 29 L7
Nashdale NSW 6 F6
Nathalia Vic. 13 L13, 30 H4
Nathan River NT 67 M12, 69 M1
Natimuk Vic. 26 F9
National Park Tas. 90 C3, 93 J7
Native Dog Flat Vic. 14 B11, 32 I7
Natone Tas. 94 G6
Nattai NSW 4 I11, 7 J8, 14 I1
Nattai National Park NSW 4 I12, 7 J9, 14 H2
Natte Yallock Vic. 27 M11
Natural Arch National Park *see* Springbrook National Park
Natural Bridge Qld 75 E13
Natya Vic. 12 G9, 29 L8
Nauiyu NT 64 B12, 66 D8
Naval Base WA 52 B7
Navarre Vic. 27 L10
Navigators Vic. 20 D4, 25 P4, 30 A13
Nayook Vic. 21 P7
Neale Junction WA 57 N2
Neales Flat SA 36 H1, 39 M7
Nebo Qld 79 K6
Nectar Brook SA 39 J1, 40 I11
Neds Corner Vic. 28 C3
Needles Tas. 95 J9
Neerabup National Park WA 52 A2, 54 C3, 56 B8
Neerdie Qld 77 P5
Neerim Vic. 21 P8, 22 H5
Neerim East Vic. 21 Q8
Neerim Junction Vic. 21 P7
Neerim South Vic. 21 P8, 22 H5
Neeworra NSW 8 E4, 76 H13
Neika Tas. 90 H7, 93 L9
Neilborough Vic. 27 Q8, 30 C7
Neilborough East Vic. 27 Q8, 30 C7
Neilmongle NSW 11 Q2, 76 D13
Neilrex NSW 8 F13
Nelia Qld 85 K4
Nelligen NSW 14 H6, 17 N6
Nelly Bay Qld 81 P12
Nelshaby SA 39 J3, 40 I13
Nelson NSW 5 L6

Nelson–Red Cliffs 103

Nelson Vic. 24 A7, 48 I13
Nelson Bay NSW 7 O4
Nelungaloo NSW 6 D5
Nemingha NSW 9 J11
Nene Valley SA 48 H12
Nepabunna SA 41 L4
Nerang Qld 75 G11, 77 Q10
Nerriga NSW 6 I12, 14 H4, 17 N1
Nerrigundah NSW 14 G8, 17 L10, 33 Q2
Nerrin Nerrin Vic. 25 K5
Nerrina Vic. 20 D4, 25 O3, 30 A13
Nerring Vic. 20 A3, 25 M3
Netherby Vic. 12 C13, 26 D5
Nethercote NSW 14 G11, 33 Q8
Neuarpurr Vic. 26 B10, 48 I8
Neurea NSW 6 F4
Neuroodla SA 41 J8
Neurum Qld 74 D7
Nevertire NSW 6 C1, 8 B13
Neville NSW 6 G7
New Angledool NSW 8 B4, 76 F13
New Beith Qld 75 C8
New Brighton NSW 9 Q2
New England NSW 9 M7
New England National Park NSW 9 N9
New Gisborne Vic. 20 H3, 22 B1, 30 E12
New Italy NSW 9 Q4, 77 Q13
New Mollyann NSW 8 F12
New Norcia WA 54 D1, 56 C6
New Norfolk Tas. 90 F4, 93 K8
New Residence SA 39 P7
New Town Tas. 89 A2
New Well SA 39 O7
Goodnight Scrub National Park Qld 77 N3
Newborough Vic. 21 R10, 23 J7
Newbridge NSW 4 A6, 6 G7
Newbridge Vic. 27 P10, 30 A8
Newbury Vic. 20 F3, 25 Q2, 27 Q13, 30 C12
Newcastle NSW 7 N4
Newcastle Waters NT 68 I6
Newdegate WA 56 G9
Newfield Vic. 25 K10
Newham Vic. 20 H2, 22 B1, 30 E12
Newhaven Vic. 21 M13, 22 E9
Newland SA 37 G8
Newlands WA 53 H7, 54 D9
Newlyn Vic. 20 D3, 25 P2, 27 P13, 30 B12
Newman WA 58 D6
Newmarket Qld 74 G12, 75 D5
Newmerella Vic. 33 J13
Newnes NSW 4 G1, 7 J5
Newnes Junction NSW 4 G4
Newport NSW 5 P6
Newry Vic. 23 M5
Newrybar NSW 9 Q3
Newstead Vic. 27 P12, 30 B10
Newton Boyd NSW 9 N6
Newtown Vic. 20 B5, 25 N4
Ngallo Vic. 28 A11, 39 R11, 48 I3
Ngangalala NT 67 L5
Ngapal SA 39 L6
Ngarigo NSW 16 B13
Nguiu NT 66 D4
Ngukurr NT 67 L10
Ngunarra NT 69 N8
Nhill Vic. 26 D7
Nhulunbuy NT 67 P5
Ni Ni Vic. 26 E6
Niangala NSW 9 K11
Nicholls Point Vic. 12 D7, 28 G3
Nicholls Rivulet Tas. 90 F10, 93 K10
Nicholson Vic. 23 Q4, 32 G13
Nicoll Scrub National Park Qld 75 G13
Niemur NSW 13 J10, 29 Q10
Nierinna Tas. 90 G8
Nietta Tas. 94 H8
Nightcap National Park NSW 9 Q2, 77 Q12
Nightcliff NT 64 C2
Nildottie SA 39 N8, 48 E1
Nile Tas. 95 M10
Nillup WA 53 D11
Nilma Vic. 21 P10, 22 H7
Nimbin NSW 9 Q2, 77 Q12
Nimmitabel NSW 14 E10, 33 N5
Ninda Vic. 27 J1, 29 J12
Nindigully Qld 8 D1, 76 H11
Nindoominbah Qld 75 D11
Nine Mile Vic. 27 M7
Ninety Mile Beach Vic. 23 N9
Ningaloo Marine Park WA 55 A4
Ningaloo Reef WA 55 B4
Ningi Qld 74 H8, 75 E1
Ninnes SA 39 J6
Ninyeunook Vic. 27 M5
Nipan Qld 77 J2
Nippering WA 54 H8
Nirranda Vic. 25 J10
Nirranda South Vic. 25 J10
Nitmiluk Gorge NT 66 G10
Nitmiluk National Park NT 66 G9
Nobby Qld 77 N10
Noccundra Qld 87 L10
Noggojerring WA 52 I1, 54 E2
Nonda Qld 85 K4
Noojee Vic. 21 Q7, 22 I4
Nook Tas. 94 I8
Nookanellup WA 54 G9
Noonamah NT 64 E4, 66 E6
Noonameena SA 39 M12, 48 D4
Noonbinna NSW 6 E8, 14 D1
Noondoo Qld 8 C2, 76 G12
Noora SA 12 A8, 28 A5, 39 R7
Nooramunga Vic. 31 K6
Noorat Vic. 25 K8
Noorinbee Vic. 14 E13, 33 N11
Noorinbee North Vic. 14 E13, 33 N11
Noorong NSW 12 I11, 29 P11
Noorongong Vic. 31 Q5, 32 D3
Noosa Heads Qld 74 H1, 77 Q6
Noosa National Park Qld 74 G2
Noosaville Qld 74 G1
Nora Creina SA 48 F10
Noradjuha Vic. 26 F10
Norah Head NSW 5 Q2
Noraville NSW 5 Q2
Nords Wharf NSW 5 R1
Normanton Qld 80 C8, 83 I8
Normanville SA 37 D7, 39 K11, 48 B3
Normanville Vic. 27 N3
Nornakin WA 54 H4
Nornalup WA 54 F13
Norseman WA 57 J8
North Adelaide SA 35 C4
North Arm Qld 74 F3
North Beach SA 38 I5
North Berry Jerry NSW 6 B11, 13 R9
North Bourke NSW 11 N5
North Bruny Island Tas. 90 I11, 93 M10
North Dandalup WA 52 D9, 54 D5, 56 C9
North Flinders Ranges SA 41 L5
North Haven NSW 9 O12
North Hobart Tas. 89 A4, 90 H6
North Lilydale Tas. 95 M7
North Maclean Qld 75 D8
North Melbourne Vic. 19 A3
North Molle Island Qld 79 K3
North Motton Tas. 94 H7
North Pinjarra WA 52 C10, 54 C5
North Richmond NSW 5 K5
North Scottsdale Tas. 95 N6
North Shields SA 38 D8
North Star NSW 8 I3, 77 K12
North Stradbroke Island Qld 75 H5, 77 R9
North Sydney NSW 5 O8
North Tamborine Qld 75 E10
North West Island Qld 79 Q10
North Yunderup WA 52 B10, 54 C5
Northam WA 52 H2, 54 E3, 56 D7
Northampton WA 56 A3
Northbridge WA 51 C4
Northcliffe WA 54 D12, 56 D12
Northdown Tas. 95 J6
Northwood Vic. 20 I1
Norton Summit SA 36 C10
Norwell Qld 75 F9
Norwin Qld 77 M9
Notley Hills Tas. 95 K8
Notting WA 54 I5
Notts Well SA 39 O7
Nowa Nowa Vic. 32 H12
Nowendoc NSW 9 L12
Nowie North Vic. 29 M10
Nowingi Vic. 28 G6
Nowley NSW 8 E7
Nowra NSW 7 K11, 14 I4
Nowra Hill NSW 7 J11, 14 I4
NSW Jervis Bay National Park NSW 7 K11, 17 R1
Nturiya NT 70 I5
Nubba NSW 6 D10, 14 B3
Nubeena Tas. 91 M10, 93 N10
Nug Nug Vic. 31 O8, 32 B5
Nuga Nuga National Park Qld 76 G2
Nugent Tas. 91 M4, 93 N7
Nuggetty Vic. 27 P11, 30 B9
Nulla Vale Vic. 20 I1
Nullagine WA 58 E3
Nullan Vic. 26 I7
Nullarbor National Park SA 42 C7, 57 R7
Nullarbor Plain SA & WA 42 C3, 57 O6
Nullarbor Roadhouse SA 42 G7
Nullawarre Vic. 25 J10
Nullawil Vic. 12 G13, 27 L4
Numbla Vale NSW 14 D10, 33 L5
Numbugga NSW 14 G10, 33 P6
Numbulwar NT 67 N9
Numeralla NSW 14 F8, 16 H10, 33 O2
Numinbah Valley Qld 75 F12
Numurkah Vic. 13 M13, 30 I4
Nunamara Tas. 95 M8
Nundle NSW 9 K12
Nundroo Roadhouse SA 43 J8
Nunga Vic. 28 H9
Nungarin WA 54 I1, 56 F7
Nungurner Vic. 23 R5, 32 G13
Nunjikompita SA 43 P10
Nuraip SA 49 G5
Nurcoung Vic. 26 E9
Nurina WA 57 O6
Nurinda Qld 74 A7
Nuriootpa SA 36 F4, 39 M8, 49 G4
Nurom SA 39 J3
Nurrabiel Vic. 26 G11
Nutfield Vic. 21 L4
Nyabing WA 54 I8, 56 F10
Nyah Vic. 12 G10, 29 M10
Nyah West Vic. 12 G10, 29 M10
Nyallo Vic. 26 I3, 28 I13
Nyarrin Vic. 29 J11
Nyirripi NT 70 D6
Nymagee NSW 11 O12
Nymboi–Binderay National Park NSW 9 O7
Nymboida NSW 9 O7
Nymboida National Park NSW 9 N6
Nymbool Qld 81 L8
Nyngan NSW 11 R10
Nyora Vic. 21 O11, 22 G8
Nypo Vic. 26 F3, 28 F13
O'Connell NSW 4 C5
O'Malley SA 42 G4
Oak Beach Qld 81 M6
Oakbank SA 36 D10, 37 I1
Oakdale NSW 5 J11, 7 J8, 14 I1
Oakey Qld 77 N9
Oakey Creek NSW 8 G12
Oaklands NSW 13 O11
Oaklands SA 38 I9
Oakleigh Vic. 21 K7, 22 D4
Oaks Tas. 95 L9
Oakvale Vic. 27 N4
Oakwood Tas. 91 M10, 93 N10
Oasis Roadhouse Qld 81 K11
Oatlands Tas. 93 M5
Ob Flat SA 48 H12
Oberne NSW 6 C13, 14 A6
Oberon NSW 4 E7, 6 I7
Obi Obi Qld 74 E4
Obley NSW 6 E4
OBX Creek NSW 9 O6
Ocean Grove Vic. 20 G10, 22 A7, 25 R8
Ocean Shores NSW 9 Q2, 77 Q12
Ockley WA 54 G6
Oenpelli NT 65 R1, 66 I5
Officer Vic. 21 M9
Ogilvie WA 56 A3
Ogmore Qld 79 M9
Olary SA 41 P10
Old Adaminaby NSW 14 D8, 16 D9, 33 K1
Old Bar NSW 7 P1
Old Beach Tas. 90 H4, 93 L8
Old Bonalbo NSW 9 O2, 77 P12
Old Bowenfels NSW 4 G5
Old Junee NSW 6 C11, 13 R9, 14 A4
Old Noarlunga SA 36 A12, 37 F3, 39 K10, 48 B2
Old Tallangatta Vic. 31 R4, 32 D2
Old Warrah NSW 8 I12
Oldina Tas. 94 F6
Olinda NSW 6 I4
Olinda Vic. 21 M7, 22 E4
Olio Qld 85 M7
Olympic Dam Village SA 40 F4
Ombersley Vic. 20 C10, 25 O8
Omeo Vic. 14 A12, 32 F8
Ondit Vic. 20 B10
One Arm Point WA 60 I6
One Tree NSW 13 K7
Ongerup WA 56 F11
Onslow WA 55 D3
Oodla Wirra SA 39 M2, 41 L12
Oodnadatta SA 46 B6
Oodnadatta Track SA 45 P5, 46 E11
Ooldea SA 42 I4
Ooma Creek NSW 6 D7
Ooma North NSW 6 D7
Oombulgurri WA 61 P4
Oonah Tas. 94 F7
Oondooroo Qld 85 L7
Oorindi Qld 84 H4
Ootann Qld 81 K8
Ootha NSW 6 B5, 13 R3
Opalton Qld 85 L10
Ophir NSW 6 G5
Opossum Bay Tas. 90 I8, 93 M9
Ora Banda WA 56 I5
Orange NSW 6 G6
Orangeville NSW 5 J10
Oranmeir NSW 14 F7, 17 K6
Orbost Vic. 33 J12
Orchid Beach Qld 77 Q2
Ord River WA 61 Q5
Orford Tas. 91 N2, 93 O6
Orford Vic. 24 G8
Organ Pipes National Park Vic. 20 I5, 22 C3
Orielton Tas. 91 K4, 93 M7
Ormeau Qld 75 F9
Ormiston Gorge NT 70 H8
Orpheus Island (Goolboddi) Qld 81 O11
Orpheus Island National Park Qld 81 O11
Orroroo SA 39 L1, 41 K12
Orrtipa-Thurra NT 71 N6
Orrvale Vic. 30 I6
Orton Park NSW 4 B4
Osbornes Flat Vic. 31 P5, 32 B3
Osbourne NSW 6 A13, 13 P11
Osmaston Tas. 95 K9
Osmington WA 53 D9, 54 B9
Osterley Tas. 93 J5
Otago Tas. 90 H5, 93 L8
Otford NSW 5 M12
Ottaba Qld 74 A9
Otway National Park Vic. 25 N12
Oura NSW 6 C12, 13 R10, 14 A5
Ourimbah NSW 5 P3, 7 M6
Ournie NSW 14 B8, 32 G1
Ouse Tas. 93 J6
Outer Harbor SA 36 A8
Outtrim Vic. 21 O13, 22 G9
Ouyen Vic. 12 E10, 28 H9
Ovens Vic. 31 O7, 32 B5
Overland Corner SA 39 P6
Overlander Roadhouse WA 55 C11
Ovingham SA 35 B2
Owanyilla Qld 77 P4
Owen SA 36 A1, 39 K7
Owens Gap NSW 7 K1
Oxenford Qld 75 F10
Oxley NSW 12 I7, 29 Q3
Oxley Vic. 31 M6
Oxley Wild Rivers National Park NSW 9 M10
Oyster Cove Tas. 90 G9, 93 L10
Ozenkadnook Vic. 26 C10
Paaratte Vic. 25 K10
Pacific Palms NSW 7 P2
Pacific Paradise Qld 74 G4
Packsaddle Roadhouse NSW 10 C7
Paddington NSW 3 I12, 5 O8
Paddys River NSW 6 I10, 14 H3
Padthaway SA 48 H7
Pages Flat SA 37 F5
Paignie Vic. 28 G9
Painted Desert, The SA 45 R7
Pakenham Vic. 21 M9, 22 F6
Palana Tas. 92 A9
Palgarup WA 54 D10
Pallamallawa NSW 8 H5
Pallarang Vic. 28 C9
Pallarenda Qld 81 P12
Pallarup WA 56 H10
Palm Beach NSW 5 P6
Palm Cove Qld 81 M6
Palm Grove NSW 5 P3
Palm Valley NT 70 H9
Palm Valley *see* **Finke Gorge National Park**
Palmdale NSW 5 P3, 7 M6
Palmer SA 36 H9, 39 M9, 48 D1
Palmer River Roadhouse Qld 81 K4
Palmers Island NSW 9 Q5
Palmers Oakey NSW 4 D2
Palmerston NT 64 D3, 66 D5
Palmerville Qld 81 J4
Palmwoods Qld 74 F4
Paloona Tas. 94 I7
Paluma Range National Park Qld 81 N11
Pambula NSW 14 G11, 33 Q7
Pambula Beach NSW 14 G11, 33 Q7
Pampas Qld 77 M10
Panitya Vic. 28 A10, 39 R10, 48 I3
Panmure Vic. 25 J9
Pannawonica WA 55 F3
Pantapin WA 54 H3
Panton Hill Vic. 21 L5, 22 E3
Pappinbarra NSW 9 N11
Papunya NT 70 G7
Paraburdoo WA 55 H5, 58 A6
Parachilna SA 41 J6
Paradise Tas. 94 I8
Paradise Vic. 25 N12
Paradise Vic. 27 K10
Paradise Beach Vic. 23 O7
Parattah Tas. 93 M5
Pardoo Roadhouse WA 60 D12
Parenna Tas. 93 R12
Parilla SA 39 Q10, 48 H3
Paringa SA 12 A7, 39 Q6
Paris Creek SA 36 D13, 37 I4
Park Beach Tas. 91 K6
Parkers Corner Vic. 23 J5
Parkerville WA 52 E4
Parkes ACT 15 D9
Parkes NSW 6 D5
Parkham Tas. 95 J8
Parkhurst Qld 79 N10
Parkside SA 35 H13
Parkside Tas. 95 Q8
Parkville NSW 7 K1
Parkville Vic. 19 B1
Parkwood Vic. 24 E4
Parliament House ACT 15 C11
Parndana SA 38 H12
Parnella Tas. 95 R8
Parrakie SA 39 P11, 48 G3
Parramatta NSW 5 M8, 7 L7
Parrawe Tas. 94 E7
Paru NT 66 D4
Paruna SA 12 A9, 39 Q8, 48 H1
Parwan Vic. 20 G5, 22 A3, 25 R4
Paschendale Vic. 24 D4
Paskeville SA 39 J6
Pastoria Vic. 20 H1
Pata SA 39 Q8
Patchewollock Vic. 12 D11, 28 G11
Pateena Tas. 95 L9
Paterson NSW 7 M3
Patersonia Tas. 95 M8
Patho Vic. 30 D3
Patonga NSW 5 O5
Patrick Estate Qld 74 C12
Patyah Vic. 26 C10
Paupong NSW 14 D10, 33 K5
Pawleena Tas. 91 K4, 93 N7
Pawtella Tas. 93 M5
Paxton NSW 7 L4
Paynes Crossing NSW 7 L4
Paynes Find WA 56 E4
Paynesville Vic. 23 Q5
Paytens Bridge NSW 6 D6
Peaceful Bay WA 54 F13, 56 D12
Peachester Qld 74 F6
Peak Charles National Park WA 56 I9
Peak Crossing Qld 75 A8, 77 P10
Peak Downs Qld 78 I8
Peak Hill NSW 6 D4
Peak Hill WA 58 C10
Peak Range National Park Qld 78 I9
Peak View NSW 14 F8, 16 I10, 33 O1
Peake SA 39 O11, 48 F3
Peakhurst NSW 5 N9
Pearcedale Vic. 21 L10, 22 E7
Pearshape Tas. 93 Q13
Peats Ridge NSW 5 O3, 7 L6
Pebbly Beach NSW 14 H6, 17 O6
Peebinga SA 12 A9, 28 A8, 39 R9, 48 I1
Peechelba Vic. 31 M4
Peechelba East Vic. 31 M4
Peel NSW 4 C3, 6 H6
Peelwood NSW 4 A11, 6 G8, 14 F1
Peep Hill SA 39 M6
Pegarah Tas. 93 Q12
Pekina SA 39 K2, 41 K12
Pelham Tas. 90 E1, 93 K6
Pelican Waters Qld 74 H6
Pella Vic. 26 F4
Pelorus Island (Yanooa) Qld 81 O11
Pelverata Tas. 90 F8, 93 K9
Pemberton WA 54 D11, 56 C11
Pembroke NSW 9 O12
Penarie NSW 12 H7, 29 N4
Penguin Tas. 94 H6
Penguin Island WA 52 A8
Penna Tas. 91 K4, 93 M8
Penneshaw SA 39 J12
Pennyroyal Vic. 20 C12
Penola SA 24 A3, 48 I10
Penong SA 43 M9
Penrice SA 49 H5
Penrith NSW 5 K7, 7 K7
Penrose NSW 7 J10, 14 H3
Penshurst Vic. 24 H6
Pentland Qld 78 C3, 85 R3
Penwortham SA 39 L5
Penzance Tas. 91 O9
Peppermint Grove WA 56 G11
Peppers Plains Vic. 26 G6
Peregian Beach Qld 74 H2, 77 Q6
Perekerten NSW 12 I9, 29 P8
Perenjori WA 56 C4
Perenna Vic. 26 E5
Pericoe NSW 14 F12, 33 P8
Perisher NSW 14 C9, 16 B12, 33 J4
Peronne Vic. 26 C9
Perponda SA 39 O9, 48 F2
Perroomba SA 39 K2, 41 J12
Perry Bridge Vic. 23 O6
Perth Tas. 95 L9
Perth WA 51, 52 C4, 54 C4, 56 C8
Perthville NSW 4 B5, 6 H6
Petal Point Tas. 95 P5
Petcheys Bay Tas. 90 E10
Peterborough SA 39 L2, 41 L13
Peterborough Vic. 25 K11
Petersville SA 38 I7
Petford Qld 81 L7
Petina SA 43 P11
Petrie Qld 74 F10, 75 D3
Petrie Terrace Qld 73 B3
Pewsey Vale SA 49 F10
Pheasant Creek Vic. 21 L3, 22 E2, 30 H13
Phillip Island Vic. 21 L12, 22 E9
Phils Creek NSW 6 F9, 14 E2
Piallaway NSW 8 I11
Piambie Vic. 29 M7
Piangil Vic. 12 G10, 29 M9
Piangil North Vic. 12 G10
Piawaning WA 56 D6
Pickertaramoor NT 66 D4
Picnic Bay Qld 81 P12
Picola Vic. 13 L13, 30 G3
Picola North Vic. 13 L13, 30 G3
Picton NSW 5 J11, 7 K9, 14 I2
Picton WA 53 G4
Piednippie SA 43 P12
Pier Millan Vic. 12 F10, 29 J10
Piesseville WA 54 G7
Pigeon Hole NT 68 E4
Pigeon Ponds Vic. 24 E2, 26 E13
Piggabeen NSW 75 H13
Piggoreet Vic. 20 B5, 25 N4
Pikedale Qld 9 L2, 77 M12
Pilbara, The WA 55 I3, 59 B4
Pilcherra Bore SA 39 P10, 48 G2
Pillar Valley NSW 9 P6
Pilliga NSW 8 E8
Pillinger Tas. 92 E4
Pilot Hill NSW 16 A5
Pimba SA 40 F6
Pimpama Qld 75 F9
Pimpinio Vic. 26 G8
Pindar WA 56 C3
Pine Creek NT 64 I13, 66 F8
Pine Hill Qld 78 G4
Pine Lodge Vic. 30 I5
Pine Point SA 38 I8
Pine Ridge NSW 8 I12
Pinery SA 36 A2, 39 K7
Pingaring WA 56 F9
Pingelly WA 54 F5, 56 D9
Pingrup WA 56 F10
Pinjarra WA 52 C10, 54 C6, 56 C9
Pinnacles, The WA 56 B6
Pinnaroo SA 12 A11, 28 A10, 39 R10, 48 I3
Pioneer Tas. 95 P6
Pioneer Bend SA 38 H12
Pipalyatjara SA 44 B2, 59 R11, 70 B13
Pipers Brook Tas. 95 M6
Pipers Creek Vic. 20 G2
Pipers Flat NSW 4 E3
Pipers River Tas. 95 L6
Pira Vic. 12 G10, 29 M10
Piries Vic. 21 R1, 31 L11
Pirlangimpi NT 66 C3
Pirlta Vic. 28 F4
Pirron Yallock Vic. 20 A11, 25 M9
Pithara WA 56 D6
Pitt Town NSW 5 L6
Pittong Vic. 20 A5, 25 M4
Pittsworth Qld 77 N9
Pittwater NSW 5 P6
Plainland Qld 74 A13
Platts NSW 14 F12, 33 N8
Pleasant Hills NSW 6 A13, 13 P11
Plenty Tas. 90 E3, 93 K7
Plush Corner SA 49 H4
Pmara Jutunta NT 70 I5
Poatina Tas. 93 K1, 95 K11
Point Clare NSW 5 P4
Point Labatt Conservation Park SA 43 P13
Point Leo Vic. 21 K12
Point Lonsdale Vic. 20 H11, 22 B7
Point Lookout Qld 75 I5, 77 R9
Point Nepean Vic. 22 B7
Point Pass SA 39 M6
Point Samson WA 55 G1, 58 A1
Point Talburpin Qld 75 G7
Point Turton SA 38 H9
Pokataroo NSW 8 D5
Police Point Tas. 90 E11, 93 K11
Policemans Point SA 39 N13, 48 E5
Polkemmet Vic. 26 F9
Pomborneit Vic. 25 M9
Pomona Qld 74 E1, 77 P6
Pomonal Vic. 24 I1, 26 I12
Pompapiel Vic. 27 Q7, 30 B6
Pompoota SA 36 I10
Ponde SA 36 I10
Pondooma SA 38 G4
Pontville Tas. 90 H3, 93 L7
Pontypool Tas. 93 O5
Poochera SA 38 A1, 40 A12, 43 R12
Pooginagoric SA 48 H7
Poolaijelo Vic. 24 B2, 26 B13, 48 I10
Poona National Park Qld 77 P4
Pooncarie NSW 12 E4
Poonindie SA 38 D8
Pootilla Vic. 20 D4
Pootnoura SA 45 P9
Poowong Vic. 21 O11, 22 G8
Poowong East Vic. 21 P11
Popanyinning WA 54 F6
Popran National Park NSW 5 O3
Porcupine Gorge National Park Qld 78 A3, 85 P3
Porcupine Ridge Vic. 20 E2, 25 Q1, 27 Q12, 30 C11
Porepunkah Vic. 31 P8, 32 C6
Pormpuraaw Qld 80 D1, 82 A13
Porongurup WA 54 H12
Porongurup National Park WA 54 H12
Port Adelaide SA 36 A8, 39 K9, 48 B1
Port Albert Vic. 23 L10
Port Alma Qld 79 O11
Port Arthur Tas. 91 N10, 93 N10
Port Augusta SA 40 I11
Port Bonython SA 38 I2, 40 I12
Port Broughton SA 39 J4
Port Campbell Vic. 25 K11
Port Campbell National Park Vic. 25 K11
Port Clinton SA 39 J7
Port Davis SA 38 I3, 39 J3, 40 I13
Port Denison WA 56 B4
Port Douglas Qld 81 M5
Port Elliot SA 37 H8, 39 L11, 48 C3
Port Fairy Vic. 24 G9
Port Franklin Vic. 23 J10
Port Gawler SA 36 A6, 39 K8
Port Germein SA 39 J2, 40 I13
Port Gibbon SA 38 G5
Port Hedland WA 58 C1, 60 B13
Port Hughes SA 38 I6
Port Huon Tas. 90 E10, 93 K10
Port Jackson NSW 5 O8
Port Julia SA 38 I8
Port Kembla NSW 7 K10
Port Kenny SA 38 A3, 43 Q13
Port Latta Tas. 94 E4
Port Lincoln SA 38 D8
Port MacDonnell SA 48 H13
Port Macquarie NSW 9 P12
Port Minlacowie SA 38 H9
Port Neill SA 38 E6
Port Noarlunga SA 36 A12, 37 E3, 39 K10, 48 B2
Port Pirie SA 39 J3, 40 I13
Port Rickaby SA 38 H8
Port Sorell Tas. 95 J6
Port Stephens NSW 7 N4
Port Victoria SA 38 H7
Port Vincent SA 38 I9
Port Wakefield SA 39 J6
Port Welshpool Vic. 23 K10
Port Willunga SA 36 A13, 37 E4
Portarlington Vic. 20 H9, 22 B6
Porters Retreat NSW 4 D10, 6 H8, 14 G1
Portland NSW 4 E3, 6 I6
Portland Vic. 24 D9
Portland Roads Qld 82 F7
Portsea Vic. 20 I11, 22 B8
Potato Point NSW 17 N10
Potts Point NSW 3 I8
Pottsville NSW 9 Q1, 77 Q11
Pound Creek Vic. 22 H10
Powelltown Vic. 21 O7, 22 G4
Powers Creek Vic. 24 C1, 26 C12
Powlett Plains Vic. 27 P8, 30 A6
Powlett River Vic. 21 N13
Powranna Tas. 93 L1, 95 M10
Pozieres Qld 9 M2, 77 N11
Prairie Qld 78 B4, 85 P4
Prairie Vic. 27 Q6, 30 C5
Pranjip Vic. 30 I8
Pratten Qld 77 N10
Precipice National Park Qld 77 J3
Premaydena Tas. 91 M9, 93 N10
Premer NSW 8 G12
Preolenna Tas. 94 E6
Preston Tas. 94 H7
Preston Beach WA 52 A12, 54 C6
Pretty Gully NSW 9 N3, 77 O12
Prevelly WA 53 B10
Price SA 39 J7
Primrose Sands Tas. 91 L6, 93 N9
Princetown Vic. 25 L11
Priory Tas. 95 Q8
Prooinga Vic. 29 K8
Propodollah Vic. 26 D6
Proserpine Qld 79 J3
Prospect Hill SA 36 C13, 37 H4
Proston Qld 77 N5
Puckapunyal Vic. 30 G10
Pudman Creek NSW 6 F10, 14 E3
Pullabooka NSW 6 C7
Pullut Vic. 26 G4
Punchmirup WA 54 G9
Punthari SA 36 I8
Punyelroo SA 39 N8
Pura Pura Vic. 25 L5
Puralka Vic. 24 B6, 48 I12
Purfleet NSW 7 P1, 9 N13
Purga Qld 75 A8
Purlewaugh NSW 8 F11
Purnim Vic. 24 I9
Purnong SA 39 N9, 48 E1
Purnululu National Park WA 61 Q8
Putty NSW 7 K5
Pyalong Vic. 21 J1, 30 F10
Pyap SA 39 Q7
Pyengana Tas. 95 P8
Pygery SA 38 C2, 40 B13
Pymble NSW 5 N7
Pyramid Hill Vic. 12 I13, 27 Q5, 30 B4
Pyrmont NSW 3 A7
Quaama NSW 14 G9, 17 L13, 33 Q4
Quairading WA 54 G4, 56 E8
Quakers Hill NSW 5 L7
Qualco SA 39 O6
Quambatook Vic. 12 H12, 27 N4
Quambone NSW 8 B10
Quamby Qld 84 G3
Quamby Brook Tas. 95 J9
Quandary NSW 6 B9, 13 R7
Quandialla NSW 6 C8, 14 A1
Quandong Roadhouse NSW 10 C12
Quantong Vic. 26 F9
Queanbeyan NSW 6 G13, 14 E5, 16 H3
Queenscliff Vic. 20 H10, 22 B7
Queenstown Tas. 92 E3, 94 E12
Quellington WA 52 I3, 54 F3
Quilpie Qld 87 O7
Quinburra NSW 14 E12, 33 M9
Quindalup WA 53 C7
Quindanning WA 54 E7
Quinninup WA 54 D11
Quinns Rocks WA 52 B2, 54 C3
Quirindi WA 53 B8
Quirindi NSW 9 J12
Quoiba Tas. 94 I7
Quorn SA 40 I10
Rabbit Flat Roadhouse NT 68 C11, 70 C1
Raglan NSW 4 C4
Raglan Qld 79 O12
Raglan Vic. 25 M2, 27 M13
Railton Tas. 94 I8
Rainbow Vic. 12 D13, 26 F4
Rainbow Beach Qld 77 Q5
Rainbow Flat NSW 7 P1
Raleigh NSW 9 P8
Raluana Vic. 27 J9
Ramco SA 39 O6
Raminea Tas. 90 E12, 93 K11
Ramingining NT 67 L5
Ranahan NT 70 D3
Ranceby Vic. 21 P12, 22 H8
Rand NSW 13 P12, 31 N1
Randell WA 57 J6
Ranelagh Tas. 90 E7, 93 K9
Ranford WA 52 G12
Ranga Tas. 92 B11, 95 Q1
Rankins Springs NSW 13 O6
Rannes Qld 79 M12
Rannock NSW 6 B10, 13 R8
Rapid Bay SA 37 C8, 39 J11, 48 A3
Rappville NSW 9 P4, 77 P13
Rathdowney Qld 9 P1, 75 B13, 77 P11
Rathmines NSW 7 M5
Rathscar Vic. 27 N11
Raukkan SA 39 M11, 48 D3
Ravensbourne National Park Qld 77 O8
Ravensdale NSW 5 O1
Ravenshoe Qld 81 M8
Ravensthorpe WA 56 H10
Ravenswood Qld 78 G2
Ravenswood Vic. 27 Q10, 30 C9
Ravenswood South Vic. 27 Q11, 30 C10
Ravensworth NSW 7 L3
Rawdon Vale NSW 7 M1
Rawlinna WA 57 N6
Rawson Vic. 23 J5
Raymond Terrace NSW 7 N4
Raywood Vic. 27 Q8, 30 C7
Red Banks SA 36 B4
Red Beach Qld 82 B6
Red Cliffs Vic. 12 D7, 28 G4

Red Gum Flat–Taralga

Red Gum Flat SA 49 B13
Red Hill Vic. 21 J11, 22 D8
Red Hill South Vic. 21 K11
Red Hills Tas. 95 J9
Red Jacket Vic. 23 J3
Red Range NSW 9 M6
Red Rock NSW 9 Q7
Redbank Vic. 27 M11
Redbank Plains Qld 75 C7
Redbanks SA 39 M5
Redcastle Vic. 30 E9
Redcliffe Qld 74 H10, 75 E3, 77 Q8
Redesdale Vic. 30 D10
Redhill SA 39 J4
Redland Bay Qld 75 G7, 77 Q9
Redmond WA 54 H12
Redpa Vic. 94 B4
Reedy Creek SA 48 F9
Reedy Creek Vic. 21 K2, 30 G11
Reedy Dam Vic. 26 I4
Reedy Flat Vic. 14 B13, 23 R1, 32 G10
Reedy Marsh Tas. 95 J8
Reefton NSW 6 B9, 13 R7
Reekara Tas. 93 Q11
Reesville Qld 74 E5
Regans Ford WA 54 C1, 56 C7
Regatta Point Tas. 92 D3, 94 D12
Reid ACT 15 F4
Reid WA 57 Q6
Reid River Qld 78 F1
Reids Creek Vic. 31 O5, 32 A3
Reids Flat NSW 6 F9, 14 E1
Reidsdale NSW 17 L5
Rekuna Tas. 90 I3, 93 M7
Relbia Tas. 95 M9
Remarkable Rocks SA 38 F13
Remine Tas. 92 C2, 94 D11
Rendelsham SA 48 G11
Renison Bell Tas. 92 D1, 94 E10
Renmark SA 39 G6
Renner Springs NT 65 M3
Rennie NSW 13 O12, 31 L2
Retreat Tas. 95 M6
Revesby NSW 5 M9
Rheban Tas. 91 O3, 93 O7
Rheola Vic. 27 O9
Rhyll Vic. 21 L12, 22 E9
Rhymney Reef Vic. 25 J2, 27 J13
Rhyndaston Vic. 93 M6
Rhynie SA 39 K5
Riana Tas. 94 G6
Rich Avon Vic. 27 K8
Richlands NSW 4 E13, 6 I9, 14 G2
Richmond NSW 5 K6, 7 K7
Richmond Qld 85 M4
Richmond Vic. 91 J4, 93 M7
Richmond Range National Park NSW 9 O3, 77 P12
Riddells Creek Vic. 20 H3, 22 B1, 30 E12
Ridgelands Qld 79 N10
Ridgeway Tas. 90 H6
Ridgewood Qld 74 E5
Ridley Tas. 94 G6
Riggs Creek Vic. 31 J8
Ringa WA 52 G1, 54 E2
Ringarooma Tas. 95 O7
Ringtail Qld 74 F1
Ringwood Vic. 21 L6, 22 E4
Ripley Qld 75 B8
Ripplebrook Vic. 21 O10, 22 G7
Risdon Vale Tas. 90 I5, 93 L8
River Derwent Tas. 93 L8
River Heads Qld 77 P4
River Torrens SA 35 F7, 36 A9
Riverside Tas. 95 L8
Riversleigh Fossil Field Qld 83 C12
Riverstone NSW 5 L6
Riverton SA 39 L6
Riverview Qld 75 B6
Roadvale Qld 75 A10, 77 P10
Robe SA 48 E9
Robertson NSW 7 K10, 14 I3
Robertstown SA 39 M6
Robigana Tas. 95 L7
Robinson River NT 69 P4
Robinvale Vic. 12 F8, 29 J6
Rocherlea Tas. 95 L8
Rochester SA 39 K5
Rochester Vic. 30 E6
Rochford Vic. 20 H2, 22 B1, 30 E12
Rock Flat NSW 14 E9, 16 G12, 33 N4
Rockbank Vic. 20 H5, 22 B3
Rockhampton Qld 79 N11
Rockingham WA 52 B7, 54 C4, 56 C8
Rockleigh SA 36 G10
Rockley NSW 4 B7, 6 H7
Rocklyn Vic. 20 E3, 25 P2, 27 P13, 30 B12
Rocksberg Qld 74 E9, 75 B1
Rockvale NSW 9 M8
Rocky Cape Tas. 94 E4
Rocky Cape National Park Tas. 94 F4
Rocky Creek NSW 8 H7
Rocky Crossing Qld 76 D10
Rocky Dam NSW 9 J4, 77 K13
Rocky Glen NSW 8 G11
Rocky Gully WA 54 F11
Rocky Hall NSW 14 F11, 33 O7
Rocky Plains NSW 16 D11
Rocky River NSW 9 K9
Rocky River SA 38 E13
Rodney NSW 14 E11, 33 M7
Roebourne WA 55 G1, 58 A2
Roebuck Roadhouse WA 60 H8
Roelands WA 53 H4, 54 E7
Roger Corner SA 38 I9
Roger River Tas. 94 C5
Roger River West Tas. 94 C5
Rokeby Tas. 91 J6, 93 M8
Rokeby Vic. 21 P9, 22 H6
Rokewood Vic. 20 B7, 25 O6
Rokewood Junction Vic. 20 B6, 25 N5
Roland Tas. 94 H8
Roleystone WA 52 D6
Rollands Plains NSW 9 O11
Rolleston Qld 76 G1, 79 J13
Rollingstone Qld 81 O12
Roma Qld 76 H6
Romsey Vic. 20 I2, 22 B1, 30 E12
Rookhurst NSW 7 N1, 9 L13
Rooty Hill NSW 5 L7
Roper Bar NT 67 K10
Roper Bar Store NT 67 K10
Rorruwuy NT 67 O5

Rosa Glen WA 53 C10, 54 B10
Rosebery NSW 92 E1, 94 E10
Rosebery Vic. 26 H4
Rosebery East Vic. 26 I3
Rosebrook Vic. 24 H9
Rosebud Vic. 21 J11, 22 C8
Rosedale NSW 17 N7
Rosedale Qld 77 N2
Rosedale SA 36 E5, 49 B7
Rosedale Vic. 23 L6
Rosegarland Tas. 90 E3
Roseneath Vic. 24 B3
Rosenthal NSW 7 N3
Roses Tier Tas. 95 O9
Rosevale Qld 77 O10
Rosevale Vic. 95 K8
Rosevears Tas. 95 L8
Rosewhite Vic. 31 P7, 32 B5
Rosewood NSW 14 B7
Rosewood Qld 77 P9
Roseworthy SA 23 Q4, 32 F13
Roslyn NSW 6 H10, 14 F3
Roslynmead Vic. 30 D4
Rosny Park Tas. 90 I6, 93 L8
Ross Tas. 93 M3, 95 N12
Ross Creek Vic. 20 C4, 25 O4
Ross River Homestead NT 71 K8
Rossarden Tas. 93 O1, 95 O10
Rossbridge Vic. 25 J3
Rossi NSW 6 H13, 14 F6, 17 J4
Rossmore NSW 5 K9
Rossville Qld 81 L3
Rostron Vic. 27 L10
Roto NSW 10 M3
Rottnest Island WA 54 B4, 56 B8
Rouchel Brook NSW 7 L2
Rowella Tas. 95 K7
Rowena NSW 8 E6
Rowland Vic. 27 Q4, 30 B2
Rowland Flat SA 36 E5, 49 D8
Rowsley Vic. 20 F5, 22 A3, 25 R4
Roxby Downs SA 40 F4
Royal George Tas. 93 O2, 95 P11
Royal National Park NSW 5 N11, 7 L9
Royalla ACT 6 G13, 14 E6, 16 G4
Ruabon WA 53 F7
Rubicon Vic. 21 P2, 22 H1, 31 K12
Ruby Vic. 21 P12, 22 H9
Rubyvale Qld 78 H11
Rudall SA 38 E5
Rudall River National Park WA 58 H4
Ruffy Vic. 30 I10
Rufus River NSW 12 B6, 28 C2
Rugby NSW 6 F9, 14 E2
Rukenvale NSW 9 P2, 77 P11
Rules Point NSW 16 D13
Running Stream NSW 6 I5
Runnyford NSW 17 M6
Runnymede Tas. 91 K3, 93 M7
Runnymede Vic. 30 E6
Rupanyup Vic. 26 I9
Rupanyup North Vic. 26 I8
Rupanyup South Vic. 26 I9
Rushworth Vic. 30 G7
Russell ACT 15 H8
Russell Island Qld 75 G7
Russell River National Park Qld 81 N7
Rutherglen Vic. 13 O13, 31 N4
Ryanby Vic. 29 L10
Ryans Creek Vic. 31 M8
Rydal NSW 4 F5
Ryde NSW 5 N8
Rye Vic. 20 I11, 22 C8
Rye Park NSW 6 F10, 14 D3
Rylstone NSW 6 I4
Ryton Vic. 23 J9
Sackville North NSW 5 L4
Saddleworth SA 39 L6
Safety Bay WA 52 B7
Safety Beach NSW 9 P7
Safety Beach Vic. 21 J11, 22 D7
St Albans NSW 5 M2, 7 L6
St Albans Vic. 20 I5
St Andrews Vic. 21 L4, 22 E2, 30 H13
St Arnaud Vic. 27 L9
St Aubyn Qld 77 N8
St Clair NSW 7 L3
St Fillans Vic. 21 N4, 22 G2, 31 J13
St George Qld 76 G10
St Georges Basin NSW 7 K12, 14 I5, 17 Q2
St Germains Vic. 30 G5
St Helena Island Qld 75 F4
St Helena Island National Park Qld 74 H12, 75 F4
St Helens Tas. 95 Q8
St Helens Vic. 24 G8
St Ives NSW 5 N7
St James Vic. 31 K5
St Kilda SA 36 A7
St Kilda Vic. 21 J7
St Kitts SA 36 G3
St Lawrence Qld 79 L8
St Leonards Vic. 20 I9, 22 B6
St Marys NSW 5 L7
St Marys Tas. 95 Q10
St Patricks River Tas. 95 M8
St Pauls Qld 82 C1
St Peter Island SA 43 N10
Sale Vic. 23 N6
Salisbury NSW 7 M2
Salisbury SA 36 C8, 39 L9, 48 B1
Salisbury Vic. 26 E7
Salisbury West Vic. 27 P8, 30 A7
Sallys Corner NSW 7 J10, 14 H3
Sallys Flat NSW 6 H5
Salmon Gums WA 55 J7
Salmon Ponds Tas. 90 E4
Salt Creek SA 39 N13, 48 D5
Salter Springs SA 39 L6
Saltwater River Tas. 91 L8, 93 N9
Samford Tas. 74 F11, 75 C4, 77 P9
San Remo Vic. 21 M13, 22 F9
Sanctuary Point NSW 7 K12, 14 I5, 17 R2
Sandalwood SA 39 P9, 48 G1
Sandergrove SA 37 I5
Sanderston SA 36 H8
Sandfire Roadhouse WA 60 F12
Sandfly Tas. 90 G7, 93 L9
Sandford NSW 7 N3, 77 M13
Sandford Vic. 24 C4
Sandgate Qld 74 G11, 75 D4

Sandhill Lake Vic. 27 O3, 29 O13
Sandigo NSW 13 P9
Sandilands SA 38 I8
Sandon Vic. 20 D1, 25 P1, 27 P12, 30 B11
Sandringham Vic. 21 J7
Sandsmere Vic. 26 C6
Sandstone WA 56 G2
Sandy Bay Tas. 89 D11, 90 I6
Sandy Beach NSW 9 P7
Sandy Creek SA 36 D6, 49 A8
Sandy Creek Vic. 31 O5, 32 D3
Sandy Creek Upper Vic. 31 Q6, 32 C4
Sandy Flat NSW 9 M4, 77 N13
Sandy Hill NSW 9 N3, 77 O13
Sandy Hollow NSW 7 J2
Sandy Point NSW 6 I12, 14 G4, 17 M1
Sandy Point Vic. 22 I11
Sangar NSW 13 N12, 31 L1
Sapphire NSW 9 K6
Sapphire Qld 78 H11
Sapphiretown SA 38 I12
Sarah Island Tas. 92 D5
Sardine Creek Vic. 14 C13, 33 J11
Sarina Qld 79 L6
Sarina Beach Qld 79 L6
Sarsfield Vic. 23 Q4, 32 F13
Sassafras NSW 7 J11, 14 H4, 17 O1
Sassafras Tas. 95 J7
Sassafras East Tas. 95 J7
Savage River Tas. 94 D8
Savage River National Park Tas. 94 D7
Savenake NSW 13 N12, 31 L2
Sawpit Creek NSW 33 K3
Sawtell NSW 9 P8
Sawyers Valley WA 52 E4
Scaddan WA 57 J10
Scamander Tas. 95 Q9
Scarborough NSW 5 M12, 7 K9
Scarborough Qld 74 H10, 75 E2
Scarborough WA 52 B4, 54 C3, 56 C8
Scarsdale Vic. 20 B5, 25 N4
Scheyville NSW 5 L6
Scheyville National Park NSW 5 L5
Schofields NSW 5 L7
Schouten Island Tas. 93 Q5
Schreibereau SA 49 E7
Scone NSW 7 K1
Scotsburn Vic. 20 D5, 25 P4
Scott National Park WA 53 D12, 54 B11, 56 C11
Scotts Creek Vic. 25 K10
Scotts Head NSW 9 P9
Scottsdale Tas. 95 N7
Scottville Qld 78 I3
Sea Elephant Tas. 93 R12
Sea Lake Vic. 12 F11, 27 J1, 29 J12
Sea World Qld 75 G11
Seabird WA 54 C2
Seacombe Vic. 23 O6
Seaford Vic. 21 K9
Seaforth Qld 79 K4
Seaham NSW 7 N5
Seal Bay Conservation Park SA 38 H13
Seal Rocks NSW 7 P3
Seaspray Vic. 23 N8
Seaton Vic. 23 L5
Seaview Vic. 21 P11, 22 H7
Sebastian Vic. 27 Q8, 30 C7
Sebastopol NSW 6 C10, 13 R8, 14 A3
Sebastopol Vic. 20 C4
Second Valley SA 37 C8, 39 J11, 48 A3
Sedan SA 36 I5, 39 M8
Sedgwick Vic. 27 R10, 30 C9
Seelands NSW 9 P6
Seisia Qld 82 C3
Selbourne Tas. 95 K8
Seldom Seen Roadhouse Vic. 14 C12, 32 I8
Sellheim Qld 78 E2
Sellicks Beach SA 37 E5, 39 K10, 48 B3
Sellicks Hill SA 37 E5
Separation Creek Vic. 25 O11
Seppeltsfield SA 36 E4, 39 L8, 49 D4
Serendip Sanctuary Vic. 20 G8
Serpentine Vic. 27 P7, 30 A6
Serpentine WA 52 D6, 54 D5
Serpentine National Park WA 52 D8, 54 D5, 56 C8
Serviceton Vic. 26 A7, 48 I7
Settlement WA 54 B4
Seven Mile Beach Tas. 91 J6, 93 M8
Sevenhill SA 39 L5
Seventeen Seventy Qld 79 Q13
Severnlea Qld 9 M2, 77 N12
Seville Vic. 21 M6, 22 F4
Seymour Vic. 30 G10
Seymour Tas. 93 Q1, 95 Q11
Shackleton WA 54 H3
Shadforth NSW 6 G6
Shady Creek Vic. 21 Q9, 22 I6
Shallow Crossing NSW 17 N5
Shannon Tas. 93 J3, 95 J12
Shannon Vic. 19 D10
Shannon WA 54 E11
Shannon National Park WA 54 E11, 56 D12
Shannons Flat NSW 14 D7, 16 E8
Shannonvale Vic. 32 E7
Shark Bay WA 55 A9
Shaw Island Qld 79 K3
Shay Gap WA 58 E1, 60 D13
Shays Flat Vic. 27 L11
Shea-Oak Log SA 36 D4, 49 A5
Sheans Creek Vic. 31 J9
Sheep Hills Vic. 26 I7
Sheffield Tas. 94 I8
Shelbourne Vic. 27 P10, 30 B9
Shelford Vic. 20 D8, 25 P6
Shelley Vic. 14 A8, 32 F2
Shellharbour NSW 7 L11
Shelly Beach Tas. 91 O2, 93 O7
Sheoaks Vic. 20 E7, 25 Q6
Shepherds Flat Vic. 20 E2
Shepparton Vic. 30 I6
Sherlock SA 39 O10, 48 F3
Sherwood NSW 4 G6
Shipley NSW 4 G6
Shirley Vic. 25 L3
Shoal Bay NSW 7 O4
Shoal Point Qld 79 L5
Shoalhaven Heads NSW 7 K11

Shooters Hill NSW 4 E9, 6 I8, 14 G1
Shoreham Vic. 21 K12, 22 D8
Shotts WA 54 D8
Shute Harbour Qld 79 K3
Sidmouth Tas. 95 K7
Sidonia Vic. 22 I11, 30 E11
Silkwood Qld 81 N8
Silvan Vic. 21 M6, 22 F4
Silver Creek Vic. 31 O6, 32 B4
Silver Sands SA 37 E5
Silverdale NSW 5 J9, 7 K8, 14 I1
Silverton NSW 10 B11, 41 R9
Simmie Vic. 30 F5
Simpson Vic. 25 L10
Simpson Desert NT & Qld 46 E4, 71 O12, 84 A12, 86 C4
Simpson Desert Conservation Park SA 46 H1, 86 A6
Simpson Desert National Park Qld 71 Q10, 84 B12, 86 B2
Simpsons Bay Tas. 90 H12, 93 L11
Simpsons Gap NT 71 J8
Singleton NSW 7 L3
Singleton WA 52 B9, 54 C5, 56 C9
Sir Edward Pellew Group NT 69 P1
Sir Joseph Banks Group SA 38 E8
Sisters Beach Tas. 94 E5
Sisters Creek Tas. 94 E5
Skenes Creek Vic. 25 O12
Skipton Vic. 25 M4
Slade Point Qld 79 L5
Slaty Creek Vic. 27 M8
Smeaton Vic. 20 D2, 25 P2, 27 P13, 30 A12
Smiggin Holes NSW 14 C9, 16 B12, 33 J4
Smithfield Qld 81 M6
Smithfield SA 36 C7
Smithlea Qld 9 K5, 77 L12
Smiths Gully Vic. 21 L4, 22 E2, 30 H13
Smiths Lake NSW 7 P3
Smithton Tas. 94 C4
Smithtown NSW 9 P10
Smokko Vic. 31 Q9, 32 C7
Smoky Bay SA 43 O10
Smythesdale Vic. 20 B5, 25 N4
Snake Range National Park Qld 78 H12
Snake Valley Vic. 20 B4, 25 N4
Snobs Creek Vic. 21 P2, 31 K11
Snowtown SA 39 J5
Snowy Mountains NSW 16 A12
Snowy River NSW & Vic. 14 C10, 33 J10
Snowy River National Park Vic. 14 C12, 33 J9
Snug Tas. 90 H9, 93 L10
Sodwalls NSW 4 F5
Sofala NSW 6 I5
Somers Vic. 21 K12, 22 D8
Somersby NSW 5 N5
Somerset Tas. 94 G5
Somerset Dam Qld 74 C9
Somerton NSW 8 I10
Somerville Vic. 21 K10, 22 E7
Sommariva Qld 76 C6
Sorell Tas. 91 K5, 93 M8
Sorrento Vic. 20 I11, 22 B8
South Arm Tas. 90 I8, 93 M9
South Bank Qld 73 C9
South Bindoon WA 54 D2
South Brisbane Qld 73 C9
South Bruny Island Tas. 90 H12, 93 L12
South Bruny National Park Tas. 93 K12
South Coast NSW 14 H11, 17 N3, 33 R10
South Cumberland Islands National Park Qld 79 L4
South East Forest National Park NSW 14 F11, 33 O8
South Forest Tas. 94 D4
South Gippsland Vic. 22 H8
South Gundagai NSW 6 D12, 14 B5
South Hedland WA 58 C1, 60 B13
South Island Qld 79 N6
South Johnstone Qld 81 N8
South Kilkerran SA 38 I7
South Kumminin WA 54 I4, 56 F8
South Melbourne Vic. 19 C13
South Mission Beach Qld 81 N9
South Molle Island Qld 79 K3
South Morang Vic. 21 K5
South Mount Cameron Tas. 95 P6
South Nietta Tas. 94 H8
South Pacific Ocean 7 Q5, 77 R2
South Perth WA 51 C12
South Riana Tas. 94 G6
South Springfield Tas. 95 N7
South Stirling WA 54 I11
South Stradbroke Island Qld 75 H9, 77 Q10
South Strathmerton Vic. 13 M13, 30 I3
South West Rocks NSW 9 P10
South Yaamba Qld 79 N10
South Yunderup WA 52 B10, 54 C5
Southbank Vic. 19 D10
Southbrook Qld 77 N9
Southend Qld 79 P12
Southend SA 48 G11
Southern Cross Vic. 24 H9
Southern Cross WA 56 G7
Southern Ocean Qld 75 G11
Southport Qld 75 G11
Southport Tas. 93 K12
Southwest National Park Tas. 90 A5, 92 F4
Southwood National Park Qld 77 J10
Sovereign Hill Vic. 20 C4, 25 O3, 30 A13
Spalding SA 39 L4
Spalford Tas. 94 H7
Spargo Creek Vic. 20 E3, 25 Q3, 30 B13
Spearwood WA 52 B6
Speed Vic. 12 E11, 26 H1, 28 I11
Speewa Vic. 29 N10
Spencer NSW 5 N4
Spencer Gulf SA 38 G7
Spicers Creek NSW 6 G3
Spilsby Island SA 38 E8
Sprent Tas. 94 H7
Spreyton Tas. 94 I7
Spring Beach Tas. 91 O2, 93 O7
Spring Hill NSW 6 G6
Spring Hill Qld 73 E2
Spring Hill Vic. 20 F2

Spring Ridge NSW 6 G2
Spring Ridge NSW 8 H12
Springbrook Qld 9 Q1, 75 F13, 77 Q11
Springbrook National Park Qld 75 F13
Springdale NSW 6 C10, 14 A3
Springfield Tas. 95 N7
Springfield Vic. 20 I2
Springhurst Vic. 31 N4
Springmount Vic. 20 D3
Springside Qld 77 M9
Springton SA 36 G7, 39 M8, 48 D1
Springvale Vic. 21 K7
Springwood NSW 5 J7, 7 J7
Staaten River National Park Qld 80 G5
Staghorn Flat Vic. 31 P5, 32 C3
Stamford Qld 85 N5
Stanage Qld 79 M7
Stanborough Vic. 93 J7
Standley Chasm NT 70 I8
Stanhope Vic. 30 G6
Stanley Tas. 94 D3
Stanley Vic. 31 O6, 32 B4
Stanmore Qld 74 E6
Stannifer NSW 9 K6
Stannum NSW 9 M5, 77 N13
Stanthorpe Qld 9 M2, 77 N12
Stanwell Qld 79 N11
Stanwell Park NSW 5 M12, 7 K9
Stanwell Tops NSW 5 M12
Starcke National Park Qld 81 L1, 82 I13
Staughton Vale Vic. 20 F6
Stavely Vic. 24 I4
Staverton Tas. 94 H8
Stawell Vic. 27 J11
Steels Creek Vic. 21 M4, 22 F2, 30 H13
Steiglitz Qld 75 G8
Steiglitz Vic. 20 E7, 25 Q5
Stenhouse Bay SA 38 G10
Stephens Creek NSW 10 B11
Steppes Tas. 93 J3, 95 K13
Stieglitz Tas. 95 R8
Stirling SA 36 C11, 37 H1
Stirling Vic. 14 A13, 23 Q2, 32 G11
Stirling North SA 38 I1, 40 I11
Stirling Range National Park WA 54 H11, 56 E11
Stockdale Vic. 23 N4, 32 D13
Stockinbingal NSW 6 C10, 14 B3
Stockmans Reward Vic. 21 Q4
Stockport SA 36 C2
Stockwell SA 36 G4, 39 M7, 49 I3
Stockyard Gully National Park WA 56 A5
Stockyard Hill Vic. 25 L3
Stokers Siding NSW 9 Q1, 77 Q11
Stokes SA 38 D7
Stokes Bay SA 38 H11
Stokes National Park WA 56 I10
Stone Hut SA 39 K3, 41 J13
Stonefield SA 39 N10, 48 E3
Stonehenge NSW 9 L6
Stonehenge Qld 85 M13, 87 M1
Stonehenge Tas. 93 N5
Stoneville WA 52 E4
Stoneyford Vic. 25 M9
Stonor Tas. 93 M5
Stony Creek Vic. 22 I10
Stony Crossing NSW 12 H10, 29 N9
Stony Point Vic. 21 L11, 22 E8
Stoodley Tas. 94 I8
Store Creek NSW 6 G4
Stormlea Tas. 91 M11, 93 N10
Storys Creek Tas. 93 O1, 95 O10
Stowport Tas. 94 G6
Stradbroke Vic. 23 M8
Stradbroke West Vic. 23 M7
Strahan Tas. 92 D3, 94 D12
Strangways Vic. 20 E1
Stratford NSW 7 N2
Stratford Vic. 23 N5
Strath Creek Vic. 21 L1, 30 H11
Strathalbyn SA 36 E13, 37 I4, 39 L10, 48 C3
Strathallan Vic. 30 I5
Stratham WA 53 F5, 54 C8
Strathblane Tas. 90 D12, 93 K11
Strathbogie NSW 9 M8
Strathbogie Vic. 31 J9
Strathbogie South Vic. 31 J9
Strathdownie Vic. 24 B5, 48 I11
Stratherne WA 54 G5
Strathewen Vic. 21 L4
Strathfield NSW 5 N8
Strathfieldsaye Vic. 27 R10, 30 C9
Strathgordon Tas. 92 F6
Strathkellar Vic. 24 F5
Strathlea Vic. 20 D1, 25 P1, 27 P12, 30 A11
Strathmerton Vic. 13 M13, 30 I3
Strathpine Qld 74 F11, 75 D3, 77 P8
Streaky Bay SA 43 N10
Streatham Vic. 25 K4
Streton WA 54 H5
Strickland Tas. 93 J5
Stroud NSW 7 N3
Stroud Road NSW 7 N2
Struan SA 48 H9
Strzelecki Vic. 21 P11, 22 H8
Strzelecki Crossing SA 47 O11, 86 F13
Strzelecki National Park Tas. 92 B12, 95 Q1
Strzelecki Track SA 47 O11
Stuart Mill Vic. 27 M10
Stuart Park NT 63 G4
Stuart Town NSW 6 G4
Stuarts Point NSW 9 P10
Stuarts Well NT 70 I10
Sturt National Park NSW 10 A2, 47 R11, 86 I13
Sue City NSW 16 B7
Suffolk Park NSW 9 R2, 77 R12
Suggan Buggan Vic. 14 C11, 33 J7
Sulphur Creek Tas. 94 G6
Summerfield Vic. 27 Q8, 30 C7
Summertown SA 36 C10, 37 H1
Summervale NSW 11 O3
Sunbury Vic. 20 I4, 22 B2, 30 E13
Sunday Creek Vic. 31 K1, 30 I1
Sundown National Park Qld 9 L3, 77 M12
Sunny Cliffs Vic. 12 D7, 28 G4
Sunny Corner NSW 4 E3
Sunnybank Qld 75 E6

Sunnyside NSW 9 M4, 77 N13
Sunnyside Tas. 94 I8
Sunnyside Vic. 32 E7
Sunnyvale SA 38 I6
Sunset Vic. 28 A9, 39 R10, 48 I2
Sunshine NSW 5 R1
Sunshine Beach Qld 74 H1, 77 Q6
Sunshine Coast Qld 74 I2, 77 R6
Sunshine Coast Hinterland Qld 77 P7
Surat Qld 76 H8
Surf Beach NSW 17 N7
Surfers Paradise Qld 75 G11, 77 Q10
Surges Bay Tas. 90 E11, 93 K10
Surprise Bay Tas. 93 Q13
Surry Hills NSW 3 E13
Surveyors Bay Tas. 90 F12, 93 K11
Sussex Inlet NSW 7 K12, 14 I5, 17 Q2
Sutherland NSW 5 N10
Sutherlands SA 39 M6
Sutton NSW 6 G12, 14 E5, 16 H1
Sutton Vic. 27 K3, 29 K13
Sutton Grange Vic. 27 R11, 30 C10
Swan Hill Vic. 12 H11, 29 N11
Swan Marsh Vic. 25 M9
Swan Reach SA 39 N8
Swan Reach Vic. 23 R4, 32 G13
Swan River WA 52 D2
Swan Valley Wine Region WA 52 D3
Swanhaven NSW 7 J12, 14 I5, 17 Q2
Swanpool Vic. 31 L8
Swanport SA 36 I12
Swansea NSW 7 N5
Swansea Tas. 93 P4, 95 P13
Swanwater Vic. 27 L9
Swanwater West Vic. 27 K8
Swanwick Tas. 93 Q4, 95 Q13
Sweers Island Qld 83 E7
Swifts Creek Vic. 14 A12, 23 Q1, 32 G9
Swing Bridge Vic. 23 L5
Sydenham Vic. 20 I4, 22 B2
Sydney NSW 3, 5 O8, 7 L8
Sydney Harbour Bridge NSW 3 E2
Sydney Harbour National Park NSW 5 P8
Sydney Opera House NSW 3 G3
Sylvania NSW 5 N10
Sylvaterre Vic. 27 Q5, 30 C4
Taabinga Qld 77 N6
Tabbara Vic. 33 K12
Tabberabbera Vic. 23 O3, 32 E12
Tabbimoble NSW 9 Q4, 77 Q13
Tabbita NSW 13 N6
Tabilk Vic. 30 G9
Table Top NSW 13 Q13, 31 P3, 32 C1
Tabooba Qld 75 C12
Tabor Vic. 24 G6
Tabragalba Qld 75 D11
Tabulam NSW 9 O3, 77 O12
Taggerty Vic. 21 O2, 22 G1, 31 J12
Tahara Vic. 24 E5
Tahara Bridge Vic. 24 D5
Tahmoor NSW 5 J12
Tailem Bend SA 39 N10, 48 E3
Takone Vic. 94 F6
Talawa Tas. 95 O8
Talbingo NSW 6 E13, 14 C6, 16 B4
Talbot Vic. 20 D1, 25 N1, 27 O12
Talbot Brook WA 52 H6, 54 E4
Taldra SA 12 A7, 39 Q7
Talgarno NSW 13 Q13, 31 Q4, 32 C1
Talia SA 38 A3
Tallageira Vic. 26 A10, 48 I8
Tallandoon Vic. 31 Q6, 32 D4
Tallangalook Vic. 31 M5
Tallangatta Vic. 31 Q5, 32 D2
Tallangatta East Vic. 32 D3
Tallangatta Valley Vic. 32 E3
Tallaroo Hot Springs Qld 80 I9
Tallarook Vic. 30 G10
Tallebung NSW 13 P2
Tallimba NSW 6 A8, 13 Q6
Tallong NSW 6 I11, 14 H3
Tallygaroopna Vic. 30 I5
Talmalmo NSW 13 R13, 14 A8, 32 E1
Talwood Vic. 8 F2, 76 I11
Tamar River Tas. 95 L7
Tamarang NSW 8 I12
Tambar Springs NSW 8 G11
Tambaroora NSW 6 G5
Tambellup WA 54 H10
Tambo Qld 76 B2
Tambo Crossing Vic. 14 B13, 23 Q3, 32 G11
Tambo Upper Vic. 23 R4, 32 G13
Tamboon Vic. 33 N13
Tamborine Qld 75 E10, 77 Q10
Tamborine Mountain Qld. 75 E10
Tamborine National Park Qld 75 E10
Tamboy NSW 7 O3
Taminick Vic. 31 J7
Tamleugh Vic. 31 J7
Tamleugh North Vic. 31 J7
Tamleugh West Vic. 30 I7
Tammin WA 56 E7
Tamrookum Qld 75 C12
Tamworth NSW 9 J11
Tanami NT 68 B11
Tandarook Vic. 25 L9
Tandarra Vic. 27 Q7, 30 C6
Tangalooma Qld 75 G2
Tangambalanga Vic. 31 Q5, 32 C3
Tangorin Qld 78 A7, 85 O6
Tangmangaroo NSW 6 F10, 14 D3
Tanja NSW 14 G10, 33 R5
Tanjil Bren Vic. 21 R7, 23 J4
Tanjil South Vic. 21 R9, 23 J6
Tankerton Vic. 21 L12, 22 E8
Tannum Sands Qld 79 P12
Tannymorel Qld 9 N1, 77 O11
Tansey Qld 77 N5
Tantanoola SA 48 G11
Tanunda SA 36 F5, 39 L8, 49 E6
Tanwood Vic. 27 M11
Tanybryn Vic. 25 N11
Tapin Tops National Park NSW 9 M12
Taplan SA 12 A8, 28 A5, 39 R8
Tappa Pass SA 49 I5
Tara NSW 6 A10, 13 Q8
Tara NT 71 J4
Tara Qld 77 K8
Taradale Vic. 20 F1, 25 R1, 27 R12, 30 C11
Tarago NSW 6 H12, 14 F4
Tarago Vic. 21 P9
Taralga NSW 6 I9, 14 G2